ABSOLUTE BEGINNER'S GUIDE

TO

iPod and iTunes,

Second Edition

Brad Miser

que®

800 East 96th Street
Indianapolis, Indiana 46240

Absolute Beginner's Guide to iPod and iTunes, Second Edition

Copyright © 2006 by Que Publishing

International Standard Book Number: 0-7897-3457-5

Library of Congress Catalog Card Number: 2005929931

Printed in the United States of America

First Printing: September 2005

08   07   06   05   4   3   2

Trademarks

All terms mentioned in this book that are known to be trademarks or service marks have been appropriately capitalized. Que Publishing cannot attest to the accuracy of this information. Use of a term in this book should not be regarded as affecting the validity of any trademark or service mark.

Warning and Disclaimer

Bulk Sales

Que Publishing offers excellent discounts on this book when ordered in quantity for bulk purchases or special sales. For more information, please contact

U.S. Corporate and Government Sales
1-800-382-3419
corpsales@pearsontechgroup.com

For sales outside the United States, please contact

International Sales
1-317-428-3341
international@pearsoned.com

Associate Publisher
Greg Wiegand

Acquisitions Editor
Stephanie J. McComb

Development Editor
Kevin Howard

Managing Editor
Charlotte Clapp

Project Editor
Seth Kerney

Production Editor
Megan Wade

Indexer
Ken Johnson

Proofreaders
Melinda Gutowski
Greg Sorvig

Technical Editor
Brian Hubbard

User Reviewer
Rick Ehrhardt

Publishing Coordinator
Sharry Lee Gregory

Interior Designer
Dan Armstrong

Cover Designer
Anne Jones

Contents at a Glance

Table of Contents

About the Author

Brad Miser has written many books about computers and related technology, with his favorite topics being anything that starts with a lower case *i*, such as the iPod and iTunes. In addition to *Absolute Beginner's Guide to iPod and iTunes, Second Edition*, Brad has written *Special Edition Using Mac OS X, v10.4 Tiger*; *Special Edition Using Mac OS X, v10.3 Panther*; *Absolute Beginner's Guide to iPod and iTunes*; *Absolute Beginner's Guide to Homeschooling*; *Mac OS X and iLife: Using iTunes, iPhoto, iMovie, and iDVD*; *iDVD 3 Fast & Easy*; *Special Edition Using Mac OS X v10.2*; and *Using Mac OS 8.5*. He has also been an author, a development editor, or a technical editor on more than 50 other titles. He has been a featured speaker on various topics at Macworld Expo, at user group meetings, and in other venues.

Brad is the senior technical communicator for an Indianapolis-based software development company. Brad is responsible for all product documentation, training materials, online help, and other communication materials. He also manages the customer support operations for the company and provides training and account management services to its customers. Previously, he was the lead engineering proposal specialist for an aircraft engine manufacturer, a development editor for a computer book publisher, and a civilian aviation test officer/engineer for the U.S. Army. Brad holds a bachelor of science degree in mechanical engineering from California Polytechnic State University at San Luis Obispo (1986) and has received advanced education in maintainability engineering, business, and other topics.

In addition to his passion for technology, Brad likes to ride his motorcycle, run, and play racquetball; playing with home theater technology is also a favorite pastime.

Once a native of California, Brad now lives in Brownsburg, Indiana, with his wife Amy; their three daughters, Jill, Emily, and Grace; a guinea pig named Buddy; and a rabbit named Bun-Bun.

Brad would love to hear about your experiences with this book (the good, the bad, and the ugly). You can write to him at bradmacosx@mac.com.

Dedication

I leave you, hoping that the lamp of liberty will burn in your bosoms until there shall no longer be a doubt that all men are created free and equal.

—Abraham Lincoln

Acknowledgments

To the following people on the *ABG iPod and iTunes* project team, my sincere appreciation for your hard work on this book:

Stephanie McComb, my acquisitions editor, who made this project possible and convinced the right people that this was a good idea and that I was the right one to write it. **Marta Justak** of Justak Literary Services, my agent, for getting me signed up for this project and providing advice and encouragement along the way. **Kevin Howard**, my development editor, who helped make the contents and organization of this book much better. **Rick Ehrhardt**, my user reviewer, who made the jump to an iPod and iTunes at just the right time and provided lots of invaluable feedback that made this book much better.

Brian Hubbard, my technical editor, who did a great job ensuring that the information in this book is both accurate and useful. **Megan Wade**, my production editor, who corrected my many misspellings, poor grammar, and other problems. **Seth Kerney**, my project editor, who skillfully managed the hundreds of files that it took to make this book into something real. **Que's production and sales team** for printing the book and getting it into your hands.

And now for some people who weren't on the project team but who were essential to me personally. **Amy Miser**, my wonderful wife, for supporting me while I wrote this book; living with an author under tight deadlines isn't always lots of fun, but Amy does so with grace, understanding, and acceptance of my need to write. **Jill**, **Emily**, and **Grace Miser**, my delightful daughters, for helping me stay focused on what is important in life. While an iPod can play beautiful music, these precious people are beautiful music given form! (And, a special thanks to **Buddy** the guinea pig and **Bun-Bun** the rabbit for their early-morning visits to cheer me up while I was working!)

We Want to Hear from You!

As the reader of this book, *you* are our most important critic and commentator. We value your opinion and want to know what we're doing right, what we could do better, what areas you'd like to see us publish in, and any other words of wisdom you're willing to pass our way.

As an associate publisher for Que Publishing, I welcome your comments. You can email or write me directly to let me know what you did or didn't like about this book—as well as what we can do to make our books better.

Please note that I cannot help you with technical problems related to the topic of this book. We do have a User Services group, however, where I will forward specific technical questions related to the book.

When you write, please be sure to include this book's title and author as well as your name, email address, and phone number. I will carefully review your comments and share them with the author and editors who worked on the book.

Email: feedback@quepublishing.com

Mail: Greg Wiegand
         Associate Publisher
         Que Publishing
         800 East 96th Street
         Indianapolis, IN 46240 USA

For more information about this book or another Que Publishing title, visit our website at www.quepublishing.com. Type the ISBN (excluding hyphens) or the title of a book in the Search field to find the page you're looking for.

INTRODUCTION

If you have been toying with the idea of getting into digital music…. If you have an iPod and aren't sure what to do with it…. If you wish you had a good way to stop messing around with a bunch of CDs when you want to listen to music…. If you've heard great things about iPods, have seen the commercials for the iTunes Music Store, and want to know what all the fuss is about, then welcome to the *Absolute Beginner's Guide to iPod and iTunes*!

Meet the Digital Music Triumvirate

In this book, you'll learn about three of the most amazing things to happen to music and digital photos since the first time someone decided that banging a stick on a rock had an appealing sound and that scratching a drawing of the day's hunt on the cave wall was a good idea. These are the iPod, iTunes, and the iTunes Music Store.

The iPod Rocks

Apple's iPod has taken the portable digital device market by storm—and for good reason. Because most of the iPods include a hard drive with up to 60GB of space, you can take your music collection wherever you go. The iPod's tools enable you to organize, customize, and listen to your music in many ways while you are on the move—in your car, at home, or working at your computer. With its tight integration with iTunes and the iTunes Music Store, managing your music is both fun and easy. Your trusty iPod can also be used as a portable drive (for example, you can use it to carry files from your home to your office), to capture sound, and to store pictures; there are numerous peripheral devices that expand its amazing capabilities even further. And, iPods are just plain cool (see Figure I.1).

If you have never used an iPod before, this book is perfect for you and will help you learn everything you need to know. If you have some experience with an iPod, this book will still help you take your iPod skills to the next level. (If you are already an iPod expert, well, you aren't likely to be picking up a book called *Absolute Beginner's Guide to iPod and iTunes* now are you!)

FIGURE I.1
Whatever iPod
model you
choose will rock
your world.

iTunes Jams

With iTunes, you can create, organize, and listen to your entire music library from your computer (see Figure I.2). iTunes enables you to build as large a Library as you have to space on your computer's hard drive to store it. Then, you can customize music playback through playlists and smart playlists, as well as create custom audio CDs in a variety of formats. It also provides other useful features, such as custom labeling and information tools, the ability to share your music on a local network, an Equalizer, and more. Because Apple's iTunes Music Store is integrated into iTunes, you can easily purchase and add music to your Library from within the application. Moreover, iTunes is the best software tool available to manage music on your iPod.

Just as with the iPod, if you have never used iTunes before, this book is perfect for you and will help you learn everything you need to know. If you have some experience, my hope is that you will learn how to get even more out of this outstanding program. Even if you have used iTunes quite a bit, you might manage to find some tidbits that will help your iTunes expertise grow.

iTunes Music Store

Using the iTunes Music Store, you can find, preview, and purchase music from a collection of hundreds of thousands of songs and download that music into your iTunes Music Library. Songs can be purchased individually or in albums, for $.99 per song (less when purchasing an entire album). Music you buy can be listened to, placed on a CD, and moved onto your iPod. Since its inception, the iTunes Music Store has rapidly become the most popular source of legal digital music on the Internet. After you have used it a time or two, you'll understand why.

FIGURE I.2

iTunes will change the way you listen to music.

Quick Guide to *Absolute Beginner's Guide to iPod and iTunes*

Absolute Beginner's Guide to iPod and iTunes provides all the information you need to get the most out of these amazing digital music tools. From the basics of listening to audio CDs with iTunes to the advanced customizing of music on an iPod and purchasing music online, this book equips you with the information you need.

The book is organized into the following three major parts, each focusing on one of the three components of the iPod/iTunes/iTunes Music Store triumvirate:

- Part I, "The iPod"
- Part II, "iTunes"
- Part III, "The iTunes Music Store"

Within each part, the chapters generally start with the basics of the topic and get more advanced as you continue. Within the chapters, the information is presented in roughly the order in which you will typically perform the tasks being described.

Speaking of tasks, this book contains many step-by-step instructions—I hope your motto will be "learn by doing." You should be able to learn how to do a task fairly quickly and relatively painlessly by following the steps using your own music and your own tools. Although my writing is so utterly fascinating that you will likely want to read this book like a good novel, try to resist that urge because you will probably get better results if you actually work with the tools while you read this book.

Of course, you can read this book from start to finish in the order in which the chapters are presented. This will work fine if you have some experience with iTunes and have some music in your iTunes Library. However, because these tools are so well integrated, you can't really use the iPod or the iTunes Music Store effectively without knowing the basics of using iTunes first.

If you are totally new to these topics, I recommend that you get a jumpstart on iTunes by reading the core iTunes chapters first, which include Chapters 13–18. Then, you should read the core iPod chapters, which are Chapters 1–6. From there, read Chapters 23–27 to get the scoop on working with the iTunes Music Store.

After you have finished these core "courses," you can read the rest of the chapters as they interest you. For example, when you are ready to burn your own CDs or DVDs, check out Chapter 20, "Burning Your Own CDs or DVDs." If you have an iPod, read Chapter 9, "Using the iPod for Images," to learn how to view photos and slideshows.

Going Both Ways

Because the iPod, iTunes, and the iTunes Music Store all work equally well on both Windows and Macintosh computers, this book covers these topics from both perspectives. So, you'll notice that some of the figures are screenshots taken on a Windows computer whereas others are taken on a Macintosh. Although the screens on these two computers look slightly different, they work very similarly, so seeing a screen on the Mac shouldn't cause a problem for you if you use a Windows computer, and vice versa. When there are significant differences between the two platforms, I explain them in the text.

Special Elements

As you read, you will see three special elements: notes, tips, and (only rarely) cautions. Also, each chapter ends with a section titled "The Absolute Minimum." Explanations of each of these are provided for you here.

note

Notes look like this. They are designed to provide you with information related to the topic at hand but not absolutely essential to it. I hope you will find the notes interesting, even if you don't find them useful immediately.

tip

Tips help you get something done more quickly and easily, or they tell you how to do a task related to what's being described at the moment. You might also find an explanation of an alternative way to get something done.

caution

If something you can do (and probably shouldn't) might end in a bad result, I warn you in a caution. Fortunately, you won't find many of these throughout the book, but when you do see one, you might want to take a close look at it.

THE ABSOLUTE MINIMUM

Finally, each chapter ends with "The Absolute Minimum" section. The contents of this section vary a bit from chapter to chapter. Examples of this content include the following:

- A summary of the key points of the chapter
- Additional tips related to the chapter's topic
- References to sources of additional information

So, now that you know all you need to about this book, it's time to strike up the band....

PART i

THE iPOD

1

TOURING THE IPOD

Apple's iPod has become one of the most popular personal digital devices ever created. When initially released, the iPod's critics said it was too expensive when compared to other digital music players and that people would never spend the additional money to get the iPod's much superior functionality and style (even the critics couldn't deny the iPod's amazing attributes). As they often are, the critics were very much mistaken. People who love music love the iPod. Its combination of features and style, and because it's simply very, very cool, led it to quickly dominate sales in its category. And with continuous improvements in features and a variety of models from which to choose, the iPod won't be slowing down any time soon.

The Apple iPod: A Lot of Hype or Really Hip?

So, what's the iPod all about?

It's about being able to take your entire music collection with you and listen to anything you want when you want to listen to it. And, using iPod's companion iTunes software, you can create and carry customized collections of your music to make getting to the specific music you want to hear even easier and more fun.

The way your music sounds on an iPod is just amazing, too. You definitely don't have to compromise music quality for portability. With the iPod, you get the best of both. If you have never heard music on an iPod before, prepare to be amazed.

That's the bottom line, but it isn't the whole story. With the iPod, you can do much more, as you will learn through the rest of this part of this book. And because of the iPod's stylish design and ease of use, you will likely want to take it with you wherever you go.

So What Is an iPod Anyway?

The iPod is a small digital device that includes memory (most models include a hard drive just like the one in your computer, only smaller), an operating system, a processor and other computer components, as well as an LCD screen (all models except the iPod shuffle), controls, and other system elements needed to deliver its amazing functionality. It also includes a rechargeable lithium battery to give you plenty of listening time, a Headphones port to which you attach audio devices (including headphones, powered speakers, and so on), and a Dock port or USB connector to enable you to move music from a computer onto the iPod and recharge its battery.

The iPod's software enables you to manage and play digital audio files. You can also use its software to set a variety of preferences, in addition to using the iPod's other built-in tools.

Even with all this, iPods are quite small. The largest iPod is only 2.4 inches wide, is 4.1 inches tall, is .75 inches thick, and weighs a mere 6.4 ounces. This is roughly the size of a deck of playing cards. The smallest model, the iPod

note

iPods can work with a variety of audio file formats, including AAC, MP3, Audible books, AIFF (Mac only), and WAV. Because you just listen to these formats on an iPod, you don't need to know that much about them to use one. However, you will want to understand these formats when you prepare music for an iPod using iTunes. If you can't wait to learn what these formats are all about, see "Audio File Formats You Might Encounter When You Use iTunes" on page **182**.

shuffle, comes in at a svelte 0.98 inches wide, 3.3 inches tall, 0.33 inches thick, and a mere 0.78 ounces, which is about the size of a pack of chewing gum.

All iPod Models Aren't Equal, But They Are All Cool

iPods come in four basic models: iPod, iPod U2, iPod mini, and iPod shuffle. All these models are definitely cool, and all perform the same basic function, which is to enable you to listen to music whenever and wherever. However, each offers specific features and options, as you will see in the following sections.

Before we get into the details of each model, let me warn you that just like the times, the iPod is a changin'. The models listed and described in this chapter are the ones available at press time. Apple regularly makes changes to existing models and introduces new models. The good news is that, even if you use a model that isn't specifically described in this chapter, the information in this book will still help you because in many ways, to know one iPod is to know them all. The controls and options might vary a bit, but most functionality is quite similar, regardless of model.

note

To get the scoop on the iPod models available right now, go to http://www.apple.com/ipod.

The iPod

The iPod is the "standard" iPod, although that word seems to imply that it is less than it really is (see Figure 1.1). The iPod offers many great features in a cool package that you will be proud to carry with you anywhere you go. In addition to your music, you can use an iPod to store your digital images and then display them on its screen or on a TV through its AV port. Because it's designed for more data, this model offers the largest hard drives.

note

With the optional iPod Camera Connector, you can connect a digital camera to your iPod and download images from the camera to the iPod.

FIGURE 1.1
The iPod will definitely rock your world.

At press time, the iPod's specifications were the following:

- A 20GB hard rated for 5,000 songs or a 60GB drive rated for 15,000 songs
- A battery rated for up to 15 hours of music playing time or up to 5 hours of slideshows with music
- A 2-inch color LCD screen
- Dock Connector, Remote Connector, and Headphone/Composite AV ports
- Dimensions of 4.1 inches by 2.4 inches by 0.63 inches and a weight of 5.9 ounces for the 20GB model or 4.1 inches by 2.4 inches by 0.75 inches and a weight of 6.4 ounces for the 60GB model
- Accessories including earbud headphones, an AC adapter, and a USB 2 cable
- A price of $299 for the 20GB model or $399 for the 60GB model

note

There is also the iPod U2 Special Edition, which is the same as the 20GB iPod in features but has a black and red case and features the signatures of U2 band members engraved on the back; it costs $329. Because it is functionally the same as the 20GB iPod, I won't mention it as a distinct model again in this book outside of this chapter.

The iPod mini

The iPod mini is smaller than an iPod (which you can probably guess from its name). Its other major characteristic is that it comes in a variety of colors (see Figure 1.2).

FIGURE 1.2

With an iPod mini, you can listen to music and make a fashion statement at the same time.

At press time, the iPod's mini offered the following:

- A 4GB hard rated for 1,000 songs or a 6GB drive rated for 1,500 songs
- A battery rated for up to 18 hours of playing time
- A choice of colors including silver, blue, pink, and green
- A 1.67-inch grayscale LCD screen
- Dock Connector, Remote Connector, and Headphone ports
- Dimensions of 3.6 inches by 2.0 inches by 0.5 inches and a weight of 3.6 ounces
- Accessories including earbud headphones, a belt clip, and a USB 2 cable
- A price of $199 for the 4GB model or $249 for the 6GB model

The iPod shuffle

Of all the iPod models and variants, the iPod shuffle is the "most" in many ways (see Figure 1.3). It is the most different from the technical point of view because it does not have a hard drive but instead uses a flash drive to store your music. The benefit to this is that it has no moving parts and will never skip, along with being even more resistant to damage. This also means it uses much less power and so can play the same amount of time with a smaller battery. The downside is that it can store much less music than any of the other models. The shuffle is the most "small" model and is less than half the size of even the iPod mini. The flipside to this is that the shuffle has no screen so you can't see information about the music you are playing or even select what you want to hear. The shuffle also uses the most different interface with your computer in that you plug it directly into a USB port. Finally, the shuffle is the most cost-efficient model.

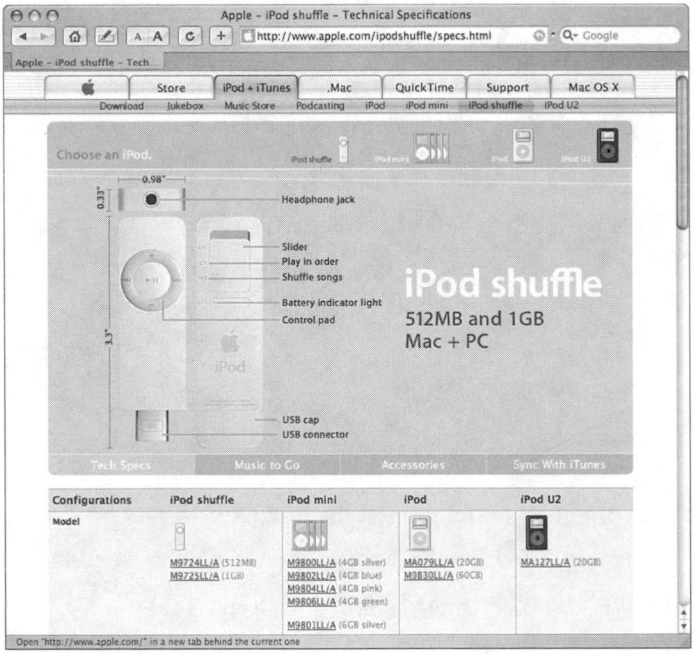

FIGURE 1.3

The iPod shuffle looks quite different from the other iPod models because it is very different from them.

The following is the skinny on this skinniest of iPod models:

- 512MB of memory rated for 120 songs or 1GB of memory rated for 240 songs
- A battery rated for up to 12 hours of music playing time
- USB connector and Headphone port
- Dimensions of 3.3 inches by 0.98 inches by 0.33 inches and a weight of 0.78 ounces
- Accessories including earbud headphones, a lanyard, and a cap for the USB connector
- A price of $99 for the 512MB model or $149 for the 1GB model

Which iPod Is Right for You?

If you already have an iPod and don't envision buying another one, you can skip to the next section. Otherwise, read on for some general guidance on choosing an iPod model.

One of the most frequent questions I get asked is, "Which iPod should I buy?" Unfortunately for me, this is also one of the hardest questions I get asked. That's because each model offers features and benefits that the others don't. And, of course, each costs a different price. There is never a clear-cut answer to this question, unless you can afford to spend only $99, in which case your only choice is the 512MB iPod shuffle (which isn't a bad choice, by the way).

Like all electronic devices, choosing an iPod is a matter of balancing features and options against cost. While I can't address your individual choice, I can provide some general guidance because each model does offer some distinct benefits.

> **note**
>
> Throughout this book, when I write about a specific model, such as an iPod mini, I will mention the model name. Otherwise, I use the term *iPod* to refer to all models. Because the shuffle is an iPod of a different feather altogether, you'll often see it excepted in generic iPod references (as in, *except the shuffle*). Confused? Hopefully you won't be as you get further into this.

If you have a digital camera and often find yourself running out of room for your photos on its memory card, an iPod can be a perfect companion for you. With an adapter, you can move photos from the camera onto the iPod and then erase your camera's card so you can take more pictures. Later, you can move the photos from the iPod onto your computer. Plus, you can view your pictures on the iPod and display them on a TV. And, the iPod offers larger disk drives, which benefits both music and photo storage. The only downside to the iPod is its price, although the 20GB model is only $50 more than the 6GB iPod mini and you get 14GB of additional disk space plus the color screen. The 60GB iPod is only $100 more than the 20GB model; you'll find that additional 40GB of space useful if you have lots of music and photos.

If the iPod's color is important to you or if you want a smaller iPod without the significant storage limitations of the shuffle, the iPod mini is your choice. The color and smaller size do come with a price, though. After a time, you'll probably find the 4GB or 6GB drive size to be a bit limiting unless you don't have a very large music collection. For $100 more than the 4GB mini or $50 more than the 6GB mini, you can get an iPod that offers 14GB more room plus a larger screen.

If you are going to be using an iPod under "extreme" conditions, such as during heavy exercise, sporting activities, or work situations, an iPod shuffle is a good choice because this model is much more resistant to damage than the other models and, with its lower cost, you are risking less by using it in these situations. Plus, it is very small so carrying it is definitely the easiest.

So, what is the bottom line? There isn't one. All iPods are a good choice. Some will fit your needs and budget better than others, but you really can't go wrong with any of them. Pick the most you can afford to spend and then get the model that fits your budget and specific needs.

What You Can Do with an iPod

The iPod is definitely a great music player, but it is much more than that, as you will learn throughout this part of the book. For now, here are just some of the great things you can do with an iPod:

- Take your entire music collection, or at least part of it, with you wherever you go.
- Play your music in many different ways, such as by album, artist, genre, song, playlist, and so on.
- Eliminate the need to carry CDs with you anywhere; using an adapter or an FM transmitter, your iPod can provide music in your home, car, or any other place you happen to be.
- View your calendar.
- Access contact information for your favorite people and companies for quick and easy reference.
- Keep track of the time and date and have a portable alarm clock.
- Listen to your favorite audio book.
- Listen to podcasts.
- Transfer information between computers or back up your important files.
- Record sound.
- Store pictures from a digital camera.
- View pictures and slideshows and play the same on a TV (iPod or iPod U2 Special Edition).

note

When choosing an iPod, consider buying more than one if your budget can support it. For example, if you have a $500 budget, you could get the 60GB iPod for general listening and photos and the 512MB iPod shuffle for exercising. This would be a great combination for most people.

note

Additional accessories are required to perform some of the tasks on this list. And not all models (most notably the shuffle) can do all of them. The shuffle is limited to only playing music (which is, of course, the primary reason to have an iPod in the first place).

The Absolute Minimum

The iPod just might be the neatest gadget ever. After you have tried one, you will likely find it to be indispensable, and you might wonder how you ever got along without it. Before we jump into configuring and using an iPod, consider the following points:

- An iPod enables you to take your music with you and listen to it any time, anywhere.

- The iPod is actually a mini computer and includes a hard drive or flash memory, an operating system, and other computer components.

- There were four types of iPods in production at press time: iPod, iPod U2 Special Edition, iPod mini, and iPod shuffle. There are also variants of all models except the iPod U2 Special Edition, such as the 512MB or 1GB iPod shuffle.

- No matter which iPod you have, you'll be amazed at all the cool things it can do from listening to music to being your own personal portable hard drive (all models except shuffle) or flash drive (shuffle).

- Current iPod models work just as well for Windows and Macintosh computers. Whether you use a Windows computer, a Mac, or both, your iPod will work great.

- Like potato chips, I'll bet you can't get by with just one iPod. After you use one model, you'll probably want to get at least one more for yourself. For example, if you have an iPod, you might want to get a shuffle for those times when device size is important. Or, if you have a mini, you might want to a get an iPod so you can download photos from a digital camera to it. And if you have a family, expect to also need a family of iPods!

2

GETTING STARTED WITH AN iPOD

Getting started with an iPod involves the following general steps:

1. Understand what is included with your iPod.

2. Charge the iPod's battery.

3. Install the iPod's software on your computer.

4. Connect the iPod to your computer and transfer music from your iTunes Library to the iPod.

5. Disconnect the iPod from your computer.

After you have performed these steps, you will be ready to learn how to use the iPod, which you'll start doing in the next chapter.

As you learned in the last chapter, there are three basic models of iPod. Considering iPods work with both Windows and Macintosh computers and how many models and variations of those there are, covering all possible combinations of iPod and computer just isn't possible. So, what I have done instead is to provide general guidelines to help you accomplish the basic tasks you need to do to get your iPod rolling (and rocking). You probably won't need to read every section in this chapter unless you use several kinds of iPods on both types of computers. Use the headings to determine which circumstances apply to you, and skip those sections that don't apply.

Exploring the iPod's Box

The iPod is so cool that even its box is stylish! In this section, you'll learn about the items included in that stylish box and how and where you use them. What you get with an iPod depends on the type and model of iPod you purchased. The following list gives you a general idea of what comes with each type of iPod:

- **The iPod**—You probably didn't need this item listed, but I like to be thorough!

- **Installation CD**—This CD contains the installer applications you will use to install the iPod's software on your computer.

- **Earbud headphones**—You can use these to listen to your iPod's music. The sound quality of the earbuds included with your iPod is remarkably good.

- **USB 2 cable**—All models except the shuffle include the cable you use to connect the iPod to a computer.

- **AC adapter**—Some models include an AC adapter you can use to power the iPod and charge its battery from a wall outlet.

- **Information pamphlets**—These provide basic information you can use to get

> **tip**
>
> As you are handling the iPod, it will turn on if you press any control. For now, turn it off again by pressing and the holding down the **Play/Pause** button until the iPod shuts off again. If you have a shuffle, ignore this because it doesn't apply.

> **tip**
>
> If you use an older Macintosh that doesn't support USB 2 devices, you'll need to purchase the Apple iPod Dock Connector to FireWire Cable. You can obtain this cable at the online Apple Store for $19. Even if your Mac does support USB 2, you might want to use FireWire instead because you probably have more USB peripherals than you have available USB ports.

started with your iPod. (Because you have this book already, you might not find these to be very useful.)

■ **Accessories**—Different iPod models purchased at different times will have different accessories included (did I use *different* in this sentence enough?). For example, the shuffle comes with a lanyard so you can wear it around your neck, while a mini includes a belt clip.

note

No matter which iPod you have, it is likely you'll want to get some accessories for it, such as a case, an FM transmitter, and so on. You'll learn about some of the more useful accessories later in this part of the book.

Charging the iPod's Battery

Like all portable electronic devices, the iPod has an internal battery. If your iPod came with an AC adapter, you should charge its battery before you start using it.

If your iPod didn't include an AC adapter, such as the iPod shuffle, skip to the next section. You'll charge its battery when you connect it to your computer.

To charge an iPod using its AC adapter, connect the USB 2 to iPod Dock connector cable to the AC adapter (USB end) and to the iPod (the larger end with the Dock connector). Then plug the power adapter into a power outlet.

When you plug the AC adapter into a wall outlet, the iPod will start up; you can tell this because an Apple logo will appear on its screen. The first time you start an iPod, a language menu will appear. Ignore this for now and just let the iPod start charging. After a moment or two, this menu will go away.

note

When you connect the Dock connector end of the cable to the iPod, the side of the connector with the icon on it should be toward you when you are looking at the iPod's face.

While the iPod is charging, a battery icon will appear on its display and the word "Charging" will appear at the top of the screen. According to Apple, the iPod's battery is charged to the 80% level in 3 hours and fully charged in 5 hours. While the iPod is charging, you can proceed with installing its software on your computer.

When the iPod is fully charged, the display will contain a "full" battery icon and the status message will be "Charged." Unplug the AC adapter and then disconnect the cable from the power adapter and from the iPod.

Installing the iPod's Software (Including iTunes)

Included in the iPod's box is a software installation CD. On this CD is the software your computer needs to be able to communicate with your iPod, along with the iTunes application you will use to manage the music you place on the iPod. You'll learn all about iTunes in Part II, "iTunes." But for now, install the software by using the steps in the section that is appropriate for the type of computer you are using (a Windows PC or a Mac).

Installing the iPod's Software on a Windows PC

If you have installed even one application from a CD, you won't have any trouble with the iPod CD, as the following steps will confirm:

1. Insert the Installation CD in your computer. The disc will be mounted on your computer, the software will begin to run, and the Choose Setup Language dialog box will appear.

2. Choose the **Language** you want to use on the drop-down list and click **OK**. Because I am linguistically challenged and can only read English, that is the language I use throughout this book. You can choose the language that works best for you.

   After you click OK, the InstallShield Wizard window will appear, and you can watch the initial installation process. When that is complete, you will see the iPod for Windows dialog box (see Figure 2.1). This dialog box might have a slightly different title depending on the iPod model you have, but it will work in the same way.

3. Read the information in the installer window and click **Next**.

4. If you have a lot of time and patience, read the license agreement; when you are done (if you are like me, you will realize it is incomprehensible and will just assume you aren't giving away your firstborn), click **Yes**. You'll see a screen recommending that you connect your iPod to your computer to see whether it needs to be formatted for your computer. You can do so if you'd like, but for now you can skip this by performing the following step.

note

If you'd rather, you can download and install a "fresh" copy of iTunes from the Internet. This is usually a good idea so you get the latest version. To get help doing that, see the section "Downloading and Installing iTunes on a Windows PC" on page **193** or "Installing and Configuring iTunes on a Macintosh" on page **198**. Then come back here and complete the iPod software installation.

FIGURE 2.1

You might see a slightly different window depending on the model of iPod you are using, but in any case, the Next button is the same.

5. Check the **Click on This Checkbox If You Wish to Continue Without Connecting Your iPod** check box and click **Next**. The iPod Serial Number dialog box will appear.

6. Enter your iPod's serial number, which can be found on the back of your iPod, and click **Next**. You will see the **Select Country or Region** dialog box.

7. Select the country or region that is most applicable to you and click **Next**. You will see the Registration Information dialog box.

8. Complete your registration information. Most of it is optional; however, you do have to provide at least a name and an email address. When you are done, click **Next**. You will see the second screen in the registration process.

9. Complete the fields about where you will use the iPod and what best describes what you do, if you'd like to. These are both optional. (Speaking of which, given how easily you can carry an iPod around with you, which is the whole point, how much sense does a question about where you will use it make?)

note

If you have trouble reading the serial number, you aren't alone. The text is very small!

tip

If the country or region you want to choose isn't listed, check the **Show All** check box and hopefully it will be then.

10. If you want to receive email from Apple, click the **Yes** radio button, or click **No** if you don't want to receive email.

11. Click **Next**. You'll see the Choose Destination Location dialog box.

12. If you want to accept the default installation location (which is `C:\Program Files\iPod\`), skipto the next step. If you don't want to accept the default installation location, click the **Browse** button and choose the location you do want to use.

13. Click **Next**. As the installer starts to work, you will see the Setup Status window. This window provides information about the installation process.

When the iPod software installation process is complete, you'll move on to the iTunes installation process.

If you already have a later version of iTunes installed on your computer, such as if you downloaded a copy from the Internet, you'll see an error dialog box that explains you already have a newer version of iTunes installed on your computer. Click **OK** to close the dialog box. You'll move to the InstallShield Wizard Complete dialog box, which prompts you to restart your computer.

If you don't have a newer version of iTunes installed already, the iTunes installation software will guide you through the installation of the iTunes software. To see the details of this installation software, see "Downloading and Installing iTunes on a Windows PC" on page **193**. When iTunes has been successfully installed on your computer, you'll move to the InstallShield Wizard Complete dialog box, which prompts you to restart your computer.

note

A pet peeve of mine is forced registration like Apple requires with the iPod. One shouldn't have to register to make a product they purchased work. Ah well, what can we do?

caution

If you have other open applications with unsaved changes, make sure you save any open documents before you restart your computer.

tip

If you installed iTunes from the iPod CD, you should immediately update the application to ensure you are working with the most current version. For information about updating iTunes, see "Keeping iTunes Up-to-date on a Windows PC Manually" on page **347**.

14. Leave the **Yes** radio button selected and click **Finish**. Your computer will restart and you'll be ready to start working with your iPod.

Installing the iPod's Software on a Macintosh

You can install the iPod's software on a Macintosh using the following steps:

1. Insert the installation CD in your Mac. It will be mounted.

2. Using the Finder, open the installation CD so you can see it folders.

3. Open the **iPod Installer** folder.

4. Double-click the icon you see in the folder, which will be the installation application.

5. Click **Continue** to allow the installer to check for the appropriate software. The install window will appear (see Figure 2.2).

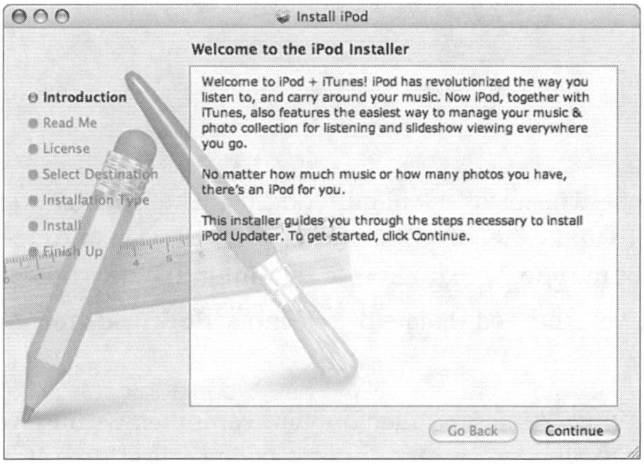

FIGURE 2.2

This is the initial screen of the iPod installer on a Mac.

6. Click **Continue**. The installer will start and you will see the next screen in the process.

7. Read the information on each screen that appears and click **Continue** to move to the next screen.

8. When you get to the license agreement prompt, click **Agree**. You'll see the Select a Destination screen.

9. Click the destination on which you want to install the iPod software. Typically, you should install the software on your active startup drive, which will be selected by default. When you select a drive, it will be marked with a green arrow to show you the drive you have selected. In the lower part of the screen, you will see information about the drive on which you have elected to install the software.

10. Click **Continue**.

11. Click **Install**.

12. If prompted to do so, authenticate yourself as an administrator and click **OK**. The installer will run. When the process is complete, you will see the installation complete screen (see Figure 2.3).

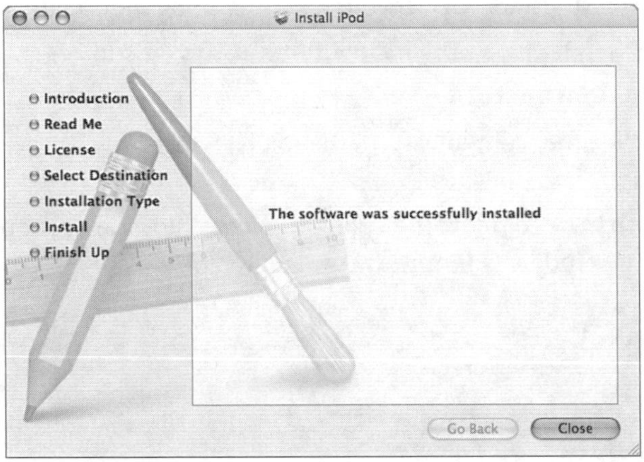

FIGURE 2.3

When you see this screen, you are done installing the iPod software on your Mac.

13. Click **Close**. The installer will quit, and the iPod Updater application will launch. To update the iPod's software, you will need to connect the iPod to your computer. You'll learn how to do that in the next section.

14. For now, quit the iPod Update by selecting **iPod Updater**, **Quit iPod Updater**.

You also need to have iTunes installed on your computer. Because you are using a Mac, you probably already have a copy installed because iTunes is installed on new Macs and as part of the Mac OS X installation. You should update the version you have installed to ensure you are using the most current version of the application. For the steps to do this, see "Keeping iTunes Up-to-date on a Macintosh" on page **347**.

If you don't have a copy of iTunes installed on your Mac already, you can install it from the iPod installation CD or by downloading a copy from the Internet. For help with those tasks, see "Installing and Configuring iTunes on a Macintosh" on page **198**.

Connecting and Configuring an iPod on Your Computer

In order to load music onto an iPod, you must connect the iPod to your computer so the music files can be moved from your iTunes Library onto the iPod. The first time you connect your iPod to your computer you'll need to configure it.

Preparing an iPod to Connect to a Computer

To connect all iPods (except the shuffle) to a computer, you use the USB 2 cable supplied with your iPod or the optional FireWire cable. All iPod cables have the Dock connector connection on one end. Connect this to the iPod's Dock connector port located on the bottom of the iPod (see Figure 2.4).

caution

To connect the Dock connector end of the cable into your iPod's Dock connector port, the icon on the Dock connect end of the cable must be "up," meaning that you see the icon when you are looking at the front face of the iPod (with the controls on it). If you try to insert the connector backwards, you can damage it.

FIGURE 2.4

You use the Dock connector port on the bottom of the iPod to connect it to a computer.

Bottom of an iPod mini   Dock connector port

Bottom of an iPod

You connect the other end of the cable to either a USB 2 or a FireWire port on your computer, depending on which cable you use and which ports your computer has. All current iPod models (except the shuffle) include a USB cable. Some previous models also included a FireWire cable, which you can also purchase separately.

The iPod shuffle has a USB connector built in to one of its ends (see Figure 2.5). To expose the connector, remove the lanyard cap from the end of the shuffle by gently pulling it off the iPod.

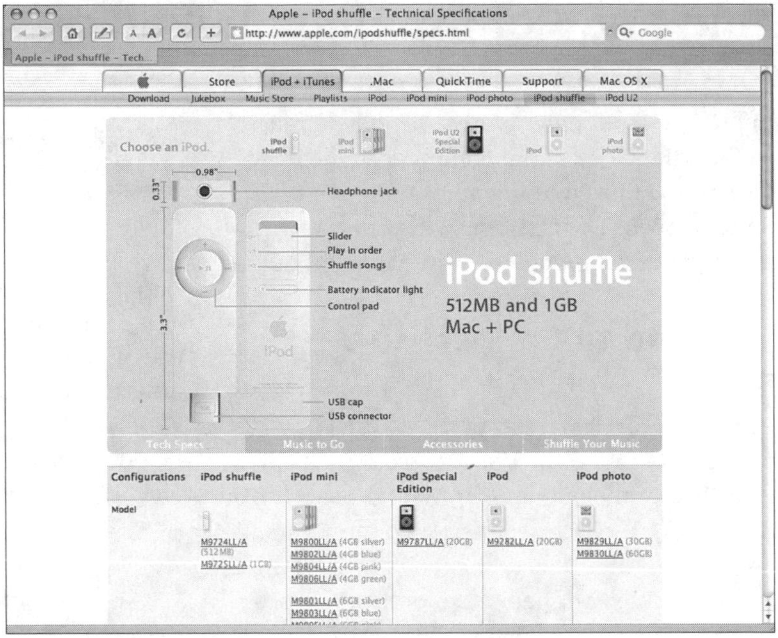

FIGURE 2.5

You don't need a cable to connect an iPod shuffle to a computer because it plugs directly into a USB port.

To connect it to your computer, simply plug it into a USB 2 port on the computer itself.

Connecting an iPod to a Computer

Connecting an iPod to a computer requires that you decide on the type of connection you will be using. There are two basic options: USB 2 or FireWire.

All modern computers (Windows and Mac) include USB 2 ports that you can use to connect an iPod to your computer. All Macs and some Windows computers include FireWire ports you can use just as well.

Although these are different connection technologies, you won't really notice any functional difference between them so it doesn't matter

caution

To use USB 2 to connect an iPod to a Mac, you must be running Mac OS X version 10.3.4 or later. If you are running an earlier version of Mac OS X, you'll need to use FireWire instead.

which you use. If you have a choice, the option you choose will likely just depend on if you have more ports available of one kind than the other.

Using USB 2 to Connect an iPod to a Computer

If you have a computer that supports USB 2—and unless you have a very old computer, it probably does—you can use USB 2 to connect your iPod to the computer. If you use a high-power USB 2 port, your iPod's battery will also be charged whenever it is connected to your computer.

A USB 2 port is a rectangular port that is fairly thin (see Figure 2.6). USB is also marked with a trident-like icon. You should use only a USB 2 port that is located on your computer's case so the port will provide enough power to charge your iPod when it is connected.

The slightly confusing thing about USB is that there are two basic kinds of USB ports: USB 1 and USB 2. And, some computers have both kinds.

Locate the USB ports on your computer's case.

caution

Not all USB ports on a computer support high power USB 2, which is what you want to use because, when you connect your iPod to your computer, the iPod's battery is also charged (it is charged when you use FireWire, too). Don't connect an iPod to a USB anywhere except on your computer's case.

FIGURE 2.6

You can use a USB 2 port to connect your iPod to your computer.

Unfortunately, you can't tell by observation whether a USB port supports USB 2 or USB 1 because the ports are identical in appearance. Check the documentation that came with your computer to determine which ports support USB 2. If you can't find that information, contact your computer's manufacturer.

If you still can't determine which ports support USB 2, try one of the USB ports on your computer's case. If the iPod's battery charges when it is connected, you have a USB 2 port. If not, you probably are using an USB 1 port. Try a different one until you locate a USB 2 port.

Plug the USB end of the USB 2 cable into the USB port on your computer. The connector will only fit one way, so if it isn't going in easily, turn the connector over. After it is connected, you'll be ready to configure your iPod. Skip to the section "Configuring an iPod on Your Computer" on page **31**.

If you use a shuffle, plug it directly into the USB 2 port. When it is connected, you'll see its status light (located at the top of the iPod shuffle on the same side as the playback controls) glow amber; this means the battery is charging. When the battery is fully charged, this light will become green. If the light doesn't light up, you need to try a different port. When you find a port that causes the light to come on, you'll be ready to configure your iPod and can skip to the section "Configuring an iPod on Your Computer" on page **31**.

tip

Diagnostic applications are available that will tell you whether your computer supports USB 2. However, these are beyond the scope of this book. You can do a web search to find to try one.

Using FireWire to Connect an iPod to a Computer

All modern Macs and many Windows PCs include FireWire ports that provide high-speed connections and power to devices such as iPods. FireWire ports are shaped like a rectangle with one end being replaced with a sort of semi-circle (see Figure 2.7).

Some previous iPod models included a FireWire cable. If yours didn't and you want to use FireWire to connect, you can purchase an iPod Dock Connector to FireWire Cable from the Apple Store (www.apple.com/store).

Locate the FireWire ports on your computer's case and connect the FireWire end of your iPod cable to it. You'll be ready to configure your iPod.

note

If your computer doesn't have any FireWire ports and does not support USB 2, you'll have to add a PCI FireWire or USB 2 card to your computer before you can connect an iPod to it.

FIGURE 2.7

When you connect an iPod to a computer using FireWire, its battery will be charged.

Configuring an iPod on Your Computer

The first time you connect an iPod to your computer, the iPod will turn on and immediately be mounted on your computer.

Depending on the iPod and computer you are using, you might be prompted that your iPod needs to be reformatted. If so, click **Update**. You'll move into the iPod Updater application, and your iPod will be prepared for use. When that process is complete, you'll see a dialog box that tells you your iPod software is up-to-date (see Figure 2.8). If you are prompted to restart your computer, do so. If not, quit the iPod Updater software on a Windows PC by clicking its **Close** box or on a Mac by selecting **iPod Updater**, **Quit iPod Updater**.

caution

Some older Windows PCs might have a four-pin FireWire port, which is quite different from the modern six-pin version. Even if you can find an adapter to be able to connect to this port, don't do so because your iPod won't charge while it is connected.

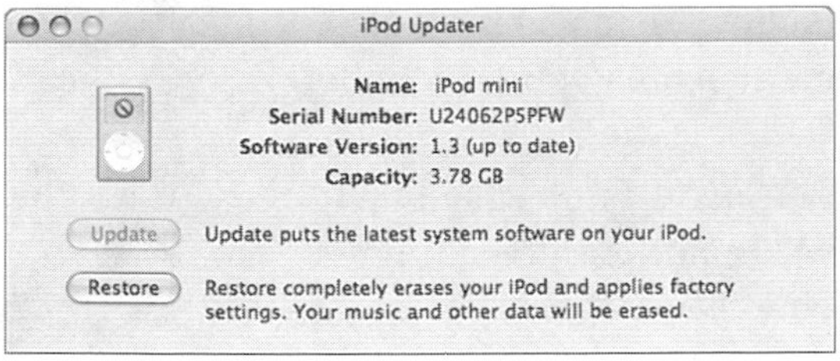

FIGURE 2.8

This updater screen tells you that the iPod's software is up-to-date.

⊗	iPod Updater

Name: iPod mini
Serial Number: U24062P5PFW
Software Version: 1.3 (up to date)
Capacity: 3.78 GB

Update — Update puts the latest system software on your iPod.

Restore — Restore completely erases your iPod and applies factory settings. Your music and other data will be erased.

After your iPod has been updated, iTunes will open and the iPod Setup Assistant will appear (see Figure 2.9). Type a name for your iPod in the text box. You can use any name you'd like; this will be the name of your iPod when it is shown in the iTunes Source List and on your computer's Desktop. Leave the **Automatically update songs on my iPod** check box checked. Then click **Next**. You'll move to the Registration screen. If you want to register your iPod, click the **Register My iPod** button and follow the onscreen instructions to complete the registration process. When you come back to the Assistant, click **Finish** (Windows) or **Done** (Mac).

tip

If you are using an iPod, the Setup Assistant will also enable you to update your photos when you update your music. For now, leave that option unchecked. You'll learn about working with iPod photos in Chapter 9, "Using the iPod for Images."

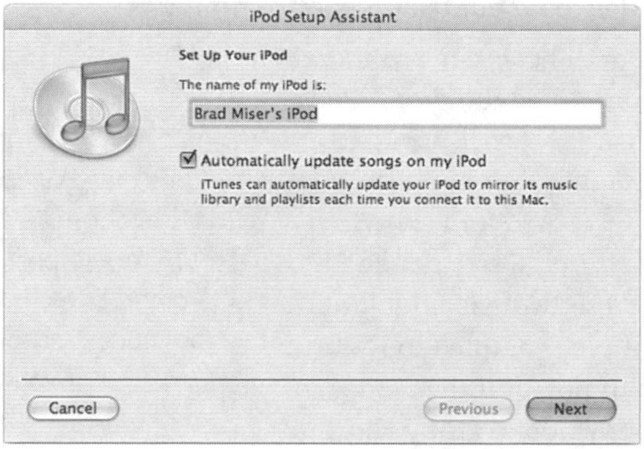

iTunes will update the iPod and transfer all the music in your iTunes Library onto the iPod—if it can.

FIGURE 2.9

The trusty iPod Setup Assistant is ready to do its work.

While music is being transferred, the iPod icon on the iTunes Source List will flash red (see Figure 2.10). You'll also see information about the transfer in the iTunes Information area at the top of the iTunes window.

If all the music in your iTunes Library will fit on the iPod, the process will complete without any further action from you. When this process is complete, you will hear a "whoosh" sound and you'll

note

If you are playing music while you transfer music to an iPod, you will see information about the music you are playing rather than information about the transfer.

see the `iPod update is complete` message in the information area at the top of the iTunes window. Click the Eject button next to the iPod's icon on the Source List. The iPod will be removed from the Source List and after a moment or two, the `OK to disconnect` message will also be displayed on the iPod's screen. When you see this message, you can disconnect your iPod from your computer. Squeeze the buttons on each side of the Dock connector end of the cable and remove the cable from the iPod; the iPod will be ready to use. You can leave the cable plugged into your computer if you want.

> **tip**
>
> If you haven't charged your iPod's battery already, you should leave your iPod connected to your computer until its battery is fully charged, which will take about 4–5 hours depending on the model you have.

FIGURE 2.10

If this book were printed in color, you would see that the iPod mini icon in the iTunes Source List is flashing red to show that music in the selected playlist is being moved onto the iPod.

iPod mini on Source List   Information area

If there is more music in your iTunes Library than can fit on the iPod, you will see a message telling you that the iPod doesn't have enough room for all your music (see Figure 2.11). You'll be prompted to have iTunes select songs that will fit onto the iPod. Click **Yes** to allow this. In this case, iTunes will create a playlist of music that will fit on the iPod and then transfer this music to your iPod. This is fine for now; in later chapters, you'll learn how to choose which music is transferred onto your iPod.

iTunes will move the playlist it created (whose name will be the name of your iPod plus the word "Selection") onto your iPod. When this process is complete, you will hear a "whoosh" sound and you'll see the iPod update is complete message in the information area at the top of the iTunes window. Click the Eject button next to the iPod's icon on the Source list. The iPod will be removed from the Source list and after a moment or two, the OK to disconnect message will also be displayed on the iPod's screen. When you see this message, you can disconnect your iPod from your computer. Squeeze the buttons on each side of the Dock connector end of the cable and remove the cable from the iPod; the iPod will be ready to use. You can leave the cable plugged into your computer if you want to.

caution

While you have an iPod connected to your computer, you will see the message Do not disconnect on the iPod's screen. You should wait until the file transfer is complete or eject an iPod before you disconnect it. You'll learn more about this in the next chapter.

FIGURE 2.11
Because I had more music than can be stored on an iPod mini, iTunes let me know about it.

The iPod "Mini iPod" cannot be updated because there is not enough free space to hold all of the songs in the iTunes music library. Would you like iTunes to choose a selection of songs to copy to this iPod?

No   Yes

Connecting an iPod to a Computer with a Dock

Dealing with a cable each time you connect your iPod to your computer is a bit of a pain. An iPod Dock provides a cradle for your iPod so you don't need to use the cable itself. When you want to transfer music to the iPod or charge its battery, you simply set it in the Dock (see Figure 2.12). The connection is made instantly and your iPod is updated while its battery charges.

You can purchase a Dock for any iPod from any retailer that carries iPod accessories or from the online Apple Store located at www.apple.com/store.

Even though it doesn't use cables, a Dock is available for the shuffle, too. This is useful when the USB port

note

A *playlist* is a collection of songs. You can use iTunes to create your own playlists and then listen to those playlists on an iPod. There are also a couple of playlists you can create and manage on the iPod itself. You'll learn about these later in this part of the book.

on your computer isn't convenient for you to reach, such as being on the back of a computer that is under a table or desk. You can place the shuffle's Dock in a more convenient location.

In addition to making it easier to connect your iPod to a computer, the Docks for various models also include other ports you might find useful. For example, Docks for iPods (and the older iPod photo models), include AV ports you can connect to a TV to display slideshows on the TV. Additionally, a Dock is the only way to use the better quality S-video connection to display an iPod's slideshows on a TV. Other Docks include an Audio out port you can connect to a home theater to play your iPod's music over a stereo system.

tip

Before you rush out and purchase a Dock, realize that if you use a case on your iPod, you'll have to remove the case to be able to place the iPod into the Dock. Depending on how hard the case is to remove, this might be more trouble than using a cable to connect. Most cases provide access to the Dock port so you can connect the cable directly to the iPod while it is in its case.

To use a Dock, connect the Dock connector end of the cable you use to connect the iPod to your computer into the Dock connector port on the Dock (instead of the port on the iPod). To connect the iPod to the computer, simply set it into the Dock. When the Dock can communicate with the iPod, you'll hear a tone and your iPod will be mounted on your computer.

When you want to disconnect your iPod from the computer, lift it out of the Dock. (You might have to place one hand on the Dock to keep it from lifting up when you lift the iPod out.)

caution

Before you pull an iPod out of a Dock, make sure the OK to disconnect message appears on the iPod's screen.

THE ABSOLUTE MINIMUM

Fortunately, a lot of the material in this chapter is useful only the first time you use your iPod. After all, installing software and connecting cables isn't all that thrilling. But it is necessary to do the thrilling stuff that starts in the next chapter. Before we leave this topic, consider the following points:

- You'll need to install the iPod's software on the CD included with it on your computer.

- The CD also contains the iTunes installer. However, you might want to download and install a copy of iTunes from the Internet so you are sure you are working with the latest version.

- To transfer music from your iTunes Library onto your iPod and to charge its battery, you connect the iPod to your computer. You can use a USB 2 or FireWire cable to do this. If you have a shuffle, you plug it directly into a USB 2 port.

- The first time you connect your iPod to your computer you'll need to do some basic setup. Fortunately, the iPod and iTunes software will guide you all the way.

- You can install more than one iPod on the same computer. For example, you might be fortunate enough to have an iPod and an iPod shuffle. If have more than one iPod, use a different name for each so you can keep them straight. You can even connect them to your computer at the same time if you have enough ports and cables available to do so.

- A Dock makes it easier to connect your iPod to your computer. It also includes a Line Out port. You can use this to connect the Dock to speakers or other audio device to play the iPod's music on that device. You'll learn more about this in Chapter 8, "Using an iPod with a Home Stereo or Car Stereo."

IN THIS CHAPTER

- Connect an iPod to headphones or speakers so you can hear its music.

- Turn on an iPod and learn about its controls.

- Tour the iPod's menus and screens.

- Light up your iPod's world with the Backlight.

- Put an iPod on hold.

- Turn off an iPod.

3

CONTROLLING AN IPOD OR IPOD MINI

The iPod is a well-designed device that is easy to control—once you understand its controls and how they work, that is. Because the iPod is likely quite different from other devices you have used, it can take a little time to get totally comfortable controlling one. That's where this chapter comes in. You'll learn about the iPod's controls and how to use them. You'll also come to know (and love) the iPod's menu structure and the major screens with which you will deal. You'll get into the details of using all these controls and screens in subsequent chapters.

In this chapter, you'll learn the specific controls on the current generation of iPods (current to when I was writing this book, that is) that you use to perform certain actions. Previous generations used different kinds of controls. For example, before the Click Wheel was standard on all iPod models, some models had separate buttons for Play and other actions. Throughout the rest of this part of the book, I'll refer to the action in general and expect that you know which control to use for your model of iPod. For example, in later chapters when a step says to play the iPod, I'll just write that you should press the Play button without telling you where it is. On all iPods except the shuffle, you'll know where it is from this chapter, and you'll learn where it is on the shuffle in Chapter 5. For other models, you'll have to figure it out, which won't be hard because the buttons are labeled with the same icons.

Getting Ready to Play

To hear the music stored on your iPod, you must attach a sound output device to it. The most common one you might think of is the earbud headphones that were included in the package.

To use these, you connect the mini-jack on the earbud cable to the Headphones port located on the top of the iPod. When you do so, you'll hear any sound coming from the iPod through the earbuds.

> **note**
>
> In this chapter, I use the term *iPod* to mean all models except the shuffle. The iPod shuffle works differently from the other iPods. If you use only an iPod shuffle, you don't need to read this chapter or the next, so move ahead to Chapter 5, "Listening to Music on an iPod shuffle."

Controlling an iPod

The primary controls for an iPod are located on its Click Wheel (see Figure 3.1).

Turning On an iPod

To turn on an iPod, press the **Click Wheel** in any location or press the **Select** button. You'll see the Apple logo on the iPod's screen, and after it starts up, you'll see the main menu.

Choosing an iPod's Language

The first time you turn on an iPod, you'll immediately move to the Language selection screen that you use to choose the language in which your iPod will display information. To choose a language, slide a finger or thumb clockwise on the **Click Wheel** to move down the language list or counterclockwise to move up the list. When the language you want to use is highlighted, press the

> **note**
>
> If you connect a set of unamplified speakers, you aren't likely to hear very much, if anything. The iPod doesn't put out enough power to drive a set of unpowered speakers.

Select button to choose it. You will then move to the main menu. You'll have to do this the first time you turn on an iPod and each time you restore it.

FIGURE 3.1

Most of the controls on an iPod mini are on its Click Wheel.

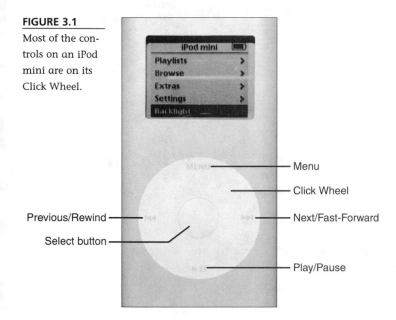

Making Selections on an iPod

The previous paragraph about selecting a language gives you the general idea of how you control an iPod. Now, let's give you a very specific idea of how you move around your iPod to make it follow your commands.

The iPod is based on menus from which you make choices. To make a choice on a menu, you slide a finger or thumb clockwise on the **Click Wheel** to move down the current menu or counterclockwise to move up the current menu. As you move up or down, a different command on the menu will be highlighted. When the command you want to use is highlighted, press the **Select** button to choose it. If the command is for another menu, that menu will appear. You can then move up and down that menu to choose another command. If the menu provides a list of songs, albums, or other categories, you can use the same process to select and play an item, such as a song.

note

Some audio devices connect to the iPod's Dock connector. Examples of these are iPod speakers, certain FM transmitters, and so on. Whenever you connect it, the point is that your iPod needs something connected to it for you to hear its music.

To move back to a previous menu, you press the **Menu** button. You move "up" one level of the menu structure each time you press the Menu button.

You'll learn the specific menus and screens you will use later in this chapter. For now, just understand how to move up and down the iPod's menu structure.

Using the iPod's Click Wheel

The iPod's Click Wheel is kind of cool because it contains both the wheel you use to move up and down the menus and the various buttons you use to control the iPod. These buttons are located at each 90° point around the Click Wheel. To use a button, you simply press down on its icon on the wheel. The button will click and the action it represents will happen.

Because there isn't a clear delineation between locations on the wheel, you don't have to be precise when you press a button. Press down close to the button's icon on the wheel and you will likely get the expected action.

When a song is playing and the Now Playing screen is displayed, you control the iPod's volume by sliding a finger or thumb on the Click Wheel clockwise to increase the volume or counterclockwise to decrease it.

When music is playing, you can also fast-forward, rewind, and rate music using the Click Wheel after you press the Select button one time to change to fast-forward or rewind mode or two times to get to the rating mode. The detailed steps to access and use these modes are covered later in this part of the book.

Looking at the iPod's Menus and Screens

Now that you have an idea of how to move around your iPod, let's get a good understanding of its menus and screens.

The steps you use to move around the iPod's menus are the following:

1. Slide your finger or thumb clockwise on the **Click Wheel** to move down a menu or counterclockwise to move up a menu. As you move your digit, different menu options will be highlighted on the screen to show that they are selected.

2. When you want to use a menu command, highlight it and press the **Select** button. That command will be active and the screen will change to reflect what you have done. For example, if you selected another menu, that menu will appear on the screen. If you selected a song, the Now Playing screen will

appear and that song will start to play. If you selected an application, that application will run.

3. To move back to a previous screen, press the **Menu** button. You'll move back to the screen you were on before the current one. Each time you press the Menu button, you'll move back one screen until you get back to the Main menu.

The Main Menu

The iPod's Main menu provides the major (dare I say *main*?) commands available to you. The specific commands you see on the Main menu by default will depend on the model of iPod you are using. For example, if you use an iPod, as shown in Figure 3.2, you'll see the Photos command, which won't appear on the iPod mini because it isn't applicable to that model.

When no music is playing, the default Main menu commands are the following:

- Music
- Photos (iPod only)
- Extras
- Settings
- Shuffle Songs
- Backlight

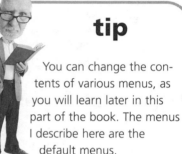

tip

You can change the contents of various menus, as you will learn later in this part of the book. The menus I describe here are the default menus.

iPod or iPod mini

FIGURE 3.2

The Main menu is a good place to start using an iPod, which is why you will move there when you first turn it on.

iPod ——————— Battery icon
Music ——————— Highlighted command
Photos ›
Extras › ——————— This arrow means you will move to another menu
Settings ›
Shuffle Songs ——————— Commands
Backlight

All these commands take you to their respective menus, except for Shuffle Songs and Backlight. The Shuffle Songs command puts the iPod in Shuffle mode where it plays songs in a random fashion (you'll learn more about this later). The Backlight command turns on the iPod's Backlight (more on this later, too).

When you are playing music, the Now Playing command appears. This command takes you to the Now Playing screen. In the upper-left corner of the screen, you'll see the Play icon if music is currently playing or the Pause icon if music has been paused.

When a menu choice leads to another menu, a right-facing arrow will appear along the right edge of the screen for that choice. If you don't see an arrow for a command, that command will cause an action to happen instead.

When there are more options on a menu than can be listed on the screen, you will see the scrollbar along the right edge of the screen; the dark part of the bar represents how much of the menu you are seeing on the screen out of the total menu, which is represented by the full bar. (Remember that to scroll up and down a menu, you use the Click Wheel.)

note

That clicking sound you hear is the iPod's way of providing additional feedback to you each time you move to a different menu option. Oh, by the way, the technical term for this feature is the Clicker.

The Music Menu and Screens

The Music command takes you to the Music menu, which provides access to a number of other menus relating to the selection of music to which you want to listen (see Figure 3.3).

FIGURE 3.3

The Music menu enables you to access your music in a number of ways.

Music	
Playlists	>
Artists	>
Albums	>
Songs	>
Genres	>
Composers	>
Audiobooks	>

The menu options you have on the Music menu are the following:

■ **Playlists**—The Playlists command takes you to the Playlists menu, which lists the playlists stored on your iPod. (If you haven't read Part II, "iTunes," *playlists* are collections of music that you create in iTunes.) On the Playlists menu, you will see each playlist you have created in iTunes and have moved to the iPod. Because each playlist represents a "menu" of the songs in that playlist, when you select it, you will see the Songs menu, which lists each song in the playlist. You'll learn how to work with the Playlists menu and screens in detail in Chapter 6, "Building an iPod's Music Library."

- **Artists**—Similar to the Playlists menu, this command takes you to a menu on which your music is organized by artist. You can choose an artist and then browse all the music by that artist that is stored on your iPod.

- **Albums**—This command and menu enable you to browse and select your music by album.

- **Songs**—This command takes you to a menu containing all the songs on your iPod, listed in alphabetical order.

- **Podcasts**—Podcasts are similar to radio broadcasts except that you can download them onto your iPod and listen to them at a time of your choosing. Selecting the Podcasts command tasks you to the podcasts stored on your iPod so that you can work with them.

- **Genres**—I'll bet you can guess that this command takes you to a menu that enables you to browse and select your music by genre.

- **Composers**—Are you detecting a pattern here? I'll leave this one for you to figure out.

- **Audiobooks**—This takes you to a menu showing all the audiobooks available on your iPod.

note

There is one playlist on the iPod that you won't find in iTunes because it wasn't created there: the On-the-Go playlist. You can create this playlist from music that is stored on the iPod. You'll learn how to use this in Chapter 4, "Listening to Music on an iPod or iPod mini."

note

If you're paying close attention, and I'm sure you are, you noticed that I didn't include a section for the Photos command. Since that is applicable only to the iPod, I cover that in Chapter 9, "Using the iPod for Images."

The Extras Menu and Screens

The Extras command takes you to the Extras menu. On this menu, you will find various options that are related only because they are on the same menu. These commands enable you to access the iPod's non-music features, such as the Clock, Calendar, and so on. You'll learn about these extras in Chapter 10, "Using the iPod's Calendar, Contact Manager, and Other Non-Music Tools."

The Settings Menu and Screens

The Settings command is like the Preferences command in most computer programs. It enables you to configure various aspects of your iPod, such as the contrast of the screen, the Clicker settings, and so on. You'll use this command to configure the Backlight, as you'll learn later in this chapter, and we'll get into it in detail in Chapter 7, "Configuring an iPod to Suit Your Preferences."

The Shuffle Songs Command

Unlike the other items described so far, this is a command that doesn't take you to a menu. Instead, it puts your iPod in Shuffle mode. You'll learn how to configure and use this command in Chapter 7.

The Backlight Command

This command turns on the iPod's Backlight if it is off or off if it is on. See the section titled "Using the iPod's Backlight" on page **45** to learn more about the iPod's Backlight.

The Now Playing Menu

The Now Playing command appears on the Main menu only when you have selected and played music. When you choose this command, you move to the Now Playing screen, which shows you the song that is currently playing (see Figure 3.4). This is an important screen because you can control various aspects of how music is playing from this screen, such as the volume level. You'll explore the Now Playing screen in detail in Chapter 4.

FIGURE 3.4
The Now Playing screen shows you the music currently playing on an iPod.

note

In Figure 3.4, you can see that the artwork associated with the music being played appears on the Now Playing screen. This only happens on an iPod with a color screen. For all other models, you won't see this.

Now Playing

1 of 44

Duck and Run
3 Doors Down
Another 700 Miles

2:28   -2:07

Using the iPod's Backlight

The Backlight lights up the iPod's screen so you can see it in dark conditions or at other times when you are having trouble reading it. You can turn the Backlight on or off manually, and you can configure it to turn off automatically after a specific period of time.

Turning On the Backlight

To turn on the Backlight, move to the **Main** menu, select **Backlight**, and click the **Select** button. The Backlight will come on and your iPod's world will be a lot brighter.

After the current backlight time passes, the Backlight will turn off automatically.

Configuring the Backlight

If you don't want to have to manually turn on the Backlight, you can set the iPod to turn it on briefly each time you press a button. This is useful because you can always see what you are doing no matter what lighting conditions are you are in. You can also have the Backlight on at all times, but I don't recommend that option because of the drain on the iPod's battery.

You can configure your iPod's Backlight settings by performing the following steps:

1. Select **Main** menu, **Settings**. You'll see the Settings screen.
2. Select **Backlight Timer**. You'll see the Backlight screen (see Figure 3.5).
3. If you want the backlight to come on each time you press a control, choose the amount of time you want it to remain on after you stop touching a control. Your options are 2, 5, 10, 15, or 20 seconds.
4. If you want the Backlight to come on only when you select the Backlight command on the Main menu, select **Off**.

caution

The Backlight uses a lot of power. To maximize the play time you get between recharges, you should use the Backlight only when you really need it or set the automatic settings so it is on only briefly.

note

To enable me to write and you to read fewer words, I've used some shorthand to indicate iPod menu selections. For example, when you see "select **Main** menu, **Settings**," this means to move to the iPod's Main menu and then to the Settings menu by highlighting the Settings command and pressing the Select button. When you see "Select **Backlight Timer**," that means to highlight the Backlight Timer command and click the Select button.

II	Backlight	▭
Off		
2 Seconds		
5 Seconds		
10 Seconds		
15 Seconds		
20 Seconds		
Always On		

5. If you want the Backlight on all the time, select **Always On**. Again, I don't recommend this option because it will drain your battery more quickly.

6. Press **Menu** twice to move back to the Main menu.

> **tip**
>
> For battery conservation, I don't recommend the 10-, 15-, or 20-second setting. Try the 2- or 5-second setting because they provide a decent length of illumination time but won't be quite so hard on your battery.

Putting an iPod on Hold

The Hold switch disables all the controls on an iPod so that you don't inadvertently press a button, such as if you carry your iPod in your pocket.

To disable the iPod's controls, slide the **Hold** switch to the left on an iPod or to the right on an iPod mini (these directions assume you are looking at the iPod's face with its top pointing up). When you do so, the area underneath the switch that was exposed when you slid it will be orange to indicate that the iPod is in the Hold mode. You'll also see the Lock icon on the iPod's screen (see Figure 3.6).

Lock icon

II 🔒	Now Playing	▭
3 of 44		
	When I'm Gone	
	3 Doors Down	
	Another 700 Miles	
3:08		-1:13

To reenable the iPod's controls, slide the **Hold switch** to the right on an iPod or to the left on an iPod mini (these directions assume you are looking at the iPod's face with its top pointing up). The orange area of the Hold switch and the Lock icon on the iPod screen will disappear and you can again control your iPod.

Turning Off an iPod

To turn off an iPod, press and hold down the **Play/Pause** button for a second or two. The iPod screen will turn off. You can turn off the iPod from any screen, regardless of whether music is playing. If you aren't playing music, iPods will turn off themselves after a period of inactivity to conserve their battery.

tip

If your iPod isn't responding to your attempts to control it, check the Hold switch to make sure it isn't active. It is amazing how easy it is to forget that you put your iPod in Hold mode and then start troubleshooting to figure why the iPod isn't working. (Not that this has happened to me of course.)

THE ABSOLUTE MINIMUM

iPods are great devices that do all sorts of cool things. Like any other piece of technology, iPod controls can require a bit of getting used to before using one becomes second nature to you. Fortunately, as you have seen in this chapter, the iPod's design does make sense, and after you gain an understanding of how the menus and screens are laid out, you won't have any trouble learning to use them in detail, which is where we are headed next. For now, review the following list to see where you've been:

- To hear your iPod's music, you need to attach an output device to it, such as headphones or powered speakers.

- You control an iPod with its Click Wheel. To select an option on a menu, you slide your finger or thumb (and why isn't the thumb included in the term *finger* anyway?) around the Click Wheel to move up or down the menu. When the option you want is highlighted, press the Select button. You can control music playback by pressing the Click Wheel near the icons on its face; for example, to play or pause music, you press the Click Wheel at the bottom of the wheel (at the 270° position for you technical types) where Play/Pause is located.

- iPods have a menu structure that enables you to access its various screens and commands; in this chapter, you saw an overview of these.

- You won't always be using an iPod in bright conditions; its Backlight helps you see the screen better.

- You turn on the Hold switch to prevent unintentionally activating commands.

- To turn off an iPod, press and hold the Play button until its screen turns off.

IN THIS CHAPTER

- Pick some music, any music.
- Control your music like a pro.
- Create and listen to an On-The-Go playlist.
- Check your battery.

4

LISTENING TO MUSIC ON AN iPOD OR iPOD MINI

In this chapter, you'll learn how to listen to and control your iPod tunes. Like any other device on which you listen to music, listening to music on an iPod is a two-step process. You first select the music you want to listen to. Then you play and control that music.

As you rock on, jazz up, classical out, and so on, you'll also find some other tasks useful, such as creating and using an On-The-Go playlist, rating your tunes, and monitoring your battery.

Selecting Music You Want to Listen To

The iPod is cool, but it isn't psychic. You need to tell it what music you want to listen to. There are two primary ways you do this: You can use playlists or you can browse the music stored on the iPod in various ways.

Selecting Music with Playlists

When you transfer music from your iTunes Library to an iPod, the playlists you have created and that are shown in the iTunes Source List come over too. You can select music to listen to by choosing a playlist using the following steps:

1. Select **Main** menu, **Music**, **Playlists**. You'll move to the Playlists menu (see Figure 4.1).

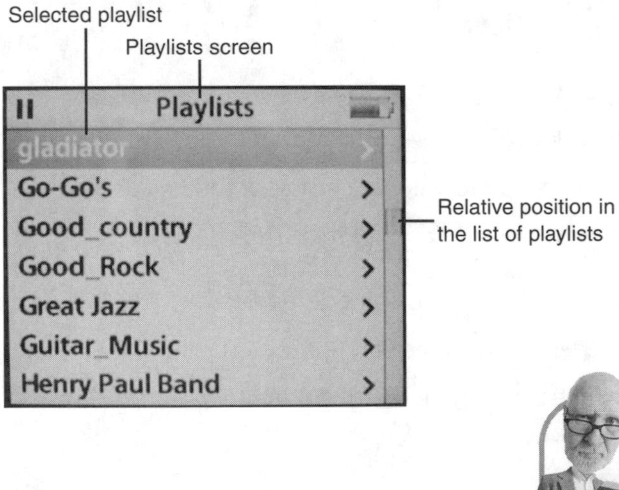

note

To play music on an iPod, you must have music stored on it. You do this by loading music into your iTunes Library and then transferring that music to the iPod. For help with the first part, see Chapters 13–18. For help with the second part, refer to Chapter 2, "Getting Started with an iPod."

Selected playlist
Playlists screen

FIGURE 4.1
Almost all the playlists you see on an iPod's Playlists menu should look familiar because they are the same playlists that appear in your iTunes Library.

‖	Playlists	▭
gladiator		>
Go-Go's		>
Good_country		>
Good_Rock		>
Great Jazz		>
Guitar_Music		>
Henry Paul Band		>

Relative position in the list of playlists

2. Highlight the playlist you want to listen to and press the **Select** button. The songs in that playlist will be shown (see Figure 4.2).

3. If you want to play the entire playlist, press the **Play/Pause** button. If you want to start with a specific song, highlight it and press the **Select** button. The

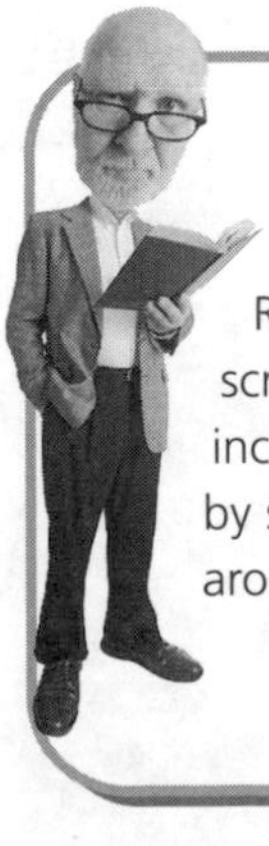

tip

Remember that you can scroll up or down any menu, including the Playlists menu, by sliding one of your digits around the Click Wheel.

Now Playing screen will appear, and the first song in the playlist or the one you highlighted will begin playing (see Figure 4.3).

Playlist title

FIGURE 4.2
This playlist is called "gladiator" because it contains the *Gladiator* soundtrack. Here, you see the list of songs in the playlist.

FIGURE 4.3
One of the songs from the selected playlist is now playing.

4. Use the techniques you'll learn throughout this chapter to control the tunes.

Browsing Your iPod's Music

Choosing music with playlists is great, and you might often find that method to be the one you end up using most because it gets you to specific music quickly. However, some music stored on your iPod might not be in a playlist, you might want to listen to all the music by a specific artist, and so on. In these cases, you can browse the music stored on your iPod to choose the music to which you want to listen. You can browse your music by the following categories:

- Artists
- Albums

tip

You can customize the iPod menu's to match your preferences. For example, if you listen to music mostly through playlists, you can move the Playlists command to the Main menu. You'll learn how in Chapter 7, "Configuring an iPod to Suit Your Preferences."

- Songs
- Podcasts
- Genres
- Composers
- Audiobooks

To browse your iPod's music, do the following:

1. Select **Main** menu, **Music**. You'll see the Music menu, which contains the categories listed previously (see Figure 4.4).

2. Highlight the category by which you want to browse your music, such as Artists to browse by artist, and press the **Select** button. You will see the menu that shows you all the music that is associated with the category you selected in step 1. For example, if you select Artists, you will see all the artists whose music is stored on your iPod (see Figure 4.5).

note

If you are wondering how this information gets associated with your music, don't wonder any longer. It all comes from your iTunes Library. See Chapter 17, "Labeling, Categorizing, and Configuring Your Music," to learn how data is associated with your music.

Music menu

FIGURE 4.4

The Music menu enables you to browse your music by various categories.

II	**Music**	
Playlists		>
Artists		— Selected category
Albums		>
Songs		>
Genres		>
Composers		>
Audiobooks		>

FIGURE 4.5

When you browse by a category, such as Artists, you will see all the music on your iPod organized by that category.

II	**Artists**	
Amy Grand/Sandi Patti		>
Andy Williams		>
Antonio Vivaldi		>
Arthur Rubinstein & Greg...		>
Avril Lavigne		>
B.B. King		>
Bach		>

3. Browse the resulting list of music that appears until you find the specific category in which you are interested; then press the **Select** button. You will see the list of contents of the category you selected. For example, when I was browsing by artist and chose B.B. King, the list of my B.B. King music was displayed (see Figure 4.6).

tip

If you select the All option on any of the category screens, all your music for that category will be shown on the next screen.

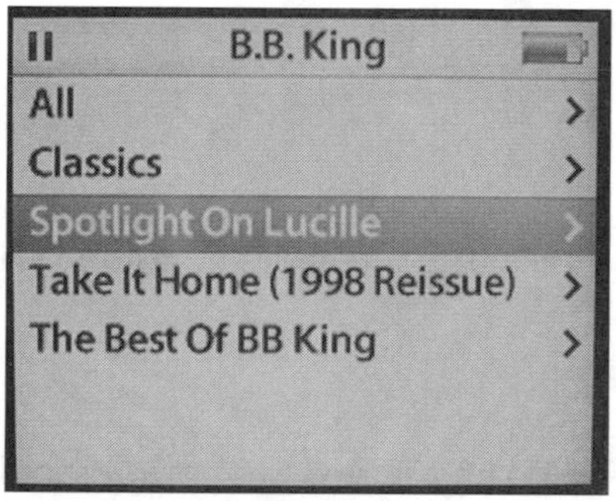

FIGURE 4.6
This screen shows all the music on this iPod by B.B. King.

❚❚	B.B. King	🔋
All		›
Classics		›
Spotlight On Lucille		›
Take It Home (1998 Reissue)		›
The Best Of BB King		›

4. To move down to the next level of detail, select an item on the current list and click the **Select** button. The resulting screen will show you the contents of what you selected. For example, I selected the B.B. King album called *Spotlight on Lucille* and saw that album's contents (see Figure 4.7).

tip

You can start playing music at any time by making a selection and pressing the Play/Pause button. The entire contents of what you select will begin to play. For example, if you select the name of an artist on the Artists list, all the music by that artist will start playing, beginning with the first song on the first album. You don't have to drill down to lower levels of detail as these steps show.

FIGURE 4.7
Here, I am looking at the contents of a specific album by B.B. King.

❚❚	Spotlight On Lucille	🔋
Slidin' And Glidin'		
Blues With B.B.		
King Of Guitar		
Jump With B.B.		
38th Stree Blues		
Feedin' The Rock		
Goin' South		

5. To play everything shown on the screen, starting at the top, press the **Play/Pause** button. To start with a specific song, select it and press the

Play/Pause button. The Now Playing screen will appear, and the first song or the song you selected will start to play (see Figure 4.8).

FIGURE 4.8
I drilled down to a specific album and pressed the Play/Pause button to hear it.

```
▶      Now Playing      ▭

1 of 12

      Slidin' And Glidin'
         B.B. King
      Spotlight On Lucille

0:03                    -3:56
```

Although the previous steps used the Artists category as an example, you can browse and select music in any of the other categories in just the same way.

Controlling Your Music

Okay, so now you have selected music and started to play it. What's next? Learn to control it, of course.

Playing the Basic Way

Here are the basic controls you can use:

- **Play/Pause button**—When music is not playing or is paused, pressing this button will cause it to play again. When music is playing, pressing this button will cause the music to pause.

- **Previous/Rewind button**—If you press this button once quickly, you will jump back to the start of the song. If you press this button twice quickly, you will jump back to the start of the previous song. If you press and hold this button, the music will rewind; release the button when you get to the point at which you want it to start playing again.

- **Next/Fast-forward button**—Press this button once and you will jump to the start of the next song. Press this button and hold it, and you will fast-forward the song; release the button when you get to the point in the song where you want to be.

tip

You can rewind or fast-forward music whether it is playing or not.

■ **Click Wheel**—When the Now Playing screen is shown, drag a digit clockwise to increase the volume or counterclockwise to decrease the volume. When you touch the Click Wheel, the Volume bar will appear on the screen to visually indicate the current volume level; the shaded part of the bar represents the current volume level (see Figure 4.9). As you change the volume, the shaded area will expand or contract, depending on whether you increase or decrease the volume. When you release the Click Wheel, the Volume bar will disappear.

FIGURE 4.9

When you touch the Click Wheel, the Volume bar appears and you can drag on the Wheel to change the volume level.

Now Playing

17 of 31

CASH

ı Comes Around   1
Johnny Cash
American IV - The ...

Volume bar

Current volume level

You can only change the volume using the Click Wheel when the Now Playing screen is shown. That is why the Now Playing option is listed on the Main menu. You can quickly jump to this screen to change the volume when you need to.

Playing the iPod Way

The basics of listening to music are cool. Now let's take a look at some of the cool iPod playback features that aren't so obvious.

You can move around menus while music is playing just like you can when it isn't. As you choose other menus, the music will continue to play until you pause it or choose different music and play that instead.

If music is playing and you move away from the Now Playing screen, such as to change a setting on a menu, you'll automatically move back to the Now Playing screen a couple of seconds after you release the Click Wheel. So, as long as music is playing, you'll always wind up back at this screen.

tip

Remember that you move "up" the menu structure by pressing the Menu button.

The Now Playing screen provides lots of information about the music that is currently playing or paused (see Figure 4.10).

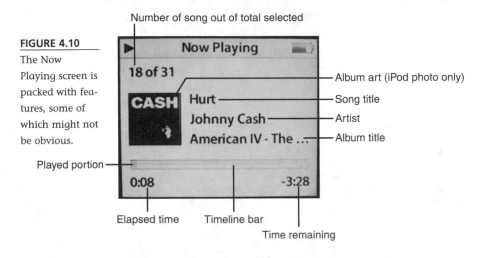

Number of song out of total selected

FIGURE 4.10
The Now Playing screen is packed with features, some of which might not be obvious.

Played portion

Album art (iPod photo only)
Song title
Artist
Album title

Elapsed time Timeline bar
Time remaining

At the top of the screen, you'll see the number of the current song out of the total you selected. For example, if you are playing the first song in a playlist containing 50 songs, this will be 1 of 50. This information helps you know where you are in the selected source.

In the center of the screen, you will see information about the song currently selected, including the song title, artist, and album. If any of this information is too long to be shown on one line, it will begin scrolling across the screen a second or two after a song starts playing. If you have artwork associated with music in iTunes and are using an iPod with a color screen, the album art will appear next to the song information.

At the bottom of the screen, you will see the Timeline bar. In the normal mode, this gives you a visual indication of the song's length and how much of the song you have played so far (represented by the shaded part of the bar). Under the left edge of the bar, you will see the amount of time the current song has been playing. Under the right end of the bar, you will see the time remaining to play (this is a negative number and counts up to zero as the song plays).

If you click the Select button one time, the Timeline bar changes to indicate that you can now rewind or fast-forward using the Click Wheel (see Figure 4.11).

note

Sometimes when song information is too long to fit onto one line, it's cut off and ellipses are used to indicate that there is more text. Frankly, I wasn't able to determine why some song information scrolls and some doesn't.

FIGURE 4.11
When the Timeline bar looks like this, you can rewind or fast-forward using the Click Wheel.

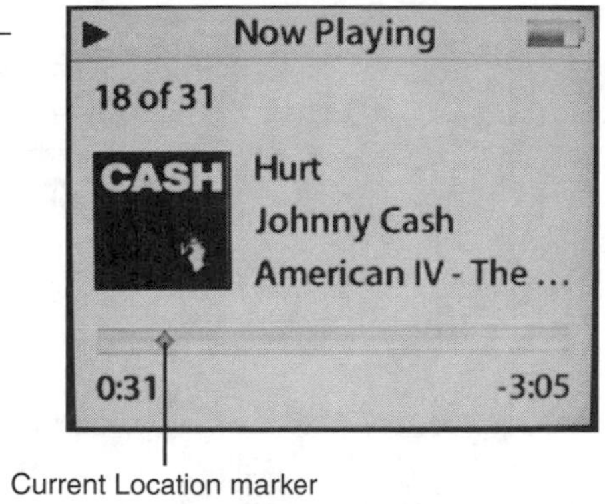

Current Location marker

When the Timeline bar is in this mode, you can drag the Click Wheel clockwise to fast-forward or counterclockwise to rewind the music. As you drag, the Current Location marker moves to its new location and the time information is updated. When you release the Click Wheel, the Timeline bar will return to its normal mode in a second or so.

If a song with artwork is playing on an iPod with a color screen and you click the Select button twice, the artwork will expand so it fills most of the screen. After a second or two, you'll return to the normal Now Playing screen.

If you click the Select button three times rapidly on an iPod with a color screen or twice on an iPod mini, the Timeline bar will be replaced by the Rating display. If the song currently playing has been rated, you will see the number of stars for that song (see Figure 4.12). If the song hasn't been rated, you see five dots instead (see Figure 4.13). You can rate the current song by dragging the Click Wheel clockwise to give the song more stars or counterclockwise to reduce the number of stars. A second or so after you stop touching the Click Wheel, the Timeline bar will return to its normal mode.

FIGURE 4.12
You can rate your music in iTunes and display the rating on your iPod.

▶   Now Playing   🔋

18 of 31

CASH   Hurt
Johnny Cash
American IV - The …

★ ★ ★ ★

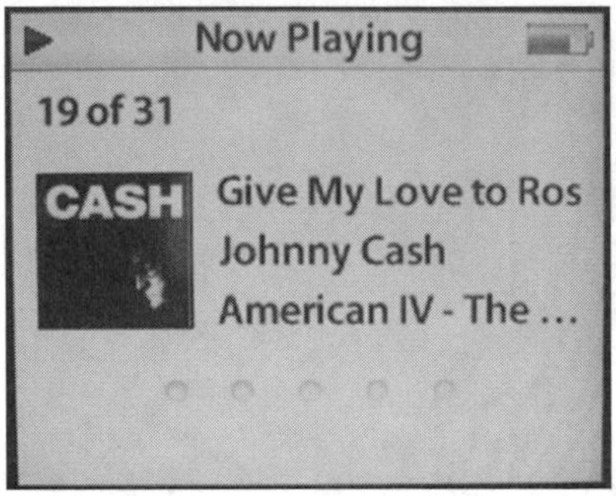

FIGURE 4.13
You can rate your iPod music by choosing one of the dots shown here.

> ▶ Now Playing
>
> **19 of 31**
>
> **CASH** Give My Love to Ros
> Johnny Cash
> American IV - The …
>
> ○ ○ ○ ○ ○

> **note**
>
> You can rate your music in iTunes. For more information on why and how you do this, see Chapter 17 for details.

The neat thing about this is that the next time you connect your iPod to your computer, the rating information you set on the iPod is carried over to that music in your iTunes Library. So, you need to rate a song in only one place.

Creating and Using an iPod On-The-Go Playlist

Working with playlists that you create in iTunes is useful, but you can also create a single playlist (called the On-The-Go playlist) on the iPod and listen to that playlist as much as you'd like. This enables you to create a playlist when you are away from your computer to listen to a specific collection of music.

> **tip**
>
> When you are viewing a playlist—including the On-The-Go playlist—that contains the song that is currently playing, it is marked with a speaker icon.

To add a song to your On-The-Go playlist, view a list—such as the list of songs on an album—on which the song is listed. Highlight the song you want to add and hold down the **Select** button until the highlighting on the song flashes. Continue adding songs using the same process until you have added a group of songs to the playlist.

To see the contents of your On-The-Go playlist, select **Main** menu, **Music**, **Playlists**, **On-The-Go**; the current On-The-Go playlist will always be at the bottom of the Playlists menu. You will see the contents of the On-The-Go playlist you have created. You can play this playlist just like any other playlist on your iPod.

When you connect your iPod to your computer, the On-The-Go playlist will be transferred into iTunes and will be available on the iTunes Source List.

If you want to clear the On-The-Go playlist, select **Main** menu, **Music**, **Playlists**, **On-The-Go**, **Clear Playlist**, **Clear Playlist** (no, that isn't a mistake, you select this command twice, but each is on a different screen). All the songs that were in the playlist will be removed, and it will become empty again. (The songs that were in that playlist are not removed from your iPod; the playlist is just cleared of those songs.)

After you have transferred the On-The-Go playlist to your iTunes Library, you can create a new On-The-Go playlist on your iPod by using the steps you learned in this section. When you connect your iPod to your computer again, this version of the playlist will also be added to your iTunes Source List, but a sequential number will be added to its name to keep the versions straight (as in On-The-Go 14).

Each time you synch your iPod with your iTunes Library and these playlists are part of the synch options, each On-The-Go playlist will be added to your iPod. You can listen to them just like other playlists.

No matter how many of these playlists you accumulate, the current On-The-Go playlist will always be the last entry on the Playlists menu.

note

As far as I know, you can't remove just a single song from the On-The-Go playlist; you have to remove all of them or none of them. Also, you can't use the same techniques to add songs to or remove playlists you created in iTunes. This works only for the On-The-Go playlist.

Monitoring an iPod's Battery

Even though the iPod's battery lasts a long time, it will eventually run out of juice and your music will come to a crashing halt. To prevent this, keep an eye on your iPod's Battery icon (see Figure 4.14). As your battery drains, the shaded part of the battery will decrease to indicate how much power you have left. When 1/4 or less is shaded, you should think about recharging your iPod. (For more information about the iPod's battery, see Chapter 12, "Maintaining an iPod and Solving Problems.")

FIGURE 4.14

This iPod mini's battery still has plenty of juice.

Battery icon

▶ Now Playing

8 of 43

When I'm Gone

3 Doors Down

2:00   -2:20

THE ABSOLUTE MINIMUM

Now you know just about everything you need to listen to music on your iPod. It isn't that difficult because the iPod's controls are well designed. Not to get controlling on you, but here are few more control points for your consideration:

- The first step in listening to music is to choose the music you want to listen to. You do this by choosing playlists or browsing your iPod's music.

- After you've selected music, you can use the pretty-obvious playback controls to control it. You also learned some useful but not so obvious ways to control it.

- After you have used it for a bit, you'll find that you can easily control an iPod with a single thumb. Often, the best way to hold an iPod is to set it in your palm and use your thumb to control it. It doesn't take long until you can navigate like a pro.

- When you use the Click Wheel to move around the iPod's screens or to control music, don't think you have to drag on it slowly or in small increments. You can move quite rapidly by dragging your finger or thumb quickly. The faster you move your finger, the faster things will happen on your iPod. You can move even faster by moving your digit in complete circles.

- You can use the On-The-Go playlist to create a playlist on the iPod.

- As you play your music, keep an eye on your iPod's battery so you don't run out of power.

In This Chapter

- Get your shuffle ready to groove.
- Turn on your shuffle, control it, and then turn it off.
- Sometimes, you need to put your shuffle on Hold.
- Keep an eye on your battery status so your shuffle doesn't run out of gas...whoops, I mean, electricity.

5

Listening to Music on an iPod Shuffle

The iPod shuffle is the newest and most different member of the iPod family. While sometimes having someone so different in a human family can be not such a good thing (you know, like that Uncle Fred no one ever talks about), the shuffle is very different in a good way. One of the "good" things about the shuffle is that it is simple to use. The previous two chapters were required to go into all the details of playing music on the other iPods, but this short chapter will tell you all you need to know about playing music on a shuffle.

Getting Ready to Play

To hear the music stored on your iPod shuffle, you must attach a sound output device to it. The most common one you might think of is the earbud headphones that were included in the package.

To use these, you connect the mini-jack on the earbud cable to the Headphone jack located on the top of the iPod shuffle (see Figure 5.1). When you do so, you'll hear any sound coming from the iPod through the earbuds.

Although you are likely to use earbuds or other headphones with an iPod shuffle, those are certainly not the only audio output devices through which you can play a shuffle's music. For example, you can also connect this jack to powered speakers to play its music on those speakers. Using an adapter, you can also connect the shuffle to a home stereo receiver, as you will learn in Chapter 8, "Using an iPod with a Home Stereo or Car Stereo."

note

Before you can play music on a shuffle, you have to put some music on the shuffle. To do that, you first need to install its software; see Chapter 2, "Getting Started with an iPod," for help with that. You also need to load music onto the shuffle, which you probably did as part of configuring it. You can also use a special iTunes tool to fill your shuffle with great tunes (see "Adding Music to an iPod shuffle" on page **82**).

FIGURE 5.1

It's easy to figure out where to plug headphones into a shuffle because there is only one option.

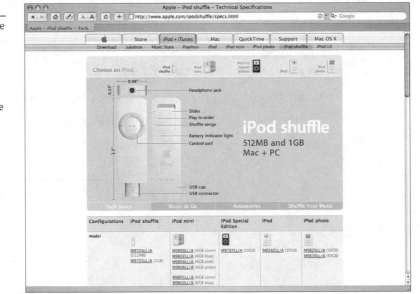

Turning On, Controlling, and Turning Off an iPod shuffle

Playing music on a shuffle couldn't be much easier. First, you choose how you want the music to play. Then, you use the shuffle's simple controls to control that music. When you are done, you turn off the shuffle.

Turning On a shuffle and Choosing How Music Will Play

One limitation of a shuffle is that you can't select the music that plays on it. You can, however, choose whether the music plays in the order you loaded it from the first song to the last or choose to have the music play at random with the iPod shuffle choosing the order in which it plays the music it contains.

Conveniently enough, when you let the shuffle know how you want the music to play back, you turn it on at the same time.

To get the shuffle going, use the slider on the back side of the shuffle's case (refer to Figure 5.1). Slide the slider one notch down to have music play straight through in the order it was loaded onto the shuffle. Slide the slider all the way down to have the shuffle, well, shuffle its music.

Notice that when you slide the slider to one of the "on" positions, a green area under the switch is exposed. This helps you know that the shuffle is turned on.

If you look at the front side of the shuffle (the side with the Control pad) while you turn it on, you'll notice that the status light (located above the Control pad) blinks green for a moment to let you know it is ready to play.

Using the iPod shuffle's Playback Controls

After the shuffle is powered up and ready to go, controlling it is a snap. You use the controls on the Control pad to play, pause, change the volume, and so on (see Figure 5.2).

The following controls are available on the Control pad:

- **Play/Pause**—When the music is stopped, pressing this makes it play. When it is playing, pressing this pauses the music.

- **Increase Volume**—Press and hold this one to increase the volume.

- **Next/Fast-Forward**—Press this once to move to the next song. Press it and hold it down to fast-forward in a song.

note

Using the Next or Previous button is affected by whether you have the shuffle set to shuffle. For example, if you have the shuffle shuffling and press the Next button, you'll move to the next song at random, not in the order in which they are loaded onto the shuffle.

- **Decrease Volume**—Press and hold this one down to decrease the volume.
- **Previous/Rewind**—Press this once to move to the previous song. Press it and hold it down to rewind a song.

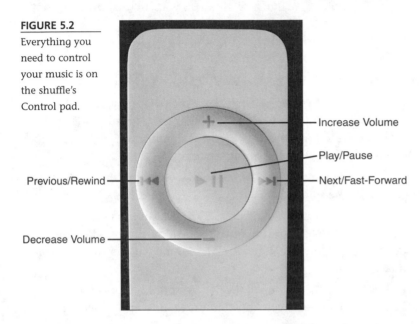

FIGURE 5.2
Everything you need to control your music is on the shuffle's Control pad.

Increase Volume

Play/Pause

Previous/Rewind

Next/Fast-Forward

Decrease Volume

Each time you press a button, the green status light on the front of the shuffle will light up to indicate that your input was received. It will go out as soon as you stop using the control.

Turning Off an iPod shuffle

When you are done playing music, you should turn off the shuffle to conserve battery power. To do so, slide the slider on the back all the way to the off position; if you don't see any green in the slider, you know the shuffle is powered down.

tip

To move to the beginning of the music on the shuffle, press the **Play/Pause** button quickly three times. That will move to the beginning of the shuffle's playlist. If you press Play/Pause again, the music will start playing from there.

Putting an iPod shuffle on Hold

Because the shuffle is so small and light, you are likely to stuff it in a pocket or other place where it might get jostled. If it gets jostled in just the right place, one of the buttons might get pushed accidentally and disrupt your musical experience. And we can't have that!

To inactivate the buttons on the shuffle, press the **Play/Pause** button and hold it for about 3 seconds. The green status light will go out and the orange one will come on. When this happens, the shuffle is in Hold mode and its controls will have no effect. If you press a button, the orange status light will light up so you know the shuffle is still in Hold mode, but the control itself will have no effect.

caution

Because the shuffle doesn't have a screen, nor does a status light remain lit while the shuffle is on, it is easy to leave it playing when you don't mean to. Remember that if you see green in the slider on the shuffle's back, it is turned on.

To make the controls active again, press and hold the **Play/Pause** button for about 3 seconds. When the green status light appears, release the button. The shuffle's controls will become active again.

Monitoring an iPod shuffle's Battery

Just like all iPods, the shuffle has an internal battery. You should monitor its charge level occasionally so you don't run out of music.

To check the shuffle's battery level, press the **Battery** button on the shuffle's backside (see Figure 5.3). The status light will illuminate. If it is green, your shuffle has plenty of charge; if it is yellow, you should think about recharging your shuffle soon. If it is red, your world is about to become a lot quieter so get thee to a USB port immediately.

Remember that every time you plug your shuffle into a computer, its battery will be charged. And, as you'll learn in Chapter 12, "Maintaining an iPod and Solving Problems," it is actually good for an iPod's battery to be charged frequently. So, it's a good idea to plug your shuffle into your computer regularly, whether you have been listening to it a lot or not.

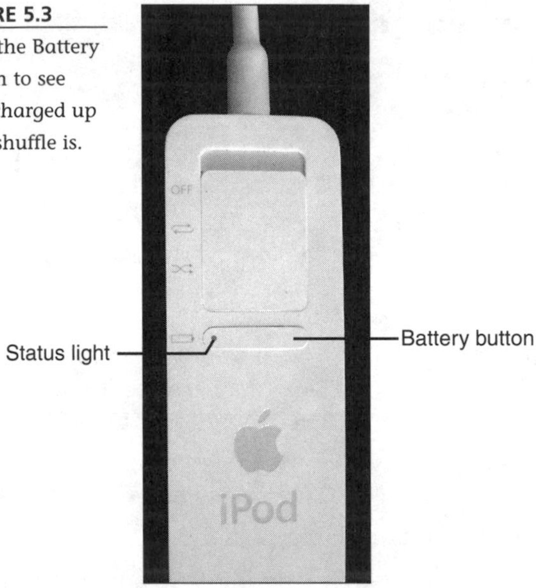

FIGURE 5.3

Press the Battery button to see how charged up your shuffle is.

Status light

Battery button

THE ABSOLUTE MINIMUM

This is a short chapter because there just isn't that much to controlling a shuffle. But, in case your mind wandered, here are the highlights:

- You can listen to a shuffle's music with the included earbuds, but you can also connect it to a set of powered speakers.

- Turn on a shuffle and choose how its music will play (straight through or shuffling) with the slider on the back of its case.

- Use the Control pad to control music playback and volume.

- Use the slider to turn off the shuffle when you are done with it.

- Use the Hold mode to prevent unintentional control presses.

- Check on the shuffle's battery every so often by pressing the Battery button on the back and looking at the status light.

- If you've read this chapter and don't have a shuffle yet, what are you waiting for? shuffles make great companions to your other iPods (don't worry, they won't get jealous).

6

BUILDING AN iPOD'S MUSIC LIBRARY

The first time you connected your iPod to your computer, all the music in your iTunes Library was transferred to your iPod automatically—that is, all the music that would *fit* within the iPod's disk or memory space limitations. If your iPod has enough storage space to hold all your iTunes music, then everything is just fine. However, as you build your iTunes Library, there may come a day when this isn't true anymore and you can't just let everything run on automatic to keep your iPod's music library current. That's where this chapter comes in. Here, you'll learn how to take control over the music stored on your iPod, especially if your iPod's storage space isn't large enough to hold all your iTunes music.

FOR IPOD SHUFFLE READERS

If you use an iPod shuffle, and only an iPod shuffle, most of this chapter doesn't apply to you. Like just about everything else you do with an iPod, you manage the music on a shuffle quite differently from how you manage music with the other iPod models. So, if you are an iPod shuffle-only user, you can skip to the section "Adding Music to an iPod shuffle" on page 82.

Creating an iTunes Music Library

As your learned in Chapter 2, "Getting Started with an iPod," and read in each of the subsequent chapters, you manage the music you store on your iPod within the iTunes application. The iTunes Library and the playlists you create within iTunes are the sources of music you listen to with an iPod. The two general steps to creating these music sources are building your iTunes Library and creating iTunes playlists.

> **note**
>
> Throughout this chapter, I assume that you have a good working knowledge of iTunes, hopefully from reading Part II, "iTunes." If you haven't read Part II yet, you need to at least read Chapter 13, "Touring iTunes," and Chapter 14, "Getting Started with iTunes," so you understand the basics of the application. However, the process of managing your iPod's music library will be much easier if you have read Chapters 13–18 before reading through the rest of this chapter.

Building an iTunes Music Library

You can get music for your iTunes Library from three main sources: audio CDs, the iTunes Music Store, and the Internet. Although the specific steps you use to add music from these various sources to your Library are a bit different, the end result is the same. Your iTunes Library will contain all the music in your collection.

I don't provide the details of building and managing an iTunes Library here because Part II is dedicated to iTunes and provides all the information you need to use this excellent application. The chapters that specifically focus on building your Library are Chapter 16, "Building, Browsing, Searching, and Playing Your iTunes Music Library," and Chapter 17, "Labeling, Categorizing, and Configuring Your Music," but you'll also want to read Chapters 13–15 to install and learn how to use iTunes.

Creating iTunes Playlists

From the earlier chapters in this part of the book, you learned that the playlists stored within iTunes are transferred to your iPod so you can listen to them. You create and manage these playlists within iTunes. Chapter 18, "Creating, Configuring, and Using Playlists," provides an in-depth look at playlists and gives you all the information you need to create and manage your playlists.

Assessing the Size of Your iTunes Library and How Much Disk Space Your iPod Has

To determine how you are going to have to manage the music on your iPod, you need to understand how large your music collection is and how much storage space is available on your iPod. This information will determine the way in which you build and maintain your iPod's music library.

> **note**
>
> Remember that there is one special playlist, called the *On-The-Go playlist*, that you can create on the iPod (except the shuffle).

Determining the Size of Your iTunes Library

You can determine how much storage space you need to move your entire music collection in just a few steps. Open iTunes. Select **Library** in the Source list. With the Browser open, select **All** in the Genre or Artist column. The iTunes window will show all the music you have placed in your Library. Look at the Source Information area at the bottom of the iTunes window (see Figure 6.1). Here, you will see the number of songs, the total playing time, and the disk space required to store all the music in your Library. The number you should be most interested in is the disk space required because that is what you use to determine whether all your music can fit onto your iPod's disk.

Determining How Much Storage Space You Have on an iPod

You have three ways to determine how large the storage space is on your iPod.

One is to refer to the documentation that came with your iPod, or perhaps you can simply remember the size of iPod you purchased. At press time, the possibilities were about 4GB or 6GB for an iPod mini, 20GB or 60GB for an iPod, or 512MB or 1GB for an iPod shuffle. This method is easy and provides a pretty good estimate of the storage capability of your iPod.

If you can't remember or want to determine the disk space on an iPod or iPod mini more accurately, you can get this information directly from the iPod itself. To do this, select **Main** menu, **Settings**, **About**. On the resulting About menu, you'll see the capacity of your iPod's disk (see Figure 6.2).

FIGURE 6.1
At this point in time, my Library required 12.78GB of disk space.

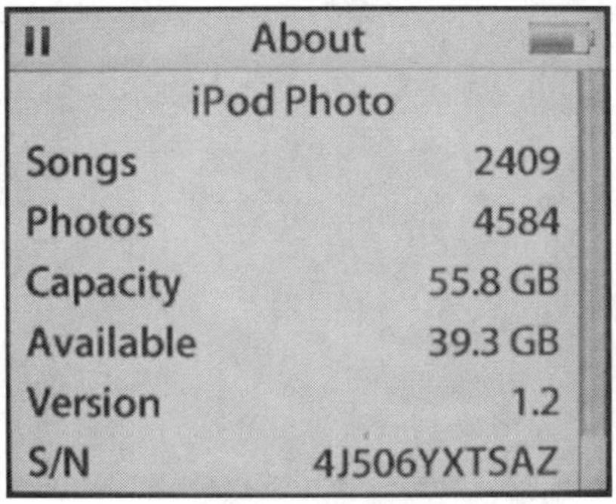

Source Information

FIGURE 6.2
This iPod has a disk capacity of 55.7GB.

The capacity shown on the About menu is the amount of storage space available for your music. Some space is required to store the files needed for the iPod to function; this is the reason the capacity you see will always be slightly less than the rated size of the iPod's disk.

You can also get information about the status of the iPod's disk by connecting it to your computer and selecting it on the Source list. Just above the Source Information area, you'll see information about the iPod's disk, including used space and free space (see Figure 6.3).

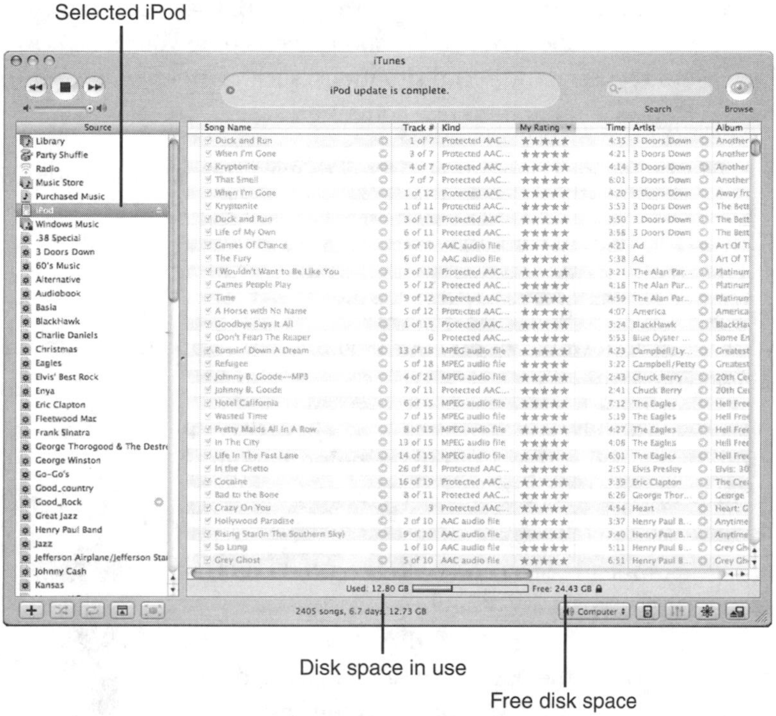

Selected iPod

FIGURE 6.3

Here you can see that this iPod has stored my entire Library with lots of room to spare.

Disk space in use

Free disk space

Understanding and Configuring iPod Synchronization Options

After you know how much space you need to store all your music (the size of your iTunes Library) and how much space is available on your iPod (its disk capacity), you can choose how you want to build and manage your iPod's music library.

Understanding Your Synchronization Options

Three basic options are available for managing the library of music on your iPod:

- **Automatically update all songs and playlists**—When you use this method, the entire process is automatic; iTunes ensures your iPod's music library is an exact copy of your iTunes Library each time you connect your iPod to your computer. This is the ideal method because you don't have to do any additional work and you always have all your music on your iPod.

- **Automatically update selected playlists only**—When you use this method, iTunes still manages the update process for you, but it updates only the specific playlists you select. This option is useful when you have more music in your iTunes Library than will fit on your iPod and don't want to have to manually update your iPod's music.

■ **Manually manage songs and playlists**—When you use this method, you manually move songs and playlists onto your iPod. This option is mostly useful in special situations, such as when you want to use the same iPod with more than one computer.

The first time you connected your iPod to your computer, an automatic method was used to move songs onto your iPod. However, if there were more songs in your iTunes Library than could be stored on your iPod, some slight of hand was done by iTunes so you wouldn't have to get into the details of this process before listening to music on your iPod. In that case, iTunes created a playlist containing a selection of your music that would fit on your iPod and iTunes moved that music to your iPod so you could listen to it.

After the first time, you need to choose the synchro-nization method you want to use. Finding the right method for you is a matter of preference, but I can provide some general guidelines for you.

If all the music in your iTunes Library will fit onto your iPod (the space required for your iTunes Library is less than your iPod's disk capacity), I rec-ommend you use the option Automatically update all songs and playlists. This option is the easiest because it requires literally no work on your part. Each time you connect your iPod to your com-puter, the update process is performed automati-cally and you will have your complete music collection available on your iPod. That's because with this option, your entire iTunes Library is moved to your iPod along with the playlists you have created. So, even if some music is not part of your playlists, it still gets moved onto the iPod.

note

Even if you have enough space on your iPod for all your iTunes music, you can still choose one of the other update options if it suits your pref-erences better.

If the size of your iTunes Library is larger than the disk capacity of your iPod, man-aging the music library on your iPod is slightly more difficult.

If your iPod isn't large enough to store your entire Library and you take full advan-tage of iTunes playlists to create collections of music to which you listen, using the option Automatically update selected playlists only is a good choice. After you choose the playlists you want to be updated, iTunes handles the process of keeping them up-to-date for you so you don't have to think about it each time you connect your iPod to your computer. Of course, you need to make sure you create and can select playlists that contain the music you want to be able to listen to on your iPod. This can require some effort, but because playlists are so useful, you will likely do that work anyway so you can listen to them on your computer. And, be aware that only music in the selected playlists is moved onto your iPod.

Finally, if you don't use a lot of playlists or you simply want to choose the specific music you want to place on your iPod, you can use the manual method to do so.

After you have determined how you want to manage your iPod's music library, you need to configure iTunes to implement your decision.

Understanding How iTunes Updates Playlists on the iPod

When iTunes updates a playlist on your iPod, it takes a "snapshot" of that playlist and places it on the iPod. If you change the playlist in some way, the next time you update your iPod, the previous "snapshot" is replaced by the new playlist.

For example, suppose you have a smart playlist that is dynamic and plays the 50 songs you have played most frequently. As you listen to songs in iTunes, the contents of that playlist change to reflect the songs you have listened to. When that playlist is moved to the iPod, it contains the songs as they were in the playlist when you per-formed the update. The playlist on the iPod will remain unchanged until you per-form the next update. At that time, if the contents of the playlist have changed, the revised playlist will replace the one currently stored on the iPod.

> **caution**
>
> If you use the same iPod with more than one computer, you need to be careful before select-ing one of the automatic methods. When you use an auto-matic method, iTunes will copy its Library onto the iPod. When it does this, it will also remove any songs on the iPod that aren't in its Library so the music on the iPod is an exact copy of the music in the iTunes Library. If you share the iPod on more than one computer, you should not use the Automatically update all songs and playlists method for both computers if you have different music in the iTunes Library on each computer. Fortunately, you can leave one com-puter set to automatic and the oth-ers set to manual.

The same principle applies when you make changes to a playlist manually. For example, if you sort a playlist to change the order in which songs play, that order will be reflected in the playlist when you update it onto your iPod. If you change the order of the songs in the playlist again in iTunes, the next time you update the iPod, the songs will play in the new order on the iPod.

Using the Automatically update selected playlists only option, when iTunes moves a playlist from its Library onto an iPod, it moves only the songs in that playlist onto the iPod. This can sometimes be confusing. For example, if you purchase an album by a specific artist and then include only some of the songs on that album in a playlist that gets moved to an iPod, only those songs by that artist in the playlist get moved onto the iPod. As an example, this can be confusing the first time you browse your iPod by artist and can't figure out why a song you know you have by that artist is not on your iPod.

Configuring iTunes to Automatically Update All Songs and Playlists

Choosing the "fully automatic" method is automatic in itself, in that this is the default option. However, should you ever need to choose this option, you can do so with the following steps:

1. Connect your iPod to your computer (remember Chapter 2!). iTunes will open automatically and the iPod will appear on the Source list.

2. Select the iPod on the **Source** list and click the **iPod Options** button (see Figure 6.4). You'll see the iPod pane of the iTunes Preferences dialog box. If you use a Mac, make sure the Music tab is highlighted.

> **tip**
>
> By default, when iTunes performs an update, it moves all the songs from each affected source onto the iPod. If you don't want specific songs to be moved onto an iPod, open the iPod Preferences dialog box and check the Only update checked songs check box. If a song's check box is not checked, it won't be included in the music moved onto the iPod during an update.

Selected iPod

FIGURE 6.4
To choose an update method, select the iPod and click the iPod Options button.

iPod Options

3. Click the **Automatically update all songs and playlists** radio button (see Figure 6.5). On a Windows computer, the **Music** tab must be selected to see this option.

4. Click **OK**. The dialog box will close, and the update will start. If your iPod can store all the music in your Library, the process will continue until the update is complete. The next time you connect your iPod to your computer or update the iPod with a command, iTunes will attempt to update its Library automatically. As long as there is enough space on your iPod, you won't need to do anything else.

> **tip**
>
> There are two other ways to open the iPod pane of the iTunes Preferences dialog box. One is to open the iPod's contextual menu and choose iPod Options. Another is to open the iTunes Preferences dialog box and click on the iPod pane.

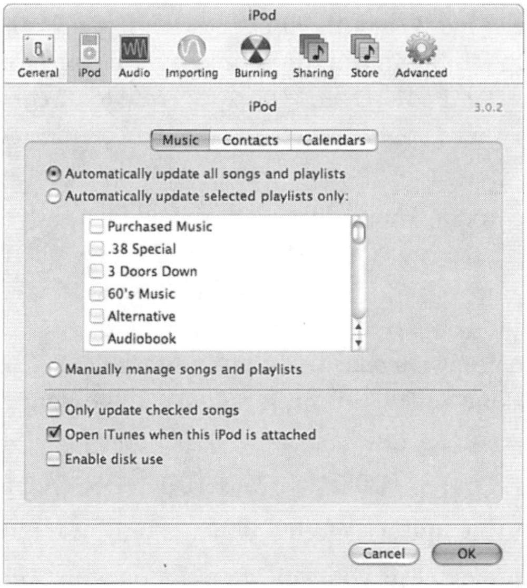

FIGURE 6.5

The iPod Preferences dialog box enables you to configure the update process for your iPod.

If your iPod doesn't have enough room to store all your music, you'll see a warning prompt telling you so. iTunes will offer to choose a selection of songs to put on the iPod.

If you click Yes in this dialog box, iTunes will create a special playlist called *nameofyouripod* Selection, where *nameofyouripod* is

> **note**
>
> If you use a Windows computer, you won't see the Contacts or Calendars tab shown in Figure 6.5. These options are available only on a Mac.

the name you gave your iPod when you configured it. This playlist contains a selection of music from your iTunes Library that will fit on your iPod. iTunes will move the music in this playlist onto the iPod to complete the update.

If you don't change the update option, iTunes will update this playlist (and only this playlist) each time you connect your iPod to your computer. (iTunes actually changes the update mode to Automatically update selected playlists only and chooses the *nameofyouripod* Selection playlist on the playlists list in the iPod Preferences pane.) You can use this playlist just like the others in your iTunes Source List, such as adding songs to it, removing songs from it, changing their order, and so on.

If you click No in the dialog box instead, the update will be aborted and you'll have to use one of the other update options.

Every time you connect your iPod to your computer, the update will be performed. You will see the update information in the Information area of the iTunes window, and the iPod icon will flash red. When the process is complete, you will see the iPod update is complete message in the Information area and the OK to disconnect message will be displayed on the iPod's screen. Then, it is safe to disconnect your iPod from your computer. Of course, you should leave the iPod connected until its battery is fully charged.

You can also activate the update manually, such as when you have added or changed the music in your Library (maybe you created a new playlist) after the automatic update was complete. You can do this by opening the iPod's contextual menu and selecting Update Songs. Or, you can select File, Update Songs on *nameofyouripod*, where *nameofyouripod* is the name of your iPod. This will perform the same update that is done when you connect your iPod to your computer.

Configuring iTunes to Automatically Update Selected Playlists

To have iTunes automatically update selected playlists only, use the following steps:

1. In iTunes, create the playlists you want to place on your iPod.

2. Connect your iPod to your computer. It will appear on the Source list, and an update determined by the current update option (such as fully automatic) will be performed.

3. Select the iPod for which you want to set an update option and click the **iPod Options** button. The iPod Preferences dialog box will appear.

4. Click the **Automatically update selected playlists only** radio button (see Figure 6.6). (If you use a Windows computer, the **Music** tab must be selected to see this option.) Just below this button you will see a list of all the

playlists configured in your iTunes Library. Next to each is a check box. If that box is checked, that playlist will be updated automatically; if that box is not checked, that playlist will be ignored.

FIGURE 6.6

You can choose the playlists that are updated automatically by checking their check boxes.

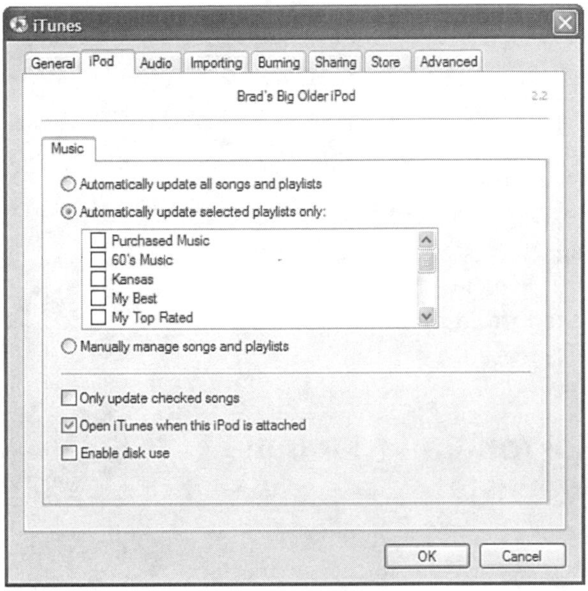

6. Click **OK**.

If the playlists you selected will all fit on the iPod, the dialog box will close and the playlists you selected will be updated on your iPod. The next time you connect your iPod to your computer, the playlists you selected will be updated automatically and you can skip the rest of these steps.

If the playlists you selected are too large to fit on the iPod, the update will start but a warning dialog box will appear (see Figure 6.7). Click **OK** to stop the update; the update can't continue because iTunes doesn't know what music to move to the iPod.

note

When you change the update method, you will see a warning prompt telling you that the current music on the iPod will be replaced by the new update method. This should be what you expect, so just click OK to clear the prompt.

FIGURE 6.7

When you see this, the playlists you selected for automatic update won't fit on your iPod.

The iPod "Mini iPod" cannot be updated because there is not enough free space to hold all of the songs in the selected playlists.

☐ Do not warn me again

OK

In this situation, you have two choices. You can deselect some of the playlists until the selected ones fit on your iPod, or you can remove songs from the selected playlists until they fit. (Remember that the only way to remove songs from smart playlists is to change their criteria.)

Configuring iTunes So You Can Manually Manage Songs and Playlists

When you choose this option, you manually place songs and playlists on your iPod. To choose this option, do the following steps:

1. Connect your iPod to your computer. It will appear on the Source list and an update determined by the current update option (such as fully automatic) will be performed.

2. Select the iPod for which you want to set an update option and click the **iPod Options** button. The iPod Preferences dialog box will appear.

3. Click the **Manually manage songs and playlists** radio button (on a Windows computer, this is located on the Music tab). You will see a prompt explaining that with this option, you must manually unmount the iPod before disconnecting it; read the information and click **OK** to close the prompt. (I'll explain what this means in a later section.)

4. Click **OK**. The dialog box will close and a brief update will be performed. An expansion triangle will appear next to the iPod on the Source list, and all the playlists stored on it will be shown under its icon. You can then manually add or remove songs or playlists (the steps to manually move music onto an iPod appear in a later section).

note

If you use the Automatically update selected playlists only option, smart playlists are even more useful because their content can be dynamic (see Chapter 18, "Creating, Configuring, and Using Playlists"). For example, you can create a playlist that automatically contains all the new music in your iTunes Library. If you choose to have this playlist updated automatically, each time you connect your iPod to your computer that playlist will be updated and so your newest music will always be placed on your iPod.

Updating Specific Songs and Playlists Automatically

If you chose the Automatically update selected playlists only option, the playlists you selected are updated on your iPod each time you connect it to your computer. To change the contents of your iPod's music library, change the contents of the playlists you have selected to update. When you connect the iPod to your computer, those playlists will be updated. For example, you can add songs to the selected playlists, remove songs from them, change a smart playlist's criteria, and so on. The next time you connect your iPod to your computer or activate the Update Songs command manually, the changes you made will be reflected on the iPod's version of those playlists.

Every time you connect your iPod to your computer, the update will be performed. You will see the update information in the Information area of the iTunes window, and the iPod icon will flash red. When the process is complete, you will see the `iPod update is complete` message in the Information area, and the `OK to disconnect` message will be displayed on the iPod's screen. Then, it is safe to disconnect your iPod from your computer.

> **note**
>
> Smart playlists can change over time automatically. These playlists will automatically change on your iPod each time you connect it to your computer. This is a great way to keep the music on your iPod fresh.

Manually Updating an iPod

If you choose the manual option, you must manually move songs and playlists onto the iPod. To do this, use the following steps:

1. Connect your iPod to your computer.

2. Select the iPod you want to update. If it isn't expanded already, click the expansion triangle next to the iPod on the **Source** list. In the iTunes Content pane, you will see all the songs in the iPod's music library. Under the iPod's icon on the Source list, you will see the playlists it contains (see Figure 6.8).

3. To add a playlist to the iPod, drag it onto the **Source** list and drop it on the iPod's icon (see Figure 6.9). When you are over the iPod, the plus sign will appear next to the pointer to show that you can release the mouse button. When you do so, the playlist and the songs it contains will be moved onto the iPod.

Songs on the selected iPod

iPod's expansion triangle

FIGURE 6.8

When you con-
figure an iPod
for manual
updating, you
can expand it on
the Source list to
see the playlists
it contains.

Playlists on the
selected iPod

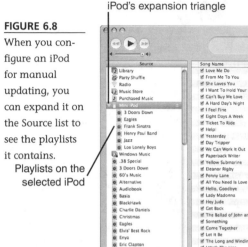

FIGURE 6.9

When you drag
a playlist into an
iPod, it and the
songs it contains
will be moved
into the iPod's
library.

4. To remove a playlist from the iPod, select it by clicking it in the list of playlists under the iPod and pressing the **Delete** key. Unless you have disabled it, you will see a prompt asking you to confirm that you want to delete the playlist. If you have disabled the warning prompt, the playlist and its songs will be removed from the iPod and you can skip step 5.

5. Click **OK**. The playlist will be deleted from the iPod.

6. To add songs to the iPod, select the source containing those songs, such as the Library. The contents of that source will be shown in the Content pane. Drag the songs you want to add from the Content pane and drop them on the iPod's icon. The songs you selected will be copied into the iPod's music library.

7. To remove songs from the iPod, select the iPod, then select the songs you want to remove in the **Content** pane, and press the **Delete** key. These songs will be deleted from the iPod and will also be deleted from any playlists on the iPod containing them.

8. When you are done updating the iPod, unmount it by selecting its icon and clicking the **Eject** button that appears next to the iPod or in the lower-right corner of the iTunes window (see Figure 6.10). After the iPod has been successfully unmounted, it will disappear from the Source list and you will see the OK to disconnect message on its screen.

tip

If you don't want to be bothered by the confirmation prompts, check the **Do not ask me again** check box.

Eject button

FIGURE 6.10

Before you disconnect an iPod that you have manually updated, you must eject it.

9. Disconnect your iPod from your computer.

You must eject an iPod that you manually update before disconnecting it because iTunes doesn't know when it should shut down any processes it is using that are related to the iPod. Because it is, in effect, a hard disk, the iPod must not be in use when you disconnect it; otherwise, its data can be damaged. When you do the update manually, you need to tell iTunes that you are done (by "ejecting" the iPod) so that it can prepare the iPod to be disconnected safely.

Adding Music to an iPod shuffle

Like in all other areas, managing the music on an iPod shuffle is different. There are different update options, and one of those is a special tool that is not available for other iPod models.

The reason for this is that, unless your music library is very small, it won't fit on a shuffle and likely not that much of it will fit because the largest memory in current shuffle models is 1GB. So, the shuffle does things a bit differently.

There are two ways to get music onto an iPod shuffle: You can use the Autofill tool to have iTunes move music onto the shuffle for you. Or, you can manually configure the songs the shuffle contains.

Prior to updating its music, configure your shuffle's preferences.

Configuring an iPod shuffle

The shuffle also has a different set of options you can configure using the following steps:

1. Plug your shuffle into an available USB 2 port on your computer. iTunes will open if it isn't already open, and the shuffle will appear on the Source list.

2. Click the **iPod Options** button, which has an iPod icon and is located to the immediate left of the Equalizer button in the lower-right corner of the iTunes window. The iPod pane of the iTunes Preferences dialog box will appear (see Figure 6.11).

note

To reiterate this slightly confusing behavior, when you delete a playlist from an iPod, only the playlist itself is removed—the songs it contains remain on the iPod. You have to select the songs and delete them to remove them from your iPod.

caution

Don't disconnect your iPod from your computer unless the OK to disconnect message is displayed on its screen. If you do so, you can damage its data. It is also safe to disconnect your iPod when the large battery charging icon or battery charged icon appears on the iPod's screen.

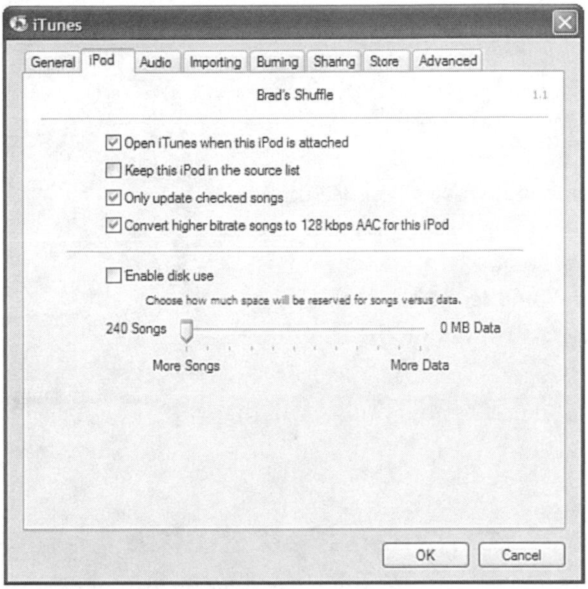

FIGURE 6.11

The iPod shuffle offers preferences that are much different from other iPod models.

```
                                    iTunes                                    ×

General | iPod | Audio | Importing | Burning | Sharing | Store | Advanced

                              Brad's Shuffle                          1.1

    ☑ Open iTunes when this iPod is attached
    ☐ Keep this iPod in the source list
    ☑ Only update checked songs
    ☑ Convert higher bitrate songs to 128 kbps AAC for this iPod

    ☐ Enable disk use
            Choose how much space will be reserved for songs versus data.
    240 Songs    ▭                                     0 MB Data

            More Songs                        More Data


                                              OK        Cancel
```

3. Set the options for the shuffle. These options are explained in the following list:

- **Open iTunes when this iPod is attached**—When this is checked, which it is by default, iTunes will open whenever you plug your shuffle into your computer.

- **Keep this iPod in the source list**—If you check this, the iPod shuffle always appears in the Source list even if it isn't plugged into the computer. You can update it just like it was connected. The next time you plug your shuffle in, it will be updated with the current music configuration.

> **note**
>
> In most cases, you can update an iPod shuffle using an USB 1 port too. But, the process will be a lot slower and might not recharge your iPod. For these reasons, you should use a USB 2 port if your computer has one.

- **Only update checked songs**—If you check this, only songs with their Song check box checked will be moved onto the shuffle.

- **Convert higher bitrate songs to 128 kbps AAC for this iPod**—This option is useful if you have a lot of music that uses a higher-quality encoder, such as Apple Lossless. With this option checked, when you put music like this on the shuffle, it is converted into the 128Kbps AAC format so that it takes up less memory. You should leave this option checked so you can get the maximum amount of music on your shuffle.

- **Enable disk use**—You use this check box and slider to configure a shuffle so you can use it as a flash drive. You'll learn about this in Chapter 11, "Taking the iPod Further."

4. Click **OK**. The preferences you set will take effect.

tip

You also open the iPod pane by opening the shuffle's contextual menu and selecting iPod Options. Or, you can open the iTunes Preferences dialog box and click the iPod tab.

Using Autofill to Put Music on an iPod shuffle

Using the Autofill tool, you provide the parameters for an update and iTunes takes care of moving music to or from the shuffle as needed based on your criteria.

To perform an Autofill update, do the following steps:

1. Plug your shuffle into an available USB port. iTunes will open (assuming you left this preference on).

2. Select the shuffle on the **Source** list. The Autofill tool will appear at the bottom of the Content pane (see Figure 6.12).

FIGURE 6.12

You can use the Autofill tool to place music onto an iPod shuffle.

3. Choose the source of music you want to place on the shuffle on the **Autofill from** pop-up menu. You can choose your Library or any of your playlists. When it autofills your shuffle, iTunes will choose only music from the selected source.

4. If you don't want all the songs currently on the shuffle to be replaced by the Autofill, uncheck the **Replace all songs when Autofilling** check box. If this check box is checked, the entire contents of the shuffle are replaced. If it isn't checked, iTunes will try to add the Autofill songs until the shuffle's memory is full.

5. If you want to Autofill with songs selected at random from the source you selected in step 3, leave the **Choose songs randomly** check box selected. If you uncheck this check box, Autofill will select songs in the order in which they are listed in the source you selected in step 3 and add them to the shuffle until its memory is full.

6. If you rate songs and want Autofill to choose higher-rated songs more frequently, leave the **Choose higher rated songs more often** check box selected. This option is only available when you use the random option described in step 5. If you uncheck this box, Autofill will select songs truly at random and ignore your ratings.

7. Click **Autofill**. The Content pane will fill with the songs that Autofill has selected and the update process will start (see Figure 6.13). It will continue until the shuffle's memory is as full as it can get or until all the music you selected has been moved onto the shuffle, whichever comes first. The amount of your shuffle's memory that is being consumed will be shown on the bar just above the Source Information area at the bottom of the iTunes window.

> **tip**
>
> If you have elected the random option, each time you click Autofill, a new set of songs will be placed on your shuffle.

8. When the update process is complete, click the **Eject** button next to the shuffle's icon on the Source list or the one located in the bottom-right corner of the iTunes window.

9. Unplug the shuffle from your computer and enjoy some tunes! (Of course, you should leave the shuffle plugged in to charge its battery.)

> **caution**
>
> Don't unplug a shuffle if its orange status light is flashing. That means an update is in progress.

FIGURE 6.13

This shuffle is getting filled up with the good stuff.

If you checked the preference to keep your shuffle on the Source list, its icon will remain after you have unplugged it. The only way to tell this is that when the shuffle isn't plugged in, the Eject buttons don't appear (because there isn't anything to eject). You can still use the Autofill tool to manage your shuffle's music. When you plug it in the next time, that music will be moved onto your shuffle.

Manually Adding Songs to an iPod shuffle

You can also add songs to a shuffle manually by performing the following steps:

1. Plug your shuffle into an available USB port. iTunes will open (assuming you left this preference on), and the shuffle will appear on the Source list.

2. Select the source containing music that you want to place on the shuffle. You can move music from the Library or any playlist.

3. Drag the songs you want to place on the shuffle from the **Content** pane onto the shuffle's icon. When the pointer is over the shuffle, its icon will be highlighted. Release the mouse button and the songs will be copied onto the shuffle (see Figure 6.14).

4. Continue dragging songs from your sources until you have added all you want or until the shuffle's memory is full.

tip

You can combine methods. For example, you can use Autofill and then manually add more songs. However, if you have the Replace all songs when Autofilling check box checked, each time you Autofill all the songs currently on the shuffle will be replaced.

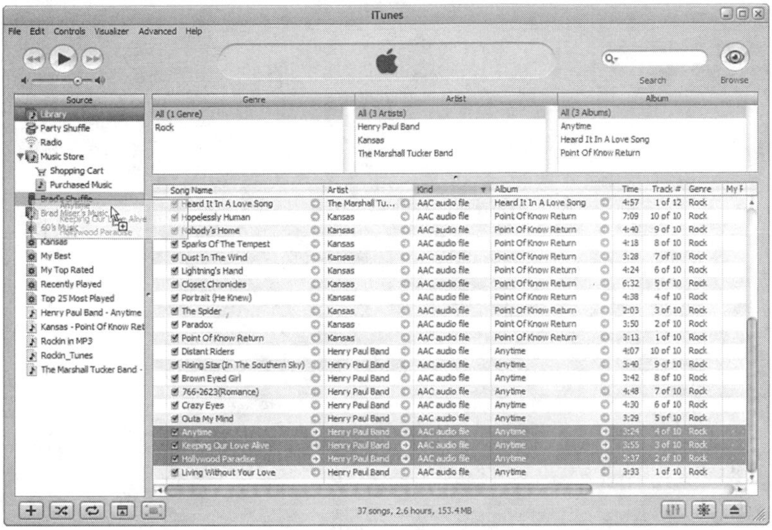

FIGURE 6.14

You can drag songs from any source onto the shuffle's icon to add those songs to it.

Removing Songs from an iPod shuffle

You can also manually remove songs from the shuffle whether you put them there manually or they were added by Autofill. Select the shuffle on the **Source** list and then select the songs you want to delete. Press the **Delete** key. If you are prompted, click **Remove** and the songs will be removed from the shuffle. If you have previously checked the **Do not ask me again** check box, you won't see any prompt that the songs will be immediately removed.

THE ABSOLUTE MINIMUM

Managing the music on your iPod is essential if you are to be able to listen to the music you want to when the mood strikes you. Fortunately, maintaining your iPod's music library isn't all that hard. As you build and maintain your iPod's music library, keep the following points in mind:

- You use the iTunes application to create the music library on your iPod.
- You can determine the amount of used and free space on the iPod's hard disk in a number of ways, including by using the iPod's About command. This is important so you know whether you can fit all your music on your iPod.
- There are three ways to synchronize the music in your iTunes Library and on your iPod.
- When you use the "fully automatic" option, this is done for you automatically and your iPod will be updated with your current iTunes Library each time you connect the iPod to your computer.
- You can also choose to have only specific playlists updated automatically.
- You can manage the music on your iPod manually as well.
- If you have more than one iPod, such as an iPod and an iPod mini, you can choose different update options for each. For example, you might want to use the Automatically update selected playlists only option for the iPod mini and the fully automatic option for the iPod.
- Most of this list doesn't apply to the shuffle. You update its music using the Autofill tool or by manually configuring its music.

7

CONFIGURING AN iPOD TO SUIT YOUR PREFERENCES

iPods are personal devices; because they are, you can customize them to work the way you want them to. You can control many aspects of how your iPod works by using the Settings menu (way back in Chapter 3, "Controlling an iPod or iPod mini," you learned how to use this menu to configure your iPod's backlight—that was only the beginning!). In this chapter, you'll learn about many of these settings that you can use to customize an iPod to suit your personal preferences.

Configuring Music Playback

Several of the iPod's settings relate to the way in which music plays. These include Shuffle, Repeat, Sound Check, and the Equalizer. If you only use an iPod shuffle, you can skip this chapter because none of its information is applicable to the shuffle.

Shuffling Music

There are two ways to shuffle music on your iPod. You can configure music to shuffle using the Shuffle settings. You can also use the Shuffle Songs command that is on the Main menu by default.

Shuffling Music with Shuffle Settings

You can use the iPod's Shuffle feature to have songs play in a random order. To shuffle music, use the following steps:

1. Select **Main** menu, **Settings**. You'll see the Settings menu.

2. Highlight the **Shuffle** command (see Figure 7.1).

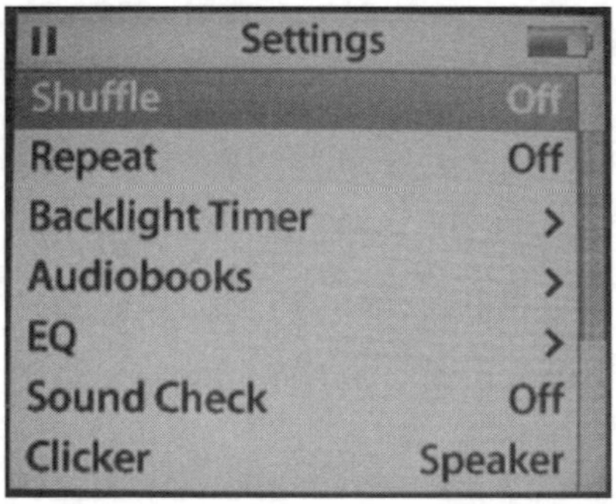

> **note**
>
> In the opening paragraph, I included the word *many* because you won't learn about all the available settings in this chapter. Some are covered in the chapters related to the features controlled on the Settings menu, such as the Contacts setting, which is covered in Chapter 10, "Using the iPod's Calendar, Contact Manager, and Other Non-Music Tools."

FIGURE 7.1

You can use the Shuffle setting to have an iPod play your music in a random order.

II	Settings	🔋
Shuffle		Off
Repeat		Off
Backlight Timer		>
Audiobooks		>
EQ		>
Sound Check		Off
Clicker		Speaker

3. If you want the songs within a selected Browse category or playlist to play in a random order, press the **Select** button once. The Shuffle setting will become Songs. This causes the iPod to shuffle the songs within a music source when you play it.

4. If you want the iPod to select random albums when you select a Browse category or playlist, press the **Select** button twice. The Shuffle setting will become Albums. This causes the iPod to select an album randomly, play all

the songs on the album that are stored on the iPod, select another album randomly, and repeat this pattern until you turn off Shuffle again.

5. Select the music you want to play in a randomized fashion and play it. On the Now Playing screen, you'll see the Shuffle indicator to remind you that you are in Shuffle mode (see Figure 7.2).

6. To disable the Shuffle feature, move back to the Settings menu and press the **Select** button until you see Off next to the Shuffle setting. Your music will again play in a linear fashion.

> **note**
>
> The options you see on the Settings menu will vary among iPod models so don't be concerned if you don't see the exact same list of options on your iPod that you see in this chapter's figures.

Shuffling Music with Shuffle Settings

By default, the Shuffle Songs command appears on the Main menu. The command shuffles all the music on your iPod. This is different from the Shuffle setting you learned about in the previous section because you can select a specific source with that option. With the Shuffle Songs command, you can only shuffle through all your iPod's music. To shuffle this way, select **Main** menu, **Shuffle Songs**. When you play your iPod's music, you'll see the Shuffle indicator on the Now Playing screen. Music will move from one song to the next at random.

FIGURE 7.2

The Shuffle indicator reminds you that you are playing in the Shuffle mode.

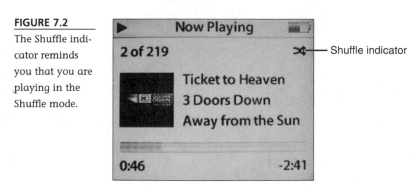

Shuffle indicator

There is some interaction between this command and the Shuffle setting. If you have Off as the Shuffle setting, this command does what I described in the previous two paragraphs. If the Shuffle setting is Songs, both are doing the same thing and work as expected. If the Shuffle setting is Albums, using the Shuffle Songs command randomly selects an album, plays all the songs on that album, chooses another album, plays all its songs, and so on.

When you want to stop shuffling music after you have selected the Shuffle Songs command, you have to select and play a music source, such as a playlist, an artist's music, and so on.

Repeating Music

The Repeat feature enables you to repeat an individual song as many times as you'd like or to repeat all the songs in a selected music source as many times as you can stand.

To repeat the same song ad infinitum, select **Main** menu, **Settings**. Highlight **Repeat** and press the **Select** button once so that One is displayed next to the Repeat setting. Select the song you want to hear and play it. It will play and then play again until you pause the iPod or choose a different song. While the song plays, the Repeat One indicator will appear on the Now Playing screen (see Figure 7.3).

> **note**
>
> The Shuffle feature works on any source of music you select, including playlists or any of the Browse categories, such as Artists, Albums, Genre, and so on. When you use the Songs mode, all the songs will be selected and play in a random fashion.

FIGURE 7.3
You can make the same song play over and over until you just can't take it anymore.

Repeat One indicator

> **note**
>
> Like the Shuffle feature, the Repeat feature works with any music source you select, including playlists or any of the Browse categories.

To repeat all the songs within a selected music source, select **Main** menu, **Settings**. Highlight **Repeat** and press the **Select** button twice so that All is displayed next to the Repeat setting. Select the music source (such as a playlist) you want to hear and play it. It will play and then repeat until you pause the iPod or select a different music source. While the music source plays, the Repeat All indicator will appear on the Now Playing screen (see Figure 7.4).

Repeat All indicator

FIGURE 7.4

You can use the Repeat All mode to repeat all the songs in a selected music source, such as a playlist.

To turn off Repeat, select **Main** menu, **Settings**. Highlight **Repeat** and press the **Select** button until Off is displayed next to the Repeat setting. Music will again play one time through and then stop.

The Repeat feature also interacts with the Shuffle Songs command. If Repeat is Off, Shuffle Songs plays all the songs on your iPod once (randomly of course). If Repeat is set to One and you use the Shuffle Songs command, one song will be selected and played until you stop it or the iPod runs out of battery. If Repeat is set to All and you select Shuffle Songs, all the songs are played at random and then start over again and play in the same order until you stop playing or the iPod runs out of power.

> **note**
>
> When you have Repeat set to One, don't be fooled by the 1 of X indicator on the Now Playing screen. "X" will continue to be the number of songs in the selected source, but the number of the current song (such as 1 of) won't change because that song gets repeated.

Using Sound Check

iTunes' Sound Check feature causes songs to play back at the same relative volume level—if you have ever been jolted out of your chair because of one song's volume level being much higher than the next one, you know why this is a good thing. Using the iPod's Sound Check setting, you can cause the iPod to use the volume levels set by iTunes when Sound Check is on.

To use Sound Check, make sure it is active on the Audio pane of the iTunes Preferences dialog box. Then, connect your iPod to your computer so the iPod's music will be updated, or you can perform a manual update if that is how you have configured iTunes for your iPod. After the update is complete, on the iPod select **Main** menu, **Settings**. On the Settings menu, highlight **Sound Check** and press the **Select** button. The Sound Check setting will become On to show you that it is in use. When you play music back, it will play at the same relative volume level.

To return the volume level to the "normal" state, select **Main** menu, **Settings**. Highlight **Sound Check** and press the **Select** button so that off appears as the Sound Check setting.

Using the iPod's Equalizer

The iPod also has a built-in Equalizer you can use to improve (*improve* being a relative term, of course) the music to which you listen. The iPod includes of number of presets designed to enhance specific kinds of music and other audio sources. To use the iPod Equalizer, do the following steps:

1. Select **Main** menu, **Settings**.

2. Highlight the **EQ** setting and press the **Select** button. You'll see the EQ menu (see Figure 7.5). On this menu, you will see all the available presets. The list is pretty long, so you will need to scroll down to see all your options. The presets include those designed for specific styles of music, such as Acoustic, Classical, Jazz, and so on, as well as for situations in which you might be using your iPod to play music, such as Small Speakers.

FIGURE 7.5
Choose an Equalizer preset on the EQ menu to activate it.

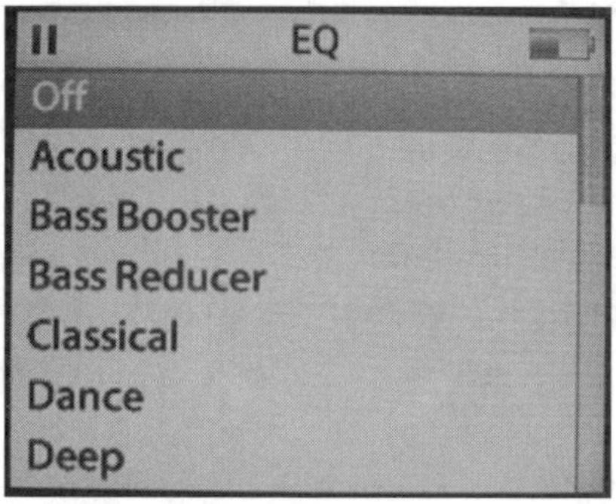

3. Highlight the preset you want to use and press the **Select** button. You'll return to the Settings menu. When you play music, the Equalizer will adjust the volume levels of various frequencies to enhance certain frequencies and to reduce the levels of others.

> **note**
>
> If you have created your own presets on the iTunes Equalizer, they won't be available on your iPod. The iPod includes a set of presets, and those are all you can use. Fortunately, the list of presets is quite large, so this isn't much of a limitation.

Setting Up Your Main Menu Preferences

You can configure the commands on the iPod's Main menu to customize it to suit your preferences. For example, suppose you frequently browse your music by artist. You can add the Artists command to the Main menu so you don't have to drill down through the Music menu to get to this category you use frequently. To configure your Main menu, do the following steps:

1. Select **Main** menu, **Settings**. The Settings menu will appear.

2. Highlight **Main Menu** and press the **Select** button. You'll see the Main menu (see Figure 7.6). On this menu, each command is listed along with its current Main menu state. If On is listed next to a command, it appears on the Main menu. If Off is listed next to a command, it doesn't appear on the Main menu. The commands are grouped into categories, including Music, Extras, and so on.

FIGURE 7.6
You can add items to the Main menu by turning them on or remove them by turning them off.

‖	Main Menu	
Music		On
Playlists		Off
Artists		Off
Albums		Off
Songs		Off
Audiobooks		Off
Genres		Off

3. To add a command to the Main menu, highlight it and press the **Select** button so that On is listed next to that command (see Figure 7.7). That command will then appear on the Main menu.

FIGURE 7.7
When On appears next to a command, such as the Artists command, it will be on the Main menu.

‖	Main Menu	
Music		On
Playlists		Off
Artists		On
Albums		Off
Songs		Off
Audiobooks		Off
Genres		Off

4. To remove a command from the Main menu, highlight it and press the **Select** button so that Off is listed next to that command. That command will not appear on the Main menu.

5. Repeats step 3 or 4 for each command until you have set all the commands you want on the Main menu to On and all those you don't want to appear on the Main menu to Off. When you view the Main menu, your command preferences will be in effect (see Figure 7.8).

tip

To return the Main menu to its default commands, select **Main** menu, **Settings**, **Main Menu**, **Reset Main Menu**. Select **Reset** again to confirm the command. The iPod's Main menu will be just like it was when you first powered it up.

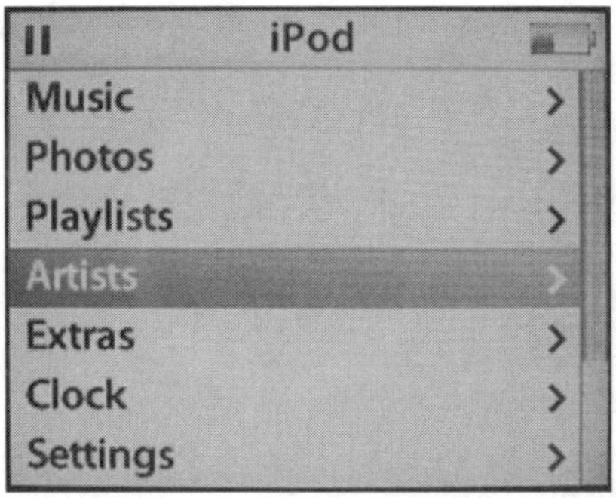

FIGURE 7.8
Using the Main menu settings, I customized the Main menu on this iPod (notice that I can use the Artists command on the Main menu to more quickly browse this iPod's music by artist).

```
II            iPod           ▭
Music                          >
Photos                         >
Playlists                      >
Artists                        >
Extras                         >
Clock                          >
Settings                       >
```

Setting the Screen's Contrast

On an iPod mini, you can adjust the contrast of the iPod's screen so it's easier to read. To do this, select **Main** menu, **Settings**, **Contrast**. You'll see the Contrast menu, which consists of the Contrast slider (see Figure 7.9). Drag the **Click Wheel** clockwise to increase the contrast (which makes the text and background darker) or counterclockwise to decrease the contrast (which makes the text lighter). As you drag, the shaded part of the Contrast bar indicates the current relative contrast level. When you think you have a setting that suits you, move to other menus to see whether the setting is correct for your eyes and viewing conditions. Otherwise, continue to adjust it until it is correct.

FIGURE 7.9
Increasing the
contrast of the
iPod's screen can
make it easier to
read.

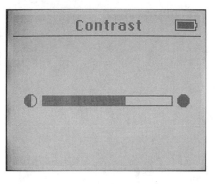

Setting the Sleep Timer

You can configure your iPod to turn itself off
automatically after a specific period of time
passes. To do this, use the following steps:

1. Select **Main** menu, **Extras**, **Clock**,
   Sleep Timer. You'll see the Sleep menu,
   which consists of a list of sleep time periods, from Off (meaning that the Sleep
   Timer is turned off) to 120 Minutes
   (meaning that the iPod will shut off in 2
   hours).

2. Select the **Sleep Timer** setting you want by highlighting it and pressing the
   Select button.

tip

You can reset an iPod's
contrast to the default setting by pressing and holding
the **Menu** button for about
4 seconds.

When you have the Sleep Timer on and view the Now Playing screen, the current
amount of time until the iPod sleeps is shown at the top of the screen (see Figure
7.10). When the counter reaches zero, the iPod will turn itself off. This happens
regardless of whether you happen to be listening to music at the time. So, if your
iPod suddenly shuts off and you don't first see a battery low warning, this is likely
the reason.

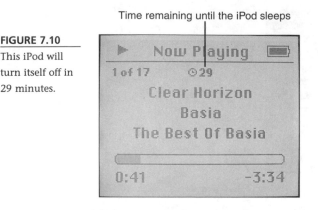

FIGURE 7.10

This iPod will turn itself off in 29 minutes.

Time remaining until the iPod sleeps

Configuring the Clicker

As you select various menu options, your iPod "clicks" to give you audible feedback. There are two ways the clicker can sound: through the iPod's internal speaker or through the Headphones jack. You can also turn off the Clicker or have it play in both ways at the same time. To configure the Clicker, select **Main** menu, **Settings**. Then highlight the **Clicker** option and press the **Select** button until the setting you want is selected. You have the following options:

- **Off**—The Clicker is silent.
- **Speaker**—The Clicker plays through the iPod's speaker only.
- **Headphones**—The Clicker plays through the Headphones jack only.
- **Both**—The Clicker plays through the iPod's speaker and the Headphones jack.

Working with the iPod's Language

When you first turned on your iPod, you selected the language in which you wanted it to communicate with you. In most cases, you will never need to change that initial setting. However, you can if you do need to for some reason.

To choose a different language, select **Main** menu, **Settings**, **Language**. You'll see the Language menu (see Figure 7.11). Highlight the language you want your iPod to use and press the **Select** button. The menus will change and use the language you selected.

FIGURE 7.11

If I were multi-lingual, more of these settings might be useful, but because I am language limited, only one is applicable.

Returning an iPod to That Factory-Fresh Feeling

On occasion, all your work configuring your iPod might not be what you intended. Fortunately, you can return the iPod settings to their default values with a single menu command.

To do this, select **Main** menu, **Settings**, **Reset All Settings**. You'll see the Reset All menu. Highlight **Reset** and press the **Select** button. Your iPod's menus and all other settings will be returned to their default condition. You'll see the Language menu you use to select the language you want your iPod to use. Do so and you'll move to the Main menu.

tip

If you accidentally select a language you can't read, you can use the information in the next section to reset the language even if you can't read the iPod's menus.

If you have set your iPod to use a language you can't read, you can reset it by selecting the Settings command, which is the fourth command on the Main menu (by default) and then selecting the last command on the Settings menu (which is the Reset All Settings command). On the resulting menu, choose the second command and press the **Select** button to reset the iPod. Of course, if you have customized the Main menu, the Settings command might or might not be the fourth one down. When you customize the Main menu, it is a good idea to remember where that command is, just in case.

THE ABSOLUTE MINIMUM

In this chapter, you've explored many of the options on the Settings menu and learned a number of ways to make your iPod suit your personal preferences. Check out the following list to review what you have learned and to pick up a few more pointers:

- Use the Shuffle, Repeat, Sound Check, and Equalizer to configure how music plays on your iPod.

- You can determine which commands appear on the Main menu by using the Main menu settings.

- Use the Contrast setting to set the contrast of the iPod's screen for an iPod mini.

- Use the Sleep Timer to have your iPod go to sleep automatically.

- If you don't like the clicking sound the iPod makes when you press a button, you can turn it off.

- Your iPod is multilingual; use the Language settings to determine which language your iPod uses.

- You can restore your iPod to its factory settings with the Reset All Settings command.

- The About command on the Settings menu provides important information about your iPod, including its name, its disk capacity, its available space, the software version installed on it, its model, and its serial number.

- The Date & Time settings enable you to configure and work with your iPod's clock. You'll learn about those settings in Chapter 10.

- You use the Contacts setting to choose how contacts on your iPod are displayed. You'll learn about that in Chapter 10, too.

- The Legal setting takes you to the oh-so-useful Legal screen, which contains lots of legalese you can read should you have absolutely nothing else to do.

IN THIS CHAPTER

- Listen to your iPod with a home stereo.
- Use your iPod as a home stereo.
- Listen to your iPod with a car stereo.

8

USING AN IPOD WITH A HOME STEREO OR CAR STEREO

One of the cool things about an iPod is how versatile it is. You can use one to play music just about anywhere and in about any situation. In fact, the iPod can be the one constant in your musical universe. Wherever you go, you can take your trusty iPod along to provide the soundtrack for your life. That's because you can interface an iPod with other devices to play your iPod's music through those devices. In this chapter, we'll look at two of the most common music components with which you might want to listen to your iPod's music: your home sound system and your car stereo. You'll also see how the iPod can easily be transformed into a home stereo or boombox.

Using an iPod with a Home Stereo

You can connect your iPod to your home stereo and then listen to your iPod's music over that stereo. There are two fundamental ways you can do this: using wires or by using an FM transmitter.

Hard-Wiring an iPod to a Home Stereo

You can connect your iPod to your stereo system using cables similar to those you use to connect other audio components, such as a lowly CD changer. After you have connected the iPod to your amplifier/receiver, you can listen to it just like that lowly CD changer or DVD player.

The only challenge to this is choosing and connecting the proper cables to get the output of your iPod connected to the input of your receiver. Fortunately, this isn't all that challenging. You just need a cable that connects the Headphones jack on your iPod to an audio input port on your home stereo receiver. In most cases, you need a cable that has a stereo mini-jack on one end and two RCA connectors on the other end. The mini-jack connector goes into the Headphones jack on your iPod, while the RCA connectors go into the audio input ports on your home stereo's amplifier/receiver.

Although this section is focused on connecting an iPod to a home stereo receiver, the same techniques enable you to connect an iPod to many other audio devices, such as boomboxes.

The cable you need is available in just about any store that carries home electronics. Or, you can buy a kit that includes all the cables you need to connect your iPod to other devices, such as the Apple iPod Stereo Connection Kit with Monster Cable (available at the Apple online store).

There are two basic ways to connect an iPod to a home stereo using a cable: You can connect the iPod directly to the cables or you can use a Dock. Each method has its pros and cons.

Connecting an iPod Directly to a Home Stereo

To connect an iPod to a stereo receiver, simply plug the mini-jack end of a Mini-jack to RCA cable into the iPod's Headphones port. Then connect the RCA connectors to the audio input ports on the receiver. Figure 8.1 shows a diagram of a typical connection scheme.

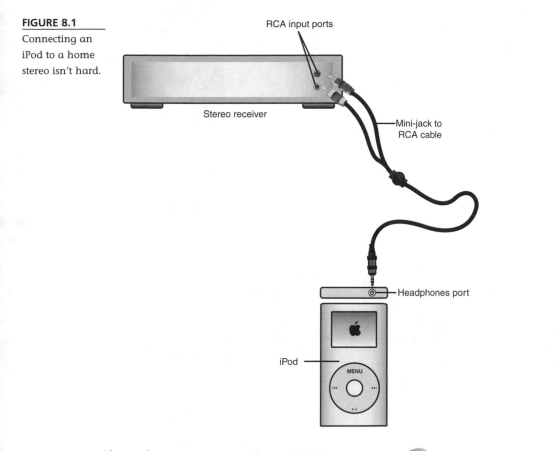

FIGURE 8.1

Connecting an iPod to a home stereo isn't hard.

RCA input ports

Stereo receiver

Mini-jack to RCA cable

Headphones port

iPod

MENU

If you also want to power the iPod while it is connected to the receiver, connect the Dock connector port to the Dock connector end of a USB or FireWire cable. Then connect the USB or FireWire end of that cable to an AC adapter and plug the adapter into a wall outlet.

Pros: Easy setup; inexpensive.

Cons: Somewhat messy because you need to have a cable connected to the receiver, whose input ports typically aren't accessible, so you leave the cable connected and "loose"; you need a separate power adapter and cable to charge the iPod while using it with the stereo.

tip

If you want to use a shuffle to play music on a stereo system, you can plug an AC adapter into a wall socket and then plug the shuffle into the USB port on the adapter. This will charge the shuffle while you play its music.

Using a Dock to Connect an iPod to a Home Stereo

The best way to connect an iPod to a home stereo is to first use a Mini-jack to RCA cable to connect a Dock to the stereo and then use the USB 2 or FireWire cable to connect the Dock to an AC adapter (see Figure 8.2). Then, you can connect the iPod to the stereo by simply placing it in the Dock. When connected, your iPod also charges, so you don't have to worry about running out of battery power.

tip

You can use any input port on a receiver to accept an iPod's input. For example, you can connect the cable to the CD ports, Aux input ports, and so on. Any ports that include a left and right channel will work.

FIGURE 8.2

Using a Dock to connect an iPod to a home stereo enables you to connect the iPod to a stereo by simply placing the iPod into the Dock.

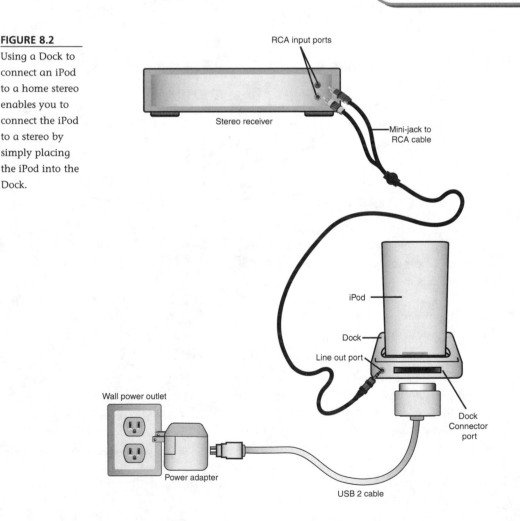

RCA input ports

Stereo receiver

Mini-jack to RCA cable

iPod

Dock

Line out port

Dock Connector port

Wall power outlet

Power adapter

USB 2 cable

Pros: Easy setup; clean installation because you don't have loose wires—after it's set up, you only need to have the Dock exposed; it's easiest to use because you connect the iPod to the stereo by placing it in the Dock.

Cons: Relatively expensive because, to be practical, you need to have a Dock and an AC adapter dedicated to this purpose, which means buying at least one Dock and AC adapter or purchasing an Apple iPod Stereo Connection Kit with Monster Cable.

Broadcasting iPod Music over FM

You can use an FM transmitter to broadcast your iPod's music on standard FM radio frequencies. Then, you can tune in the frequency on which you are broadcasting on any receiver, such as the tuner in your stereo system's receiver, to listen to your music.

Obtaining an FM Transmitter

To broadcast your iPod's music over FM, you need a transmitter that connects to your iPod and then sends its output over the airwaves. Because you are more likely to use one of these devices in your car, they are covered later in this chapter.

Broadcasting iPod Music to a Home Stereo

Depending on the type of FM transmitter you use, setting up an iPod and FM transmitter so you can tune in your iPod's music requires from little to no work. You simply plug the transmitter into your iPod's Headphones or Dock Connector port and play your iPod. Then, you set the tuner you are going to use to listen to the same frequency over which you are broadcasting your iPod's output.

Pros: Using an iPod with any audio device that can receive FM is easy; simple setup and use; no messy wires.

Cons: Subject to interference; it can be difficult to find an unused FM station in a metropolitan area.

Playing an iPod over a Home Stereo System

After you have installed or connected the components necessary to send your iPod's output to a home receiver, listening to your iPod's music is as simple as simple gets (however simple that is). On the receiver, select the iPod source, such as an Aux input or the FM tuner tuned to the frequency on which you are broadcasting your iPod's output. Then use the iPod controls to play the music and use the receiver's controls to set the volume level.

Typically, if you connect the iPod through its Headphones jack, you should leave the iPod's volume set at a mid-range point when using it with a home receiver. That prevents any distortion that might occur when the iPod is using its maximum output level. If you connect it via the Dock Connector port, the volume level on the iPod doesn't matter.

Using an iPod in this way is no different from other sources, such as a standard CD player.

Using an iPod As a Portable Home Stereo or Boombox

If you want to be able to listen to your iPod without headphones, use it as a home stereo, or use it as a portable boombox, you can obtain a set of iPod speakers. Typically, the iPod drops into a Dock-like port on the speakers. When powered via an AC adapter, the iPod also charges while you are using it. Some speakers can be battery powered too, so you can use the iPod boombox anywhere.

Many iPod speakers are available, and most offer similar features. My favorite is the Altec Lansing IM3c (see Figure 8.3). These speakers are about the size of a small hardcover book and fold flat for easy storage. They can be run on the included AC adapter or on batteries. The unit also includes a remote control so you can control the iPod music from a distance. But the best part about these amazing speakers is how good they sound; you won't be sacrificing anything for the unit's small size. I take my set with me whenever I travel so I can have my own stereo system in hotel rooms or wherever I happen to be.

FIGURE 8.3

Altec Lansing IM3c speakers are small and compact, but the sound they produce is anything but small.

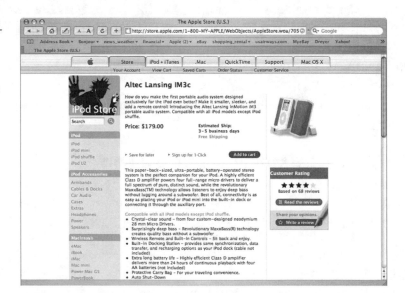

If the cost of a set of speakers like this is prohibitive for you, you can purchase an inexpensive set of computer speakers and plug them into the Headphones jack on the iPod. You'll need to make sure you get a powered set of speakers because the iPod won't be able to provide enough volume to unpowered speakers.

Using an iPod with a Car Stereo

Being able to take all your music with you on an iPod is cool everywhere, but no place more so than in your car. Forget trying to carry CDs with you (if you are like me, you never have the one you really want to listen to anyway). Just grab your iPod and you are ready for the open road.

Getting Sound from an iPod to a Car Stereo

There are two basic ways to get the output from your iPod to your car stereo: use a cassette adapter or use an FM transmitter.

note

One of the features I like best about the IM3c speakers is that they also include a Line In port to which you can connect other devices. For example, when watching DVDs on my laptop computer, I connect its audio output to the IM3c speakers. This provides much better sound quality than the tinny speakers on most laptops.

Connecting an iPod to Your Car Stereo with a Cassette Adapter

A cassette adapter looks like a standard cassette, but it also has a wire coming from it that ends in a mini-jack. You connect this plug into the iPod's Headphones port. There are many brands and types of cassette adapters, and you can obtain one through most electronics retailers.

You then insert the cassette into a standard cassette player that is installed in many cars and use the car stereo's controls to play it.

When that is done, you can control the music from the iPod, just as if you were listening to it with headphones.

Cassette adapters are convenient, but don't be surprised if the sound quality doesn't seem as good as you get when you listen to a CD or an FM radio station. These adapters often cause music to sound a bit muted. If this bothers you, try an FM transmitter instead.

The other issue is that cassette players are going the way of 8-tracks and other obsolete devices. Once common, cassette players are seldom installed in new vehicles because CDs are better on all counts.

Connecting an iPod to Your Car Stereo via FM

You can also use an FM transmitter to broadcast your iPod's output. Then, you use your car's tuner to tune into the frequency you are broadcasting on. At that point, you can play your iPod and listen to its output over your car radio.

Many types of FM transmitters are available. The best units provide the ability to transmit over all available FM frequencies, power the iPod while it is broadcasting, and hold the iPod securely. My current favorite is the Digital Lifestyle Outfitters TransPod FM All-In-One Car Solution (see Figure 8.4). This unit includes a variety of attachment devices, including a solid boom that plugs directly into your car's power outlet (in the old days, this used to be where the cigarette lighter was installed). The unit holds your iPod securely and recharges it whenever you drop it into the TransPod's iPod bay. It has a digital tuner so selecting any FM frequency is a snap (it also enables you to memorize your favorite broadcast channels). When you use the boom to connect the unit to power, you don't have any wires to mess around with. Just drop the iPod into the unit and you're ready to play.

> **tip**
>
> Combined with a good frequency, broadcasting your iPod's music over FM results in the best sound quality. In fact, it might be so good that it will sound much better than it does when you use headphones.

FIGURE 8.4

The DLO TransPod enables you to listen to your iPod in the car while powering it and holding it securely.

Powering and Charging an iPod While You Are on the Road

You can power and charge your iPod while you are on the road by obtaining and using an auto power adapter. These devices plug into the 12-volt power outlet that is available in all cars and connect to the Dock port on your iPod to power it. Many of these devices are available, too.

If you use FM to broadcast your iPod's music, try to get a unit that also powers your iPod. Otherwise, you'll need a separate power adapter. If you use a cassette adapter, you'll likely also want a separate power adapter to keep your iPod charged when you use it in the car.

Mounting an iPod in Your Car

Finding a good spot to place your iPod in your car is probably the most difficult part of using an iPod in a car. You need the iPod within arm's reach, but you don't want it sliding around or falling off the dash. So, you want it close to you but want it held firmly, too. Let's see, what is designed to keep something in place but needs to be close enough to reach? Yep, you got it. A cup holder. It is likely that you have one or more of these near your radio and within arm's reach. The odds are that one of these is a good place to keep your iPod while you are driving.

caution

If you use wires, such as a power and cassette adapter, be sure you route them such that they don't interfere with any of your car's controls. It is easy to get them wrapped around something without knowing it until you are in a bad spot.

You can just drop the iPod in a cup holder. Depending on the size and configuration of the cup holder and the size of your iPod, this might work just fine. However, in most cases, you should put your iPod in a holder or case before doing this to protect it from scratches and to keep it from bouncing around. Several devices are designed to hold your iPod in a cup holder securely, such as the Belkin TuneDok Car Holder for iPod.

In what is probably a familiar song by now, if you use an FM transmitter, get one that also holds the iPod securely. The TransPod does this and so does the Griffin Technology RoadTrip.

caution

If the cup holder you use is in plain sight from outside the car, make sure you remove your iPod and put it out of sight before you leave your vehicle. An iPod in plain sight will tempt any thief who happens by your car.

Controlling an iPod While You Are on the Road

If there is one dangerous topic in this book, this is it. Playing around with an iPod while you are driving is not a good idea. It is very easy to get focused on the iPod instead of where you are going, and your day can suddenly be ruined. To practice safe iPodding while you are on the road, consider the following tips:

caution

Take the information in this section seriously. Listening to music is not worth risking your life or property, not to mention the others who share the road with you (myself included!).

- **Choose the music to which you are going to listen while you are stopped**—The iPod's screen is just not large enough to be able to see it clearly and look around you at the same time. Choosing music is at least a one-hand and two-eye operation. That doesn't leave much left for driving. So fire up your iPod, connect it to the radio with a cassette adapter or configure the FM transmitter, choose your music source and play it, place your iPod in its holder, and then drive.

- **Consider creating playlists for driving**—You can make these long enough so you never have to change the music that is playing while you drive.

- **If you must fiddle with your music while you drive, at least use a remote control**—You can't change the music source with these devices, but you can change the volume, skip to the next song, and so on.

- **Remember that you don't need to change the volume on the iPod itself**—Set it at mid-level and leave it alone. Use your car radio's controls instead. (If you use an FM transmitter that connects to the iPod's Dock Connector port, you don't need to bother with the iPod's volume control at all.)

- **Keep your iPod secure, as explained in the previous section**—Nothing is more distracting than the thought of your precious iPod flying around the car as you drive. If that does happen, remember that fixing you and your car (plus other people) will cost a lot more than a new iPod!

- **Remember the road rule of the day: Road first, music last.**

THE ABSOLUTE MINIMUM

Using an iPod with a home or car stereo is easy to do and lets you listen to your iPod's music in many situations. Perhaps the best way to do this is to use an FM transmitter so you can tune in your iPod's music on your car radio or receiver's tuner. If you do this, check out the following pointers:

- Don't worry about other people being able to listen to your music when you use an FM transmitter. These devices have very limited range. If you are in a vehicle, someone might be able to pick up your iPod station if his vehicle is right next to yours; however, as soon as you separate even a few feet, he will lose the signal.

- Because you move around a lot when you drive, finding a good (meaning never used) FM frequency to use while you are on the road can be a challenge, especially if you are in a large metropolitan area. If a frequency isn't being used directly, it still might suffer bleed-over from stations on other frequencies. If you choose a frequency that is being used or has bleed-over, your iPod's music might be interrupted occasionally. For best results, select a station you think is unused and listen to it for a while as you drive around. (Yes, you will feel kind of silly listening to static, but hey, it will help in the long run.)

- When you find a good candidate for an unused frequency, set one of your radio's buttons to that frequency so you can easily return to it. If you use an FM transmitter in more than one car, you might want to set it on the radio in each one.

- Don't be surprised if you still have occasional static while using FM, even if you find a good unused station. Hopefully, you will be able to find a station with which this is a rare occurrence, but it is likely to happen once in a while. If you can't find a frequency/transmitter combination that works satisfactorily, try using wires or the cassette adapter method instead.

- Remember that, as you move among different areas, there are different radio frequencies being used. You might have to use different frequencies in the different areas in which you drive.

USING THE IPOD FOR IMAGES

The current pinnacle of the iPod line is the iPod itself. There are a number of reasons for this, including the color screen, bigger hard drives, and so on. One of the coolest things about an iPod is that it can work with photos as well as it does music.

iPods and Photos

What does *work with* photos mean? That means you can

- Use iTunes to move photos from a computer onto an iPod.
- View photos on the iPod individually or in slideshows.
- Use an iPod to display photos and slideshows on a TV.
- Connect a digital camera to an iPod and move photos from the camera to the iPod, where you can view them (with an optional iPod Camera Connector).
- Move photos from the iPod onto a computer.

Moving Pictures onto an iPod

To view photos on an iPod, you have to move them onto the iPod. There are three ways to do this:

- Use a supported application to move images onto an iPod via iTunes.
- Manually move photo files from a computer onto an iPod.
- Transfer photos from a digital camera onto an iPod.

Card readers for iPods enable you to transfer photos from the memory cards in digital cameras onto your iPod. You can use these devices with any iPod (except the shuffle) to store photo files on the iPod. However, you can't view photos on the iPod with this method. You can only use the iPod to transport those files, in which case, this is like using the iPod as a disk with any other kind of computer file. While this is useful in some cases, this isn't covered in this chapter. The focus here is on using the iPod to view photos along with transporting them.

Using an Application to Move Pictures from a Computer onto an iPod

With a supported application, you can transfer photos from your photo albums onto an iPod. To use this technique, you must store your photos in one of the following applications:

■ Adobe Photoshop Album, version 1.0 or later (Windows)

■ Adobe Photoshop Elements, version 3.0 or later (Windows)

■ iPhoto, version 4.0.3 or later (Macintosh)

If you use an application other than one of these to manage your photos, you can still move those photos onto an iPod; you just have to manage them outside the application itself, which you'll learn how to do in the next section.

If you do have one of these applications, use the following steps to move images from the application onto an iPod:

note

These steps use iPhoto on a Mac as an example. Using Photoshop Album or Elements on a Windows PC works similarly.

1. Connect the iPod to your computer.

2. Select the iPod on the **Source** list and click the **iPod Options** button.

3. Click the **Photos** tab. You'll see the Photos synchronization tools (see Figure 9.1).

FIGURE 9.1

Use the Photos tab of the iPod Options dialog box to move photos from a supported application onto an iPod.

4. Check the **Synchronize photos from** check box.

5. On the pop-up menu, choose the application you want to use. If you use a Mac, select **iPhoto**. If you use a Windows PC, select either **Photoshop Album** or **Photoshop Elements**.

6. If you want to move all the photos and photo albums stored in the selected application onto your computer, click the **Copy all photos and albums** radio button and skip the next step.

7. If you want to move only selected photo albums onto the iPod, click **Copy selected albums only** and then click the check box next to each album you want to import.

8. If you also want to move full-resolution photo files onto the iPod, check **Include full-resolution photos**. When viewing photos on an iPod, it uses an optimized version of the photo to display on the screen. If you want to use the iPod to move full-resolution files, say from one computer to another, this option will copy those files onto the Photos folder on the iPod. You can then use the iPod as a disk to move the files from that folder onto a different computer.

9. Click **OK**. The dialog box will close and the photos you selected will be moved onto the iPod, ready for you to view.

> **tip**
>
> If you look closely at Figure 9.1, you'll notice that the iPod menu appears at the top of the pane. That's because I had two iPods connected to the computer at the same time. You can use this menu to choose the iPod you want to configure. In this example, I have the iPod called iPod Photo selected.

Moving Image Files from a Computer onto an iPod

If you don't use a supported photo application, you can still transfer images onto an iPod for viewing. This requires slightly different steps, as you will see here:

1. Prepare the photos you want to move onto the iPod using the application you use to transfer photos from a digital camera.

2. Create a folder on your computer.

3. Copy or move the photo files into the folder you created in the previous step.

4. Connect the iPod to your computer.

5. Select the iPod on the **Source** list and click the **iPod Options** button.

6. Click the **Photos** tab. You'll see the Photos synchronization tools.

7. Check the **Synchronize photos from** check box.

> **tip**
>
> You can use an iPod to back up your photo files by checking **Include full-resolution photos**. Each time you synch your iPod, copies of your photo files will be placed on your iPod. If you ever need to recover them on your computer, you can use the iPod as a disk to do so.

8. On the pop-up menu, select the folder in which you placed the photos you want to move onto the iPod. The menu will show the folder you selected (see Figure 9.2).

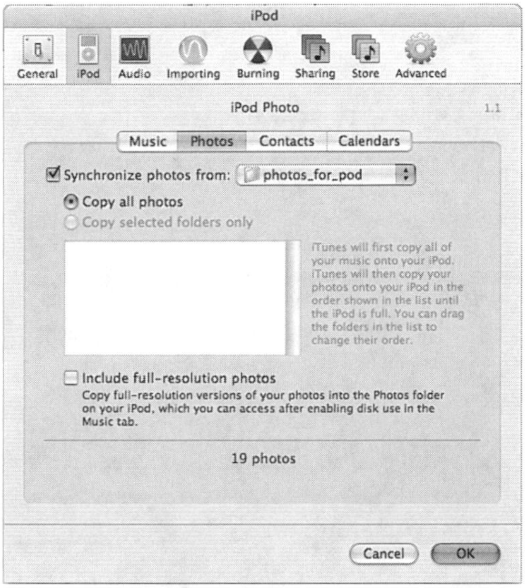

FIGURE 9.2

The menu next to the Synchronize check box shows the name of the folder containing images I want to move onto an iPod.

9. If you also want to move full-resolution photo files onto the iPod, check **Include full-resolution photos**. When viewing photos on an iPod, it uses an optimized version of the photo to display on the screen. If you want to use the iPod to move full-resolution files, say from one computer to another, this option will copy those files onto the Photos folder on the iPod. You can then use the iPod as a disk to move the files from that folder onto a different computer.

10. Click **OK**. The dialog box will close and the photos you selected will be moved onto the iPod, ready for you to view.

Moving Photos from a Digital Camera onto an iPod

Using the iPod Camera Connector accessory (available at the online Apple Store), you can connect the USB cable you use to transfer images from your digital camera to your computer to also transfer them onto an iPod (see Figure 9.3). In addition to being able to view those images on the iPod, you can also transfer them from the iPod to your computer.

FIGURE 9.3

Using the iPod
Camera
Connector, you
can transfer
images directly
from a digital
camera onto an
iPod.

To transfer photos from a digital camera to an
iPod, use the following steps:

1. Connect the iPod Camera Connector to
   the Dock port on the iPod.

2. Connect the USB cable for your camera
   to the camera and to the iPod Camera
   Connector, and put your camera in
   transfer mode. On the iPod, you'll see
   the Import screen. On this screen, you'll
   see the number of photos that are ready
   to transfer and how much disk space
   they will consume.

3. Highlight the **Import** command and
   press the **Select** button. The photos will be
   imported onto the iPod. On the Photo Import screen, you'll see a thumbnail
   of each image as it is moved from the camera onto the iPod.

   When the process is complete, you'll see the Import Done screen.

4. To exit the Import mode, select **Done**. You'll move to the Photo Import
   screen that shows each import session identified by Roll (see Figure 9.4). For
   each roll, you'll see the number of photos imported.

tip

This is a great way to
expand the number of
images you can capture
without a computer. If you
fill up your camera's memory
card, you can move the
images on that card to the
iPod, erase the card, and then
shoot more photos.

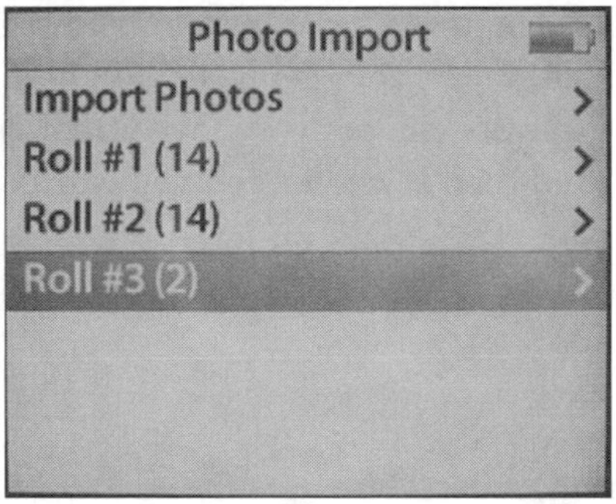

FIGURE 9.4

So far, I've used
the iPod Camera
Connector to
import three
"rolls" of photos
from my camera
onto this iPod.

Photo Import	
Import Photos	>
Roll #1 (14)	>
Roll #2 (14)	>
Roll #3 (2)	>

tip

If you want to stop the process before it is complete and save the images you have imported so far, select **Stop** and **Save**. If you don't want to save any of the images, select **Cancel**.

After you have imported images from a camera onto the iPod, you can work with them on the iPod (to view them or move them to a computer), just like photos you move onto the iPod with one of the other methods, which brings us to the next section.

To erase the camera's memory card, select **Erase Card**. Then select **Erase Card** again on the Erase Card screen.

Viewing Photos on an iPod

After you have stored photos on an iPod, using any of the methods you learned earlier in this chapter, you can view them using the following steps:

1. Select **Main** menu, **Photos**. You'll see the Photos menu (see Figure 9.5). On this menu, you'll see the photos you have imported to the iPod organized in photo albums if you used a compatible application to import them. If you've imported photos using an iPod Camera Connector, you'll also see the Photo Import option, which leads you to images you have imported from a camera.

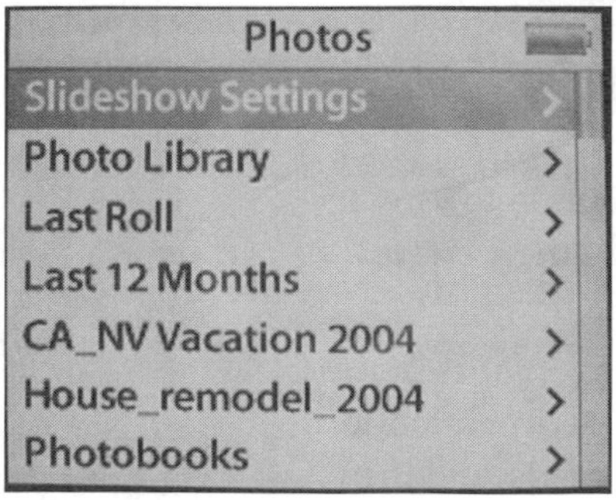

FIGURE 9.5

When I imported
photos onto this
iPod, I used the
iPhoto applica-
tion, so I see my
photo albums on
the iPod.

Photos	
Slideshow Settings	>
Photo Library	>
Last Roll	>
Last 12 Months	>
CA_NV Vacation 2004	>
House_remodel_2004	>
Photobooks	>

2. Select the source of the photos you want to view. For example, to view the images in a photo album, select it on the menu. To see all the images on the iPod, select **Photo Library**. To see images you have imported from a camera, select **Photo Import** and then select the roll you want to view.

3. Press the **Select** button. You'll see thumbnails of all the images in the selected source (see Figure 9.6). The current image will be indicated by a yellow box.

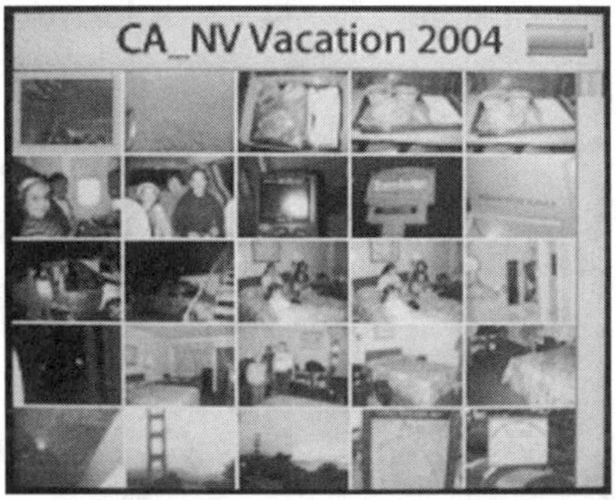

FIGURE 9.6
Here, I've selected a photo album and can see thumbnails of the images it contains.

4. Use the **Click Wheel** to move to the image you want to view.

5. Press the **Select** button. The image you selected will fill the iPod's screen (see Figure 9.7).

FIGURE 9.7
This image is filling the iPod's screen.

6. Press the **Fast Forward** button to view the next image in the source or the **Rewind** button to view the previous image.

7. When you are done viewing images in the selected source, press the **Menu** button to move back to the source's menu and then press **Menu** again to move back to the Photos menu.

note

When you get to the last photo in the source, pressing the Fast Forward button won't do anything. That's how you know you have seen all the images in the source.

Viewing Slideshows on an iPod

You can view the images on your iPod in a slideshow. There are two general steps to do this. First, configure the slideshow options. Then, watch the show.

Setting Up an iPod Slideshow

To configure a slideshow, perform the following steps:

tip

If you press the Play or Select button when you are viewing an image, you'll jump to the Slideshows menu.

1. Select **Main** menu, **Photos**, **Slideshow Settings**. You'll see the Slideshow Settings menu (see Figure 9.8).

FIGURE 9.8

Your iPod offers a number of options for its slideshows that you can configure on the Slideshow Settings menu.

Slideshow Settings	
Time Per Slide	>
Music	>
Repeat	Off
Shuffle Photos	Off
Transitions	>
TV Out	Ask
TV Signal	NTSC

2. Select the option you want to configure and press the **Select** button.

3. Use the resulting menu to choose the specific options you want to configure. See Table 9.1 for a description of the available settings.

TABLE 9.1   Slideshow Settings Options

Setting	What It Does	Options
Time Per Slide	Controls the amount of time each image is displayed	Manual; means you must press the Fast Forward button to advance the slideshow
		2, 3, 5, 10, or 20 seconds; plays the image for the selected amount of time

Table 9.1   (continued)

Setting	What It Does	Options
Music	Chooses the music that should be played when the slideshow is playing	From iPhoto (Mac only); plays the music associated with the source in iPhoto
		Now Playing; uses the music currently playing
		Off; no music
		Playlist name; plays the selected playlist
Repeat	Repeats the slideshow	Off; don't repeat the slideshow
		On; repeats the slideshow
Shuffle Photos	Displays photos at random	Off; plays the photos in order
		On; displays the images randomly
Transitions	Chooses the transition used between photos	Off; no transition is used
		Random; uses a random transition between each image
		Transition name; uses the selected transition between all images
TV Out	Sets the iPod to play to a TV	Ask; displays a prompt for you to select to play to a TV each time you play a slideshow
		On; always sets to display on a TV
		Off; always sets to play on the iPod only
TV Signal	Chooses a format for the signal sent to a TV	NTSC; uses the NTSC format (standard for the United States)
		PAL; uses the PAL format (standard for Europe)

4. Press the **Menu** button to move back to the Photos menu.

Playing an iPod Slideshow

To view a slideshow, perform the following steps:

1. Select **Main** menu, **Photos**. You'll see the Photos menu.

2. Highlight the source of the images you want to view in a slideshow. The options are the same as when you are viewing images individually.

3. Press the **Play** button. The slideshow will play using the current slideshow settings (see Figure 9.9). Sit back and enjoy the show!

4. When the last image in the slideshow appears, press the **Menu** button to return to the slideshow.

Using an iPod to Display Slideshows on a TV

Using the optional iPod AV Cable, you can connect your iPod to a TV and display slideshows on the TV (see Figure 9.10). Connect the cable to your iPod and to the RCA input jacks on your television. Then, play a slideshow using the TV Out option set to Yes, or select the Ask option and then select the TV On option. The slideshow will be played on the TV.

note

If you configure slideshows with the Manual setting, you'll need to press the Fast Forward button to advance the images in the show.

FIGURE 9.10

FIGURE 9.10

Using this cable, you can display images and slideshows on a TV.

You can use the iPod Dock for this as well. The benefit of this is that you can use an S-video cable to connect the Dock to your television, which will improve the quality of the images on the TV. Then, you connect the Audio out port on the Dock to the Audio In ports on the TV. Drop your iPod in the Dock and play a slideshow.

While a slideshow plays, you'll see full-screen images on the TV. On the iPod, you'll see thumbnails of the previous, current, and next images. You'll also see how many images are in the slideshow and the amount of time remaining for each image being displayed (see Figure 9.11).

FIGURE 9.11

While you're watching a slideshow on a TV, you'll see the Slideshow screen on the iPod.

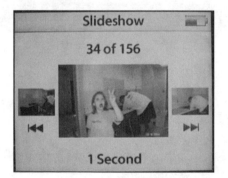

Moving Photos from an iPod onto a Computer

You can move photos from an iPod to a computer. For example, you might want to move images you have moved from a camera onto the iPod to your photo collection on your computer or move images from one computer to another.

tip

You can stop the slideshow by pressing the Menu button.

Using an Application to Move Photos from an iPod onto a Computer

You can transfer photos from the iPod to a computer just like you do from a digital camera. The steps to do this are as follows:

1. Connect the iPod to your computer, just as you do when you want to update it.

2. Open the application you use to import images from your digital camera.

3. Import the images from the iPod (see Figure 9.12).

FIGURE 9.12

Here I am importing images from an iPod into my iPhoto Library.

Manually Moving Files from an iPod to a Computer

You can store images on an iPod and move those to a computer similar to how you store and move any other files. To do so, perform the following steps:

1. Enable your iPod for disk use.
2. Connect your iPod to your computer.
3. Open a window on the desktop that shows the contents of your iPod (see Figure 9.13).
4. Drag the image files from the iPod to a location on your computer to copy them there.

note

If your iPod is not recognized by the application, you'll have to use the method described in the next section to move images from the iPod to your computer.

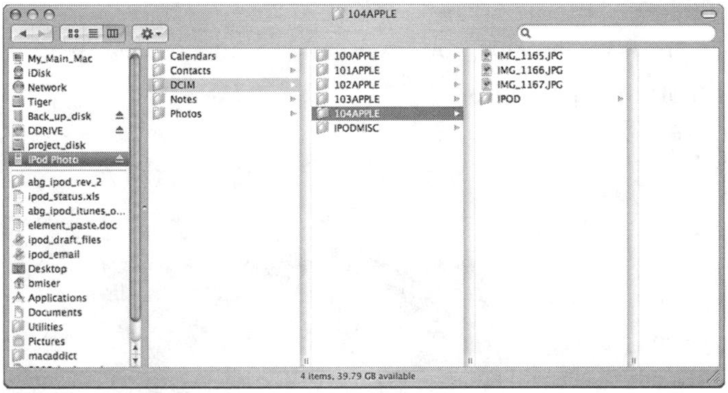

FIGURE 9.13

On this Mac, I've selected the iPod and can see the folders and files it contains.

5. Open the application you use to manage your images.
6. Import the images you copied from the iPod into that application. From this point on, the images you moved from the iPod can be used in the same way as those you imported from a digital camera.

There are a couple of locations on the iPod where your photos might be stored. If you manually moved photos from your computer onto the iPod, look in the folder you placed them in. (You might do this when you are moving image files from one computer to another.) If you imported images from a digital camera onto the iPod, the photos will be stored in the folder called DCIM (which stands for Digital Camera Images). Open this folder and you will see a folder for each import. Open a folder to access the files it contains, such as to import them into your photo application.

THE ABSOLUTE MINIMUM

The iPod is the king of the iPod family for several reasons, the foremost of which is its capability to handle photos along with music. If you are fortunate enough to have one of these amazing devices, keep the following points in mind:

- The iPod enables you to store images and view those images individually or in slideshows.

- There are three ways to move images onto an iPod so you can view them. You can use iTunes to synchronize your photos stored in a supported photo application (Photoshop Elements, Photoshop Album, or iPhoto) on your iPod. You can also use iTunes to move photos stored in a folder on your computer onto your iPod. With an iPod Camera Connector, you can download images directly from a digital camera onto an iPod.

- You can select and view images on your iPod individually.

- You can also view photos on an iPod in slideshows that can have music and transition effects.

- With the optional cable or Dock, you can connect an iPod to a TV and show your slideshows on the TV.

- You can also move photos from an iPod onto your computer. You can do this by importing its images into your photo application or from your computer's desktop.

- If you don't have a color iPod yet, what are you waiting for?

IN THIS CHAPTER

- Use your iPod like it's a $2 watch.

- Keep your appointments by placing calendar events on your iPod calendar.

- Take your contact information with you wherever you go.

- Store text gems on your iPod so you can read them at your leisure.

10

USING THE IPOD'S CALENDAR, CONTACT MANAGER, AND OTHER NON MUSIC TOOLS

The iPod is all about music, but it also can do a number of other useful things that might not be obvious. These "other things" include providing an alarm clock, displaying a calendar, showing contact information, displaying text notes, and even playing games. Although none of these features alone would make the iPod great, they are nice extras, which is, I suppose, why they are located on the Extras menu.

Keeping Track of Time with the iPod Clock

You can use your iPod to keep track of time and as a basic, but perfectly functional, alarm clock. This is handy when you travel because you don't need to carry a separate clock with you. Or, if you are like me and don't wear a watch, an iPod can help you keep track of time.

Configuring the Time on an iPod

Before you use the iPod as a clock, you need to configure its time and date. Use the following steps to do this:

note

If you only use an iPod shuffle, the information in this chapter doesn't apply and you can skip it.

1. Select **Main** menu, **Extras**, **Clock**, **Date & Time**. You'll see the Date & Time menu (see Figure 10.1).

FIGURE 10.1

You use the iPod's Date & Time menu to configure your iPod's clock.

Date & Time	
Set Time Zone	>
Set Date & Time	>
Time	12-hour
Time in Title	Off

2. Select **Set Time Zone**. You'll see the Time Zone menu.

3. Scroll on the list of time zones until you see the time zone you are in.

4. Highlight your time zone and press the **Select** button. The iPod's time zone will be set to the one you selected, and you will return to the Date & Time menu.

5. Select **Set Date & Time**. You'll see the Date & Time menu again, except that this time it will be in the set date and time mode (see Figure 10.2). The hour will be highlighted.

6. Use the **Click Wheel** to increase or decrease the hour until the correct hour is displayed.

7. Press the **Fast-forward** button so that the minute display is highlighted.

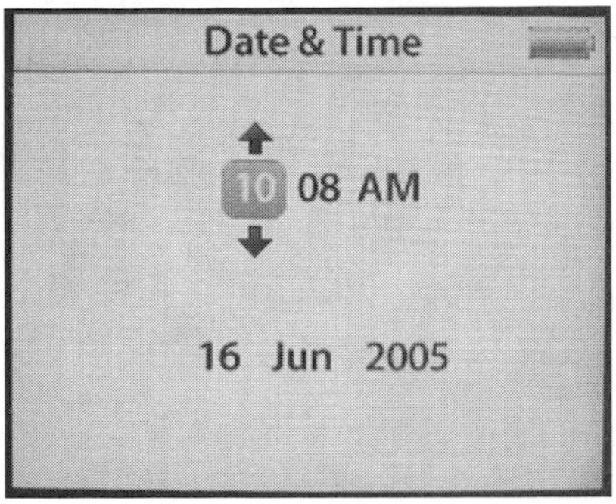

FIGURE 10.2

You use this screen to set the time and date on your iPod.

8. Use the **Click Wheel** to increase or decrease the minute until the correct minute is displayed.

9. Press the **Fast-forward** button so that the AM/PM indicator display is highlighted.

10. Use the **Click Wheel** to change the AM/PM to the correct value.

11. Continue using the **Fast-forward** button and **Click Wheel** to set the correct date, month, and year.

12. Press the **Select** button. The date and time you selected will be set, and you will return to the Date & Time menu.

13. Highlight the **Time** setting. The default value is to use a 12-hour clock.

14. To use a 24-hour clock, press the **Select** button. The Time setting will become 24-hour, and a 24-hour clock will be used.

15. To display the time in the menu title area, highlight **Time in Title** and press the **Select** button. The Time in Title setting will become On, and the time will be displayed in the title bar—instead of the menu title (see Figure 10.3).

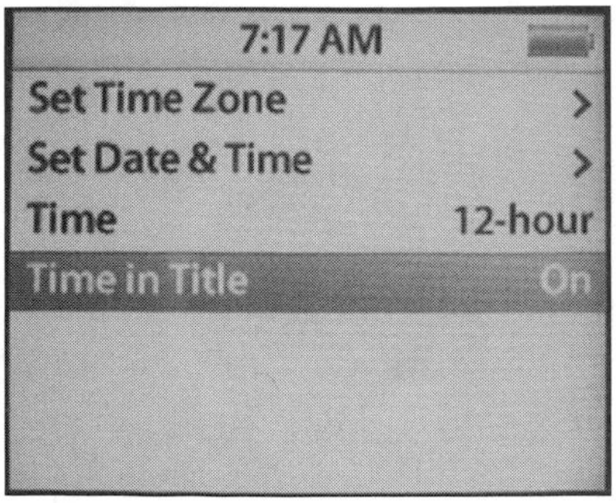

FIGURE 10.3

Placing the time in the title bar makes using an iPod as a clock much more convenient.

16. Press the **Menu** button to return to the Clock menu.

Displaying the Time on an iPod

There are a couple of ways to display the time and date on an iPod:

- Select **Main** menu, **Extras**, **Clock**. You'll see the Clock display (see Figure 10.4). In the title area, you'll see the current date, and just below the title, you'll see the current time.

FIGURE 10.4
Who says an iPod can't do everything that a $2 watch can do?

> 16 Jun 2005
>
> **7:18:39**
>
> Alarm Clock >
> Sleep Timer >
> Date & Time >

- If you turn the Time in Title setting to On (as described in step 15 in the previous list of steps), the time will be displayed in the title area of every screen a second or two after you move to a new screen. When you first move to a screen, you will see the title, but after that small amount of time passes, the title will be replaced by the current time.

> **tip**
>
> For faster access to the Clock display, add the Clock command to the Main menu. See "Setting Up Your Main Menu Preferences" on page **95**.

Setting and Controlling an Alarm

You can also use the iPod's alarm clock to wake you up or remind you of an important time. To set an alarm, perform the following steps:

1. Select **Main** menu, **Extras**, **Clock**, **Alarm Clock**. You'll see the Alarm Clock screen (see Figure 10.5). By default, the alarm is turned off, which is indicated by the Off setting.

2. Highlight **Alarm** and press the **Select** button. The Alarm setting will become On, and the alarm will be active.

3. Highlight **Time** and press the **Select** button. You'll see the Alarm Time screen.

4. Use the **Click Wheel** to select the time you want the alarm to sound. Drag clockwise to increase the time or counterclockwise to decrease it.

FIGURE 10.5

You use this screen to set your iPod's alarm.

5. When the correct alarm time is set, press the **Select** button. You'll return to the Alarm Clock menu.

6. Highlight **Sound**. By default, the alarm sound setting will be Beep, which you can hear even if you don't have earphones or speakers connected to the iPod. If you choose a different sound, you have to have speakers or headphones attached to the iPod to hear the alarm.

tip

Even though you set the alarm by the minute, you can get to any time quickly by rapidly dragging around the Click Wheel in full circles.

7. If you want to have a playlist start playing instead, press the **Select** button. You'll see a list of playlists on your iPod.

8. Highlight the playlist you want to use as the alarm sound and press the **Select** button. You'll return to the Alarm Clock menu.

9. Press the **Menu** button. You'll return to the Clock display. A bell icon will appear on the right side of the time to indicate that the alarm is set.

When the appointed time comes along, your iPod will turn on and play the beep sound or the selected playlist.

If you combine an iPod with a set of speakers, such as the Altec Lansing IM3cs that I recommended in Chapter 8, "Using an iPod with a Home Stereo or Car Stereo," it becomes a very nice bedside alarm clock. This is especially useful when you frequently stay in hotel rooms in which you can find a bewildering variety of alarm clocks, each of which requires different steps to set. With your iPod, you don't need to bother with those. Just set its alarm and drop it into the speakers. You can then wake up to your favorite tunes.

Planning Your Days with the iPod Calendar

You can use an iPod to display a calendar, and you can add events on a calendar application, such as Outlook or iCal, to the iPod calendar so you can view those events.

Setting Up Your iPod Calendar

To start using your calendar, you need to add information to it.

Moving Calendar Information from Outlook to an iPod (Windows)

You can manually move events from Outlook to your iPod by first exporting them from Outlook and then mounting your iPod as a hard disk and dragging the events into the iPod's Calendars folder. However, this process is painfully manual and you aren't likely to want to use it very often.

A better approach is to use an iPod application that can automate this process for you; one example is iPod Agent, available at www. ipodsoft.com. These applications take most of the pain out of moving events to your iPod's calendar.

Most of these applications work similarly; I'll use iPod Agent as the example in this section.

> **caution**
>
> Unless you are an incredibly light sleeper, don't expect the beep sound to wake you up. It isn't very loud and doesn't play very long. You'll have better luck if you connect your iPod to speakers and use a playlist instead.

After you have downloaded and installed iPod Agent on your computer, use it to move events to your iPod by performing the following steps:

1. Open Outlook and configure your calendar if it isn't configured already.

2. Launch **iPod Agent**.

3. Click the **Calendar** icon in the iPod Agent toolbar. You'll see the iPod Agent window (see Figure 10.6).

4. Click **Settings**. You'll see the Outlook Calendar Settings dialog box (see Figure 10.7).

5. Use the number of days box to enter the number of days in the future that you want moved onto your iPod. You can type a number or use the arrow buttons. Enter **0** to move all future events onto the iPod.

6. If you want to move past appointments on the iPod, check the **Include past appointments** check box and enter the number of days of past appointments you want to be moved in the box.

7. If you want recurring appointments included, check the **Include recurring appointments** check box.

8. If you want appointments saved as individual files, check the **Save each appointment as an individual file** check box.

9. If you want an error message to be displayed if an appointment can't be moved, check the **Display message if unable to export appointment** check box.

10. Click **OK**. The dialog box will close and you'll move back to the iPod Agent window.

11. Check the check boxes next to each Outlook folder you want to synchronize. When you do this, the folder will expand and any subfolders it contains will be shown. These are selected by default.

> **note**
>
> Because of space limitations, I have included coverage of the most popular calendar applications on each platform. You can use similar steps to add calendar information from other applications to an iPod. The iPod's Calendar feature is limited, but even so, it can be useful.

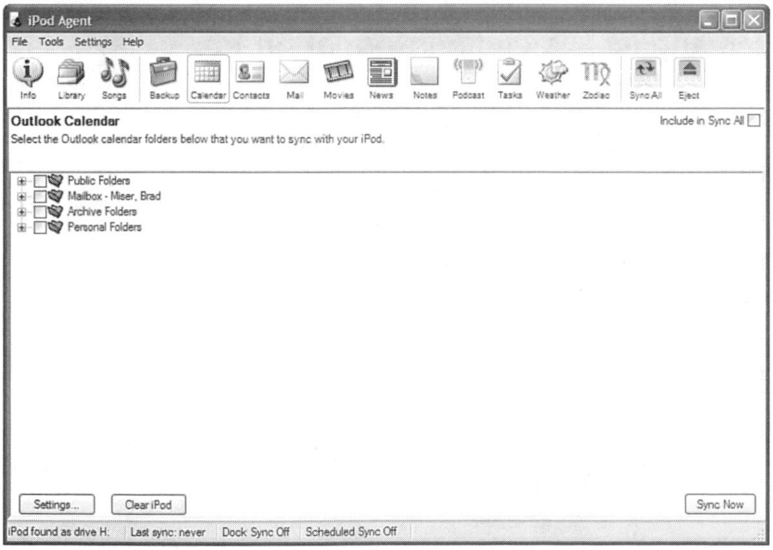

FIGURE 10.6

When you click the Calendar button on the iPod Agent toolbar, you can select the items you want to synchronize in Outlook with your iPod.

12. If you don't want a subfolder synchronized, uncheck its box.

13. Click **Sync Now**. The information you selected will be moved to your iPod.

FIGURE 10.7
Use this dialog
box to configure
how you want
your Outlook
calendar moved
onto an iPod.

Outlook Calendar Settings

Synchronize the calendar information in Calendar on your iPod with Microsoft Outlook on this computer.

Indicate how many days in the future to include appointments from (0 indicates all)

☐ Include past appointments

Indicate how many days in the past to include appointments from (0 indicates all)

☑ Include recurring appointments

☐ Save each appointment as an individual file

☑ Display message if unable to export appointment

Cancel   OK

After you have moved information to the iPod, skip
to the section called "Viewing Your iPod Calendar"
on page **138** to learn the steps to access that information on the iPod.

Moving iCal Calendar Information to an iPod (Mac)

Mac OS X includes the iCal calendar application;
you can synchronize the information it contains
with your iPod so you can view your calendar on
the iPod. This is built in to iTunes so you don't
need any additional software to keep your iPod
calendar current. Because iCal is "native" to Mac
OS X, it is used as the example in this section.

If you use a different calendar application, you
might need to use a manual process to move events to the iPod. First, export the
events from the application. Then, mount your iPod as a disk and copy the events
to the iPod Calendar's folder. There are also applications that will perform this task
for you.

Synchronizing your iCal calendar on your iPod is straightforward, and you can
even configure this to happen each time you connect your iPod to your Mac. Follow
these steps:

1. Connect your iPod to your Mac and open **iTunes** if it doesn't open automatically.

2. Select the iPod and click the **iPod Options** button.

> **note**
>
> Depending on how
> your Outlook is configured,
> you might get warnings when iPod
> Agent attempts to access its data.
> You must allow this access for the
> synchronization to work.

3. Click the **Calendars** tab. You'll see the Calendars synchronization tools. You also see the list of calendars you have created in iCal.

4. Check the **Synchronize iCal calendars** check box (see Figure 10.8).

FIGURE 10.8

You can use the Calendars tab of the iPod Settings dialog box to select iCal calendar synchronization options.

iPod

General   iPod   Audio   Importing   Burning   Sharing   Store   Advanced

iPod Photo   1.1

Music   Photos   Contacts   **Calendars**

☑ Synchronize iCal calendars
 ⦿ Synchronize all calendars
 ○ Synchronize selected calendars only:

☐ vacation
☐ Bike Rides
☐ Work

Cancel   OK

5. If you want all your iCal calendars moved onto the iPod, click the **Synchronize all calendars** radio button.

6. If you want to move only some of your calendars onto the iPod, click the **Synchronize selected calendars only** radio button and check the check box for each calendar you want to move onto the iPod.

7. Click **OK** to close the iPod Options dialog box. The calendar information you selected will be moved onto the iPod. Each time you update your iPod, the changed information in iCal will be moved to the iPod automatically.

note

Explaining the details of using iCal is beyond the scope of this book. For help, see my book *Special Edition Using Mac OS X, v10.4 Tiger*.

Viewing Your iPod Calendar

To view your iPod calendar, do the following steps:

1. Select **Main** menu, **Extras**, **Calendars**. You'll see the Calendars menu (see Figure 10.9). If you have moved multiple calendars onto the iPod, you'll see them listed on the screen.

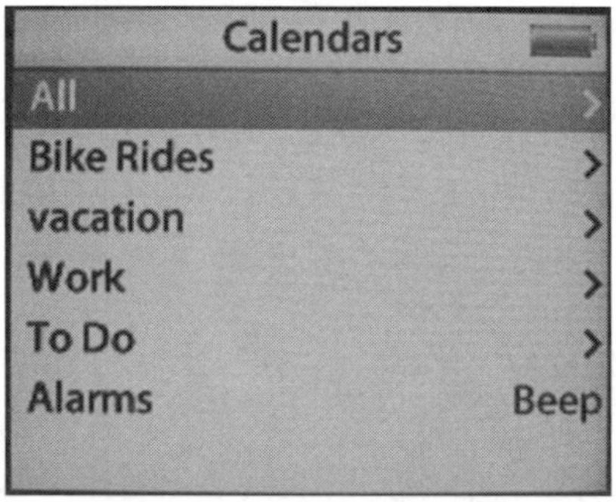

FIGURE 10.9

Choose a calen-
dar to view it.

2. Highlight the calendar you want to view and press the **Select** button. If you want to see all the calendar events, select **All**. You'll see the Calendar display (see Figure 10.10). The current date is highlighted. Dates with one or more events scheduled are marked with a black box (monochrome iPods, such as the iPod mini) or a red flag (color iPods).

FIGURE 10.10

Dates with an
event are marked
with a black box
or a flag in the
lower-right
corner of the
date box.

Date with event

3. To get details for an event, use the **Click Wheel** to move to the date in which you are interested. As you move away from the current date, its box will take on a lighter shade and the currently selected date will be highlighted in the darker shade.

tip

You can move to the next month by pressing the Fast Forward button or to previous months by pressing the Rewind button. You can also use the Click Wheel to scroll to future or past months.

4. When the date in which you are interested is highlighted, press the **Select** button. The events for that date will be listed.

5. To see the detailed information for an event, highlight it and press the **Select** button. You'll see the detailed information for that event (see Figure 10.11).

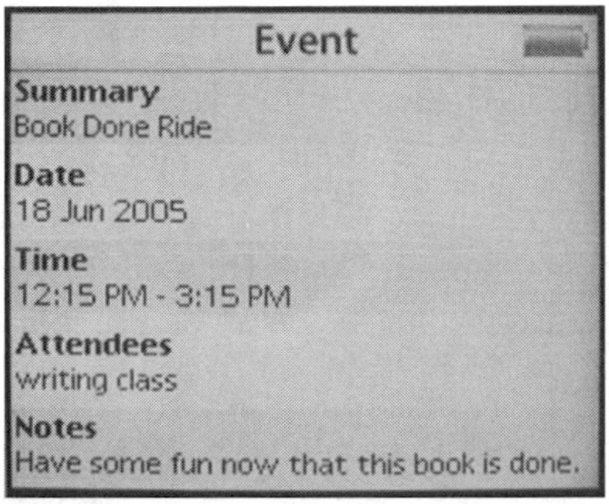

FIGURE 10.11

Here, I am viewing the details for an event on my iPod's calendar.

```
                    Event               ▄▄
Summary
Book Done Ride
Date
18 Jun 2005
Time
12:15 PM - 3:15 PM
Attendees
writing class
Notes
Have some fun now that this book is done.
```

6. Use the **Menu** button to move back to the list of events (one press) or back to the calendar (two presses).

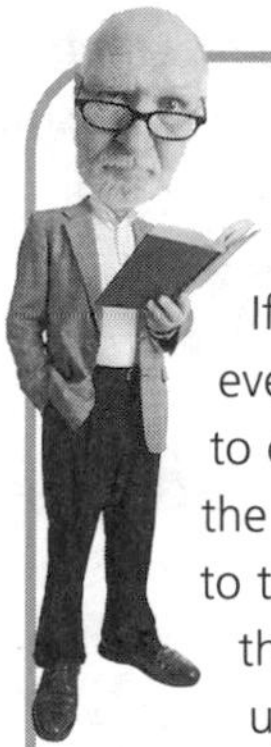

The iPod calendar also picks up event alarms for the events you place on it. To configure the event alarm, open the **Calendars** menu and scroll until you see the **Alarms** option. Set this to **Beep** to hear the beep sound for an event alarm, **Silent** to see a silent alarm, or **Off** to turn off the event alarm.

To change events on or delete them from your iPod, change or delete them in the calendar application you use (such as Outlook or iCal) and synchronize your iPod. The iPod enables you to view your calendar information, but you can't change it on the iPod itself.

tip

If you are looking at an event several months prior to or after the current date, the easiest way to get back to the current date is to use the Menu button to move up to the Calendars menu again and then select the calendar. When you return to it, you'll be in the current month.

Using an iPod to Keep an Address Book

The iPod's Contacts tool is analogous to its Calendar. Storing contacts on an iPod makes accessing phone numbers, email addresses, and other information fast and easy.

Configuring Your iPod Contacts

As with the calendar, the first step you need to take is to move contact information from your computer to the iPod.

Moving Contact Information from Outlook to an iPod (Windows)

You can manually export contact information from Outlook and place the results files in the Contacts folder on your iPod. However, this is time-consuming. It is much better to use an application that will automate the process of moving contact information from Outlook to your iPod.

iPod Agent is a good example of these applications. The steps to synchronize contact information using iPod Agent are similar to those you use to move calendar information.

Refer to "Moving Calendar Information from Outlook to an iPod (Windows)" on page **134** for the detailed steps to configure a calendar synchronization. When moving contact information, click the Contacts button on the iPod Agent toolbar instead. When you open the Settings dialog box, you'll see slightly different options, but they are just as easy to configure.

When you have configured the contacts synchronization, click **Synch Now** to move the contact data to your iPod.

Moving Address Book Contact Information to an iPod (Mac)

Address Book is Mac OS X's built-in contact information manager. It is also designed to be synched with your iPod from within iTunes. The steps to do this are nearly identical to those you use to configure calendar synchronization.

Refer to "Moving iCal Calendar Information to an iPod (Mac)" on page **136** for the detailed steps to synchronize calendar information. The steps to synchronize contacts are nearly the same. The only difference is that you use the Contacts tab of the iPod Options dialog box. Just like the calendar, you can choose to sync all contact information or only part of it. When the iPod is updated, this information is moved onto it automatically.

Configuring How Contacts Appear

When it comes to displaying contact information on an iPod, you have two options. To select an option, select **Main** menu, **Settings**, **Contacts**. You'll see the

tip

If you check the Include in Sync All check box when the Calendar or Contacts option is selected, those will be updated each time you click the Sync All button on the toolbar. This enables you to update all your Outlook information at the same time.

Contacts preferences screen. This screen has two options. Use the **Sort** option to choose how contacts are sorted on the screen. Use the **Display** option to determine how contacts are displayed on the screen. In both cases, your choices are First Last, which lists the first name followed by the last name, and Last First, which places the last name fist and the first name last.

To select an option, choose the setting and press the **Select** button to toggle the option.

Viewing Your Contacts

To view your contacts, perform the following steps:

1. Select **Main** menu, **Extras**, **Contacts**. You'll see the list of contacts sorted by your sort preference (see Figure 10.12).

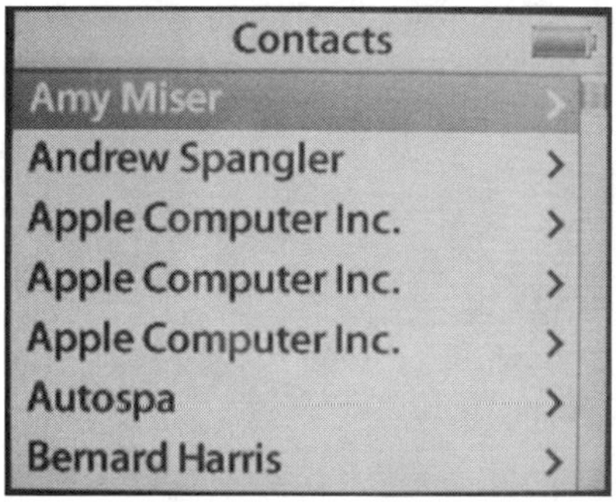

FIGURE 10.12

This screen displays a list of contacts stored on your iPod.

```
           Contacts        ▬
 Amy Miser                   >
 Andrew Spangler             >
 Apple Computer Inc.         >
 Apple Computer Inc.         >
 Apple Computer Inc.         >
 Autospa                     >
 Bernard Harris              >
```

2. To view a contact's detailed information, highlight the contact in which you are interested and press the **Select** button. You'll see a screen showing all the information for that contact (see Figure 10.13).

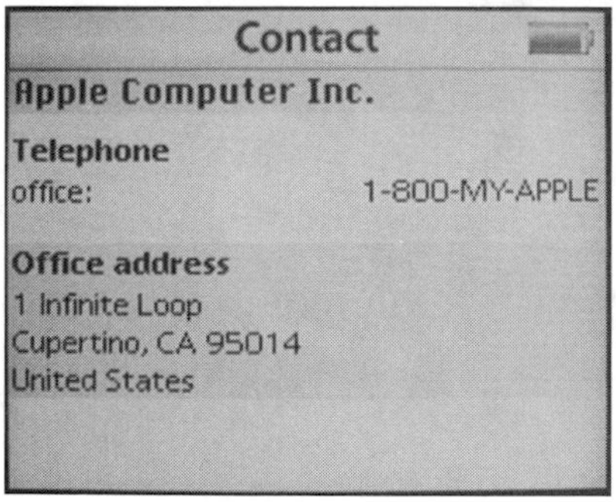

FIGURE 10.13

Here's contact information for a close, personal friend of mine.

```
           Contact         ▬
 Apple Computer Inc.
 Telephone
 office:            1-800-MY-APPLE

 Office address
 1 Infinite Loop
 Cupertino, CA 95014
 United States
```

3. Scroll down the screen to see all the information for the contact.

Using the iPod to Store and Display Text

You can also store and display text files on your iPod. For example, you might want to store instructions to perform a task that you have trouble remembering how to do or the directions to a location on your iPod for easy reference.

Creating Notes for an iPod

To create a note on an iPod, use any word processor or other application that can create a text file (the filename extension should be .txt). Create the text you want to store on the iPod and save it as a TXT file.

Moving Notes to an iPod

Connect your iPod to your computer and place the text file you created in the Notes folder on the iPod's hard drive. (To do this, you need to configure your iPod so it can be used as a hard drive; see Chapter 11 to learn how to do this.)

Reading Notes on an iPod

After you have placed text files in the Notes folder, you can read them by selecting **Main** menu, **Extras**, **Notes**. You'll see the Notes screen, which contains a list of all the text files in the Notes folder on your iPod. To read a note, highlight it and press the **Select** button. You'll see the note's text on the screen (see Figure 10.14). Scroll down the screen to read all the text if you need to.

In case you are wondering, there isn't a typo in the word *isn't* in the figure. The iPod didn't display the apostrophes in this note. I have heard that it does display them fine in some cases.

FIGURE 10.14

Hopefully, you'll put your iPod's Notes feature to better use than I did.

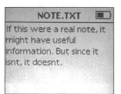

NOTE.TXT

If this were a real note, it might have useful information. But since it isnt, it doesnt.

THE ABSOLUTE MINIMUM

Although the features in this chapter probably aren't the reason you bought and use an iPod, they are a nice bonus you can take advantage of without too much work on your part. Check out this list of features:

- You can use your iPod as a clock and even as an alarm clock. This is probably the most useful extra feature, at least in my book (which you happen to be reading right now).

- You can store calendar events on your iPod's calendar to make it a handy way to keep track of where you are supposed to be and when you are supposed to be there.

- Forget carrying around a paper list of contact information; store the names, addresses, email addresses, and phone numbers of people you need to contact on your iPod and they will be with you whenever your iPod is.

- Although the iPod's screen is too small to make reading long sections of text pleasant, you can store short text notes on your iPod and read them while you're on the move.

- Lest you think these extra features are all work and no play, select **Main** menu, **Extras**, **Games**. Sure, none of these iPod games will challenge *Halo* on the Xbox for the Best Game Ever title, but they might help you kill a few minutes of time.

11

TAKING THE IPOD FURTHER

The iPod is one amazing device, isn't it! It excels as a music player and does so much more. As you learned in Chapter 8, "Using an iPod with a Home Stereo or Car Stereo," the iPod can also replace your home and auto CD player. In Chapter 10, "Using the iPod's Calendar, Contact Manager, and Other Non-Music Tools," you learned how to use the iPod to manage time, calendar, and contact information. This chapter extends your education in iPod utility and includes five more uses for your trusty iPod, including downloading and listening to podcasts, using the iPod as a hard drive or flash drive, using the same iPod with more than one computer, using an iPod to record sound, and moving music from an iPod onto a computer.

Working with Podcasts

Podcasts are radio-like broadcasts that you can download to your iPod and listen to. Podcasts are provided in segments, which are called episodes. When you listen to a podcast, you listen to specific episodes. There are a bewildering number of podcasts available on just about every topic you can imagine and some that you probably can't imagine. You can subscribe to the podcasts to which you want to listen and then move those podcasts onto your iPod so you can listen to them just like music you have added to it.

Just like music, you can build your podcast library in iTunes and then move those podcasts from iTunes onto your iPod to listen to them. This section explains how to move podcasts onto an iPod and then listen to them. To learn how to use iTunes to subscribe to podcasts, see "Subscribing and Listening to Podcasts" on page **254**.

Moving Podcasts onto an iPod

After you have subscribed to podcasts in iTunes, you have three ways to move those podcasts onto an iPod. These are analogous to how you move music onto an iPod. You can have all your podcasts moved onto an iPod automatically, you can have only selected podcasts moved onto your iPod automatically, or you can manually move podcasts onto an iPod.

If you use an iPod shuffle, you can only use the manual option to move podcasts onto it.

Automatically Moving All Your Podcasts onto an iPod

To have all of your podcasts moved onto an iPod automatically, perform the following steps:

1. Connect your **iPod** to your computer, select it on the Source list, and click the **iPod Options** button. The iPod Options dialog box will appear.

2. Click the **Podcasts** tab (see Figure 11.1).

3. Click the **Automatically update all Podcasts** radio button. You'll see a warning explaining that if you do this, you'll replace all of the podcasts currently on your iPod with those in your iTunes music library; click **OK** to clear the warning (assuming that is ok with you of course).

4. On the **Update** pop-up menu, choose which episodes you want to be updated. Choose **All episodes** if you want all the episodes of all your podcasts to be moved onto the iPod. Choose **Only checked episodes** if you only want podcasts who check boxes are checked to be moved onto the iPod. Choose **Only most recent episode** if you want only the newest episode of the podcast to be moved onto your iPod. Or choose **Only unplayed episodes** if you want only those podcasts that you haven't listened to yet to be moved onto the iPod.

5. Click **OK**. Your iPod will be updated according to the options you selected. Each time your iPod is updated, your podcasts will be too.

Automatically Moving Selected Podcasts onto an iPod

You might not want all of your podcasts to be moved onto your iPod all the time, especially if you have an iPod with memory limitations. You can choose to move only selected podcasts to your iPod automatically by performing the following steps:

1. Connect your iPod to your computer, select it on the Source list, and click the **iPod Options** button. The iPod Options dialog box will appear.

2. Click the **Podcasts** tab.

3. Click the **Automatically update selected Podcasts only** radio button. You'll see a warning explaining that if you do this, you'll replace all of the podcasts currently on your iPod with those in your iTunes music library; click **OK** to clear the warning (assuming that is ok with you of course). In the box, you'll see the podcasts in your iTunes music library (see Figure 11.2).

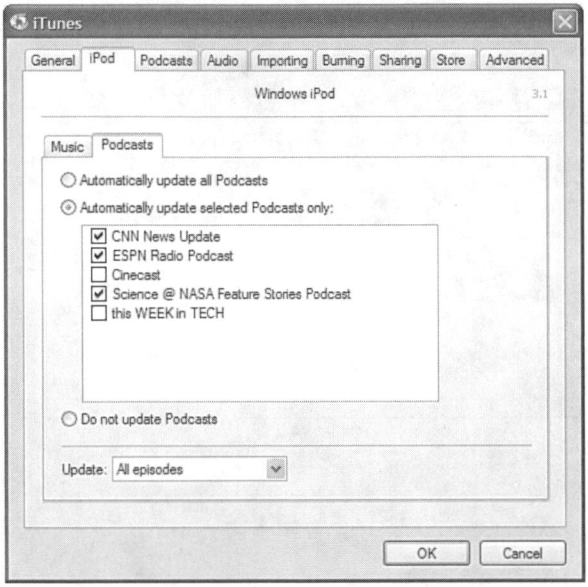

FIGURE 11.2

You can select
specific podcasts
to be moved
onto an iPod
automatically by
checking their
check boxes.

4. Check the **check box** next to each podcast you want to be moved onto the iPod automatically.

5. On the **Update** pop-up menu, choose which episodes you want to be updated. Choose **All episodes** if you want all the episodes of all your podcasts to be moved onto the iPod. Choose **Only checked episodes** if you only want podcasts who check boxes are checked to be moved onto the iPod. Choose **Only most recent episode** if you want only the newest episode of the podcast to be moved onto your iPod. Or choose **Only unplayed episodes** if you want only those podcasts that you haven't listened to yet to be moved onto the iPod.

6. Click **OK**. The selected podcasts will be moved onto the iPod and will be updated automatically each time you update the iPod according to the update preferences you selected.

Manually Moving Podcasts onto an iPod

You can also manually move podcasts from iTunes onto an iPod if you don't want to use one of the automatic options for some reason (if you use an

> **note**
>
> You can manually move podcasts onto an iPod regardless of the update option selected on the Podcasts pane of the iPod Options dialog box.

iPod shuffle, this is your only option). To manually move podcasts onto an iPod, use the following steps:

1. Connect your iPod to your computer.

2. In iTunes, select **Podcasts** on the Source list. You'll see all of the podcasts to which you are subscribed.

3. Drag the episode that you want to move onto an iPod from the Content pane onto the iPod's icon on the Source list (see Figure 11.3). That episode will be copied onto the iPod.

FIGURE 11.3

If you drag a podcast from the Content pane onto an iPod's icon on the source list, it will be copied onto the iPod.

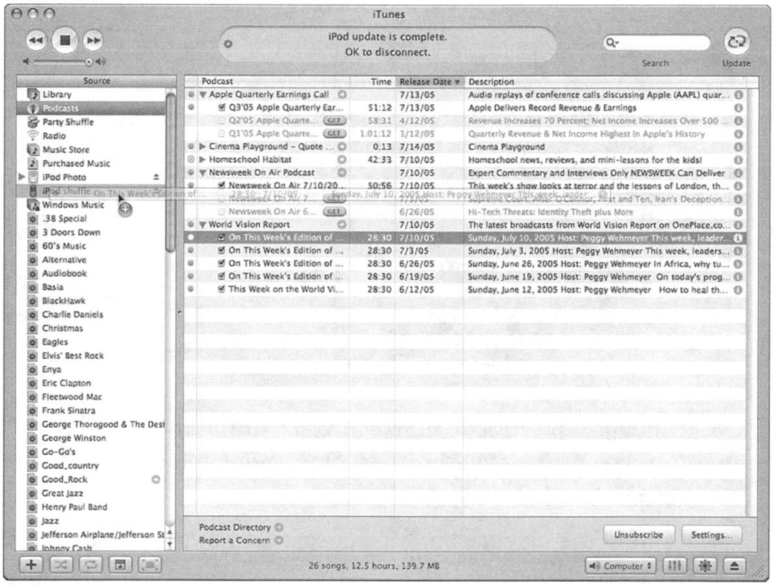

4. Continue manually moving episodes onto the iPod until you have added all that you want to be able to listen to on the iPod.

Listening to Podcasts onto an iPod

After you have moved podcasts onto an iPod, perform the following steps to listen to them:

1. Choose **Main Menu**, **Music**, **Podcasts**. You'll see the Podcasts menu that lists all of the podcasts stored on your iPod (see Figure 11.4).

2. Highlight the podcast to which you want to listen and press the **Select** button. You'll move to the episode menu for the podcast you selected; the menu name will be the name of the podcast. Here, you'll see all of the episodes of the podcast that are stored on the iPod (see Figure 11.5).

FIGURE 11.4

The Podcasts menu contains all of the podcasts you have downloaded to your iPod.

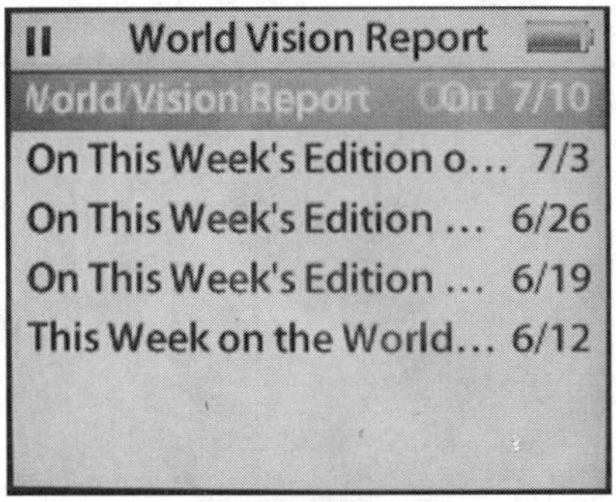

Podcasts

Apple Quarterly Earnings Call >
Cinema Playground - Quot... >
Newsweek On Air Podcast >
World Vision Report >

FIGURE 11.5

This menu shows all of the episodes of a podcast that have been downloaded to this iPod.

World Vision Report

World Vision Report On 7/10
On This Week's Edition o... 7/3
On This Week's Edition ... 6/26
On This Week's Edition ... 6/19
This Week on the World... 6/12

3. Highlight the episode to which you want to listen and press the **Select** button. The podcast will begin to play and you'll move to the Now Playing screen.

4. Control the playback of the podcast using the same controls you use to listen to music.

Removing Podcasts from an iPod

How you remove podcasts from an iPod depends on the update options you have selected.

If you use the fully automatic option, all the podcasts on your iPod will be replaced each time you update the iPod.

When you use the "selected episodes" option, the episodes of the podcasts you chose to update will be replaced each time you update the iPod.

You can also manually remove episodes from an iPod with the following steps:

tip

From the Now Playing screen, click the **Select** button twice to see a text summary of the episode to which you are listening.

1. On all iPods except the shuffle, click the **Podcasts** icon listed underneath the iPod's icon on the iTunes Source list. On an iPod shuffle, select its icon on the Source list and then scroll in the content pane until you see the episodes that you want to remove.

2. Select the episodes that you want to delete from the iPod.

3. Press the **Delete** key. The episodes you selected will be deleted from the iPod.

Using an iPod As a Portable Hard Drive

Here's some news for you: The iPod is a fully functional, portable hard drive. In addition to using the iPod's hard drive to store music, you can also use it just like any other hard drive you connect to your computer. Because you use USB 2 or FireWire to connect it, an iPod has speedy performance, too.

The uses for an iPod as a hard drive are almost endless; following are a few examples:

- **A transport drive**—Have files you want to move from one computer to another? No problem. Connect your iPod to one computer, copy files to it, connect it to the second computer, and copy files from the iPod onto that computer.

- **Extra storage space**—Need a few extra GB of disk space? No problem. Connect your iPod and you have it.

- **Temporary backup drive**—Have some important files you want to back up? Place them on an iPod and there you go.

Enabling an iPod to Be Used As a Hard Drive

To be able to use an iPod as a hard drive, you need to configure it within iTunes by using the following steps:

1. Connect your iPod to your computer. iTunes will open, and your iPod will be shown in the Source list.

2. Select the iPod and click the **iPod Options** button. You'll see the iPod Options dialog box (see Figure 11.6).

3. Check the **Enable disk use** check box. You'll see a warning prompt that explains that, if you enable disk use, you'll have to manually unmount the iPod before disconnecting it.

note

Just like any other drive you might use, you can work on files while they are stored on an iPod.

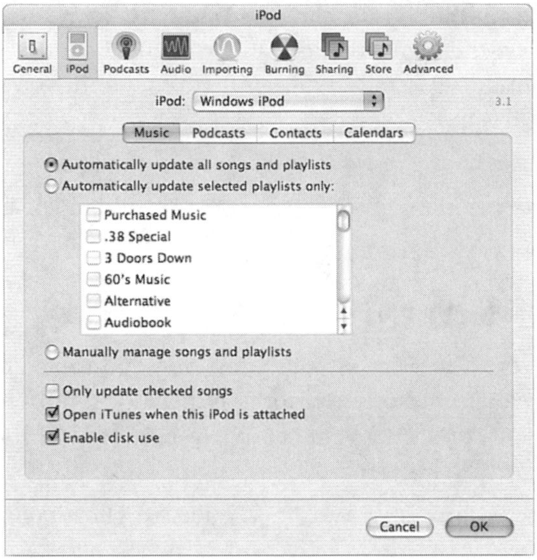

FIGURE 11.6

You use the iPod Preferences dialog box to enable your iPod to act as a hard drive.

4. Click **OK** to close the warning prompt.

5. Click **OK** to close the iPod Preferences dialog box.

Using an iPod As a Hard Drive

After you have enabled this functionality, you can use an iPod as a disk by performing the following steps:

1. Connect your iPod to your computer. iTunes will open, and if you have configured automatic updating, the iPod will be updated.

2. On your computer's desktop, open a new window and select the iPod, which will be listed just like other hard drives in your system (see Figures 11.7 and 11.8).

3. To copy files onto the iPod, drag them from other locations on your computer and drop them onto the iPod.

4. When you are done moving files to or from the iPod, eject it. You can do this from the computer's desktop by selecting the iPod and selecting the **Eject** command or from within iTunes by selecting the iPod from the

> **note**
>
> If you don't enable an iPod to be used as a disk, you won't be able to see it from your computer's desktop. Only within iTunes will you be able to see the iPod when it is connected to your computer.

Source list and clicking one of the **Eject** buttons. The iPod will be unmounted, and you can disconnect it from your computer.

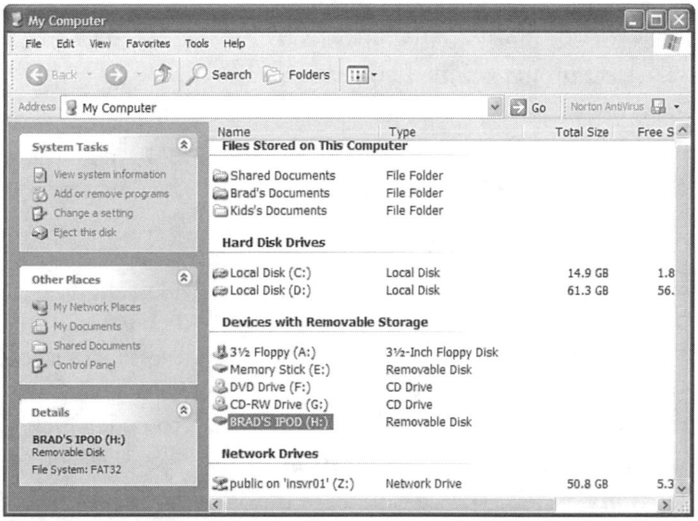

FIGURE 11.7

In the My Computer folder, you will see your iPod, which is listed in the Devices with Removable Storage section.

FIGURE 11.8

In the Mac's Finder, an iPod looks and works like other drives, too.

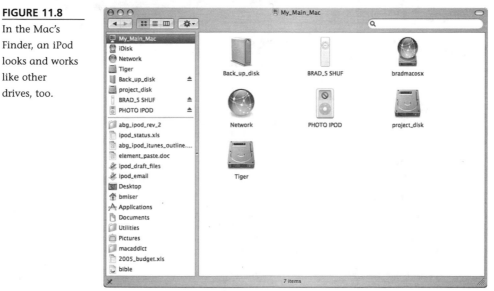

Using an iPod shuffle As a Flash Drive

Even though it doesn't have a hard drive, you can use the shuffle to store files as a USB flash drive. This works similarly to the other iPod models. First, set up the shuffle to be used as a drive. Then, use it.

Configuring an iPod shuffle As a Flash Drive

To prepare an iPod shuffle to be a flash drive, perform the following steps:

1. Plug the shuffle into your computer. iTunes will open and the shuffle will appear on the Source list.

2. Select the shuffle and click the **iPod Options** button. The iPod pane of the iTunes Preferences dialog box will appear (see Figure 11.9).

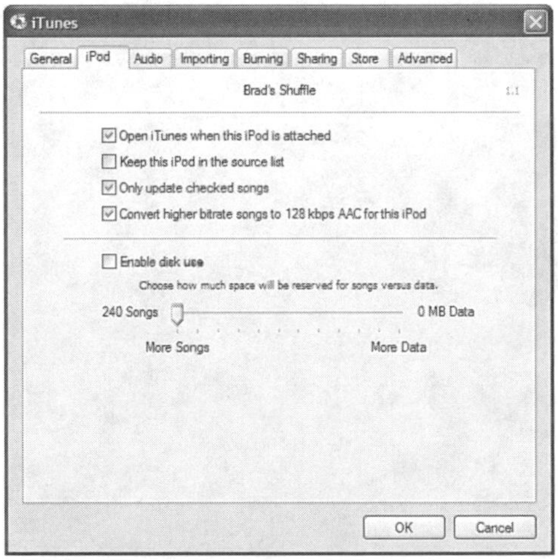

caution

When you have enabled an iPod to be used as a disk, you must manually eject it before disconnecting it from your computer. If you don't, you can damage the data stored on it. To let you know this, the `Do not disconnect` message will appear on the iPod's screen when it is mounted on your computer. Don't disconnect your iPod until you have ejected it and the `OK to Disconnect` message appears on its screen.

FIGURE 11.9

When you select a shuffle and open its options, you can configure it as a flash drive.

3. Check the **Enable disk use** check box and click **OK** in the resulting dialog box (which warns you that you must manually eject the shuffle before unplugging it when you use it as a drive). This enables your shuffle to become a USB flash drive.

4. Use the slider to set the amount of memory that should be reserved for songs. A portion of its memory must be dedicated to the flash drive function

to serve this purpose. Any memory you allocate for this won't be available for music. As you move the slider, the information at each end of the slider will show you how much memory you have allocated for each purpose.

5. Click **OK** to close the Preferences dialog box.

Using an iPod shuffle As a Flash Drive

After you have configured it for disk use, using a shuffle as a disk is simple:

1. Plug the shuffle into your computer. iTunes will open and the shuffle will appear on the Source list. The shuffle will also be mounted on your desktop just like hard drives and other storage devices you use.

2. Move to your computer's desktop and locate the shuffle; it will have the name you gave it during the initial configuration process (or as close as your computer can come to it to create a valid disk name).

3. Open the shuffle just as you would any other storage device (see Figure 11.10).

FIGURE 11.10
The shuffle appears on the list of removable storage devices and can be used just like one of them.

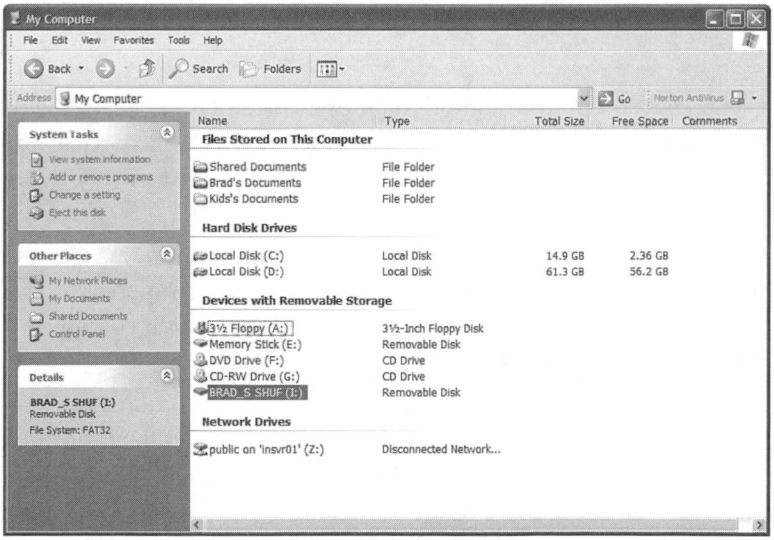

4. To add files to the shuffle, drag them from your desktop onto its folder.

5. When you are done using the shuffle as a disk, eject it from the desktop or by clicking one of the **Eject** buttons in iTunes (one is next to the shuffle on the Source list while the other is in the lower right corner of the iTunes window).

Using an iPod with More Than One Computer

Because the iPod is so very portable, you might use it with more than one computer—especially when you use it as a portable drive, as you learned how to do in the previous two sections. And because iTunes is free, there is no reason you can't install it on every computer you use.

Using an iPod with more than one computer presents only one minor complication: When you configure an iPod to be automatically updated (either with the full automatic or the selected playlist option), you link it to the iTunes Library on the machine you configured the update on. When you connect the iPod to another machine that also has automatic updating set, you will see a warning prompt that explains that the iPod is linked to another iTunes Library (see Figure 11.11).

FIGURE 11.11

This warning prompt explains that the iPod is already linked to another iTunes Library.

The iPod " iPod" is linked to another iTunes music library. Do you want to change the link to this iTunes music library and replace all existing songs and playlists on this iPod with those from this library?

☐ Do not ask me again

No   Yes

If you click Yes in this prompt, the music currently on the iPod will be replaced by the music stored on the computer to which the iPod is connected and the link will be changed to the current iTunes Library. If you don't want to replace the iPod's music, click No.

If you want to move music to the iPod from more than one iTunes Library, you'll need to select the Manual update option on each computer with which you use it. This option doesn't link the iPod to any Library, so you can move songs from multiple Libraries onto the same iPod.

If you just want to be able to use the iPod as a disk, choose one computer to link the iPod to for music. Each time you connect it to a different computer, just click No in the warning prompt to leave the music on the iPod alone. The iPod will be mounted on that computer and you can use it as a disk. You'll also be able to manually move music from that computer's iTunes music library onto the iPod.

Using an iPod to Capture Sound

With a recording accessory, you can use the iPod to record your voice or other sounds. This can be a handy way to capture information on-the-fly for use later. For example, if you use a vehicle for business use, you might want to use the iPod to keep a verbal log of that use that you can document on paper later.

Choosing a Voice Recorder for an iPod

To record sound on an iPod, you need to obtain a voice recorder accessory. At least two of these units are available: the Belkin iPod Voice Recorder and the Griffin Technology iTalk iPod Voice Recorder.

The Belkin unit is the one I focus on here (see Figure 11.12). This unit retails for about $35 and enables you to access the recording features that are already built in to the iPod's software.

Installing the Belkin iPod Voice Recorder

Installing the Voice Recorder couldn't be easier. Simply plug the unit into the iPod's Headphones and Remote ports. When you do so, you'll see the Voice Memo screen (see Figure 11.13). That's all there is to setting up the Voice Recorder.

note

There are some funky ways you can record a few seconds of sound without a voice recorder unit, but it requires more maneuvering than you are likely to want to do except as a novelty. If you are interested in this method, use Google to search the Internet for this information.

note

Unfortunately, the Belkin Voice Recorder doesn't work with an iPod mini or shuffle.

FIGURE 11.12

The Belkin iPod Voice Recorder enables you to use your iPod to record your voice and other sound.

FIGURE 11.13

When you connect a Voice Recorder to your iPod, you'll see this Voice Memo screen.

Recording Sound on an iPod

To record sound, use the following steps:

1. Move to the Voice Memo screen; if you aren't there already, select **Main menu**, **Extras**, **Voice Memos**, **Record Now**.

2. Highlight **Record** and press the **Select** button. Your iPod will begin recording, and the counter on the Voice Memos screen will begin counting the time of the current recording. At the same time, the Pause and Stop and Save commands will appear on the screen (see Figure 11.14).

3. Speak into the voice recorder. Whatever sound you make will be recorded.

tip

You aren't limited to recording your own speech; you can record any sound that is close enough to be picked up by the microphone in the voice recorder.

FIGURE 11.14

As you record, your iPod displays the length of the recording you are making.

4. To pause the recording, highlight **Pause** and press the **Select** button. The counter and recording will pause.

5. To resume recording from where you left off, highlight **Resume** and press the **Select** button. Your iPod will start recording again.

6. When you are done recording, highlight **Stop and Save** and press the **Select** button. The recording process will stop, and you'll move back to the Voice Memos screen on which your recording will be listed. It will be named with the date and time on which you made it (see Figure 11.15).

FIGURE 11.15

On the Voice Memos screen, you'll see the recordings you have made.

You can repeat the previous steps to continue recording sound until you have captured all that you are interested in or until you run out of disk space to store the sound you have recorded—whichever comes first.

Working with Sound You Have Recorded

There are a number of things you can do with sounds you have recorded. These include the following:

- You can play sounds you have recorded by highlighting the sound you want to hear on the Voice Memo screen and pressing the Play button. You'll see the Now Playing screen, and the sound will play.

note

Because you install the voice recorder in the Headphones port, you must remove it to connect headphones to the iPod to be able to listen to sound you have recorded.

■ You can delete sounds you have recorded by highlighting the sound you want to delete and pressing the **Select** button. You'll see a screen with Play and Delete options. Select **Delete** and then select **Delete Memo** on the resulting screen. The sound you recorded will be deleted.

■ The next time you connect your iPod to your computer, the sounds you recorded will be uploaded into your iTunes Library. To find them, search for the dates on which you recorded the sounds; the sounds you recorded on those dates will be shown in the Content pane (see Figure 11.16). After a recorded sound is in your Library, you can work with it just like the songs in that Library. For example, you can play the sounds, add them to playlists, put them on CD, and so on.

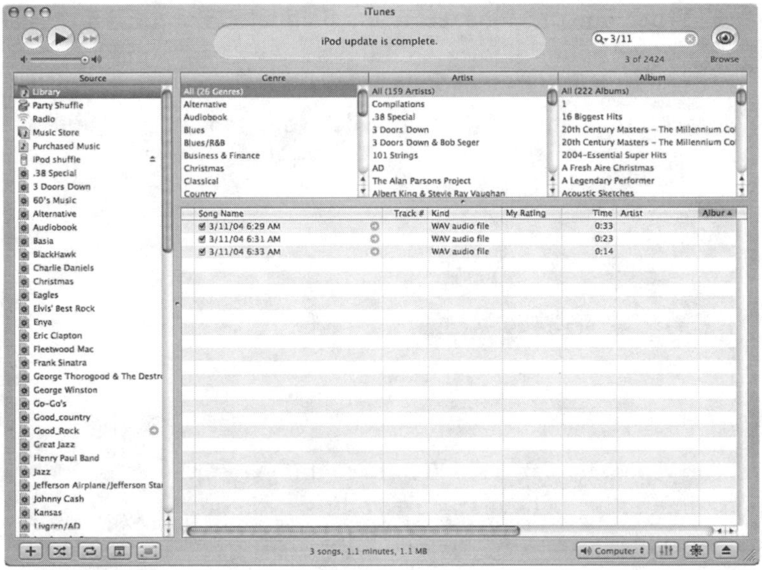

FIGURE 11.16

These are sounds I recorded on an iPod.

■ You can also directly access the recording files you made by connecting the iPod to a computer and opening it as a hard drive from the desktop. Then you open the Recordings folder, and you will see one WAV file for each recording stored on the iPod. You can play these WAV files or import them into an audio application for editing or other purposes.

Using an iPod to Move Your Music Collection from One Computer to Another

In this book, I encourage people to write to me, which they do. There is one question I am asked much more than any other, and that is, "How do I move my music from an iPod to my computer?" My answer is that using iTunes, you can't. iTunes is designed for one-way transfer, from the computer to an iPod. I suspect this is to help protect the copyright of purchased and other music.

If your iPod has enough disk space to store the music you have imported onto it *and* all the music files in your iTunes Library, you can mount your iPod as a hard disk, copy your iTunes folder from your computer onto the iPod, connect the iPod to another computer, copy the iTunes folder onto that computer, and import the music files into the iTunes Library on the second computer.

There are two issues with this approach, though. One is that you have to have enough room on your iPod for two versions of all your songs. The other is that it is a pain to import all that music into another iTunes Library.

Applications are available that will enable you to move music from your iPod to a computer and provide lots of other features.

If you use a Windows computer, several applications can recover the music on your iPod and copy it to a computer. One example is iPod Agent, available at www.ipodsoft.com.

After you launch iPod Agent and get into the main interface, you will see the iPods connected to your computer (see Figure 11.17). You can then move the music on the iPod onto your computer.

> **caution**
>
> Don't use these applications to copy your music for people who aren't entitled to it. Just because an application can do this doesn't mean it is something you should do.

> **note**
>
> If you read Chapter 10, you should remember iPod Agent because this is the application I recommended for Windows users who are going to use their iPods as PDAs with a Windows computer.

If you use a Macintosh computer, you can download iPod Rip from www.thelittleappfactory.com. When you install and open the application, you can work with the iPods connected to your computer (see Figure 11.18). You can use the Recover iPod feature to restore an iPod's music on your Mac.

Providing detailed steps for these applications is beyond the scope of this book, but both are relatively simple to use and include help systems if you have questions about how they work.

One of the nice things about these applications is that they, in effect, turn your iPod into a backup system for your music (assuming your entire iTunes Library fits on your iPod, of course). Should anything happen to your iTunes Library, you can move the music from the iPod back onto your computer to restore it. I still recommend that you back up on disc, though.

As the makers of iPod Agent warn you when you launch the application, iTunes will delete any music on your iPod that isn't in its Library if you have enabled your iPod to sync automatically. When you connect the iPod to your computer and iTunes begins to open, hold down the **Shift+Ctrl** keys until the iPod appears on the Source list. This will prevent iTunes from performing an update.

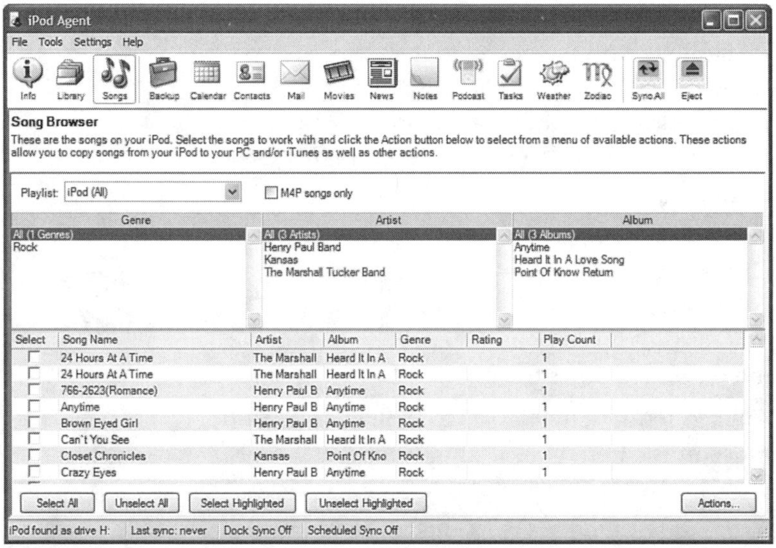

FIGURE 11.17

You can use iPod Agent to copy music from an iPod onto a computer among many other tasks.

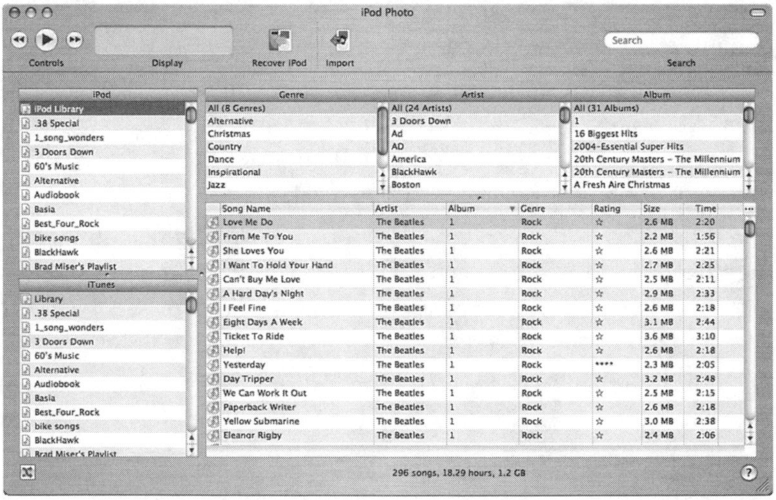

FIGURE 11.18

iPod Rip enables you to transfer music from an iPod onto a Macintosh.

THE ABSOLUTE MINIMUM

As you can see, the iPod is much more than just the world's best portable music player. As you live with your iPod, you'll likely come to appreciate its other uses, which include the following:

- Putting podcasts on your iPod enables you to listen to radio-like programs of your choice at any time and in any location.

- Using your iPod as a portable hard drive or flash drive just might be one of the best reasons to have an iPod. The ability to carry gigabytes of data on a device the size of a deck of playing cards is very useful indeed.

- You can use an iPod with more than one computer; just be aware of the update option you use. Otherwise, you might find the contents of your iPod being replaced when you didn't intend them to be.

- Adding a voice recorder to an iPod is a great way to use it to record sounds, such as voice memos or reminders.

- You can move music from an iPod onto a computer, but without an additional application, it isn't the easiest task in the world. Fortunately, there are applications designed to do just this for both Windows and Macintosh computers.

IN THIS CHAPTER

- Maximize your iPod's battery life and durability.
- Update or restore your iPod's software.
- Identify and solve iPod problems.

12

MAINTAINING AN iPOD AND SOLVING PROBLEMS

The iPod is a well-designed device, and it is more likely than not that you won't ever have any trouble with it, especially if you practice good battery management and keep its software up-to-date. In this chapter, you'll learn how to do those two tasks, plus you'll also learn how to handle any problems in the unlikely event they do occur.

Maintaining Your iPod's Power

Like any other portable electronic device, your iPod literally lives or dies by its battery. When not connected to a power source, your iPod's battery is the only thing standing between you and a musicless life. Fortunately, working with your iPod's battery isn't very difficult, but it is something you need to keep in mind.

Monitoring and Maximizing Battery Life

The Battery icon in the upper-right corner of the screen always tells you what your battery's status is at any point in time for all iPods except the shuffle.

When your iPod is running on battery power, the amount of shading within the icon provides a relative—and I do mean *relative*—indication of your battery's current state (see Figure 12.1). As you use battery power, the shaded part of the

> **note**
>
> There has been a lot of controversy regarding the iPod's battery, including several lawsuits and some awards from those lawsuits. Getting into the details of the iPod battery's legal and other history isn't the point of this section. Unless you have an older iPod, you'll probably not encounter any battery problems anyway.

battery will decrease until your iPod runs out of gas. When it does, you'll see an icon of a battery with an exclamation point that indicates your iPod is out of power and that the battery will have to be charged before you can use the iPod again.

Battery icon

FIGURE 12.1
Keep an eye on the battery icon to make sure you don't run out of juice while you're on the move.

Determining the state of the iPod shuffle's battery is much harder (not really). On the back of the shuffle, press the Battery Status button. The small light next to the button will illuminate. If it is green, you are good to go. If it's orange (Apple calls this *amber*), you are running somewhat low and should recharge when you can. If it is red, you are close to being empty and need to recharge ASAP. If the light doesn't appear at all, your shuffle is out of power and you are out of luck if you want to listen to music.

To maximize your iPod's playing time per battery charge, you can do the following:

- Keep the iPod's software up-to-date (you'll learn how later in this chapter).

- Use the Hold feature (the Hold switch on the iPod and iPod mini or press and hold the Play button for 3 seconds on the shuffle) to prevent your iPod's controls from being unintentionally activated when you carry it around. You'd be amazed how easy it is for the iPod to be turned on and start playing without you knowing it, especially if you carry it in your pocket, backpack, or computer bag. (It's no fun trying to listen to tunes only to find out your iPod's battery has been accidentally drained—not that this has ever happened to me, of course.)

- When you aren't listening, don't keep your iPod playing; press the Pause button to stop the music. Playing music uses power at a greater rate than not playing music.

- Put your iPod to sleep by turning it off when you aren't using it. The Sleep, or Off, mode uses the least amount of power. (You can press and hold the Play/Pause button to turn off the iPod. You can also add the Sleep command to the Main menu if you prefer to use that instead. You can turn a shuffle off by using the slider on its back.)

- Keep backlighting at a minimum level. Backlighting is very helpful to be able to see the iPod's screen, especially in low-light conditions. However, it does use additional power, so you should use it only as necessary to maximize battery life. When you don't need it, such as in daylight conditions, turn it off. When you do need it, set it such that it remains on only a few seconds when you press a control.

- Minimize track changes. Each time you change tracks, the iPod uses more power than it would just playing tracks straight through. Likewise, using the Shuffle mode consumes power at a faster rate because the iPod's disk has to be accessed more frequently.

note

The batteries on different iPod models and different generations of the same models are rated for different amounts of playing time. At press time, the iPod's battery is rated for up to 15 hours (music only, 5 hours for slideshows with music), the iPod mini's for up to 18 hours, and the shuffle's for 12 hours. Of course, these ratings are based on ideal conditions, which means the iPod plays straight through for these periods with no controls being used, no backlighting, and so on. Should you expect to get that much time under actual conditions? Probably not. Later in this section, you'll learn how to test your iPod's battery to ensure it is in good condition.

- Turn off the Equalizer. The Equalizer uses more power than playing music without it.
- Every 30 recharges or so, fully drain and recharge the battery.
- Keep the iPod at a comfortable temperature. Using the iPod in very cold or very hot conditions lowers its battery life.

> **tip**
>
> When an iPod is turned off, it still uses some power. For example, its internal clock keeps ticking. And, it takes some power to maintain the iPod's memory. If you don't use your iPod for 14 days or more, you should charge its battery to keep it ready to play.

Charging an iPod's Battery

Fortunately, there are a number of ways to charge your iPod's battery, including the following:

- If your iPod includes an AC adapter, use it to charge the iPod's battery.
- Connect the iPod to a high-power USB 2 or a FireWire port either directly with a cable or via a Dock. This has the benefit of updating your iPod at the same time you charge its battery.
- Plug the shuffle into a high-power USB 2 port on a computer's case.
- Use a power adapter designed for 12-volt sources, such as the power outlets in your vehicle, along with the iPod's AC adapter to charge the iPod on the move.

The iPod lets you know it is charging in two different ways.

When your iPod's battery is charging via a connection to a computer, the Battery icon will include a lightning bolt symbol and display a filling motion from the left to the right of the icon (see Figure 12.2). When the battery is fully charged, the icon will be completely filled and the motion will stop.

Battery being charged

FIGURE 12.2

This iPod is getting its battery charged via a FireWire cable.

Do not disconnect.

When you charge your iPod's battery through a separate power adapter only, the battery icon fills the iPod's screen and flashes (see Figure 12.3). When the process is complete, the battery icon remains steady and the fully charged message appears.

FIGURE 12.3

This iPod is being charged with the power adapter.

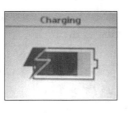

When you are charging a shuffle, its status light will be orange while the battery is charging. When it's fully charged, the light will be green.

According to Apple, it takes only 2 hours (iPod shuffle, iPod mini) or 3 hours (iPod) to charge a drained battery to 80% of its capacity. It can take up to 4 hours (iPod shuffle) or 5 hours (iPod) to fully charge a drained battery.

Getting More Life Out of an iPod's Battery

The iPod uses a lithium-ion batter. Any battery, including the iPod's, will eventually wear out and no longer provide the power it once did. In my research, most lithium-ion batteries are rated for 300–500 charges. In this context, a charge can't be precisely defined, but it does include a full discharge and then a full recharge. A partial charge doesn't "count" as much, but the precise relationship between the amount of charge and how much that charge "counts" can't be specified.

Batteries like that in the iPod actually last longer if you don't let them fully discharge before you recharge them. Frequent "topping off" will not reduce the battery's life and in fact is better for your battery than letting it run very low on power before you recharge it.

Every 30 recharges or so, do run your iPod until it is completely out of power and then perform a full recharge. This will reset the battery's power gauge, which tends to become more inaccurate if the battery is never fully discharged.

note

Unlike some other rechargeable batteries, lithium-ion batteries don't have a memory, which means their performance is not degraded by not being fully discharged and then recharged each time.

note

The fact that the iPod's battery will eventually wear out is nothing unique to the iPod. All batteries die eventually and must be replaced. However, some early iPods (the Original iPod for one) did have major battery problems that have left the iPod with a now-underserved reputation for having defective batteries.

It doesn't hurt the battery to do frequent and short recharges, such as by placing the iPod in a Dock every day after you are done using it.

However, you should be sure to run the iPod on battery power for significant periods of time. If you constantly run the iPod from the power adapter or while it is in the Dock connected to a power source, the iPod's battery's performance will degrade.

Solving Battery Problems

Frankly, your iPod's battery will eventually wear out. You'll know this by the time it can play on battery power becoming shorter and shorter. And, the battery is the most likely problem you might experience.

Testing Your iPod's Battery

If your iPod doesn't seem to play for a reasonable amount of time, you should test it to get an idea of what its current battery life is. Test your iPod by performing the following steps:

1. Fully charge your iPod.

2. Remove the iPod from the charger so it is running on battery power.

3. Make a note of the current time.

4. Use the Settings commands to turn off the Equalizer, Shuffle, and Backlight.

5. Set **Repeat** to **One**; on the shuffle, use the slider to have music playback straight through.

6. Select an album or a playlist and play it.

7. Let the iPod play until it runs out of power. While the iPod is playing, don't use any of its controls. Anytime you cause the iPod to perform an action, you cause it to use additional power. In this test, you are attempting to determine what its maximum life is so you can compare it to the rated life.

8. When the iPod stops playing and the low power icon appears in the display, make a note of the time.

9. Calculate the battery life by figuring out how much time passed since you started the iPod playing (compare the time you noted in step 8 with what you noted in step 3).

The rated life of iPod batteries changes regularly, but when I wrote this, the following ratings applied:

> **tip**
>
> If you are testing an iPod, use the slideshow with music mode because the test will be done much more quickly.

- **iPod shuffle**—Rated for up to 12 hours of playing time. If yours lasts more than

8–10 hours, your battery is in good shape. If it won't last more than 6 hours, you likely have a battery problem.

- **iPod mini**—Rated for up to 18 hours of playing time. If yours lasts more than 14–16 hours, your battery is in good shape. If it won't last more than 8, you likely have a battery problem.

- **iPod**—Rated for up to 15 hours of music playing time or 5 hours of slideshows with music. If yours lasts more than 8–12 hours of music or 2–3 hours of slideshows, your battery is in good shape. If it won't last more than these general guidelines, you likely have a battery problem.

Getting Help from Apple for iPod Battery Problems

If your iPod doesn't play for the expected time, the battery probably needs to be replaced. If the iPod is still under warranty (1 year without the AppleCare Protection Plan or 2 years with it), Apple will replace the battery for free. If the iPod is not under warranty, Apple will replace the battery for you (currently this costs $99 plus $6.95 shipping). To get more information and start this process, go to www.apple.com/support/ipod/power/ and click the **iPod battery service request form** link.

> **note**
>
> Batteries are manufactured items, which means they aren't always made just right. You should test your new iPod's battery life to ensure yours is performing up to snuff prior to the warranty expiring.

Updating or Restoring an iPod's Software

Apple is continually improving the iPod's software to add features, make it even more stable, and so on. You should periodically check for new iPod software and, when you find it, install it on your iPod—this is called *updating* the iPod's software.

When you are having major problems with your iPod or just want to completely reformat it, you can also *restore* its software to return it to factory settings.

You do both of these tasks in the same way, as the following steps show:

1. Open a Web browser and move to www.apple.com/ipod/download/. You'll see the iPod Updater page (see Figure 12.4). Along the right side of the screen you'll see a table listing each model of iPod and the current software version. If your iPod is already using the most current version, you don't need to download or install the iPod Updater application because it is already installed on your computer and so you can skip to step 6.

2. Click the radio button for either **Windows 2000 or XP** or
   Mac OS X and then click **Download iPod
   Software Update**. The download
   process will start automatically; if not,
   click the link to manually start it.

3. Notice the name of the application you
   downloaded and where you stored it on
   your computer.

4. Launch the iPod Updater installer application you downloaded—in some cases, it
   will run automatically after you download it.

5. Follow the onscreen instructions to install
   the iPod Updater application on your computer.

6. Connect the iPod you want to update or restore to your computer.

7. Launch the iPod Updater application. To do this on a Windows computer,
   select **Start** menu, **All Programs**, **iPod**, **iPod Updater** (with the most
   recent date), **iPod Updater**. On a Mac, open the **Applications**, **Utilities**,

caution

According to Apple, your
iPod will be replaced
with an equivalent
model rather than just
the battery being
replaced. Make sure you have all
the data you need from your iPod
before you send it in for service.

and **iPod Software Updater** folders. Then open the iPod Updater application with the most recent date.

When the iPod Updater launches, it will locate the iPod connected to your computer and display information for it, such as its name, serial number, software version, and capacity (see Figure 12.5).

tip

To see the current version of iPod software installed on your iPod, select **Main** menu, **Settings**, **About**. On the About screen, you will see the version of iPod software you are currently using next to the Version label. On the shuffle, use the iPod update application to see which software version is currently installed.

FIGURE 12.5

You use the iPod Updater application to update your iPod's software or to restore it to original condition.

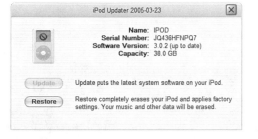

8. If you want to install the latest version of the iPod software on your iPod, click the **Update** button. If the most current version is already installed, the Update button will be inactive and you'll see (up to date) in the software version information section. If you want to restore your iPod, click **Restore** instead.

9. Follow the onscreen instructions to complete the update or restore process.

After you have updated your iPod, you can continue using it as you did before the update.

If you restored your iPod, you will have to perform an update from iTunes to load your music back onto it. You'll also have to replace any calendar or contact information you want to store on it.

Identifying and Solving iPod Problems

Okay, I admit it. The iPod isn't perfect. Once in a while, it might not act the way you expect it to. Hey, no one or no technology is perfect, after all.

caution

When you restore an iPod, all of its data is erased, including its music, calendar data, contacts, and so on. If you have stored files on the iPod that aren't stored elsewhere too, make sure you copy the files you want to save from the iPod to another location before you restore it.

In this section, you'll read some information that will help you in the event you do experience problems.

Solving iPod Problems

Troubleshooting iPod problems isn't all that different from troubleshooting other kinds of problems. First, observe exactly what is happening. Determine what you are doing and how the iPod is responding or not responding, as the case may be. Then, use the information in the following sections to see whether you can solve the problem yourself.

Checking the Basics

We all do things that can be classified as something less than intelligent once in a while. And using the iPod can result in a few of these events, so use the following list to ensure you haven't done anything to shoot yourself in the foot:

- If the iPod won't respond to any controls, make sure the Hold feature isn't active. The Hold feature does just what it is supposed to—it prevents everything from working. It can be rather embarrassing to panic that your precious iPod has suffered a major failure only to realize that the Hold switch is on. (Of course, you understand that this has never happened to me personally.) If you use a shuffle, press a control; if the status light flashes orange, hold is on. Also on a shuffle, make sure the slider isn't in the Off position.

- If the iPod won't turn on, connect it to an AC power adapter or to a high-powered USB 2 or FireWire port on a computer. It might simply be that the battery is out of power. Remember that the iPod uses some battery power when you aren't using it, and after 14 days or so, it might not have enough battery power to wake up. Sometimes the empty battery icon will appear when you try to turn on a fully discharged iPod—and sometimes it won't. Use the Battery Status light on a shuffle to check its charge; if the light doesn't illuminate, the shuffle must be recharged before you can use it.

- If the Hold feature isn't on but the iPod won't respond to commands, try connecting the iPod to a computer. If it mounts, you probably just need to do a minor reset to get it to work again.

Resetting an iPod

If you can't get an iPod to do anything (and you've checked the Hold feature) or if it is behaving badly or locks up, try resetting it. When you reset an iPod, its temporary memory is cleared but your data (music) isn't affected.

How you reset an iPod depends on the specific model you are using. Fortunately, resetting the current models is relatively easy; you have to jump through some hoops for older models. You should check the documentation that came with your iPod to see how to reset it.

To reset current iPods, press and hold both the **Menu** and **Select** buttons for about 6–10 seconds until you see the Apple logo on the iPod's screen. This indicates that the reset process was effective.

To reset a shuffle, turn it off, wait 5 seconds, and then turn it on again using the slider on its back.

If you are using an older model and don't have its documentation, visit www.apple.com and click the **Support** tab. Then, search for "reset iPod." Open one of the documents that contains information about resetting an iPod. This will either provide you with the steps you need or lead you to documentation that does.

After your iPod is reset, it should work normally. If not, you should try restoring it.

Restoring an iPod

As you read earlier, you can also use the iPod Updater application to restore an iPod. When you restore an iPod, its memory is erased and a clean version of its software is installed. The purpose is to configure the iPod with factory settings that will likely solve many problems you are having.

For the steps to perform a restore, refer to "Updating or Restoring an iPod's Software" on page **171**.

Solving the Folder/Exclamation Point Icon Problem

In some situations, your iPod will display a folder and exclamation point icon on its screen. When it does so, this indicates there is a problem and you won't be able to use the iPod until you solve it. Unfortunately, this icon doesn't relate to one specific problem but can result from an incorrect software version being installed, which is easily remedied via a restore using the iPod Updater application. It can also be due to something being wrong with the iPod's disk, which will require a repair.

caution

Restoring an iPod also deletes any data you have stored in its memory (hard drive or flash memory), so be sure you have any data that is unique to the iPod backed up before you restore it. As long as all of the music on the iPod is in your iTunes music library, you don't have to worry about its music because that will be replaced the next time you connect it to your computer to perform an update from iTunes.

tip

Resetting or restoring an iPod is the solution to almost all the problems you will be able to solve yourself. Whenever you have a problem, always try to reset the iPod first. If that doesn't work, try to restore it. In the vast majority of situations, one of these will solve the problem.

Fortunately, while the cause of the problem won't be clear to you, the solutions available should be. First, try to reset the iPod. If that doesn't work, try to restore it. In most cases, one of these two actions will solve the problem. If not, your iPod probably needs to be repaired or replaced. See the section "Getting Help with iPod Problems" to see what to do next.

Solving the "I Can't See My iPod in iTunes" Problem

If you connect your iPod to your computer but it doesn't appear in the Source list, this means iTunes can't find your iPod. This can happen for a number of reasons. Use the following steps to troubleshoot this problem:

1. With your iPod connected to your computer, restart the computer and then open **iTunes**. This will sometimes get the devices communicating again. If you see your iPod on the Source list, you are good to go. If not, continue with the next step.

2. With your iPod connected to your computer, open the **iPod Updater** application. If it recognizes your iPod, this means your computer and iPod can communicate, which is a good thing. If the Update button is active, update your iPod's software. If not, restore its software instead. Then, repeat step 1. If iTunes still doesn't show the iPod, download and reinstall iTunes.

3. If the iPod Updater doesn't recognize your iPod and instead displays the message `Connect an iPod to your computer to update it`, there is a communication problem between your computer and the iPod. Try plugging the iPod into a different USB 2 or FireWire port. If the two devices still can't communicate, there is a problem either with the iPod or with your computer. You'll probably need some help to solve either of these issues.

Getting Help with iPod Problems

Although I probably could have added a few more pages to this book with specific problems you might encounter and potential solutions to those problems, that would have been wasteful for two main reasons. First, it is likely you won't ever experience the problems I would include. Second, Apple maintains an extensive iPod website from which you get detailed information about iPod problems. You can use this information to solve specific problems you encounter (that aren't solved with the information in the previous sections, such as a reset).

To access this help, use a web browser to move to www.apple.com/support/ipod. On this page, you can search for help, read FAQs, and get other information that will help you solve iPod problems (see Figure 12.6).

FIGURE 12.6

Need iPod help?
You got it.

A number other websites might be helpful to you as well. These include www.ipodlounge.com and www.ipodhacks.com. You can also use www.google.com to search for iPod problems; you'll find no shortage of web pages on which those problems are discussed. It is highly likely that someone else has faced and solved the same problem you are having.

tip

Feel free to write to me with questions about your iPod or to ask for help with problems you are having with your iPod. You can reach me at bradmacosx@mac.com.

The Absolute Minimum

The iPod is what we hope most technology will be—it just works and works well. Here are some pointers to help you keep your iPod in tune:

- Understand your iPod's battery and use the practices described in this chapter to keep it maintained properly.

- Keep your iPod's software current by using the update software Apple releases periodically.

- If you do run into problems, check the last section in this chapter for help in solving them. Fortunately, many problems are easy to solve with a reset or restore. If those don't work, lots of help is available to you.

PART II

iTunes

13

TOURING iTUNES

With not-very-sincere apologies to Mr. Edison, Apple's iTunes is the best thing to happen to music since the phonograph. This amazing application enables you to do things with your music you might have never dreamed possible. Of course, you can use iTunes to listen to audio CDs, but that is certainly nothing to write home (or a book) about. Any two-bit boombox can do that. That basic task is barely a warm-up for iTunes. If you have never used iTunes before, prepare to be impressed (and if you have used iTunes before, be impressed anyway).

What You Can Do with iTunes

I could fill a book (or at least Part II of this book) with all the great things you can do with iTunes. Following are some examples just to whet your appetite:

- Listen to audio CDs.

- Listen to Internet radio and podcasts.

- Store all the music you like in a single place so you never need to fuss with individual CDs again.

- Search and organize all this music so listening to exactly the music you want is just a matter of a few mouse clicks (and maybe a few key presses).

- Create custom albums (called *playlists*) containing the specific songs you want to hear.

- Create custom albums (called *smart playlists*) that are based on a set of criteria, such as all the jazz music you have rated at four or five stars.

- Use the iTunes built-in Equalizer to make your music just right.

- Burn your own music CDs to play in those oh-so-limited CD players in your car, a boombox, or in your home.

- Share your music collection with other people over a wired or wireless network; you can listen to music other people share with you as well.

Audio File Formats You Might Encounter When You Use iTunes

As you work with digital music and other audio files, you'll encounter a number of file formats you need to understand. This is important because each of these formats offers specific benefits and limitations that impact what you do with your music. For example, some file formats offer better music quality versus file size than others. You definitely don't need to have all the specifications for each of these formats committed to memory (nor will you find them in this book); instead, all you need is to be able to distinguish between them and to be able to choose the format that is the most appropriate for what you are trying to do.

Most audio file formats are *encoded*. This means specific compression algorithms (because this is a computer book, I am required by contract to use that word at least once) are used to reduce the size of the audio file without—hopefully anyway— lowering the quality of the resulting sound very much. The higher the compression that is used, the lower the quality of the resulting music when it is played back. Note that the words *higher* and *lower* are relative. Often, it takes a musical expert to tell the difference between encoded and unencoded music, but even if it is imperceptible to us mere mortals, it does exist.

When it comes to digital audio files, one trade-off always has to be made. And that is *file size* versus *sound quality*. When you add thousands of songs to your iTunes Library, you can easily consume gigabytes of disk space. Although you might have a humungous hard drive in your computer, you might also have other files you want to store on it, such as photos, Word documents, and so on. Even I realize that computers can be used for more than just music.

To keep the amount of disk space required to store your music to a minimum, you must encode it. When you do, you choose the settings you want to use to encode that music. The more encoding you apply, the less space the music will consume, but the lower quality the playback will be. You will quickly find a happy medium between file size and how the music sounds to you.

You'll learn about encoding music in more detail later in the book, but for now, you should read the following sections so you can become comfortable with the various audio file formats you will encounter.

CD Audio

The CD Audio format was the world's first widely used entry in the digital audio format life cycle. The creation of this format was the start of the CD revolution. Instead of vinyl albums, which were a pain to deal with and included lots of hisses, pops, and other distractions when played, listeners began enjoying digital music. In addition to being easier to handle than LPs, CDs provided a much better listening experience and were—and are—much more durable than records. They also sounded much better than cassettes and could be just as portable.

Eventually, CD Audio made its way to computers, which now can provide all the music-listening enjoyment of a home stereo plus much more, thanks to applications such as iTunes.

Although you can use iTunes to listen to your audio CDs, typically you will just convert those CDs into one of the newer digital formats and store that content on your computer's hard disk so you don't have to bother with a CD when you want to listen to music. You will also use this format when you put your iTunes music on your own audio CD so you can play your iTunes music when you are away from your computer.

> **caution**
>
> Some audio CDs use copyright-protection schemes that prevent you from listening to them on a computer (with the idea being that you won't be able to make copies of the songs for illegal purposes). Unfortunately, not only do these CDs not work in your computer, but they also can actually cause damage. Before playing a CD in your computer, check the CD's label carefully to make sure it doesn't contain any warnings about playing the CD in a computer or state that the CD is copy-protected. If it does have these warnings, don't try to use the CD in your computer.

MP3

Even if this book is your first foray into the wonderful world of digital music, you have no doubt heard of MP3. This audio file format started, literally, an explosion in music technology that is still reverberating and expanding today.

MP3 is the acronym for the audio compression scheme called *Moving Picture Experts Group (MPEG) audio layer 3*. The revolutionary aspect of the MP3 encoding scheme was that music data could be stored in files that are only about 1/12 the size of unencoded digital music without a noticeable degradation in the quality of the music. A typical music CD consumes about 650MB of storage space, but the same music encoded in the MP3 format shrinks down to about 55MB. Put another way, a single 3.5-minute song shrinks from 35MB on audio CD down to a paltry 3MB or so in MP3 format. The small size of MP3 files opened up a world of possibilities.

For example, MP3 enabled a new class of portable music devices. Because MP3 files can be stored in small amounts of memory, devices with no moving parts can store and play a fair amount of music; these were the early MP3 players, such as the Rio. Then came other devices containing small hard drives—can you say iPod?—that can store huge amounts of music, enabling you to take your entire music collection with you wherever you go. These devices are extremely small and lightweight, and their contents can be easily managed.

> **note**
>
> Because MP3 files are relatively small, storing an entire music collection in a small amount of disk space is possible, thus eliminating the need to bother with individual CDs. Using a digital music application such as iTunes, you can easily store, organize, and access an entire music collection on your desktop or laptop computer.

You will encounter many MP3 files on the Internet, and with iTunes, you can convert your audio CDs into the MP3 format so that you can store them in iTunes and put them on an iPod.

AAC

The successor to MP3 is called *Advanced Audio Coding (AAC)*. This format is part of the larger MPEG-4 specification. Its basic purpose is the same as the MP3 format: to deliver excellent sound quality while keeping file sizes small. However, the AAC format is a newer and better format in that it can be used to produce files that have better quality than MP3 at even smaller file sizes.

Also, as with MP3, you can easily convert audio CD files into the AAC format to store them on a computer and add them to an iPod. What's more, you can convert

AAC files into the Audio CD or MP3 format when you want to put them on a CD to play on something other than your computer, such as a car stereo.

The AAC format also enables content producers to add some copy-protection schemes to their music. Typically, these schemes won't have any impact on you (unless of course, you are trying to do something you shouldn't).

One of the most important aspects of the AAC format is that all the music in the iTunes Music Store is stored in it; when you purchase music from the store, it is added to your computer in this format.

WAV

The *Windows Waveform (WAV)* audio format is a standard on Windows computers. It has been widely used for various kinds of audio, but because it does not offer the "quality versus file size" benefits of the MP3 or AAC formats, it is mostly used for sound effects or clips people have recorded from various sources. Millions of WAV files are available on the Internet that you can play and download.

You can load WAV files into iTunes, and you can even use iTunes to convert files into the WAV format. However, because MP3 and AAC are much newer and better file formats, you aren't likely to want to do this very often. Occasionally, you might want to add WAV files to your iTunes music collection; this can be easily done, as you will learn later in this book.

AIFF

The *Audio Interchange File Format (AIFF)* provides relatively high-quality sound, but its file sizes are larger than MP3 or AAC. As you can probably guess from its name, this format was originally used to exchange audio among various platforms.

> **tip**
>
> If you ever want to find a sound byte from your favorite movie or TV show, you can probably do so at one of the many WAV websites. One example is www.wavcentral.com. Interestingly enough, even the sound clips on these sites have mostly been converted into MP3.

As with the WAV format, because the MP3 and AAC formats provide a better sound quality versus file size trade-off, you aren't likely to use the AIFF format. The most typical situation in which you might want to use it is when you want to move some music or sound from your iTunes collection into a different application that does not support the MP3 or AAC format.

Apple Lossless

The Apple Lossless format is the only encoding option supported by iTunes that doesn't sport a fancy acronym. The goal of this format is maximum sound quality.

As a result, files in this format will be larger than in AAC or MP3. However, Apple Lossless files will be slightly smaller than AIFF or WAV files.

The Apple Lossless format provides very high-quality music but also larger files sizes. If you have a sophisticated ear, high-quality sound systems, and discriminating taste in music (whatever that means), you might find this format to be the best for you. However, because storing music in this format requires a lot more space on your computer and on an iPod, you will probably use the AAC or MP3 format more.

The iTunes Music Library

Earlier, you read that one of the great things about iTunes is that you can use it to store all your music on your computer. This is done with the iTunes Library (see Figure 13.1). This is the place in which you store all the music and sounds you import into iTunes, such as from audio CDs or other sources. You can then browse or search your Library to find the music you want to listen to or work with.

FIGURE 13.1

The iTunes Library is the one place to go for all the good music in your life.

As you use iTunes, you will frequently be accessing your Library; it will often be your first stop when you do things with your music, such as creating playlists or burning CDs.

Where Does All That Music Come From?

You have three primary sources of the music and sounds from which you will build your iTunes Library:

- **Audio CDs**—You can add music from your audio CDs to the iTunes Library. In iTunes lingo, this process is called *importing*.

- **The Internet**—You can download music, podcasts, and other audio files from the Internet and add those files to your iTunes Library.

- **The iTunes Music Store**—Part III, "The iTunes Music Store," is dedicated to this source, and for good reason. Using the iTunes Music Store, you can search for, preview, and purchase music online and add that music to your Library. You can also choose and subscribe to podcasts from the bewilderingly large selection available.

> **note**
>
> iTunes uses a civilized term (*importing*) for the process of converting an audio CD into a different format and adding the resulting music to your Library. The more traditional term for converting audio CD music into the MP3 format is *ripping*. I kind of like *ripping* myself, but because *importing* is the term iTunes uses, I guess we will go with that.

Playlists: Customizing Your Music Experience

I've saved one of the best features of iTunes for nearly last—*playlists*. Playlists enable you to create custom collections of music from the songs in your iTunes Library. (If you think of a playlist as a custom CD without the disc itself or size limitation of a disc, you will be very close.)

When you create playlists, you can mix and match music to your heart's content. For example, you can build your own "greatest hits" collections that include multiple artists, music genres, and so on. You can repeat the same song multiple times in the same playlist, and you can get rid of songs you don't like by not including them in the playlists you listen to. What's more, you can create a playlist to include a specific amount of music from a single CD or endlessly repeat all the music in your Library.

Basically, you can use playlists to organize a collection of songs in any way you choose. You can then listen to your playlists, put them on a CD, or move them to an iPod.

You'll learn all you need to know about playlists in Chapter 18, "Creating, Configuring, and Using Playlists."

The Other Members of the Band: The iPod and the iTunes Music Store

When it comes to citizenship, iTunes definitely gets an A+ because it plays so well with others.

If you have read Part I, "The iPod," you know that the iPod might just be the coolest portable electronic device ever to hit the streets. Although the iPod is indeed an awesome piece of technology, it wouldn't get very far without a tool to manage the music it contains. iTunes is that tool. iTunes and the iPod go together like a 1-2 combination punch, peanut butter and jelly, jalapenos on a pizza, Bing Crosby and Bob Hope (well, you get the idea). Using iTunes, you can determine which parts of your music library are on the iPod. iTunes manages moving the music files to the iPod and organizing them, so the process is simple (from your perspective anyway). In fact, iTunes will manage the process for you automatically if you prefer; when you connect your trusty iPod to your computer, iTunes will recognize it and then synchronize the music it has in your Library with that on your iPod.

When you get to Part III, you will learn in detail about the last part of the digital music triumvirate: the iTunes Music Store. With the iTunes Music Store, you can shop for music to add to your Library. When you find songs you'd like to have, you can purchase and download them into your iTunes Library with just a couple of mouse clicks. And you can do all this from within iTunes itself. It feels like the iTunes Music Store is just an extension of iTunes, which, in fact, it is. You access the iTunes Music Store from within iTunes, and the Store uses an interface that looks very similar to the iTunes interface. So, once you know iTunes, you won't have any problems with the iTunes Music Store.

THE ABSOLUTE MINIMUM

Now that you have met iTunes, I hope you are jazzed (pun intended) to get into it and start making its musical magic work for you. In the chapters following this one, you'll learn how to do everything from listening to audio CDs and Internet radio to building playlists to sharing your music over a network. Here are the major topics you learned about in this introduction to iTunes:

- You can use iTunes to do just about anything you want to with your music, from listening to CDs to putting your entire music collection on your hard drive to managing the music on an iPod.

- The primary audio file formats you are likely to use with iTunes are AAC and MP3. However, you can also use WAV, AIFF, and the Apple Lossless format when you want to maximize sound quality or for other purposes (such as to export music to another application).

- The iTunes Music Library is where you store and can work with all your iTunes music.

- You can get music for your iTunes Library from audio CDs, the Internet, and the iTunes Music Store.

- You add and listen to podcasts using iTunes and then move those podcasts to an iPod.

- You can use playlists to create and listen to customized collections of music.

- iTunes works seamlessly with the iPod and the iTunes Music Store.

- Learn how to install iTunes on a Windows PC.

- Open the application and do some basic configuration.

- Do the same on a Macintosh.

- Get comfortable with the iTunes interface; to know it is to love it.

- Figure out what my least favorite iTunes feature is.

14

GETTING STARTED WITH iTUNES

It's time to put iTunes through it paces so you can see and hear for yourself what it can do. Fortunately, you will find that iTunes is not only so well designed that it is easy to use, but it is just as easy to install on your computer.

In the first part of this chapter, you'll learn how to install and launch iTunes. Although using iTunes on a Windows PC and on a Macintosh are nearly identical, there are slight differences in how you install the applications on each platform. So, I've included an installation section for each kind of computer. It should go without saying, but I will say it anyway just in case: You don't need to read both installation sections. Just read the section that is applicable for the type of computer you use. (Of course, if you are fortunate enough to have both kinds of computers, you'll want to install iTunes on each and will need to read this entire chapter.)

After you have installed and launched iTunes, read the section "Getting to Know iTunes," where you'll get the grand tour of the amazing iTunes features you will be using throughout the rest of this part of the book.

Installing iTunes on a Windows PC

Over the years, Apple has produced a few applications designed for both Windows PCs and Macintoshes. Thank goodness for Windows users that iTunes is also in this group. (Few of Apple's other attempts are worthy of much mention, but iTunes is definitely a crossover hit!)

To use iTunes on a Windows computer, you must be running Windows 2000 or Windows XP. If you are running Windows 98, Me, or 95, you are out of the iTunes game. (Of course, those older versions of Windows are really old and you should be using a newer version for more reasons than just the ability to run iTunes!)

You have two primary ways to get a copy of iTunes and install it on your computer. (The good news is that neither way will cost you any more money than you have already spent.) First, if you have purchased an iPod, which is a likely case given that you are reading a book about iPods, a copy of iTunes is provided on the CD included with every iPod. Second, if you don't have an iPod or don't have the CD that came with it for some reason, you can download iTunes from the Internet.

note

In case you are wondering, about the only other successful application Apple has produced for Windows computers is the database program FileMaker Pro. This originally was developed by a subsidiary of Apple called Claris. Claris spun out from Apple and is now known as FileMaker, thus giving the company the same name as its most popular product. Apple has also produced a technology that is widely used on Windows PCs: QuickTime.

Downloading and Installing iTunes on a Windows PC

Even if you have a copy on the iPod CD, it can be better to download a copy of iTunes from the Internet to install it on your computer. That's because the application is periodically updated to add new features and bug fixes. When you download a copy from the Web, you get the latest and greatest version. When you install a copy from the CD, you get the latest and greatest version when the CD was produced, which might not be the current latest and greatest.

If you want to download and install a copy of iTunes, perform the following steps:

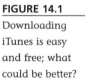

note

For information about installing iTunes from the CD included with iPods, refer to "Installing the iPod's Software on a Windows PC" on page **22**. If this is the option you chose, you can skip over the rest of this section and move ahead with launching the application, as I explain in "Launching and Performing the Initial Configuration of iTunes on a Windows PC," on page **196**.

1. Open your favorite web browser, such as Internet Explorer.

2. Move to http://www.apple.com/itunes.

3. Click the **Free Download** link. You will see the Download page.

4. Scroll down the page until you see the Download iTunes section (see Figure 14.1).

FIGURE 14.1

Downloading iTunes is easy and free; what could be better?

5. Click the **Windows 2000 or XP** radio button.

6. Uncheck the boxes for the Apple newsletters you don't want to receive (they are both checked by default). For example, the *New Music Tuesday* newsletter lets you know about music that has been added to the iTunes Music Store. If you want that information, leave its check box checked.

7. Enter your email address if you left either of the check boxes checked; if you unchecked both of them, you can leave this blank.

8. Click **Free Download iTunes**. In most cases, you will see the Security Warning dialog box. If you don't have your web browser configured to present this, you will move directly to the Save As dialog box, in which case you can skip the next two steps.

9. In the Security Warning dialog box, click **Run** to indicate that you want to download and run the iTunes Installer. You'll see yet another Security Warning dialog box.

10. Click **Run**. The InstallShield Wizard will open and start the installation process. After a moment or two (if you connect to the Internet with a dial-up connection, it might be quite a bit longer than a moment or two), you will see the iTunes Installer window (see Figure 14.2).

FIGURE 14.2

Working through the iTunes Installer is mostly a matter of reading and clicking Next.

11. Read the information in the Installer window and click **Next**.

12. If you have a lot of time and patience, read the license agreement; when you are done, click **Yes** if you agree or **No** if you don't. (If you don't agree, you can skip the rest of these steps and the rest of this part of the book because you won't be able to use iTunes.)

13. In the resulting Information window, you can read information about iTunes, such as what it can do and what you need to install it. Because you have this book, you don't really need to read this information, but it can't hurt to do so! When you are done reading, click **Next**. You'll see the Setup Type window (see Figure 14.3).

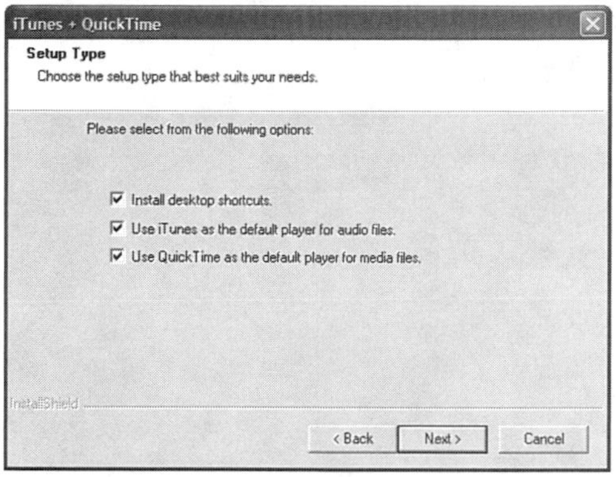

FIGURE 14.3

As you install iTunes, you have several options, such as whether you want iTunes to be the default player for audio files.

14. Check the following options to make them active or uncheck them to make them inactive:

- **Install desktop shortcuts**—This option places a shortcut to iTunes on your desktop. Unless you don't like desktop shortcuts for some reason, you should usually leave this option checked.

- **Use iTunes as the default player for audio files**—This option causes iTunes to be used to play most audio files you access on the Internet, your computer, CDs, and so on. If you prefer to use another application, such as Window Media Player, uncheck this check box. However, I recommend that you leave it checked for now. You can always change the default application to something else after you have become comfortable with iTunes (not that you'll want to!).

- **Use QuickTime as the default player for media files**—If you select this option, the QuickTime Player application will be used when you view video or other multimedia content. Just like the previous option, if you prefer to use a different application, uncheck this check box.

15. Click **Next**. You'll see the Choose Destination Location dialog box.

16. If you want to accept the default installation location (which is C:\Program Files\iTunes\), skip the rest of this step. If you want to change the installation location, click the **Browse** button and select the location you do want to use. When that location is selected, click **OK**.

17. Click **Next**. You'll see a window advertising something, such as the AirPort Express Base Station or the iPod. (Even with as much as I like these products, it doesn't seem quite right to stick in an ad that stops the installation process, but what can you do?)

18. Click **Next**. As the Installer starts to work, you will see the Setup Status window. This window provides information about the installation process (see Figure 14.4).

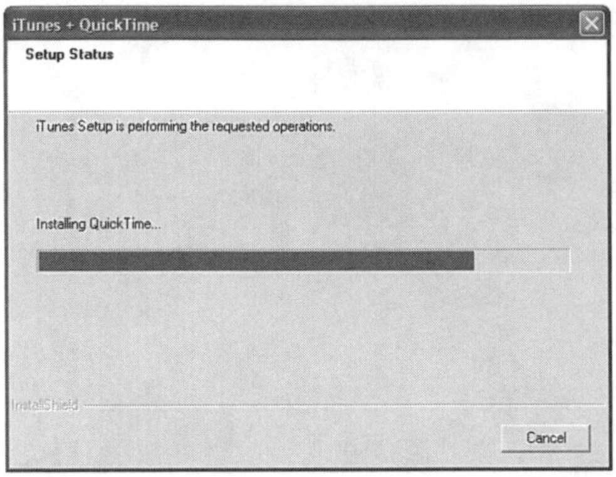

FIGURE 14.4

Here, you can see that the iTunes Installer is currently installing QuickTime.

When the process is complete, you will see the Installation Successful window.

19. Click **Finish**. iTunes will be ready for you to enjoy.

Launching and Performing the Initial Configuration of iTunes on a Windows PC

Whichever path you have taken to this point, I am sure all is well and you are ready to start cutting your teeth on iTunes.

To open the application and perform the initial configuration (which you need to do only the first time you open the program), follow these steps:

1. Open iTunes. You have several ways to do this. You can use the desktop icon to open it (assuming you chose to have an icon placed there). You can also select **Start**, **All Programs**, **iTunes**, **iTunes** to launch the application from the Start menu. Or, you can click the shortcut that was conveniently placed in the taskbar for you.

tip

If you find yourself opening iTunes every time you use your computer—and you probably will—consider adding it to the list of startup programs so it will open automatically when you turn on your computer.

After you have used one of these methods, the iTunes window will open. The first time you launch the application, the iTunes Setup Assistant will appear (see Figure 14.5). The helpful assistant will guide you through the few configuration decisions you need to make before you start working with the application. As with other assistants, you will move through the iTunes Setup Assistant by reading its information, making choices, and clicking the Next button.

FIGURE 14.5

The iTunes Setup Assistant appears the first time you open the application; get a good look at it because you won't be seeing it again.

2. Click **Next** to move to the Find Music Files screen. The purpose of this screen is to indicate whether you want iTunes to search your Music folder to find any existing music and then add that music to your iTunes Library. If you have music in this folder, I recommend that you let iTunes add it to your Library.

   If you want iTunes to search for music on your computer, click the **Yes** radio button (which isn't really necessary because it is the default selection) and then click **Next**.

   If you want to skip this search, click **No** and then click **Next**.

3. Use the Keep iTunes Music Folder Organized window to indicate whether you want iTunes to automatically rename and organize the music in your iTunes Music folder when you change that music's information (such as genre).

   Unless you have a very specific reason not to want this feature, click **Yes** and then click **Next**.

   If you do have some reason why you don't want iTunes to rename or move your music files, click **No** and then click **Next**.

4. Use the iTunes Music Store window to determine whether you want to move to the iTunes Music Store immediately after the Setup Assistant is done.

   Because you will learn about the iTunes Music Store in detail in Part III, "The iTunes Music Store," click the **No** radio button and click **Finish**.

   The Setup Assistant will run and you will see the iTunes window (see Figure 14.6). If you indicated that you want iTunes to find any music in your Music

> **note**
>
> After the first time you launch iTunes, you won't ever need to access the Setup Assistant again because you can configure iTunes using its Preferences command.

folder and add it to the iTunes Library, you will see the music the application found.

FIGURE 14.6
Okay, so the iTunes window doesn't look so exciting yet; soon, there will be lots of great music to listen to.

Now you are ready to learn about the major elements of the iTunes window. Unless you also have a Macintosh on which you also want to install iTunes, you can skip ahead to the section "Getting to Know iTunes" on page **201**. However, because my writing is so scintillating (don't you love that word?), I wouldn't blame you if you read the next section even if you don't have a Mac!

Installing and Configuring iTunes on a Macintosh

Because iTunes is developed by Apple, it is as integrated into the Macintosh operating system as much as any application can be. You have a number of ways to get iTunes installed on your Mac, including the following:

■ **Install Mac OS X**—When you install Mac OS X, iTunes is also installed. If you have installed OS X on your Mac, you don't need to do any installation, but you should make sure you have the current version

> **note**
>
> Not to push my other books (okay, to push my other books), but if you need help with Mac OS X in general, see *Special Edition Using Mac OS X, v10.4 Tiger* (catchy title, huh?).

installed (to do so, see the section "Keeping iTunes Up-to-date on a Macintosh" on page **347**).

■ **Buy a new Mac**—Okay, this might be the most expensive option, but, hey, you get a free Mac with your copy of iTunes!

■ **Install iTunes from the iPod software CD**—The software installation CD included with an iPod also enables you to install iTunes. For help with this option, refer to the section "Installing the iPod's Software on a Macintosh" on page **25**.

■ **Buy a copy of the Apple iLife suite**—In addition to iTunes, you'll get iMovie, iPhoto, iDVD, and GarageBand.

■ **Download and install iTunes from the Internet**—You can always download and install the latest version of iTunes from the Internet. The steps you need to do that are in this section.

If you have installed Mac OS X on your computer, you probably don't need to do any installation because it is likely that you already have iTunes installed on your machine.

To use one of the CD options, just insert the CD, launch the installer, and follow the onscreen instructions.

If you don't already have some version of iTunes installed on your Mac, you can download and install a copy from the Internet. This is often the best option because you are sure to get the most current version of the application.

The process for downloading and installing iTunes on a Mac is almost identical to what you use to download and install iTunes on a Windows computer. To save a few trees, I haven't included the steps to do this on a Mac. Just refer to the section "Downloading and Installing iTunes on a Windows PC" on page **193**. The most important difference is that you should choose to download the version for Mac OS X (as if you couldn't guess that!). After that, just follow the onscreen instructions.

You have a number of ways to open iTunes on a Mac, including the following:

■ Click the iTunes icon on the Dock.

■ Open the Applications folder and double-click the iTunes icon.

■ Insert an audio CD into your Mac; by default, iTunes is set to launch whenever you mount an audio CD.

The first time you open iTunes, you will need to work through a basic configuration of the application. Following are the steps you need to perform:

1. Launch **iTunes**. You will see yet another License Agreement screen. (I guess Apple was kidding with the others.)

2. Click **Agree**. You will see the iTunes Setup Assistant, which will guide you through the rest of the process (see Figure 14.7).

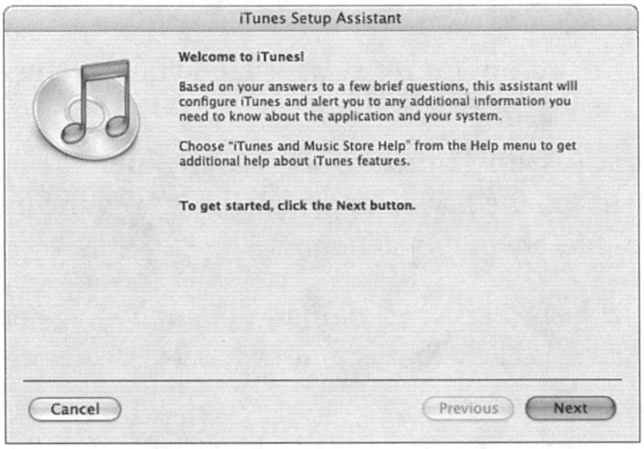

FIGURE 14.7

The iTunes Setup
Assistant lives
up to its name.

3. Click **Next**. You will see the Internet Audio Settings window. These settings control whether iTunes is the default application for audio content from the Internet and whether iTunes should automatically connect to the Internet when it needs to.

4. Click both **Yes** radio buttons and then click **Next**. You'll see the Find Music Files window.

5. If you want iTunes to search for music on your Mac and then add that music to the iTunes Library, click **Yes**. If you don't want this to happen, click **No**. Then click **Next** and you'll see the iTunes Music Store window.

6. Because we will explore the iTunes Music Store in detail later, click the **No** radio button and then click **Done**. The iTunes window will open (see Figure 14.8) and you will be ready to tour the application, as you will do in the next section.

FIGURE 14.8

There aren't any songs in the Library yet, so this iTunes window looks a bit boring; we'll soon fix that!

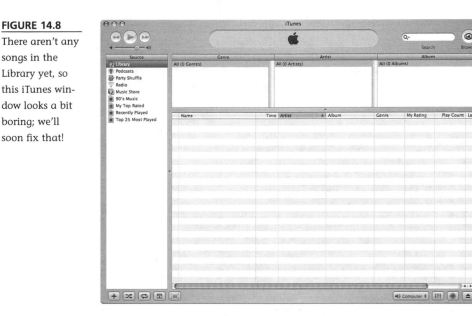

Getting to Know iTunes

The required but mundane work of installing iTunes on your computer is done. Now, let's take a quick tour so you get the overall feel of this excellent application. In the following chapters, you'll get down and dirty (well, because we are dealing with electrons here, there isn't really any dirt, but you know what I mean) with the details.

Seeing Through the iTunes Window

The iTunes window, like the windows on your house, consists of a number of panes (see Figure 14.9). Let's take a quick look at each of these.

On the far left of the iTunes window is the Source list. On this list, as you might suspect from its name, are the sources of music with which you can work. To work with a source, such as a CD or the iTunes Music Store, you select it by clicking it. When you select a source, its contents will appear in the Content pane and Browser (if you have the Browser open for a selected source). In Figure 14.9, I have selected the Library as the source; its contents are shown in the Browser at the top of the window, while the list of individual songs that make up the Library is at the bottom of the window.

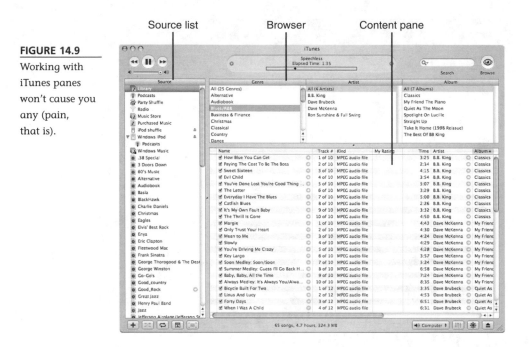

FIGURE 14.9

Working with
iTunes panes
won't cause you
any (pain,
that is).

You will use many types of sources, including the
Library, Podcasts, the Radio, the iTunes Music Store,
audio CDs, an iPod, playlists, and more. As we work
though the rest of this part of the book, you will get
experience with all these kinds of sources.

The Browser presents the contents of the selected
source at a summary level, by genre, artist, and
album. You can view the contents of the selected
source by clicking it in the appropriate column. For
example, in Figure 14.9, I have selected the
Blues/R&B genre. The Artist column then shows all
the artists whose music I have in the selected genre.
The Album column shows all the albums for the
selected artists.

The Browser can be shown or hidden. For example,
take a look at Figure 14.10, which shows the iTunes
window with the Browser hidden.

> **note**
>
> Different sources have
> different icons in the
> Source list. For example, the
> Library has a yellow box containing
> a music note, whereas playlists
> have a blue box with a musical
> note and smart playlists have a
> purple box with a gear.

FIGURE 14.10

Where, oh where, has my Browser gone? Where, oh where, can it be?

In the lower part of the iTunes window (or filling it if the Browser is hidden) is the Content pane. This area lists each song in the selected source. For each song, you will see a variety of information, such as Song Name, Track #, Time, Artist, and so on. You can choose the information you see on this list. The order in which songs are listed in the Content pane is the order in which they will play when you play the selected source.

Referring to Figure 14.9, you can see that a number of songs by B.B. King are among those listed in the Content pane.

tip

We will get to working with the Browser later, but for now know that you can open and close it by clicking the Browse button or by selecting Edit, Show Browser or Edit, Hide Browser.

Controlling Your Music

Surrounding those panes are the controls you use to work with and get information about your music. At the top of the window, from left to right, you will see the following areas (see Figure 14.11):

- **Playback controls**—Here, you can see the familiar Play/Stop, Fast Forward, and Rewind buttons along with the Volume Control slider. These work as you probably expect them to.

FIGURE 14.11

At the top of the iTunes window are a number of controls you can use to play and manage your music.

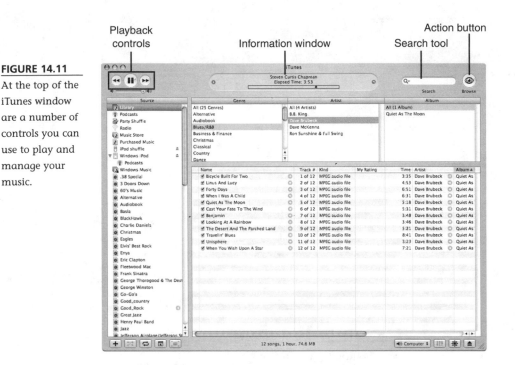

- **Information window**—In the center of the top part of the iTunes window is the Information window. In this area, you will see a variety of information about what you are doing at any point in time. For example, when you are playing music, you will see information about the music currently being played. When you import music, you will see information about the import process. When you download music from the iTunes Music Store, you'll see information about the download process.
- **Search tool**—You use the Search tool to search for songs.
- **Action button**—The Action button changes depending on the context you are in. For example, if you have selected the Library, it becomes the Browse button, which you use to open or close the Browser. If you select a playlist, it becomes the Burn button, which enables you to burn a CD or DVD.

When you move to the bottom of the iTunes window, you will see the following (see Figure 14.12):

FIGURE 14.12

Not to be out-
done by the top,
the bottom of
the iTunes win-
dow is chock full
of good stuff,
too.

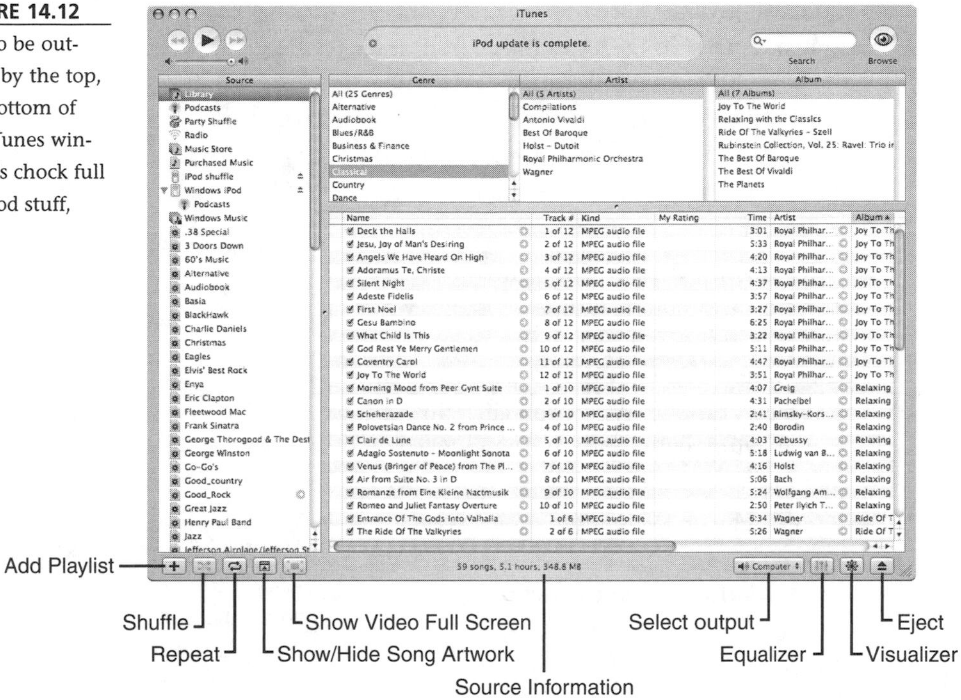

- **Add Playlist button**—You can use this button to create your own playlists.
- **Shuffle and Repeat buttons**—You use the Shuffle button to shuffle the music in the selected source so it doesn't play in the listed order. You can use the Repeat button to cause songs to repeat within a selected source.
- **Show/Hide Song Artwork button**—Songscan have album art associated with them. When you click this button, you will see the Art Album box at the bottom of the Source pane. In it will appear any art associated with the currently selected song.
- **Show Video Full Screen button**—Yes, you can also view certain types of video content, namely QuickTime movies, within iTunes. When you click this button, iTunes will disappear and the movie will fill the screen while it plays. When it is done, iTunes will appear again.
- **Source information**—This information shows number of songs, total playing time, and disk space of the selected source. This becomes useful at certain times, such as when you are burning a CD or building a playlist.
- **Select Output menu**—This menu appears when an AirPort Express Base Station is available; you can choose to output iTunes music to your computer speakers or to a base station. When you choose a base station, you can

connect powered speakers to it or connect to a stereo to hear your iTunes music in that location. You'll learn about this cool feature later in this book.

- **Equalizer button**—This button opens the Equalizer window, which provides a graphic equalizer.

- **Visualizer button**—Okay, this was one of the most promoted features of iTunes when it was initially released (which seems like a long time ago), but I didn't get it then, and I still don't today. When you click this, the iTunes window fills with a graphic display reminiscent of the 1960s (see Figure 14.13).

- **Eject button**—When you have selected an ejectable source, such as an audio CD, you can click this button to eject it.

note

Because I don't see much value (not even entertainment value) in the Visualizer, I won't be mentioning it again in this book. You can play with it by using the Visualizer menu if you want to. Oh, by the way, the images you see in the Visualizer are not related to any music that might be playing anyway. Want proof? Fire up the Visualizer with no music playing; it looks just like it does when music is playing.

FIGURE 14.13

Just because I don't think the Visualizer is groovy, there is no reason you can't dig it.

THE ABSOLUTE MINIMUM

You are well on your way to total iTunes nirvana. If you have read this chapter, you should be hip to the following iTunes jazz:

- You have a number of ways to install iTunes on your computer—whether it's a Mac or a Windows PC. The best way is to download and install it from the Internet.

- No matter how you installed iTunes, make sure you keep it up-to-date (we'll get to that in Chapter 22, "Maintaining iTunes and Solving Problems").

- When you first open iTunes, you work through several configuration settings using the iTunes Setup Assistant. However, you can change these settings at any time using the iTunes Preferences dialog box, which you will be working with throughout the rest of this part of the book.

- The iTunes window is an elegant mix of functionality and good interface design. As you learn more about the application, you will likely be impressed. The primary components of the iTunes window are its controls, the Information area, the Source list, the Browser, and the Content pane.

- Although iTunes is one of my favorite applications and I use it constantly, it sports one of the silliest features that was ever part of an application. What is it?

15

LISTENING TO AUDIO CDS AND INTERNET AUDIO WITH ITUNES

The basic reason to have and use iTunes is to listen to music and other audio, such as podcasts or Internet radio streams. Which, not coincidentally, is the basic point of this chapter. Here, you will learn how to use iTunes to listen to a couple of sources: audio CDs and Internet radio. The good news is that once you know how to use iTunes to listen to these two sources, you know how to listen to other sources you will use as well, such as songs in your playlists, on an iPod, and from shared music.

After you become an iTunes-playing guru, we'll take a look at some of the ways you can configure iTunes to suit your playing preferences.

Listening to an Audio CD

What iTunes has in common with its much less-sophisticated cousins the boombox and the standard CD player is the capability to play audio CDs. Although the basic function is the same, iTunes has several tricks in its bag to make listening even better. So, grab a CD and give it a try:

1. Open **iTunes**.

2. Insert an audio CD into your computer. In a moment, the CD will be mounted on your computer and will appear and be selected in the Source list (see Figure 15.1).

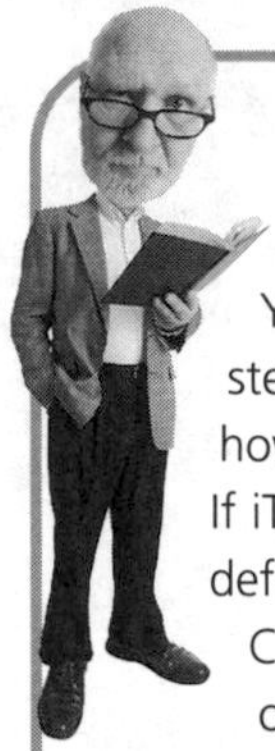

A CD is the
selected source

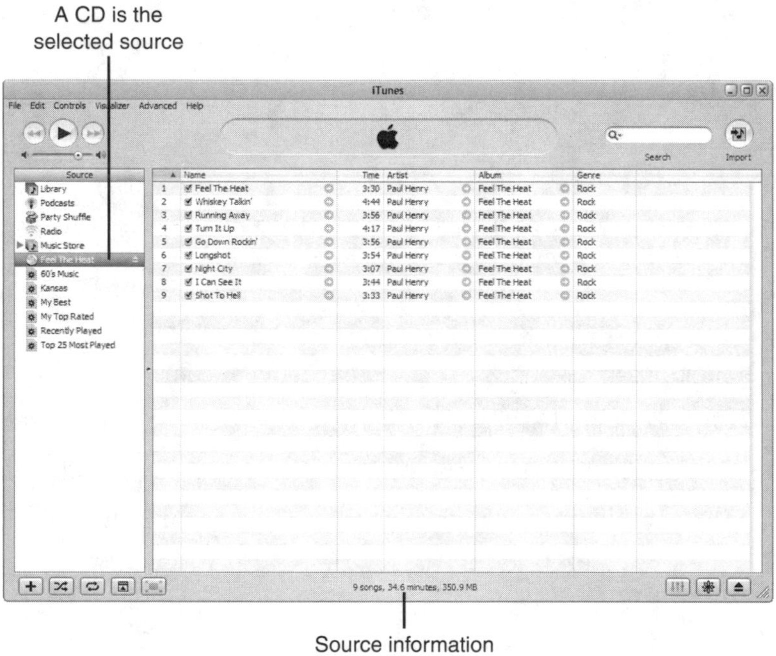

FIGURE 15.1

When a CD appears on the Source list, it awaits your listening pleasure.

Source information

By default, iTunes will automatically connect to the Internet and attempt to identify the CD you have inserted. If it finds it, it will display the CD's information, including the CD name, track names, times, artist, and genre, in the Content pane (in Figure 15.1, you can see the CD's information has been found). This is really cool because iTunes does most of the labeling work for you; this comes in handy when you want to search or browse for music to create playlists or just to listen to specific tracks.

If iTunes finds information for a CD, it remembers that information and displays it each time you insert the CD.

At the bottom of the iTunes window is the Source Information display. This will show you the total number of songs on the CD, how long it plays, and the total disc space used.

If the CD's information isn't located, you can add it yourself (see Chapter 17, "Labeling, Categorizing, and Configuring Your Music").

note

If you don't want iTunes to check for a CD's information automatically, you can disable this feature, as you will learn a little later in this chapter.

3. To play the CD, do any of the following: click the **Play** button in the upper-left corner of the window (when a CD is playing, this becomes the Pause button); select **Controls**, **Play**; or press the **spacebar**.

The CD will begin to play. As a song plays, a speaker icon appears next to it in the Content pane to indicate it is the current song, and information about that song appears in the Information window (see Figure 15.2).

Song currently playing   Information window

FIGURE 15.2

You can tell this CD is playing because the Play button has become the Pause button and the speaker icon shown next to the song currently being played.

	Name	Time	Artist	Album	Genre
1	Feel The Heat	3:30	Paul Henry	Feel The Heat	Rock
2	Whiskey Talkin'	4:44	Paul Henry	Feel The Heat	Rock
3	Running Away	3:56	Paul Henry	Feel The Heat	Rock
4	Turn It Up	4:17	Paul Henry	Feel The Heat	Rock
5	Go Down Rockin'	3:56	Paul Henry	Feel The Heat	Rock
6	Longshot	3:54	Paul Henry	Feel The Heat	Rock
7	Night City	3:07	Paul Henry	Feel The Heat	Rock
8	I Can See It	3:44	Paul Henry	Feel The Heat	Rock
9	Shot To Hell	3:33	Paul Henry	Feel The Heat	Rock

9 songs, 34.6 minutes, 350.9 MB

4. Control the volume of the sound by dragging the **Volume** slider to the left to turn it down or to the right to turn it up. You can also control the volume by selecting **Controls**, **Volume Up** or **Controls**, **Volume Down**. For yet another option, press the **Ctrl+Up arrow** and **Ctrl+Down arrow** keys on Windows PCs or the ⌘**+Up arrow** and ⌘**+Down arrow** keys on Macs to set the volume from the keyboard.

To mute the sound, select **Controls**, **Mute**. On Windows PCs you can press **Ctrl+Alt+Down arrow**, whereas on Macs you can press **Option+⌘+Down arrow** to do the same thing.

5. To pause a song, click the **Pause** button; select **Controls**, **Pause**; or press the **space-bar**.

That's it. You now know everything you need to listen to an audio CD. However, there are lots more ways to control the tunes, some of which are in the following list:

note

Using the Volume slider within iTunes only changes the volume of iTunes relative to your system's volume. If you can't make the music loud or quiet enough, check your system volume level.

- Double-click any song to play it. When you do that, the speaker icon will jump to the song which you double-clicked and it will play.

- When a song is playing and you click and hold the Rewind or Fast Forward button, the song will rewind or fast-forward until you release the button.

- If a song is not playing or a song is playing but you single-click (but don't hold the button down) the Rewind or Fast Forward button, the previous or next song, respectively, will be selected. You can also select Controls, Next Song or Controls, Previous Song to move to the next or the previous song. And for yet another method to do the same thing, you can press the Ctrl+Right arrow and Ctrl+Left arrow keys on a Windows PC or the ⌘-Right arrow and ⌘-Left arrow keys on a Mac to move to the next or previous song.

- You can set a default action for iTunes to perform each time you insert a CD into your computer. You do this with the iTunes Preferences dialog box, which you will be using throughout this part of the book. Select **Edit**, **Preferences** (Windows) or **iTunes**, **Preferences** (Mac). The Preferences dialog box will appear. The Preferences dialog box has several panes that you access by clicking the related tab (Windows) or icon (Mac). Click the **General** tab (Windows) or **General** icon (Mac). Use the **On CD Insert** drop-down list to choose the default action iTunes should perform when it recognizes an audio CD. Show Songs just displays the list of tracks on the

CD. Begin Playing starts playing the CD as soon as it is mounted on your computer (this does the same thing as clicking the Play button). Import Songs adds the selected songs on the CD to your Library. Import Songs and Eject does the same thing as Import Songs, but it ejects the CD when all its tracks have been added to your Library. (You'll see the value of the last two settings in the next chapter.)

■ To remove a CD from your computer, select it in the Source list and select **Controls**, **Eject Disc**; press **Ctrl+E** (Windows) or ⌘**+E** (Macintosh); or click the **Eject** button located in the lower-right corner of the iTunes window.

Viewing Information While Listening to Tunes

You can view different information in the Information window, such as the name, artist, and album of the currently playing song. When you first view this window, it contains a timeline bar that represents the total length of the song being played (see Figure 15.3). A black diamond (the Playhead) indicates the relative position of the music you are hearing at any point in time compared to the total length of the song.

note

When you "freeze" information in the Information window, it remains frozen until the next track is played, at which point it starts rotating again.

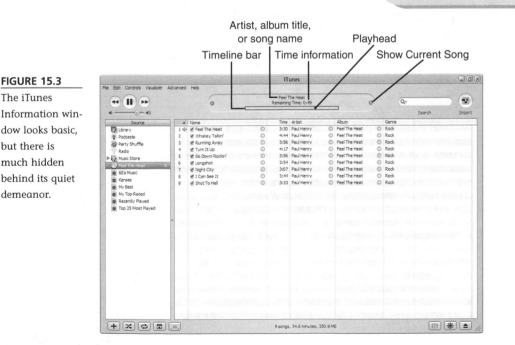

Artist, album title, or song name
Timeline bar | Time information
Playhead
Show Current Song

FIGURE 15.3
The iTunes Information window looks basic, but there is much hidden behind its quiet demeanor.

At the top of the Information window is a line of text. What appears here changes over time; it automatically rotates between the artist's name, album name, and name of the song currently playing. You can freeze this display on a specific attribute, such as song name, by clicking the text. Each time you click, the information will change from album to artist to song name. Whichever one you last clicked will remain showing in the window.

Underneath the album, artist, and song name line is time information. This can display the elapsed time (the amount of time a song has been playing), remaining time (the amount of time a song has left), or total time (the song's total length). Unlike the name information, this display does not rotate among these values. You can set the value being displayed by clicking the text; each time you click, a different time value will be shown until you have rotated among all three values.

If you click the Show Current Song button, the song currently playing will be selected; this is indicated by it becoming highlighted in blue. This can be handy when you are working with other music while listening to a song because you can click this button to quickly return to the song that is playing.

Finally, if you click the Change Display button, the display will become a graphical representation of the volume levels at various frequency groups (see Figure 15.4). You can return to the title information by clicking the button again.

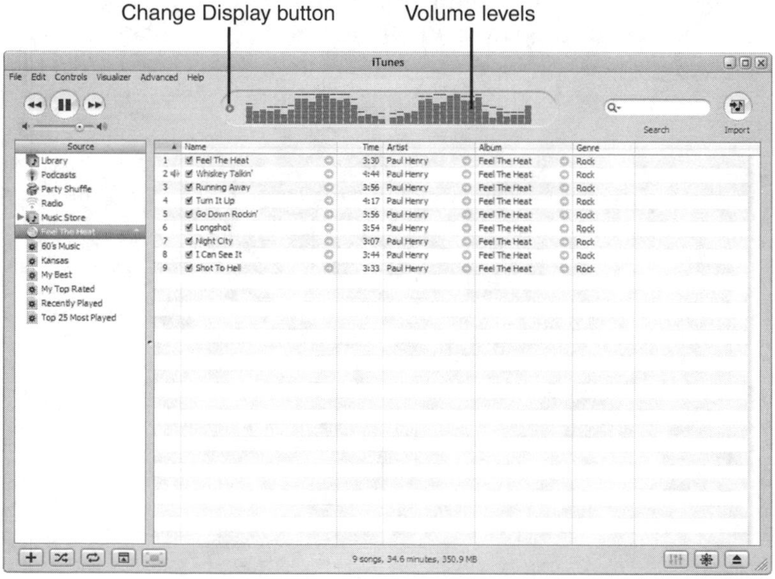

Change Display button   Volume levels

FIGURE 15.4

Why would you want to use the volume level display in the Information window? No real reason, but it does look kind of cool.

Controlling the Tunes

Playing an audio CD from start to finish and controlling the volume are useful and required tasks, but with iTunes you can take control of your music so that you hear only what you want to hear, in the order in which you want to hear it. In the following sections, you'll see how iTunes lets you take control of your tunes. For example, in the next section, you'll learn how to choose the songs you want to hear.

> **note**
>
> The neat thing about the Information window is that it changes based on the context of what you are doing. You have seen how it works when you listen to music. When you add music to your Library, the information and tools in the window become those you use for the import process.

Choosing the Songs You Hear

Let's face it, you probably don't like every song on a CD no matter how much you like the CD on the whole. With iTunes, you can choose the songs that play when you play the CD. You can cause a song to be skipped by unchecking its check box (see Figure 15.5). When the CD plays, it will skip over every song whose check box is unchecked.

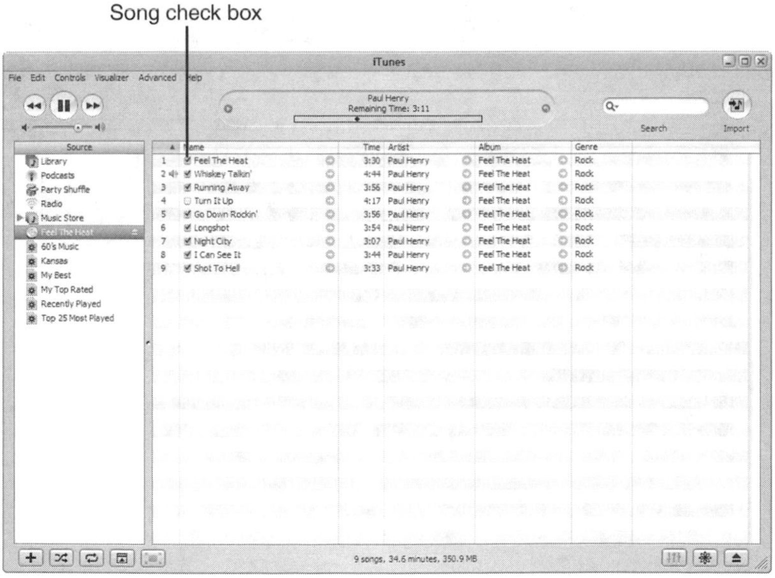

Song check box

FIGURE 15.5

Here, the song "Turn It Up" will be skipped because its Select check box is unchecked (of course, this is only an example; all the songs on this CD are excellent).

To have iTunes include and thus play the song again the next time you play the CD, simply check its check box again.

Choosing the Order in Which Songs Play

iTunes determines the order in which songs play by the order in which they are shown in the Content pane, starting from the top of the pane and moving toward the bottom. By default, songs are listed and therefore play in the order they appear on the CD, from track 1 to the last track on the disc. However, you can make songs on a CD play in any order you choose. You have a couple ways to do this.

tip

Along with a CD's information, iTunes remembers the settings you make for a CD and reuses them each time you insert and play the CD. This includes skipping songs, changing the order in which they play, and so on. Cool!

You can change the order in which songs are listed in the Content pane (and thus the order in which they play) by dragging the songs up or down in the pane (see Figure 15.6). When you change the order of the songs in the pane, you change the order in which they will play.

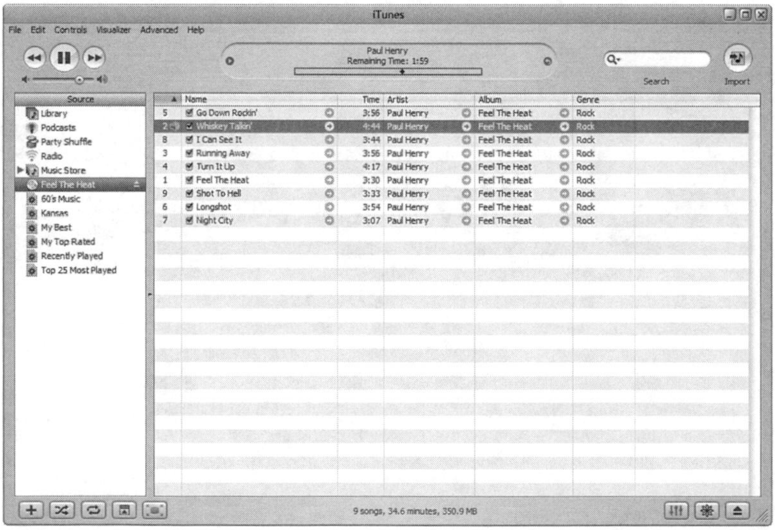

FIGURE 15.6
Order! Order! Compare the order of the songs in this figure with the previous one; listening to the CD now will be an entirely different experience.

You can also change the order of tracks by sorting the Content pane by the various attributes shown, such as Track Number, Song Name, Time, Artist, and so on. You can do this by clicking the column heading of the attribute by which you want to sort the list. When you do so, the tracks will be sorted by that column (see Figure 15.7). To change the direction of the sort (from ascending to descending or from descending to ascending), click the **Sort Order** triangle; the sort direction will be reversed and the songs will be reordered accordingly. Just like when you manually move songs around, they will play in the order in which they are listed in the pane.

The Content pane is sorted by this column

Sort Order triangle

FIGURE 15.7

Now the order of the songs is based on their length; in this case, the longest song on the CD will play first, then the next longest second, and so on.

The column by which the pane is sorted is indicated by the column heading being highlighted in blue—this defaults to the first column, which is the Track Number (which, by the way, is the only unnamed column because it applies only to audio CDs and to no other sources). (When a CD is the source, the Track Number column is always the first or leftmost column in the Content pane.) When you select a different column, its heading becomes blue to show that it is the current sort column.

You can also tell which column is the current sort column by the Sort Order triangle. It only appears in the sort column. When the triangle is pointing down, the sort is descending. When the triangle is pointing up, the sort is ascending.

tip

To return a CD to the default order, click the first column and then make the Sort Order triangle point down. This returns the CD to play by track number.

Getting Random

For a little variety, you can have iTunes play songs in a random order. This feature is called Shuffle. To use this feature, click the **Shuffle** button located at the bottom of the window (second one from the left) or select **Controls**, **Shuffle**. The songs will be reordered in the Content pane and will play in the order in which they are listed (hopefully in a random fashion). The Shuffle button will be highlighted in blue to indicate that it is active.

To return the CD to the order you have set for it (or its original order if you haven't changed it), click the **Shuffle** button again or select **Controls**, **Shuffle**.

There is a preference setting that determines whether songs are shuffled by song or album, which you will learn about later. (Because all the songs on a CD are from the same album, this setting has no impact when you shuffle a CD's songs. It does become important when shuffling your Library or a playlist.)

Repeating Tracks

Sometimes, you just can't get enough of the music to which you are listing. In that case, you can set iTunes to repeat an entire CD once or to repeat only a single song. To repeat your tunes, check out these pointers:

- To have iTunes repeat an entire CD, select **Controls**, **Repeat All** or click the **Repeat** button located at the bottom of the window (third one from the left). The Repeat button will become highlighted to show you that it is active, and the CD will repeat when you play it.

- To repeat only the selected song, select **Controls**, **Repeat One** or click the **Repeat** button a second time. A "1" will appear on the Repeat button to indicate that only the current song will be repeated.

- To turn off the repeat function, select **Controls**, **Repeat Off** or click the **Repeat** button until it is no longer highlighted in blue.

note If you have manually reordered a CD by dragging songs up and down in the Content pane, that order is remembered and used when you sort the CD by the first column (Track Number). To put songs back in their original order, drag them so that track 1 is at the top, track 2 is next, and so on.

note If you used the menu to shuffle a disc, you will notice that the Shuffle command on the menu has a check mark next to it. This check mark shows you that the command is currently active. When it isn't, the check mark will disappear. This is true of other settings as well, such as Repeat.

Controlling iTunes from the Desktop

Using the controls you have seen so far is fine, but you might not want to have the iTunes window foremost all the time. You must be able to see iTunes to control it, right? Wrong!

Controlling iTunes from the Windows System Tray

When iTunes is running on a Windows machine, an iTunes icon is displayed in the System Tray. Right-click this icon and you will see an iTunes menu (see Figure 15.8). At the top

> **tip**
>
> Using Repeat, you might hear a song you don't like all that much more than once. Remember to uncheck the Select check box for any songs you don't want to hear. They will be skipped no matter how you play the CD.

of the menu is the Show iTunes command; select it to move into the iTunes window. Just under this command is the Now Playing section that provides information about the music that is currently playing (if no music is playing or selected, you won't see this section in the menu). You can use the commands on this menu just as you can from within iTunes itself. For example, you can skip to the next song by selecting Next Song. After you select a command, you can move off the menu and it will disappear. This is a handy way to control iTunes without having to make its window active or even being able to see it.

FIGURE 15.8
You can control iTunes even if you can't see it.

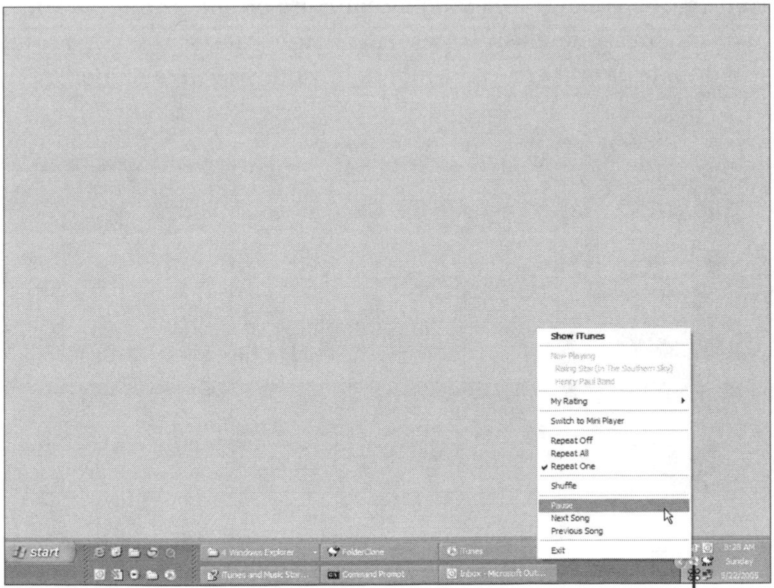

iTunes icon in the System Tray

If you don't want the iTunes icon to appear in the System Tray for some reason, you can remove it. Open the iTunes Preferences dialog box (**Ctrl+,**), click the **Advanced** tab, uncheck the **Show iTunes icon in system tray** check box, and click **OK**. The icon will no longer appear in your System Tray.

Controlling iTunes from the Mac's Dock

The iTunes icon on the Mac OS X enables you to control iTunes at any time even when the iTunes window is in the background, when its window is minimized, or when the application is hidden. When you Ctrl-click the iTunes Dock icon (or right-click if you have a two-button mouse), the iTunes menu will appear (see Figure 15.9). At the top of this menu is the iTunes command that will move you into the iTunes window. Just under that is the Now Playing section that provides information about the song currently playing (if no music is selected or playing, you won't see this section). You can control iTunes by selecting a command on the iTunes Dock menu. For example, you can pause the music by selecting Pause. After you select a command, the menu will disappear and you can get back to what you were doing.

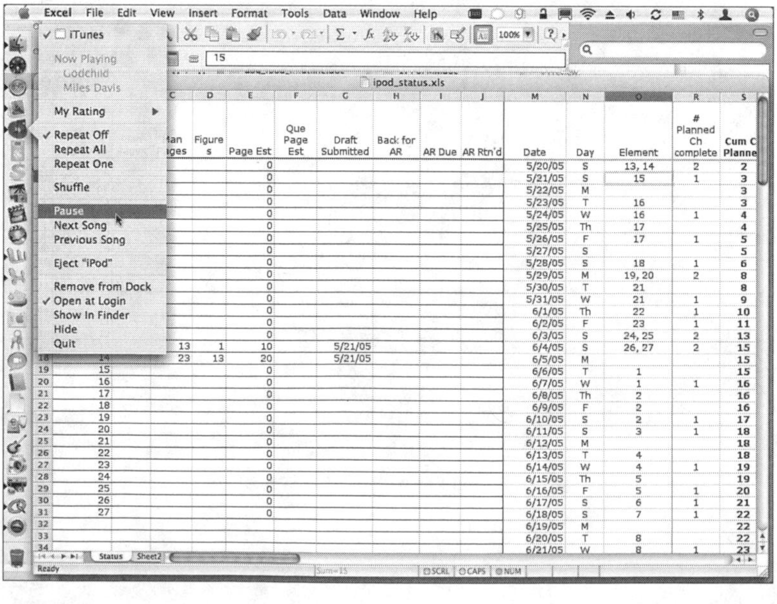

tip

To keep iTunes out of the way, open it and select a source, such as an audio CD. Then configure and play the source. Minimize (Windows) or hide (Mac) the iTunes window so it no longer appears on your desktop. Then, you can use the iTunes System Tray icon menu (Windows) or iTunes Dock icon menu (Mac) to control it—for example, to pause your tunes when you receive a phone call.

FIGURE 15.9

On the Mac, you use its Dock menu to control iTunes even when you can't see the application, such as when you are working with Excel.

Controlling iTunes on a Mac with the iTunes Widget

Version 10.4 of the Mac OS introduced the cool Dashboard function that provides quick access to miniapplications called *widgets*. One of the default widgets enables you to control iTunes.

First, configure the iTunes widget to appear when you use the Dashboard by performing the following steps:

1. Press your **Dashboard** key on the keyboard; by default on desktop Macs, this is the F12 key. Mobile Macs use other keys depending on the model you are using. The Dashboard will appear. If the iTunes widget appears, you can skip the rest of these steps.

2. Click the + located in the lower-left corner of the desktop. The Dashboard bar will appear.

3. Drag the iTunes widget from the bar onto the location on your desktop where you want it to be when you open the Dashboard.

4. Close the Dashboard by pressing its key.

When you want to use the iTunes widget, open the Dashboard by pressing its key. Your widgets will appear, including the iTunes widget (see Figure 15.10). Some of the controls look slightly different than they do within iTunes, but they work in the same way. Use the controls, such as rotating the Volume wheel to change volume, and then hide the Dashboard again by pressing its key or clicking someplace else.

FIGURE 15.10

The iTunes widget is another way to control iTunes when you aren't working with the application directly.

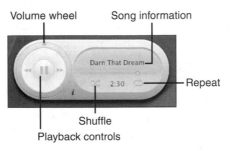

Volume wheel   Song information

Darn That Dream

2:30 — Repeat

Shuffle

Playback controls

One control that isn't so obvious is the ability to select a music source from within the iTunes widget. Open the widget and wait for a moment or two (just how long is a moment, anyway?). An *i* will appear at the bottom of the widget near its center. Click this button and you will see a Source pop-up menu. Choose a source (such as your Library or a playlist) on this menu and click **Done**. You can play the source by clicking the widget's Play button and control the music with the other widget controls.

Listening to Internet Radio

iTunes supports Internet "radio" stations; you can choose one of the available stations and listen to its content similarly to how you listen to a radio station over the air. (The stations are actually websites that offer streaming audio files in various formats, but they are analogous to radio, so using that as a model is a good way to think about them.) iTunes offers a number of genres from which you can choose, such as pop, classic rock, jazz, and so on. Listening to one of these stations is much like listening to a CD (or any other source for that matter).

Playing Your iTunes Radio

To tune in iTunes radio, perform the following steps:

1. Open iTunes and select the **Radio** source by clicking it. iTunes will retrieve a list of all the available stations and the Content pane will contain the list of available genres. The column headings will be updated to be appropriate to the content. For example, you will see Stream, Bit Rate, and Comment.

2. Click the expansion triangle for the genre in which you are interested (see Figure 15.11). iTunes will connect to the Internet to update the list of channels for the genre you selected, and the genre will expand. You will see the various channels it contains. Look at the stream name, bit rate, and comment for the channels to decide which you want to try. Usually, the Comment column will provide a description of the kind of music the stream contains.

note

This is likely obvious to you from the title of this section, but your computer must be able to connect to the Internet to be able to listen to Internet radio.

Expansion triangle

Radio source

FIGURE 15.11

FIGURE 15.11

Many of these
radio stations
(called streams)
don't include
commercials.

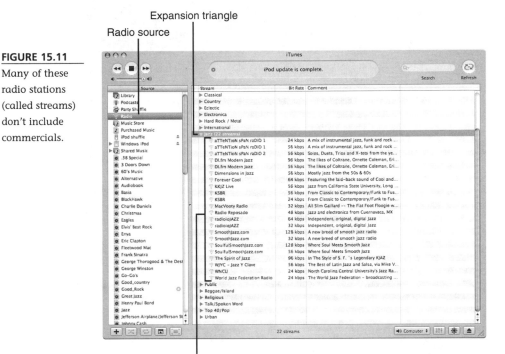

Expanded genre

3. To play a channel, select it and click **Play** or
double-click the stream you want to hear. The
channel will begin to play; this will be
instantaneous if you have a fast connection
to the Web, or there will be a slight delay if
you use a dial-up connection. Just like
when you play a song on a CD, the speaker
icon will appear next to the channel to
which you are listening.

Also just like when you listen to a CD,
information about the channel will appear
in the Information window (see Figure
15.12). This includes the stream name, the
song currently playing, and the website
with which the channel is associated.

note

When you view the
Content pane with Radio
source, Stream provides the names
of the available channels. Bit Rate
is a measure of the quality of a
channel. The higher the bit rate,
the better the quality, but the
higher bandwidth connection you
need to play it successfully. The
Comment column contains a
description of each channel.

FIGURE 15.12
FIGURE 15.12
Smooth Jazz is
an appropriate
name for this
stream.

You can use the Volume slider to change the volume
level and the Stop button to stop playback. The
Rewind and Fast Forward buttons work a little differently from what you might expect. Rather than
moving you in the selected stream, they instead
take you to the previous or next stream, which
makes sense when you think about each stream as
being like a track on a CD.

Refreshing Your Radio

When you select the Radio source, the Action button becomes the Refresh button. When you click
this, all the genres are refreshed with the latest
content. If you leave the Radio source selected for
a long time, you might want to click the Refresh
button once in a while to see whether new channels become available. (Each time you select the
Radio source, it is refreshed, so you don't need to
click the Refresh button if you have recently
selected the Radio source.)

> **note**
>
> If you have a dial-up
> Internet connection, you
> will likely have the best results if
> you choose a channel with a bit
> rate of 56Kbps or less. If you have
> a broadband connection, you
> should select the highest bit rate
> version of the available channels
> (some channels are offered at mul-
> tiple bit-rate levels).

Configuring iTunes for a Slow Internet Connection

If you use a slow Internet connection, such as a dial-up account, traffic on the Internet can cause the stream of music to slow or even stop, resulting in pauses in the music, even if you choose a lower bit-rate channel, such as 32Kbps. If this is a problem for you, perform the following steps:

1. Select **Edit**, **Preferences** (Windows) or **iTunes**, **Preferences** (Mac). The Preferences dialog box will appear.

2. Click the **Advanced** tab (Windows) or the **Advanced** icon (Mac). The Advanced pane will appear.

3. On the Streaming Buffer Size drop-down list, select **Large**. This increases the amount of buffer space used to store a stream before it actually starts to play.

4. Click **OK**. The dialog box will close.

Hopefully, this will eliminate any pauses in the streams to which you like to listen. If not, choose a different stream or one with a lower bit rate.

Playing Around with Internet Audio

You can do a couple of other things with Internet audio using iTunes.

If you want iTunes to be used to play Internet audio by default, open the **Preferences** dialog box (**Ctrl+,** on Windows computers or ⌘**-+,** on Macs). Open the **General** pane. Then check the **Use iTunes as the default player for audio files** check box (Windows) or click the **Set** button (Mac). When your browser hits an audio file that iTunes supports, iTunes should play it.

tip

The name of the song currently playing is especially useful when you hear a song you like that you might want to add to your collection. Make a note of the song's name and artist. Then, you can look for CDs containing that song or, even better, buy it from the iTunes Music Store.

note

Don't confuse Internet radio with podcasts. Internet radio is delivered as a stream that is continuously downloaded from the Internet while it plays. Podcasts are downloaded to your computer and stored there; you don't have to be connected to the Internet to listen to a podcast, which is why you can use podcasts with an iPod. We'll get into podcasts in the next chapter.

You can also play audio streams for which you have a URL within iTunes. To do this, use the following steps:

1. Find the URL pointing to the stream to which you want to listen. Hopefully, you can copy the URL from the Address bar of the web browser because that is a lot easier than trying to remember the URL or writing it down and then typing it in.

2. Select **Advanced**, **Open Stream**. The Open Stream dialog box will appear.

3. Paste or type the URL in the **URL** field (see Figure 15.13).

> **note**
>
> There are more than just tunes on the iTunes Radio. You can also hear talk, news, and other audio content.

FIGURE 15.13
Here, I've pasted in a URL to an MP3 file that contains a line from the movie *The Matrix*.

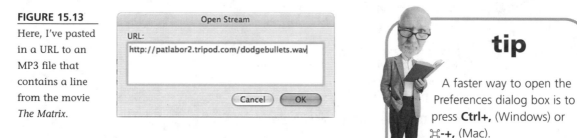

4. Click **OK**. The stream will play.

> **tip**
>
> A faster way to open the Preferences dialog box is to press **Ctrl+,** (Windows) or **⌘-+,** (Mac).

Customizing the iTunes Window

You can configure iTunes in various ways to suit your preferences. You can also change the size of the iTunes window in different ways.

Setting General iTunes Preferences

On the General pane of the Preferences dialog box are several settings you might want to use (see Figure 15.14):

- **Source Text**—Use this drop-down list to change the size of the font of the sources shown in the Source list. The options are Small (default) and Large.

> **tip**
>
> If you want to play the content to which the URL points more than once, download it to your computer and add it to the Library. You'll learn how to do this in the next chapter. You can also add a stream to a playlist by selecting it and selecting File, New Playlist from Selection.

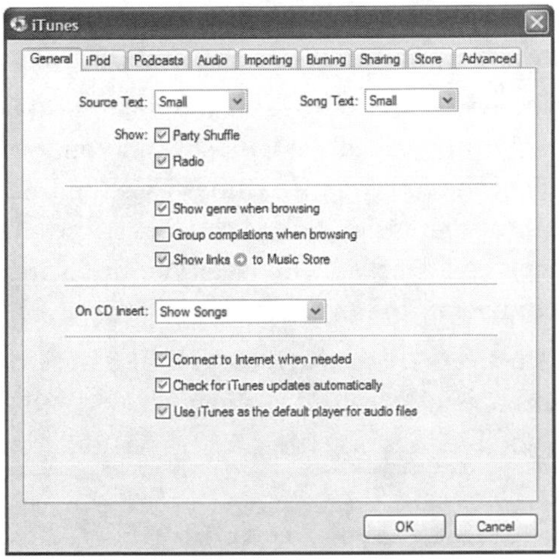

FIGURE 15.14

The General pane of the iTunes Preferences dialog box provides…, well, general preferences.

- ■ **Song Text**—This setting changes the size of the text used in the Content pane. Again, your options are Small and Large.

- ■ **Show Party Shuffle and Radio check boxes**—Earlier, you learned how to work with the Radio source. If you don't want that source to be shown, uncheck the Radio check box. The Radio source will be removed from the Source list and you won't be able to see it. Similar to this, you can uncheck the Party Shuffle check box to hide that playlist (you'll learn about this special playlist later in this part of the book) .

- ■ **Show genre when browsing**—If you read the previous chapter, you learned about the Browser. This check box controls whether the Genre column appears in the Browser (the check box is checked) or not (the check box is not checked). I like the Genre column, so I leave this checked, but if you don't, you can uncheck the check box to remove that column from the Browser.

- ■ **Group compilations when browsing**—Compilations are what iTunes calls CDs that contain music from various artists (you know, like that *Greatest TV Theme Songs from the 1970s* CD you like so much). If you check this check box, these compilations will be grouped as collections of music even though the artists might be different on one or more tracks. If you don't want your compilations grouped and prefer to have each track be grouped by artist, uncheck the check box.

- ■ **Show links to Music Store**—When this is checked, arrow buttons will appear next to songs, artists, and albums in the Content pane and in other locations. When you click one of these buttons, you'll move to related music in the iTunes Music Store. If you don't want these links displayed, uncheck the check box.

- **On CD Insert**—You learned about this earlier in this chapter and will come back to it in the next.

- **Connect to Internet when needed**—If you don't want iTunes to try to connect to the Internet automatically, such as when you are using it on a laptop, uncheck this check box. Because iTunes uses the Internet to get CD information, provide Internet radio, and access the iTunes Music Store, you should leave this check box checked whenever you are using iTunes on a computer that can connect to the Internet.

- **Check for iTunes updates automatically**—This check box controls whether iTunes checks for updates and lets you know when they are available. Because it is a good idea to use the current version, you should leave this check box checked.

- **Use iTunes as the default player for audio files (Windows) or Use iTunes for Internet music playback (Mac)**—You learned about this check box (Windows) or Set button (Mac) in the previous section.

Changing the Size of the iTunes Window

Like the windows of other applications, you can change the size of the iTunes window. For example, you might want to make the window smaller so that it doesn't consume so much desktop space (remember that you can minimize or hide the window and use its System Tray or Dock controls to control it).

Changing the Size of the iTunes Window on a Windows PC

As you use iTunes, keep in the mind the following tips for keeping the window out of your way:

- **Minimize/maximize the window**—Use the standard Minimize and Maximize controls in the iTunes window to hide it or make it full-screen size.

- **Make the window smaller**—If the iTunes window is in the resize mode (click the Maximize button so the window's size is maximized and then click it again), you can drag its resize handle to make the window smaller until it reaches the smallest possible size. Then, you can slide the window out of the way.

> **note**
>
> You have many ways to customize how contents are displayed in the Content pane. You will learn about these later in the book.

■ **Use the Mini Player**—For minimum window real estate use, put iTunes in the Mini Player mode by selecting Advanced, Switch to Mini Player; pressing Ctrl+M; or opening the iTunes System Tray menu and selecting Switch to Mini Player. The iTunes window will compress down so it is just large enough to display the playback and window controls (see Figure 15.15). To switch back to the normal iTunes window, use the window controls, press Ctrl+M, or open the iTunes System Tray menu and select Switch to iTunes Window.

> **tip**
>
> Within the iTunes window, you can change the relative width of the Source list pane versus the Content pane/ Browser or between the Browser and the Content pane by dragging the resize pane handle to the left or right or up or down. These handles are the dots that appear in the center of the bars between the panes of the window.

FIGURE 15.15
Smaller is sometimes better, when it comes to window size that is.

Changing the Size of the iTunes Window on a Mac

When you use iTunes on a Mac, you can change the window's size in the following ways:

■ **Hide the application**—Press ⌘-**H** to hide iTunes. Its window will be hidden from the desktop. You can control iTunes by using its Dock menu or widget. Click the **iTunes Dock** icon to show the window again.

■ **Toggle the size of the window**—If you click the Toggle Size button (the green "light") on the window's title bar, the iTunes window will collapse so that only the playback controls and the Information window are shown (see Figure 15.16). Click the button again to open the window to its full size.

FIGURE 15.16
On the Mac, you can quickly collapse the iTunes window to this handy size.

■ **Change the size of the window**—In either the full or collapsed state, you can change the size of the window by dragging its resize handle located in the bottom-right corner of the window.

Setting iTunes Audio Preferences

You can use iTunes Audio preferences to control how your music plays. For example, you can get rid of the gap of silence between songs or make songs play back at a consistent volume level. You can take advantage of these features by using the Audio pane of the iTunes Preferences dialog box. On this pane, you can configure the following preferences for your music (see Figure 15.17):

■ **Crossfade playback**—This effect causes one song to fade out and the next one to fade in smoothly, eliminating the gaps of silence between songs. To activate it, check the **Crossfade playback** check box and use the slider to see the amount of fade time. If you move the slider to the left, songs will fade out more quickly. If you set it to 0, there is no fading and as soon as one song ends, the next one starts. If you move the slider to the right, the fades will last longer. Click **OK** and the effect will take effect.

tip

Within the iTunes window, you can change the relative width of the Source list pane versus the Content pane/ Browser or between the Browser and the Content pane by dragging the resize pane handle to the left or right or up or down. These handles are the dots that appear in the center of the bars between the panes of the window.

tip

If you toggle the window to its reduced size and then make it even smaller with the resize handle, the window will contain only the playback controls.

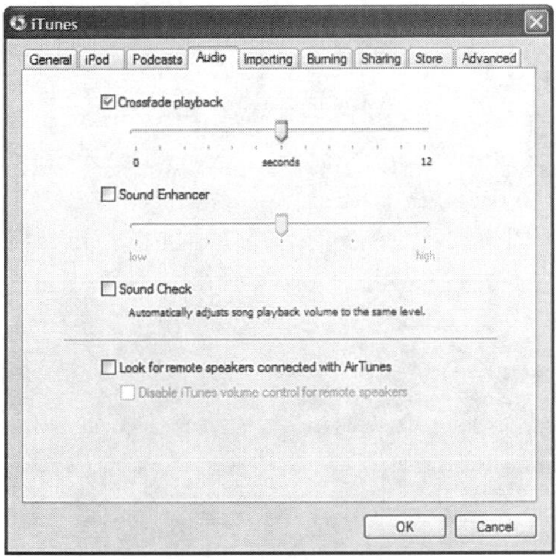

FIGURE 15.17

Control how your music sounds with the Audio preferences.

■ **Sound Enhancer**—This effect is iTunes' attempt to "add depth and enliven" the quality of your music. The actual result of this effect is a bit difficult to describe, so the best thing to do is try it for yourself. Check the **Sound Enhance** check box and use the slider to set the relative amount of enhancement. Click **OK** and then listen to some music. It if sounds better to you, increase the amount of the effect. If not, decrease it or turn it off.

■ **Sound Check**—This effect sets the relative volume level of all songs to be the same. It is useful if you have changed the relative volume level of songs (perhaps you cranked up your favorite classical tunes) and want to have all your music play at the same volume level. To implement this effect, check its check box and click **OK**. (You'll learn how to change the relative volume level of songs later in this part of the book.)

note

This Crossfade setting does not impact audio CDs. Because there is a physical gap between tracks on the CD, iTunes can't do anything about it. This setting applies to other sources, such as your Library and playlists. (So why cover it in the CD chapter you ask? Because this seemed like the place to cover the other effects, so I added this one here, too.)

note

The other controls on the Audio pane relate to broadcasting your iTunes music using an AirPort Express Base Station. You'll learn about this later, too.

THE ABSOLUTE MINIMUM

By learning how to use iTunes to play audio CDs and Internet radio, you've picked up a lot more knowledge than you might realize. That's because you use the same steps and controls to listen to other music sources, such as your Library, playlists, and so on. In the next couple of chapters, you'll learn about these other sources; once you do, you'll be able to use the techniques you picked up in this chapter to work with them.

For now, keep the following tidbits in mind:

- Many of the controls in the iTunes window work just like similar controls on a CD player.

- The iTunes Information window doesn't look like a lot, but you'll learn to really love it when you are building your Library in the next chapter.

- If a song's check box is checked, it will play. If it's not checked, the song won't play.

- You determine the songs you want to hear and the order in which you want to hear them for all your sources by the order in which they appear in the Content pane (except for the Radio source, which you have to take as it comes). Each time you insert a CD, iTunes remembers the settings you used last time and uses those settings again. Just wait until you get to playlists—you can take this concept to the extreme!

- You can repeat or randomize the music in any source, such as a CD or playlist.

- Don't forget about the iTunes System Tray (Windows) or Dock (Mac) menu. This is a great way to keep iTunes music going while not consuming any of your valuable desktop real estate. On the Mac, you can also use the iTunes widget to control iTunes without consuming lots of screen real estate.

- You can change the width of columns within the iTunes window, and you can also resize the iTunes window to make it the size you want. As you work through later chapters, you'll also learn how to customize the information you see inside the window as well.

- Listening to the Radio source provides access to lots of music available on the Internet.

- You can use iTunes Audio preferences to control the gap between songs, to equalize the relative volume of songs, and to enhance the sound you hear.

- As you view the screenshots throughout this book, you'll see examples of some of my favorite music. If you like it too, drop me an email (bradmacosx@mac.com) to let me know.

- Know the sources of all iTunes music.

- Find out where your iTunes music will be stored and change the location if it suits your fancy.

- Maximize your music's quality/file size ratio by choosing encoding options and quality levels when you import audio CDs.

- Build your iTunes Library by importing audio CDs into it.

- Browse and search your Library like a master librarian.

- Dump music you don't want cluttering up your digital shelves.

- Add podcasts to your Library so you can enjoy a mind-boggling array of content from the comfort of your computer or iPod.

16

BUILDING, BROWSING, SEARCHING, AND PLAYING YOUR iTUNES MUSIC LIBRARY

Are you ready for some real iTunes? If the material in the previous chapters covered good features of iTunes, which it did, then this chapter starts the coverage of the amazing, awesome [insert your own superlative here] features that make iTunes something to write a book about. Here is where we start taking your iTunes game to the next level, hitting some home runs, scoring touchdowns, and some other sports clichés that all good books use. It's time to start working with that mysterious Library I have mentioned a number of times but into which until now you have only had glimpses.

The iTunes Library is where you can store all your music, such as that from audio CDs and the Internet, and where any music you purchase from the iTunes Music Store is stored. After you have added music to your Library, you never have to bother with individual CDs again because you can access all your music from the Library. And, you can use the music in your Library in many ways, such as to create playlists, burn CDs, and so on.

Right now, your iTunes Library is probably sort of sad. Like a book library with no books in it, your iTunes Library is just sitting there gathering dust on its digital shelves. You will change that shortly. The first step is to add music to the Library. Then, you'll learn how to browse, search, and listen to the tunes you have added there.

Gathering Your Music from All the Right Places

If you are going to add music to your Library, you have to get it from somewhere, right? The following are the three main sources of tunes for your Library:

- **Audio CDs**—Who wants to bother with audio CDs? Wouldn't it be nice if you could store all the content of your CD collection in one place so you could listen to any music you wanted to at any time just by browsing or doing a quick search? Obviously, that is a loaded question because you already know you can use iTunes to do just that. In this chapter, you'll learn how to copy the music from audio CDs into your Library (as you'll remember from Chapter 13, "Touring iTunes," this is called *importing*) so that you never have to use the original CDs again.

- **MP3 and other audio files**—You can add audio files in just about any format to your Library. For example, there are lots of free and legal MP3 files on the Web that you can add to your own Library. In this chapter, you will learn how to add music to your Library in this way, too.

- **iTunes Music Store**—With the iTunes Music Store, you can browse and search among hundreds of thousands of songs. When you find music you like, you can purchase an entire CD's worth of songs or you can buy individual songs (can you say one-hit wonders!). When you buy a song, it

> **note**
>
> *Podcasts* are a special type of content similar to broadcast radio except that no broadcasting is involved and you have total control over what you hear (so, I guess it isn't all that similar after all). Some podcasts contain music, but there are a lot more including news, talk, and so on. You'll learn about podcasts in detail in the last section of this chapter.

is downloaded and added to your iTunes Library. Instead of ordering a CD or, even worse, buying one in a physical store, your music is available to you instantly, and you don't even have to import it. Because the iTunes Music Store is so cool, I have devoted an entire part of this book to it (Part III, "The iTunes Music Store"). In that part, you will see how to build your Library by purchasing music online.

Determining Where and How the Music Library Music Is Stored

It is much easier to organize an empty room, so it is good practice to set up the organization of your iTunes Library before you fill it with music. In this section, you'll learn how iTunes organizes the music in your Library. If its standard practices aren't good enough for you, you can change its ways to suit your own organizational preferences.

Working with the iTunes Music Folder

As you import music into the Library, files are created for each song you add (whether it's from a CD, downloaded from the iTunes Music Store, or imported from an existing file). When you first started the application, iTunes created a folder called iTunes Music in which it stores all the music it manages for you.

The default location of this folder depends on the kind of computer you are using. On Windows computers, the folder will be stored in a folder called iTunes, located within your My Music folder. On Macs, this folder is also called iTunes, but it is located in the Music folder within your Home folder.

To see the current location of the iTunes Music folder on your computer, open the **iTunes Preferences** dialog box and then open the **Advanced** pane (see Figure 16.1). At the top of this dialog box, you will see the iTunes Music Folder Location box. Within this box, you will see the path to your iTunes Music folder.

Just for fun, open your iTunes Music folder so you can see it for yourself. Use the path you see on the Advanced pane to find it. If you haven't added any music to your Library yet, it might be pretty dull. To see what a full folder looks like, check out Figure 16.2.

tip

In case you don't remember from the last chapter, you access the iTunes Preferences dialog box by pressing **Ctrl+,** (Windows) or ⌘**-,** (Macs).

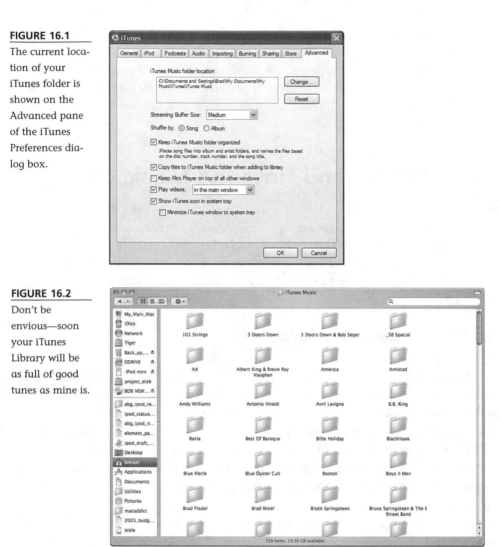

FIGURE 16.1
The current location of your iTunes folder is shown on the Advanced pane of the iTunes Preferences dialog box.

FIGURE 16.2
Don't be envious—soon your iTunes Library will be as full of good tunes as mine is.

As you can see, within the iTunes Music folder is a folder for each artist. Within the artists' folder, each album from which you have added music is shown. Within each of those album folders, the tracks you have added are individual files (see Figure 16.3). If you take a close look at Figure 16.3, you can see that the files have the extension .mp3, which means the song files for the album *The Best Of BB King* were imported in the MP3 format.

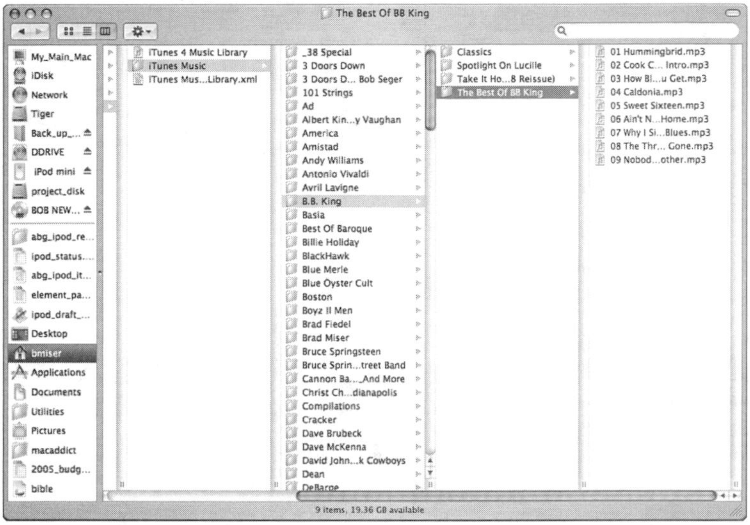

FIGURE 16.3

In this folder, you can see all the songs contained on the album *The Best of BB King* (which is an excellent album by the way, not that I am qualified to be a music critic).

Configuring the Location of the Music Folder

In most cases, the default location of your iTunes Music folder will be fine, and you don't have to do anything about it. However, there are some cases in which you will want to change the location of this folder. For example, suppose you have several hard drives in your computer and the one on which the folder is currently stored doesn't have a lot of room. Even though individual song files are relatively small, you are likely to end up with thousands or tens of thousands of them in your Library. That can add up to a lot of disk space. You might want to change the location of your iTunes Music folder so it is on a drive with more room.

To change the location of this folder, do the following:

1. Open the **Advanced** pane of the iTunes Preferences dialog box.

2. Click the **Change** button. On a Windows PC, you will see the Browse For Folder dialog box (see Figure 16.4). On a Mac, you will see the Change Music Folder Location dialog box (see Figure 16.5).

3. Use the dialog box to move to and select the folder in which you want your iTunes Music folder to be located. For example, if you want to move the folder to another hard drive, move to that drive and click the Make New Folder (Windows) or New Folder (Mac) button to create a new folder for your music.

FIGURE 16.4

You use the Browse For Folder dialog box to move to or select a new home for your iTunes Music folder.

FIGURE 16.5

The Change Music Folder Location dialog box looks a bit different from its Windows counterpart, but the purpose is exactly the same.

4. Click **OK** (Windows) or **Choose** (Mac). You'll return to the Advanced pane, and the folder you selected will be shown in the iTunes Music Folder Location area.

5. Click **OK** to close the iTunes Preferences dialog box.

Setting Other Organization Preferences

The location of the folder in which your music will be stored is likely the most important part of the organization preferences. However, you'll need to understand a couple more preferences that are alsov located on the Advanced pane of the iTunes Preferences dialog box:

note

If you already have music in your Library, changing the location of the iTunes Music folder won't hurt you. When you select a new folder, iTunes will remember the location of any previous music you have added to the Library and will update its database so that music will still be part of your Library.

- **Keep iTunes music folder organized**—This preference causes iTunes to organize your music as described earlier—that is, by artist, album, and song. Because this is a logical way to organize your music files, I recommend that you leave this option active by making sure this check box is checked.

- **Copy files to iTunes Music Folder when adding to library**—This preference causes iTunes to make a copy of audio files that already exist on your computer (such as MP3 files you have downloaded from the Internet) and places those copies in your iTunes Music folder, just like files you create by importing them from a CD. If this preference is inactive, iTunes uses a pointer to song files you are adding instead of making a copy of the files; it doesn't actually place the files in your iTunes Music folder. I recommend that you make this preference active by checking its check box. This way, all your music files will be in the same place, no matter where they came from originally.

> **tip**
>
> If you want to go back to the default location of the iTunes Music Folder, open the Advanced pane of the iTunes Preferences dialog box and click the Reset button.

If you don't have iTunes make copies of songs when you add them to your Library and then you delete or move the song files you added, iTunes will lose track of the song and you will experience the "missing song file" problem. To learn how to solve that problem, see "Solving the Missing Song File Problem" on page **348**.

> **caution**
>
> If you do have iTunes copy files to your iTunes Music folder when you add them to your Library, be aware that it does actually make a copy of the file you are adding. This means you will have two files for each song you add to the Library. After you have successfully added songs to your Library, you should delete the song files from their original locations so you aren't wasting disk space.

Understanding Encoding and Other Important Format Options

Back in Chapter 13, you learned about the major music file formats that you need to be aware of as you use iTunes. As you will recall, the two primary formats you use when dealing with music are AAC and MP3, but the Apple

Lossless format is useful when you want only the highest quality from your music. When you add music to your Library, you choose the format and then select the specific configuration of that format.

Choosing a Format Option

Although I am sure that going into the specifications for each kind of format would make for fascinating reading, there isn't really any need to get into that detail. Frankly, the benefit of using an application such as iTunes is that it manages all this complexity for you so that you don't have to be concerned with it. If you are like me, you just want to work with the music, not diddle around with complicated settings.

Generally, when you add music to your Library, you should use either the AAC or MP3 format. Because the AAC format is better (with *better* meaning that it provides higher quality music in smaller file sizes), it is usually the best choice.

If you want to have the highest quality music and file size isn't a concern for you, Apple Lossless is the way to go.

Picking Quality Levels

After you select a format, you decide the quality with which the music will be encoded. Higher quality levels mean better-sounding music but larger file sizes. If file size is not a problem, choosing a higher quality setting is the way to go. If you have relatively little disk space, you might want to experiment to see which is the lowest quality setting you can choose that results in music that still sounds good to you. If you demand the absolute best in music quality and have plenty of hard drive space to spare, Apple Lossless is a good option for you.

Your computer's hard disk space isn't the only factor you need to consider when choosing a quality level. iPods also have a hard drive or flash memory, and if you use the higher-quality encoders, such as Apple Lossless, you won't be able to fit as many songs on your iPod as with a format designed for small files, such as the AAC format.

Note that when it comes to music, quality is in the ear of the beholder. Also, it heavily depends on the type of music you listen to as well as how you listen to it. For example, if you listen to heavy metal rock using a low-quality pair of speakers (in other words, cheap speakers), quality will be less of an issue because you likely won't hear any difference

note

Nothing against heavy metal rock, of course (I like some of it myself), it's just that it usually includes lots of distortion and constant noise, which means minor flaws in the encoded music won't be as noticeable.

anyway. However, if you listen to classical music on high-quality speakers, the differences in quality levels might be more noticeable.

The trade-off for quality is always file size. The higher the quality setting you choose, the larger the resulting files will be. If you don't have disk space limitations and have a discriminating ear, you might want to stick with the highest possible quality setting. If disk space is at a premium for you, consider using a lower quality setting if you can't detect the difference or if that difference doesn't bother you.

Configuring iTunes to Import Music

Before you start adding music to your Library, choose the import options (mainly format and quality levels) you want to use. Here are the steps to follow:

1. Open the **Importing** pane of the iTunes Preferences dialog box (see Figure 16.6).

FIGURE 16.6

Here, you can see that the AAC format (the AAC Encoder) is selected.

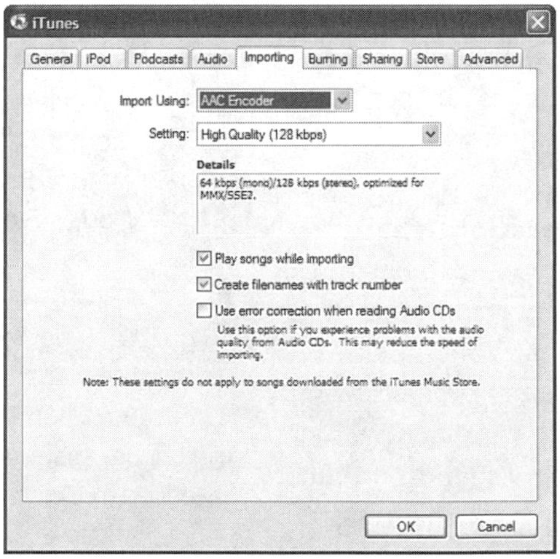

2. Select the format in which you want to add music to your Library on the **Import Using** menu. For example, to use the AAC format, select **AAC Encoder**. To use the MP3 format, select **MP3 Encoder**. Or, select **Apple Lossless Encoder** to maximize the quality of your music. The other encoder options are WAV and AIFF, but you probably won't use those options except for special circumstances, such as when you are going to use the music you encode in a different application, in which case the AIFF encoder might be a good choice.

3. Select the quality level of the encoder you want to use on the **Setting** menu. The options you see in this list depend on the format you selected in step 1. If you chose AAC Encoder, you have three quality options: High Quality, Podcast, and Custom. If you chose MP3 Encoder, you have four options:

Good Quality, High Quality, Higher Quality, and Custom. If you selected the Apple Lossless Encoder, you have only the Automatic option.

In the Details box, you will see a summary of the settings you have selected. For example, you will see the data rate of the encoder, such as 128Kbps, and the processor for which the encoder has been optimized. (Do you need to worry about these details? Not really.)

If you use the AAC encoder, the High Quality setting will likely be all you ever need.

4. If you want music you add to your Library to play while it is being added, check the **Play songs while importing** check box. This is a personal preference, and it doesn't impact the encoding process significantly.

5. If you want the files that iTunes creates when you import music to include the track number in their filenames, check the **Create filenames with track number** check box. Because this helps you more easily find files for specific songs, I recommend that you keep this preference active.

6. The **Use error correction when reading Audio CDs** check box causes iTunes to more closely control the encoding process. You should use this option only if you notice problems with the music you add to your Library, such as cracking or popping sounds. If that happens, check this check box and try the import process again.

7. Click **OK** to close the dialog box.

> **tip**
>
> In most cases, choosing an encoder isn't a difficult decision. If hard drive space is a factor for you, you use an iPod, or you don't have the ears of a music expert, the AAC encoder is the way to go. If you demand perfection, use the Apple Lossless Encoder. Because I don't have musically trained ears, I use the AAC encoder. (Although my music collection does contain a number of MP3 files that I created before the AAC format became available.)

Adding Music from Audio CDs to Your iTunes Music Library

Now that you know all you need to about configuring iTunes to build your Library, you are ready to start adding your own audio CDs to your Library.

Adding Audio CDs to Your Library

Use these steps to add a CD to your Library:

1. Configure the encoder you want to use for the import session (refer to the section "Configuring iTunes to Import Music" on page **241**).

2. Insert the CD you want to add to your Library. iTunes will attempt to identify it. When it does, the CD will appear in the Source list and will be selected (see Figure 16.7). Notice that the Action button in the upper-right corner of the screen is now the Import button.

tip

You can also select **File**, **Import** or press **Shift+Ctrl+O** (Windows) or **Shift-⌘-O** (Mac) to start the import process. You will see a dialog box that enables you to move to and select the CD you want to import.

FIGURE 16.7

iTunes is ready to add this CD to the Library.

3. If there are songs you don't want to add to the Library, uncheck their check boxes. Only songs with their check boxes checked will be imported. Unless you really hate a song or disk space is at a premium, it is generally better to import all the songs. You can use the check box in another source, such as in your Library, to cause those songs to be skipped when you play that source.

4. Click the **Import** button. It will become highlighted, and the import process will start (see Figure 16.8).

   If you left the Play songs while importing preference active, the music will begin to play as it is imported.

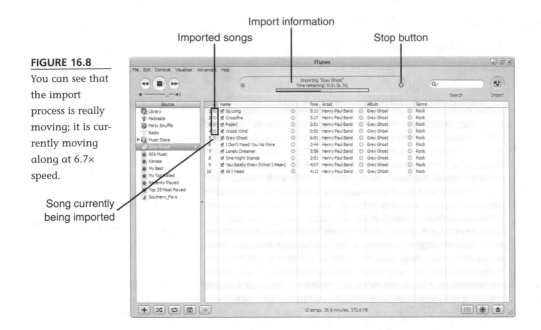

Imported songs

Import information

Stop button

FIGURE 16.8

You can see that the import process is really moving; it is currently moving along at 6.7× speed.

Song currently being imported

The Information window will show information related to the import process, such as the name of the song currently being imported and the rate at which the import process is happening.

The rate of the import process depends on the hardware you are using and the import settings. In most cases, the import process will occur at a much greater rate than the playing process. For example, with moderate hardware, you can usually achieve import rates exceeding 7×, meaning 7 minutes of music will be imported in 1 minute of time.

An orange circle with a "squiggly" line inside it marks the song currently being imported. When a song has been imported, it is marked with a green circle containing a check mark.

If you want to stop the import process for some reason, click the **Stop** button (the small *x* within a circle) in the Information window.

When the process is complete, you will hear a tone and all the songs will be marked with the "import complete" icon.

If you have the Play songs while importing preference active, the music will keep

tip

During the import process, you don't have to listen to what you are importing. You can select a different source, such as a playlist, and play it while the CD is being imported. This will slow the import speed slightly, but probably not enough to bother you.

playing long after the import process is complete (because importing is much faster than playing is). Listen for the complete tone or keep an eye on the screen to determine when all the music on the CD has been imported.

5. Eject the CD.

Building Your iTunes Music Library in a Hurry

The import process moves along pretty quickly, but you can make it even faster by following these steps:

1. Gather a pile of your CDs in a location close to your computer.

2. Set the import preferences (encoder and quality) for the import session.

3. Open the **General** pane of the iTunes Preferences dialog box.

4. Select **Import Songs and Eject** on the **On CD Insert** menu (see Figure 16.9). This causes iTunes to immediately begin the import process when you insert a CD. When the import process is complete, the CD will be ejected automatically.

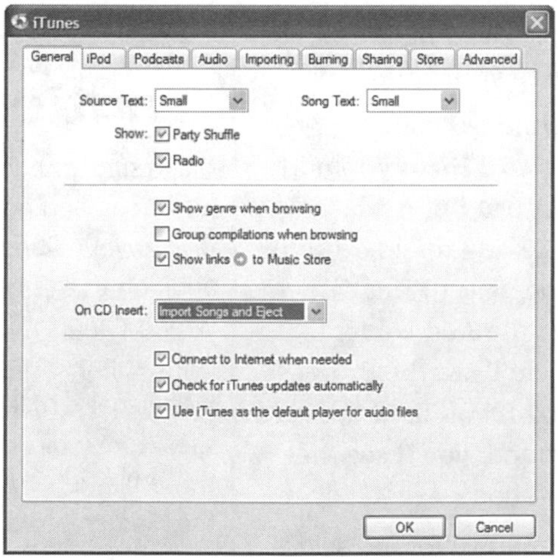

FIGURE 16.9

Choosing the Import Songs and Eject option makes adding lots of CDs to your Library as fast as possible.

5. Click **OK** to close the dialog box.

6. Insert the first CD you want to import. iTunes will start importing it automatically. When the process is complete, the CD will be ejected automatically.

7. Insert the next CD you want to import. Again, iTunes will import the music and eject the disc when it is done.

> **tip**
>
> Consider turning off the Play songs while importing preference on the Importing pane so the import process doesn't impact the music to which you are listening.

8. Repeat step 7 until all the CDs have been imported. You'll be amazed at how quickly you can build a Library, even if you have a large number of CDs.

When you are done batch importing your CDs, you might want to reset the On CD insert menu to **Show Songs** to prevent unintentionally importing a CD more than once.

Importing Audio Files into Your Library

Another potential source of music for your Library is the Internet. There are millions of audio files there, and you can download these files and add them to your Library.

Or, you might have lots of MP3 files on your computer already. You can add all these to your iTunes Library so you can use that music from within iTunes as well.

You can add music stored on your hard drive to your iTunes Library by following these steps:

1. Locate the files you want to add to your Library. For example, find the MP3 files on your hard drive or go to a website that has audio files, such as MP3 files, and download them to your computer.

2. Using iTunes on a Windows computer, select **File**, **Add File to Library** to add individual music files or **File**, **Add Folder to Library** to add a folder full of music files. On a Mac, select **File**, **Add to Library**. If you used the Add Folder to Library command, you'll see the Browse For Folder dialog box. If you used the Add File to Library command, you'll see the Add to Library dialog box.

3. Use the dialog box to move to and select the folder containing the files you want to add or to select the files you want to add to the Library.

4. Click **Open**, **OK**, or **Choose** (the name of the button you see depends on the command you use). The files you selected will be imported into your Library. If you selected a folder, all the songs it contains will be added to your Library.

caution

Make sure you don't download and add illegal files to your Library. In addition to this being the wrong thing to do, you can get prosecuted for downloading files illegally. Make sure any websites from which you get files have those files legally with permission of the files' creators.

Browsing and Searching Your Music Library

It won't be long until you have a large Library with many kinds of music in it. In fact, you are likely to have so much music in the Library that you won't be able to find songs you are interested in just by scrolling up and down the screen. In this section, you'll learn how to find music in your Library, first by browsing and then by searching.

Browsing in the Library

You've already seen the Browser a couple of times. Now it is time to put it to work:

1. Select **Library** on the Source list.

2. If the Browser isn't showing, click the **Action** button, which is now labeled Browse (it looks like an eye). The Browser will appear (see Figure 16.10). The Browser has three columns: Genre, Artist, and Album. The columns start on the left with the most general category, Genre, and end on the right with the most specific category, which is Album.

tip

If you don't see the Genre column in the Browser, open the **General** pane of the iTunes Preferences dialog box and check the **Show genre when browsing** check box.

FIGURE 16.10

The Browser offers a good way to find songs in your Library.

The contents of the "path" selected in the Browser are shown in the Content pane that now occupies the bottom part of the right side of the window. At the top of each column is the All option, which shows all the contents of that category. For example, when All is selected in the Genre column, you will see the contents of all the genres for which you have music in the Library. In Figure 16.10, you can see that I have selected All in the Genre column, Phil Keaggy in the Artist column, and Acoustic Sketches in the Albums column. This causes the Content pane to show all the tracks of album titled *Acoustic Sketches* by Phil Keaggy in the Content pane.

At the bottom of the screen, you will see Source Information for the selected source. Again, in Figure 16.10, you can see that the 19 songs shown in the Content pane will play for 1 hour and consume 61.6MB of disk space.

> **tip**
>
> You can also open and close the Browser by selecting **Edit**, **Show Browser** or **Edit**, **Hide Browser**. Pressing **Ctrl+B** (Windows) or ⌘-**B** (Mac) also works.

3. To start browsing your Library, select the genre in which you are interested by clicking it. When you do so, the categories in the other two columns are scoped down to include only the artists and albums that are part of that genre (see Figure 16.11, which shows the Jazz genre in my Library). Similarly, the Content pane now includes only jazz music. Notice in Figure 16.11 that the Source Information has been updated, too. It now shows that I can listen to one day of jazz before I run out of music.

4. To further limit the browse, click an artist in which you are interested in the Artist column. The Album column will be scoped down to show only those albums for the artist selected in the Artist column (see Figure 16.12). Also, the Content pane will show the songs on the albums listed in the Album column.

5. To get down to the most narrow browse possible, select the album in which you are interested in the Album column. The Content pane will now show the songs on the selected album.

6. When you have selected the genre, artist, and album categories in which you are interested, you can scroll in the Content pane to see all the songs included in the group of songs you are browsing.

To make the browse results less narrow again, select **All** in one of the Browser's columns. For example, to browse all your music again, click **All** in the Genre column.

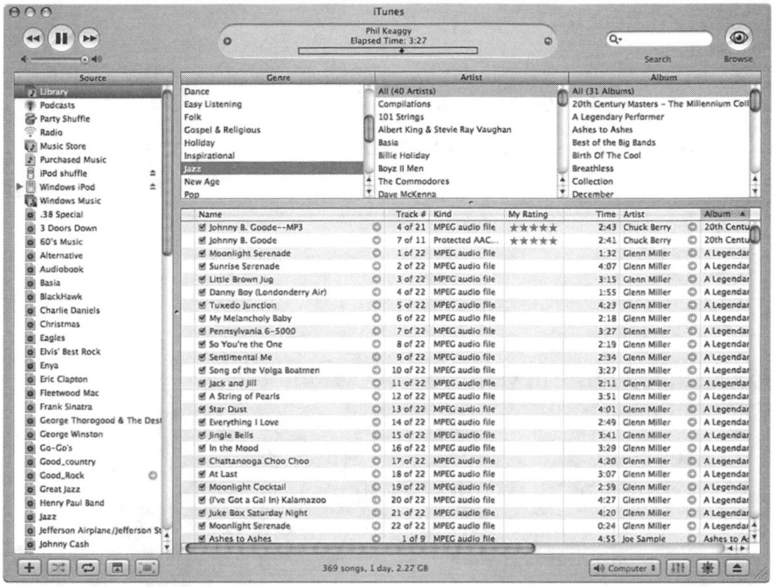

FIGURE 16.11

Because Jazz is selected in the Genre column, the Artist and Album columns and Content pane contain only the jazz that is in my Library.

FIGURE 16.12

Now I am browsing all my music in the Jazz genre that is performed by Kenny G.

Hopefully, you can see that you can use the Browser to quickly scan your Library to locate music you want to hear or work with. As you use the Browser more, you will come to rely on it to get you to a group of songs quickly and easily.

Searching Your Music Library

You can use iTunes Search tool to search for specific songs. You can search for songs by any of the following criteria:

- All (searches all possible data)
- Artists
- Albums
- Composers
- Songs

To search for music in your Library, perform the following steps:

tip

If you want to search by all data at the same time, you don't need to perform step 2 because All is the default selection.

1. Select the source you want to search (for example, click the **Library** source). As you might surmise, you can search any source in the Source list—such as a CD, playlist, and so on—by selecting it and then performing a search.

2. Click the **magnifying glass** icon in the **Search** tool (see Figure 16.13). You will see a menu containing the list of data by which you can search. The currently selected search attribute is marked with a check mark.

3. Select the data for which you want to search in the menu. When you release the mouse button, the name of the Search tool will change to reflect your selection on the menu. For example, if you select Artists to search by the Artist field, the Search tool will be labeled Search Artists.

4. Type the data for which you want to search in the field. As you type, iTunes searches the selected source and presents the songs that meet your criterion in the Content pane. It does this on-the-fly so the search narrows with each keystroke. As you type more text or numbers, the search becomes more specific (see Figure 16.14).

5. Keep typing until the search becomes as narrow as you need it to be to find the songs in which you are interested.

After you have found songs, you can play them, add them to playlists, and so on.

To clear your search click the **Clear Search** button that appears in the Search tool after you have typed in it (see Figure 16.14). The songs shown in the Content pane will again be determined by your selections in the Browser.

FIGURE 16.13

By selecting Artists on the menu, you can search the Artist field for all the songs in the selected source (in this case, the Library).

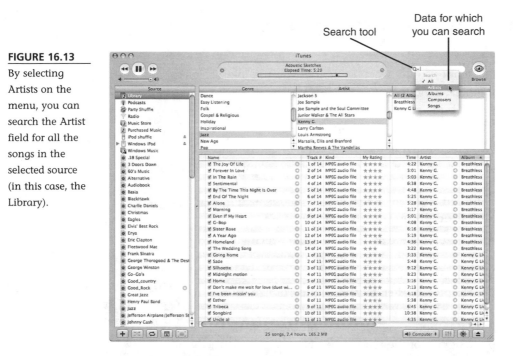

Search tool

Data for which you can search

Clear Search

FIGURE 16.14

Because I selected Artist and typed lyn in the Search tool, the Content pane shows all songs whose artist includes the text *lyn*, as in The Lyndhurst Orchestra, Lynyrd Skynyrd, and so on.

Playing Music in Your Music Library

Remember earlier when I said that you use the same listening techniques to listen to music in your Library as you do when listening to a CD? Now it's time to prove my words.

When you listen to music in your Library, you start by choosing the scope of the music you want to hear. You do this by browsing or searching for music. (If you don't know how to do this, here's a hint: Read the previous two sections.)

After you have the group of songs to which you want to listen showing in the Content pane, use the listening tools you learned about in the previous chapter to listen to your music. For example, you can click Play to play the songs, use the Repeat button to repeat them, sort the Content pane by one of the column headings to change the order in which the songs play, and so on.

Removing Tunes from the Music Library

Not all that glitters is gold, nor are all tunes that are digital good. Sometimes, a song is so bad that it just isn't worth the hard disk space it consumes.

To remove songs from your Library, ditch them with the following steps:

1. Find the songs you want to delete by browsing or searching.

2. Select the songs you want to trash. They will become highlighted to show you they are selected (see Figure 16.15).

3. Press the **Delete** or **Backspace** key. You will be prompted to confirm that you really want to delete the song you have selected.

note

When you are listening to your Library, I don't recommend that you uncheck a song's check box in the Library or move songs up and down in the list to control how they are played. Use playlists for that kind of customized listening instead (playlists are explained in Chapter 18, "Creating, Configuring, and Using Playlists"). Changes you make to songs in the Library can result in unexpected things happening if you forget to undo a change before making a playlist, burning a CD, and so on.

tip

Remember that you can stop a song from playing by unchecking its Song check box in the Content pane. If you aren't sure you want to dump a song permanently, use that method instead so you can always use the song again should you change your mind.

FIGURE 16.15

If I press the Delete key now, "Shot To Hell" will be removed from my Library.

4. If you see the warning prompt, click **Remove** to confirm the deletion. You will see another prompt asking whether you want the selected files to be moved to your Recycle Bin (Windows) or Trash (Mac) or you want to keep the files on your computer. (If you have disabled the warning prompt, you'll move directly to the second dialog box.

5. Click **Move to Recycle Bin** (Windows) or **Move to Trash** (Mac) to move the files so you can get rid of them entirely. The selected songs will be deleted from your Library, and their song files will be moved to the appropriate trash receptacle on your computer. The next time you empty that receptacle, they will be gone forever.

> **tip**
>
> In many of the prompts iTunes presents to you, you have the option of telling the application not to present those prompts again. Just look for the appropriate Do not ask me again check boxes in such prompts and check them to hide those prompts in the future.

If you just want to remove the references to files from the iTunes Library but not delete the song files, click **Keep Files**. The songs will be removed from the Library, but the song files will remain in their current locations.

254 ABSOLUTE BEGINNER'S GUIDE TO **IPOD AND ITUNES**

Subscribing and Listening to Podcasts

Podcasts are radio-like audio you can add to your iTunes Library. You can find thousands of podcasts in the iTunes Music Store. Many websites provide access to podcasts, and some exist solely for that purpose.

Most podcasts are provided in episodes you can listen to individually. When you want to be able to listen to a podcast, you subscribe to it; subscribing to a podcast causes it to be downloaded to your computer and added to your Library. You can also choose to download previous episodes if you want to.

After you have downloaded podcasts, you can listen to them on your computer, move them to an iPod, and so on.

Setting Your Podcast Preferences

Some podcast preferences should be set before you start working with podcasts. Do so with the following steps:

1. Open the iTunes Preferences dialog box and click the **Podcasts** tab (see Figure 16.16).

2. Choose how often you want iTunes to check for new episodes using the **Check for new episodes** drop-down list. The options are Every hour, Every day, Every week, or Manually. iTunes will check for new episodes according to the timeframe you select—unless you select Manually, in which case you must manually check for new episodes.

note

Of course, songs you delete probably aren't really gone forever. You can always add them back to the Library again by repeating the same steps you used to place them in there the first time. This assumes you have a copy somewhere, such as on a CD or stored in some other location. If you imported the music from your hard disk and had iTunes move the songs files to your iTunes Music folder, your only copy will reside in your iTunes Library, so make sure you have such music backed up before you delete it if you might ever want it again.

caution

You should never delete music you purchased from the iTunes Music Store unless you are absolutely sure you will never want it again or you have that music backed up elsewhere. You can download music you purchased from the store only one time. After that, you have to pay for it to download it again.

FIGURE 16.16

Use the Podcasts preferences to determine how you want your podcast subscriptions to be managed.

3. Use the **When new episodes are available** drop-down list to determine what iTunes does when it finds new episodes of the podcasts to which you are subscribed. Select **Download most recent one** if you want only the newest episode to be downloaded. Select **Download all** if you want all available episodes downloaded. Select **Do nothing** if you don't any episodes to be downloaded.

Just under the Check for new episodes drop-down list you'll see when the next check for new episodes will be performed.

4. Use the **Keep** drop-down list to determine if and when iTunes deletes podcast episodes. Select **All episodes** if you don't want iTunes to automatically remove any episodes. Select **All unplayed episodes** if you want iTunes to remove episodes to which you have listened, and select **Most recent episode** if you want iTunes to keep only the most recent episode even if you haven't listened to all of them. Select **Last X episodes**, where **X** is 2, 3, 4, 5, or 10, to have iTunes keep the selected number of episodes.

5. Click **OK**. The dialog box will close and your podcast preferences will be set.

Subscribing to Podcasts

Now that iTunes is ready to manage podcasts according to your preferences, it's time to load up your Library with podcasts of your choice. In this section, you'll learn how to subscribe to podcasts from two sources: the iTunes Music Store and the Internet.

Subscribing to Podcasts from iTunes Music Store

In addition to lots of great music, you can also access thousands of podcasts via the iTunes Music Store. Most of these podcasts are free and you don't even need an iTunes Music Store account to gain access to them.

When you access the podcasts section of the iTunes Music Store, you can browse or search for podcasts to which you can then subscribe.

To browse for podcasts in the iTunes Music Store and subscribe to them, perform the following steps:

1. Select **Music Store** on the Source list. The iTunes Music Store will fill the Content pane.

2. Click the **Podcasts** link in the iTunes Music Store. You'll move to the Podcasts home page (see Figure 16.17).

3. Scroll down the window until you see the **Categories** section. Here, you can access podcasts based on various categories, such as Arts & Entertainment, Audio Blogs, Business, Comedy, and so on.

4. Click a category in which you are interested, such as News. The Content pane will be refreshed and will become the Browse window (see Figure 16.18). The podcast Browser works just like the Browser when you browse your Library or other sources.

note

You'll also see the iPod Preferences button. If you click this, you'll move to the Podcasts tab of the iPod preferences tab. You can use the controls on this tab to configure how podcasts are moved into an iPod. For information about configuring podcast preferences for an iPod, refer to "Working with Podcasts" on page **146**.

note

In this chapter, you'll get a very focused view of the iTunes Music Store. To learn about the iTunes Music Store in detail, see Part III, "The iTunes Music Store."

FIGURE 16.17

Want podcasts? The iTunes Music Store has them!

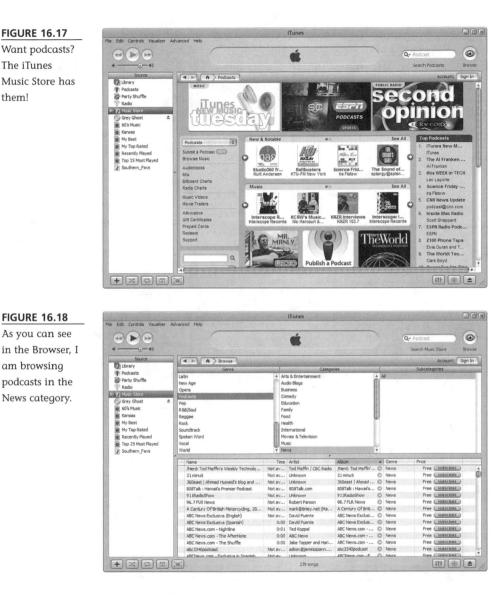

FIGURE 16.18

As you can see in the Browser, I am browsing podcasts in the News category.

5. If the category has subcategories, you'll see them in the rightmost pane of the Browser; click the subcategory in which you are interested. The Content pane will show all podcasts in the categories selected in the Browser.

6. Use the scrollbar in the Content pane to browse all the podcasts available. For each podcast, you'll see the name, time, artist, album, genre, and price information (which is free for most podcasts).

7. When you find a podcast in which you are interested, you can listen to it by selecting it and clicking the **Play** button. The podcast will begin to play.

8. When you find a podcast that you would like to listen to on a regular basis, click its **Subscribe** button. You'll see a confirmation dialog box; click the **Subscribe** button to subscribe to the podcast. You'll move to the Podcasts source in your Library and episodes will be downloaded according to the preferences you set earlier (see Figure 16.19).

9. Click the **Music Store** source to go back to browse for and subscribe to more podcasts. You'll return to your previous location in the store.

tip

You can click just about any object on the Podcasts home page to move to individual podcasts. The steps in this section are focused on browsing by category, but there are many other ways to browse for podcasts. In Part III, you'll learn more techniques to find music in the iTunes Music Store. These work for podcasts, too.

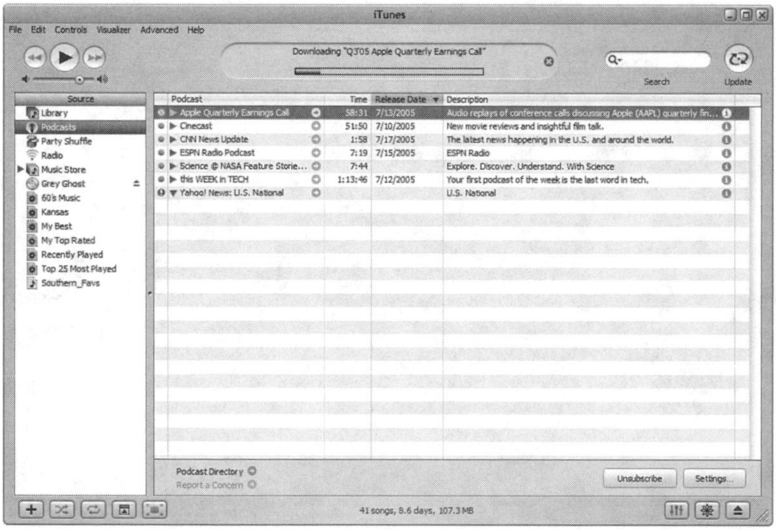

FIGURE 16.19
Here, I've subscribed to the Apple Quarterly Earnings Call podcast and the most recent episode is being downloaded to my computer.

You can also search for specific podcasts in the iTunes Music Store using the following steps:

1. Select the **Music Store** source.

2. Click the **Podcasts** link.

3. Use the **iTunes Search** tool to search for specific podcasts. This works just like it does in other contexts; select the attribute by which you want to search using the magnifying glass icon and then type search text in the box. Press the **Enter** (Windows) or **Return** (Mac) key to perform the search. The results will appear in the Content pane (see Figure 16.20).

FIGURE 16.20

Here I've
searched for pod-
casts containing
"fox;" as you
can see, a num-
ber of podcasts
were found,
many of which
are from Fox
News.

4. Use the scrollbar in the Content pane to browse all the podcasts that were found by your search. For each podcast, you'll see the name, artist, category, description, relevance to your search, and price information (which is free for most podcasts).

5. When you find a podcast in which you are interested, you can listen to it by selecting it and clicking the **Play** button. The podcast will begin to play.

6. When you find a podcast that you would like to listen to on a regular basis, click its **Subscribe** button. You'll see a confirmation dialog box; click the **Subscribe** button to subscribe to the podcast. You'll move to the Podcasts source in your Library and episodes will be downloaded according to the preferences you set earlier.

7. Click the **Music Store** source to go back to search for and subscribe to more podcasts. You'll return to your previous location in the store.

To learn how to work with podcasts to which you have subscribed, see "Listening to and Managing Podcasts" on page **262**.

Subscribing to Podcasts from the Internet

A tremendous amount of podcasts are available on the Internet, and you can subscribe to these to listen to them and download them to an iPod. The most challenging part is finding podcasts that are worth the time to listen to, but that judgment
is, of course, in the ear of the beholder.

There are two general sources of podcast websites on the Internet. One includes websites whose sole purpose is to provide access to podcasts. The other includes websites from specific organizations, such as radio shows, that provide podcasts related to those organizations. Subscribing to podcasts from either source is similar.

The following steps show you how to subscribe to a podcast accessed from a specific podcast collection website. You can use similar steps to find other podcast sites.

1. Open a web browser and move to a website that provides podcast information. For example, www.podcastalley.com contains information about thousands of podcasts.

2. Browse or search the website for podcasts that interest you.

3. Click the **Subscribe** link for a podcast in which you are interested. You'll move to an information page that provides a URL for you to subscribe to the podcast (see Figure 16.21).

4. Copy the URL that is displayed.

5. Move into iTunes.

6. Select **Advanced**, **Subscribe to Podcast**. You'll see the Subscribe to Podcast dialog box (see Figure 16.22).

7. Paste the URL you copied in step 4 into the dialog box and click **OK**. The dialog box will close and you'll move into the Podcasts source. You'll see the podcast to which you subscribed in the Content pane (see Figure 16.23).

note

Some websites provide access to podcasts only if you are paying subscriber to that site. This is true for some radio shows, for example. Some sites also provide specific tools you must use to access their podcasts. Exploring how to use these kinds of podcasts is beyond the scope of this chapter. Most such sites also provide help information to enable you to use them.

tip

If you want to explore the variety of podcast sites available, perform a Google search on the term "podcast."

To learn how to work with podcasts to which you have subscribed, see "Listening to and Managing Podcasts" on page **262**.

FIGURE 16.21

Here I am view-
ing the URL for a
podcast called
this WEEK in
TECH.

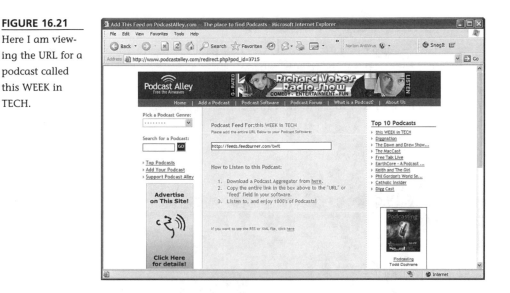

FIGURE 16.22

When you paste
a podcast's URL
into this dialog
box, you can
subscribe to it.

FIGURE 16.23

I've subscribed to
the this WEEK in
TECH podcast.

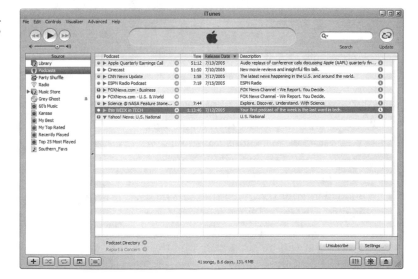

Listening to and Managing Podcasts

After you have subscribed to podcasts, you can listen to them. You can also manage the podcasts to which you have subscribed.

To work with your podcasts, click **Podcasts** on the Source list. You'll see the podcasts to which you have subscribed in the Content pane (see Figure 16.24).

Podcast with content

Downloaded episode

Expansion triangle

Information button

FIGURE 16.24

Use the Podcasts source to work with the podcasts to which you have subscribed.

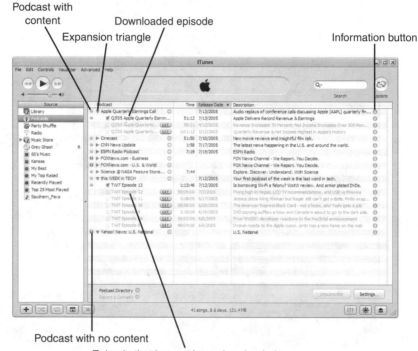

Podcast with no content

Episode that has not been downloaded

To perform various podcast actions, refer to the following list:

- To see all the episodes available for a podcast, click its expansion triangle. All the available episodes will be shown. The episodes that have been downloaded to your computer and to which you can listen will have a blue dot next to them. Those that haven't been downloaded yet will be grayed out and the Get button will be shown.

- To download an episode, click its **Get** button. The episode will be downloaded to your computer. When that process is

> **tip**
>
> Remember that you control how many episodes are downloaded to your computer using the Podcasts preferences you learned about earlier in this section.

complete, it will be marked with a blue dot and you will be able to listen to it. The Information area will present information about the download process.

■ To play an episode of a podcast, select it and click the **Play** button. The other iTunes playback controls work similarly to how the do for other sources, too.

■ To get information about an episode, click its **Information** button. You'll see the Podcast Information window that presents a summary of the episode (see Figure 16.25).

FIGURE 16.25

Here I am viewing information for an episode of the World Vision Report podcast.

tip

You can click the Settings button to jump to the Podcasts pane of the iTunes Preferences dialog box.

■ To move a website associated with a podcast, click the arrow in its **Podcast** column. If the podcast came from the iTunes Music Store, you'll move to its page in the store. If it came from outside the iTunes Music Store, you'll move to the podcast's home page on the Web.

■ Click the **Podcast Directory** link at the bottom of the Content pane to move to the Podcast home page in the iTunes Music Store.

■ To unsubscribe from a podcast, select it and click the **Unsubscribe** button. Episodes of the podcast will no longer be downloaded to your computer. You can subscribe again by clicking the Subscribe button that appears next to the podcast.

note

After you have listened to an episode, it might be removed from the Podcasts source, depending on the Keep preference set in the Podcasts pane of the iTunes Preferences dialog box. For example, if you select All unplayed episodes, episodes will be removed after you have played them.

- To remove a podcast, select it and press the **Delete** key. Click the **Move to Recycle Bin** (Windows) or **Move to Trash** (Mac) button to delete the podcasts files from your computer and from the Library or the **Keep Files** button to remove the podcast from your Library but leave its files on your computer.

- You can click the Update button to refresh the list of episodes available for each podcast to which you are subscribed.

- If a podcast has an exclamation point icon next to it, that podcast has a problem, such as no content being available. If you want to report the problem, select the podcast and click the Report a Concern link. This is available only for podcasts that are available in the iTunes Music Store.

The Absolute Minimum

Although it might not smell like a book library, your iTunes Library is at least as useful and is a heck of a lot easier to get to. In this chapter, you learned how to build and use your iTunes Library. Before we move on to the next great thing about iTunes, check out some related points of interest (well, my interest anyway; hopefully, they will be yours, too):

- Through the Audible.com service (accessible via the iTunes Music Store), you can also add audio books to your iTunes Library to listen to them on your computer and you can add them to an iPod. Working with audio book content is similar to working with music. Unfortunately, covering the details of doing so is outside the scope of this book.

- You learned that you can choose the import encoder and quality settings when you import music from audio CDs to your Library. You can import the same songs at different quality levels to experiment with various settings or to create different versions of the same song. For example, you might want a high-quality version to play from your computer and a lower-quality version with a smaller file size for a portable device. To create another version of a song, you can change the import settings and import it from a CD again. You can also reimport a song already in the Library by setting the encoding settings and adding its file (which will be located in the iTunes Music folder) to the Library, just like other music files stored on your computer.

continues

- Although we focused on the AAC and Apple Lossless Encoder formats in this chapter, in some cases you might want to use the WAV or AIFF format. For example, suppose you want to use part of a song as a sound byte in an application that doesn't support either of the primary formats but does support WAV files. You could choose the WAV format and then import the song you want to use in that format. The WAV file, which would be located in your iTunes Music folder, could then be added to the other application you are working with.

- If you are listening to music while doing something else, such as browsing your Library, you might move away from the song that is currently playing. If you want to move back to it again, select **File**, **Show Current Song** or press **Ctrl+L** (Windows) or ⌘**-L** (Mac).

- If you like to shuffle while you listen, you can determine whether iTunes shuffles by song or by album. It can be interesting when listening to the Library if you shuffle by album because iTunes will pick an album and play all the songs it contains, then pick another album, play all its songs, and so on. If you choose to shuffle by song, individual songs will be played regardless of the albums of which they are a part. To set this behavior, open the **Advanced** pane of the iTunes Preferences dialog box and click either the **Album** radio button next to the Shuffle by album or the **Song** radio button to shuffle by song.

- Podcasts are similar to broadcast radio except that you can store episodes in your iTunes Library so you can listen to them from your computer at a time of your choosing or by moving them to an iPod so you can listen on the move. iTunes includes all the tools you need to subscribe to, manage, and listen to any podcasts you can find.

- You can use the Browser with any source, although it defaults to being closed with CDs and some playlists because it usually isn't that useful in those contexts (especially when the source is a single CD). To open it for any source, just select the source you want to browse and open the Browser.

IN THIS CHAPTER

- Get to know and love tags.
- Get the details for your music.
- Label your music so you can do cool things with it, such as creating playlists based on a music's information.
- Rate your songs, set the relative volume level, and hear only the parts you want to hear.
- Don't miss out on album artwork just because you have gone digital.
- Work the Content pane like a pro.

17

LABELING, CATEGORIZING, AND CONFIGURING YOUR MUSIC

It's confession time. I admit it. This topic might not seem too exciting at first glance. Who wants to spend their time labeling and categorizing music? That is a fair question, but I hope by the time you read through this chapter, you answer that question with an enthusiastic, "I do, that's who!" Of course, I would be almost as happy even if your response is, "It might not be as fun as building my Library, but it will make my iTunes world a lot better." Think of this chapter as learning the nuts and bolts of how iTunes works so you can become an iTunes wizard later.

After you have worked through the labeling content in this chapter, I think you will find the ability to configure the songs in your Library to be pretty exciting because that is where you really start bending iTunes to your will (which isn't as dramatic as it sounds because iTunes is really pretty easy to command).

Understanding Song Tags and Knowing Why You Should Care About Them

In the previous chapter, you saw how you can browse your iTunes music collection by genre, artist, and album. This makes finding music fast and easy, even if you have thousands of songs in your Library. This functionality is enabled because each song in your Library has information—also called a *tag*—that categorizes and identifies that song for you. Genre, artist, and album are just three of the possible tags for each song in iTunes. There are many more items of information that iTunes manages.

These types of data fall into two groups: data that iTunes assigns for you and that you can't change, and data that you or iTunes assigns and that you can change.

Data that iTunes assigns and that you can view but can't change include the following:

- **Kind**—This identifies the type of file the song is, such as Protected AAC audio file, AAC audio file, MP3, and so on.

- **Size**—The amount of disk space required to store the song.

- **Bit Rate**—The quality level at which the song was encoded. Larger numbers, such as 128Kbps, are better.

- **Sample Rate**—The rate at which the music was sampled when it was captured.

> **note**
>
> Not all songs have all the data fields listed. You will only see data that is applicable to a specific song. For example, only music purchased from the iTunes Music Store has information about the purchase.

- **Date Modified**—The date on which the song file was last changed.

- **Play Count**—The number of times the song has been played.

- **Last Played**—The last time the song was played.

- **Profile**—A categorization of the song's complexity.

- **Format**—The format in which the song was encoded, such as MPEG-1, Layer 3.

- **Channels**—Whether the track is stereo or mono.

- **Encoded With**—The tools used to encode the song, such as iTunes, QuickTime, and so on.

- **ID3 Tag**—ID3 tags are data formatted according to a set of specifications. If a song's data has been formatted with this specification, the ID3 version number will be shown.

- **Purchase By, Account Name, and FairPlay Version**—If a song was purchased from the iTunes Music Store, this information identifies who purchased the music and which account was used. The FairPlay version information relates to the means by which the song is protected.

- **Where**—This shows a path to the song's file on your computer along with the filename.

Data collected for songs that you can change includes the following:

- **Name**—This is the name of the song.

- **Artist**—The person who performs the song.

- **Album**—The name of the album from which the song comes.

- **Grouping**—This is a label you can assign to group songs together in some fashion.

- **Composer**—The person who is credited with writing the song.

- **Comments**—This is a free-form text field in which you can make comments about a song.

One "kind" you will see is Protected AAC audio file. This indicates that the song was purchased from the iTunes Music Store. You will learn about this type in Part III, "The iTunes Music Store."

- **Genre**—This associates a song with its musical genre, such as jazz or classical.

- **Year**—The year the song was created.

- **Track Number**—The song's position on the CD from which it came, such as "2 of 12."

- **Disc Number**—The number of the CD or DVD. This is meaningful only for multiple-disc sets.

- **BPM**—The song's beats per minute.

- **Part of a Compilation**—This indicates whether the song is part of a compilation CD, meaning one that contains music from a variety of artists (you know, like that *Greatest TV Theme Songs from the 1970s* CD you love so much).

When you add a song to your Library, iTunes will add as much of this data as it can find for each song. However, you can add or change the data in the previous list.

So, why should you care about all this data? There are a couple of reasons.

The first is that, as you already know because you learned how to browse and search your Library in the previous chapter, this data can be used to find music in which you are interested. That reason alone should be enough to convince you that these types of data are important to you.

The second reason is that when it comes time to create playlists (which you will learn about in Chapter 18, "Creating, Configuring, and Using Playlists"), you can use song tags to determine which songs are included in your playlists. For example, you can configure a playlist to include the last 25 songs you have played from the Jazz genre. This is just a basic example—you can get much more sophisticated than this. In fact, you can include several combinations of these types of data as criteria in playlists to create interesting sets of music to listen to.

> **note**
>
> When you insert a CD, iTunes attempts to get that CD's information from the CDDB (the online CD database), which is why it connects to the Internet. If iTunes finds the CD in this database, the information for that CD is applied to the CD and carried into the Library if you import the songs from that CD into iTunes. If you purchase music from the iTunes Music Store, it also contains many of these tags.

Viewing Song Information

Now that you understand the types of data that can be associated with songs in your Library, it's time to learn how to view that information. You have three basic areas in which to view song information: the Browser, the Content pane, and the Info window.

Viewing Tags in the Browser

If you read through the previous chapter, you have already used this technique. When you view the Browser, you see the genre, artist, and album tags associated with the songs you are browsing (see Figure 17.1).

Viewing Tags in the Content Pane

Even if you don't realize it, you have also seen tags in the Content pane. The column headings you see in the Content pane are actually the tags associated with the songs you are viewing (see Figure 17.2).

FIGURE 17.1

Each column in the Browser is a tag associated with songs in your Library.

FIGURE 17.2

Each column heading in the Content pane is a tag.

You can customize the columns (tags) shown in the Content pane, as you will learn later in this chapter.

Viewing Tags in the Info Window

The Info window is probably the only area in which you haven't seen tags yet. To view the Info window, select a song in your Library and select **File**, **Get Info** or press **Ctrl+I** (Windows) or ⌘-**I** (Mac). The Info window will appear; at the top of the window, you'll see the name of the song whose information you are viewing (see Figure 17.3). This window has four panes that you will be using throughout the rest of this chapter.

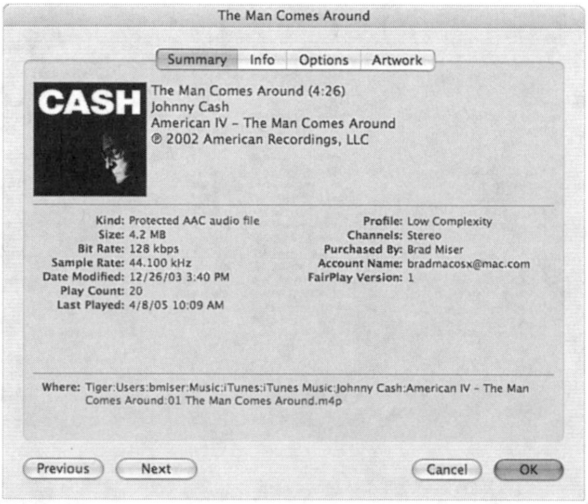

FIGURE 17.3

The Info window enables you to view the tags associated with a song, and you can change many of them.

The Summary pane provides a summary view of the song's information, starting at the top with any album art associated with the song and including its name, length, artist, and album. In the center part of the pane, you see the data iTunes manages (you can view this data, but you can't change it). At the bottom of the pane, you can see the path to the song's file on your computer.

When you click the Info tab, you will see the tags you can change (see Figure 17.4). You'll learn how to change this data in the next section.

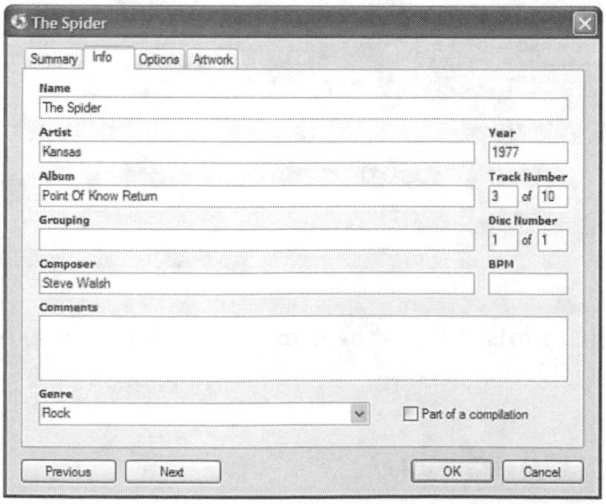

FIGURE 17.4

Although you can't change the tags shown on the Summary pane, you can change the ones on the Info pane.

The other two panes of the window, Options and Artwork, are used to configure specific aspects of a song (again, we'll get to these topics in a few pages).

You can view information for other songs without closing the window. Click **Next** to move to the next song in the source you are viewing (such as your Library) or **Previous** to move to the previous song. When you do, that song's information will be displayed in the Info window.

To close the Info window, click **OK**.

Labeling Your Music

There are a couple of places in which you can change a song's tags.

Labeling a Song in the Info Window

You can use the Info window to change a song's tags, as you can see in the following steps:

1. Open the **Info** window for the song whose information you want to change.

2. Click the **Info** tag, and the Info pane will appear.

3. Enter or change the information shown in the various fields. For example, you can change the song's name or artist. Or you might want to add comments about the song in the Comments box.

4. To change a song's genre, select the new genre from the **Genre** menu.

5. When you are done entering or changing tags, click **OK**. The Info window will close, and any changes you made will be saved.

Labeling Multiple Songs at the Same Time

You can change some tags, such as Genre, for a group of songs at the same time. This can be a faster way to entering data because you can change multiple songs at the same time. Here are the steps to follow:

note

Typically, if you have imported a CD or purchased music from the iTunes Music Store, you shouldn't change the data that came from the source, such as name, artist, album, track number, and so on. Occasionally, a CD's information will come in incorrect (such as a misspelling in the artist's name); you'll probably want to fix such mistakes. You can certainly add data in those fields that are empty.

note

One of the more useful tags is Genre. This can be used for browsing and also in playlists.

1. Select the songs whose data you want to change.

2. Open the **Info** window. You'll be prompted to confirm that you want to change the information for a group of songs.

3. Click **Yes** to clear the prompt. The Multiple Song Information window will appear (see Figure 17.5). The information and tools in this window work in the same way as they do for individual songs. The difference is that the information and settings apply to all the songs you have selected.

> **tip**
>
> If a genre by which you want to classify music isn't listed on the menu, you can add it to the menu by selecting Custom on the menu and then typing the genre you want to add. That genre will be added to the menu and associated with the current song. You can use the genres you create just like the default genres.

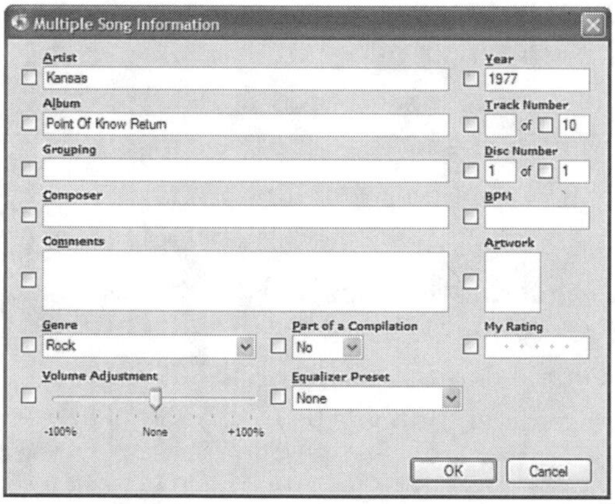

FIGURE 17.5

You can use this window to change the data for multiple songs at the same time.

4. Enter data in the fields, make changes to existing data, or use the other tools to configure the songs you have selected. As you change information, the check box next to the tag will become checked to show that you are changing that data for all the selected songs.

5. When you are done making changes, click **OK**. The window will close and the changes you made will be saved.

> **tip**
>
> To select multiple songs that are next to each other, hold down the **Shift** key while you click songs. To select multiple songs that aren't next to each other, hold down the **Ctrl** (Windows) or ⌘ (Mac) key while you click songs.

Labeling a Song in the Content Pane

You can also edit tags within the Content pane:

1. Click once on a song to select it.

2. Click once on the tag you want to edit. The tag will become highlighted to show that it is ready to be edited (see Figure 17.6).

3. Type the new information.

4. Press **Enter** (Windows) or **Return** (Mac). The changes you made will be saved.

note

You haven't yet learned about some of the fields on the Multiple Song Information window, such as My Rating, but you will soon.

FIGURE 17.6

You can also change tags from the Content pane; in this example the album name is highlighted and can be changed.

Configuring a Song's Options

You can configure a number of options for the songs in your Library, including the following:

■ **Relative Volume**—You can change a song's relative volume so it is either louder or quieter than "normal." This is useful if you like to listen to songs recorded at a variety of volume levels because the volume remains somewhat similar as you move from song to song.

- **Equalizer Preset**—You can use the iTunes Equalizer to configure the relative volume of sound frequencies. You'll learn about the Equalizer in Chapter 19, "Equalizing Your Music."

- **My Rating**—You can give tunes a rating from one to five stars. You can use ratings in various ways, such as to create criteria for playlists (such as include only my five-star songs) or to sort the Content pane.

- **Start and Stop Time**—You can set songs to start or stop at certain points in the track. This can be useful if you don't want to hear all of a track, such as when a song has an introduction you don't want to hear each time the song plays.

Configuring Song Options in the Info Window

You can configure a song's options in the Info window by performing the following steps:

1. Select the song whose options you want to set.

2. Open the **Info** window.

3. Click the **Options** tab (see Figure 17.7).

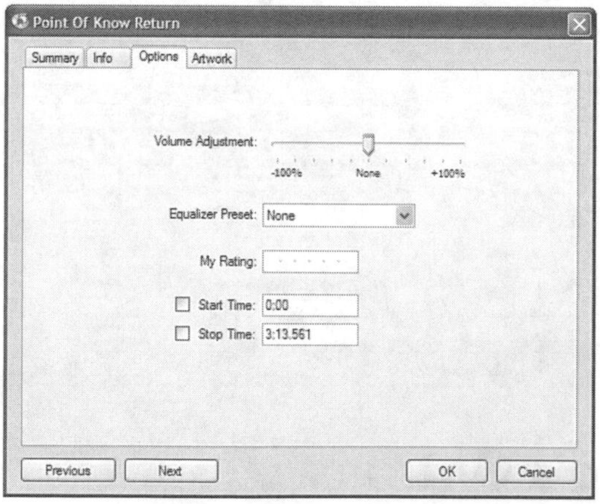

tip

Another way to open the Info window is to point to a song and right-click (or Ctrl-click on a Mac with a single-button mouse). A contextual menu will appear, from which you select Get Info.

FIGURE 17.7

Using the Options tab, you can configure a number of settings for a song.

4. To change the song's relative volume, drag the **Volume Adjustment** slider to the left to make the song quieter or to the right to make it louder.

5. To rate the song, click the dot representing the number of stars you want to give the song in the **My Rating** field. For example, to give the song three

stars, click the center (third) dot. Stars will appear up to the point at which you click. In other words, before you click you'll see a dot. After you click a dot, it becomes a star.

6. To set a start time, check the **Start Time** check box and enter a time in the format *minutes:seconds*. When you play the song, it will start playing at the time you enter.

7. To set a stop time, check the **Stop Time** check box and enter a time in the format *minutes:seconds*. When you play the song, it will stop playing at the time you enter.

8. Click **OK**. The window will close and your changes will be saved.

note

When you set a start or stop time, you don't change the song file in any way. You can play the whole song again by unchecking the Start Time or Stop Time check box.

Rating Songs in the Content Pane

You can also rate songs in the Content pane. To do so, follow these steps:

1. Scroll in the Content pane until you see the **My Rating** column (see Figure 17.8).

FIGURE 17.8

You can also rate songs from the Content pane.

2. Select the song you want to rate. Dots will appear in the My Rating column for that song.

3. Click the dot representing the number of stars you want to give the song. The dots up to and including the one on which you clicked will become stars.

Adding and Viewing Album Artwork

note

The My Rating column might not appear in the Content pane for every source. In a later section, you will learn how to choose the columns shown for a given source.

Many CD and album covers are works of art (though many aren't!), and it would be a shame never to see them just because your music has gone digital. With iTunes, you don't need to miss out because you can associate artwork with songs and display that artwork in the iTunes window.

Most of the music you purchase from the iTunes Music Store will include artwork you can view. You can also add artwork to songs and view that in the same way.

Viewing Album Artwork

To view a song's artwork, do one of the following:

tip

Yet another way to rate a song is to open its contextual menu (right-click it with a two-button mouse or Ctrl-click it with a one-button mouse). Select the **My Rating** command and then select the number of stars on the pop-up menu.

■ Click the **Show/Hide Song Artwork** button located under the Source list. The Artwork pane will appear and display the artwork associated with either the currently playing song or the currently selected song (see Figure 17.9). At the top of the artwork, you will see **Selected Song**, which indicates you are viewing the artwork associated with the selected song, or **Now Playing**, which indicates you are viewing artwork associated with the song currently playing.

■ Double-click the artwork to see a larger version in a separate window (see Figure 17.10). The title of the window will be the name of the song with which the artwork is associated.

FIGURE 17.9

You can view the artwork associated with a song in the Artwork pane.

Show/Hide Song Artwork

FIGURE 17.10

You can view a large version of a song's artwork in a separate window.

■ To choose between viewing artwork associated with the selected song or the song currently playing, click the arrow button or text at the top of the Artwork pane. The artwork will change to the other option (for example, if you click Now Playing, it will become Selected Song), and you will see the artwork for that song.

- If you select the Now Playing option, the artwork will change in the Artwork pane as the next song begins playing (unless, of course, the songs use the same artwork). When nothing is playing, you'll see a message saying so in the pane.

- If the song has more than one piece of artwork associated with it, click the arrows that appear at the top of the pane to see each piece of art.

Adding Artwork for Songs

You might want to associate artwork with a song. For example, if a song doesn't have album art associated with it (songs you import from a CD won't), you can add the art yourself. Or, you might want to add the artist's picture or some other meaningful graphic to the song.

If you burn discs for your music, you should add art to your music because you can use iTunes to print jewel case covers that include this art. You'll learn how to print with iTunes in Chapter 20, "Burning Your Own CDs or DVDs."

You can add one or more pieces of art to songs by using the following steps:

1. Prepare the artwork you are going to associate with a song. You can use graphics in the usual formats, such as JPG, TIFF, GIF, and so on.

2. Select the song with which you want to associate the artwork.

3. Open the **Info** window and then click the **Artwork** tab (see Figure 17.11). If the selected song has artwork with it, you will see it in the Artwork pane.

note

If you view the artwork in a separate window, it does not change with the music. When you open the artwork in a new window, it is static, meaning you can only view the image you double-clicked.

tip

A great source of album covers for your CDs are online CD retailers (such as Amazon.com). Most of these provide the album cover as an image when you view a CD. You can download these images to your computer and then add them to songs in your Library.

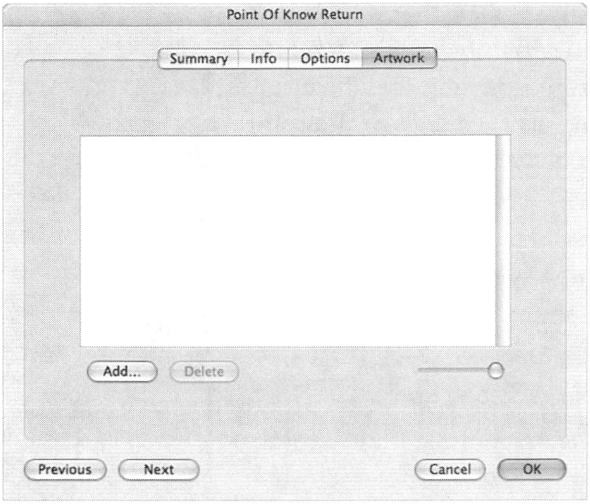

FIGURE 17.11

You use the
Artwork pane to
add artwork to a
song.

4. Click **Add**. A dialog box that enables you to choose an image will appear.

5. Move to and select the image you want to associate with the song.

6. Click **Open** (Windows) or **Choose** (Mac). The image will be added to the Artwork pane of the Info window (see Figure 17.12).

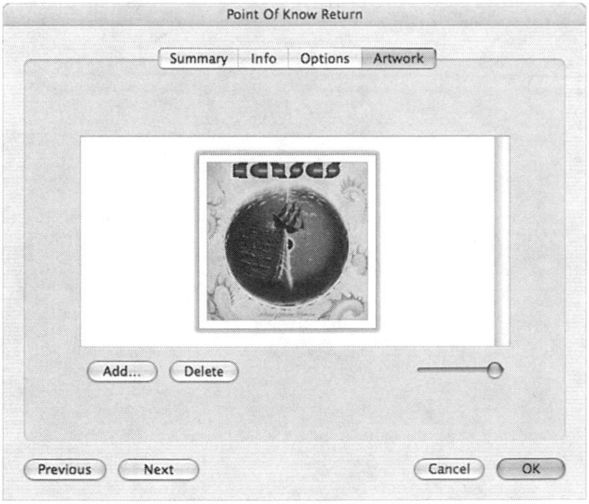

FIGURE 17.12

This song now
has album art
associated
with it.

You can use the slider under the image box to change the size of the previews you see in the window. Drag the slider to the right to make the image larger or to the left to make it smaller. This doesn't change the image;

instead, it only impacts the size of the image as you currently see it in the Info window. This is especially useful when you associate lots of images with a song because you can see them all at the same time.

7. Repeat steps 4–6 to continue adding images to the Artwork pane until you have added all the images for a song.

    The default image for a song is the one on the left of the image box.

8. To change the order of the images, drag them in the image box.

9. Click **OK**. The window will close and the images will be saved with the song (see Figure 17.13).

tip

You can associate art with multiple songs at the same time, such as for an entire CD. To do so, select multiple songs and open the **Info** window. Use the **Artwork** box on the Multiple Song Info window to add images. Either drag images onto this box or double-click it to open the image selection dialog box and then select the images you want to add to all the songs at once.

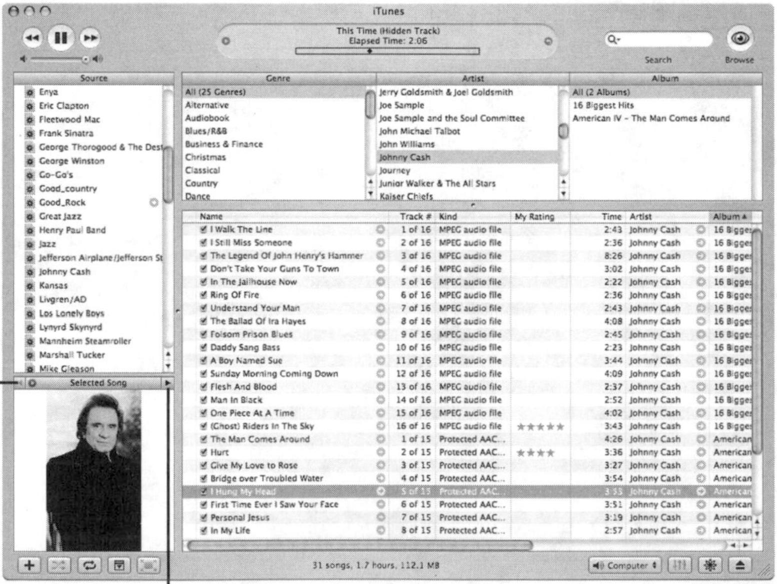

FIGURE 17.13
You can tell this song has multiple images associated with it by the arrows at the top of the Artwork pane. Click an arrow to see its other images.

View previous image

View next image

Customizing the Content Pane

There are a number of ways to customize the columns (tags) that appear in the Content pane. What's more, you can customize the Content pane for each source. The customization you have done for a source (such as a CD or playlist) is remembered and used each time you view that source.

You can select the tags (columns) that are shown for a source by using the following steps:

1. Select the source whose Content pane you want to customize. Its contents will appear in the Content pane.

2. Select **Edit**, **View Options** or press **Ctrl+J** (Windows) or ⌘-**J** (Mac). You will see the View Options dialog box (see Figure 17.14). At the top of the dialog box, you'll see the source for which you are configuring the Content pane. (In Figure 17.4, it is a playlist called Johnny Cash.) You'll also see all the available columns that can be displayed. If a column's check box is checked, that column will be displayed; if not, it won't be shown.

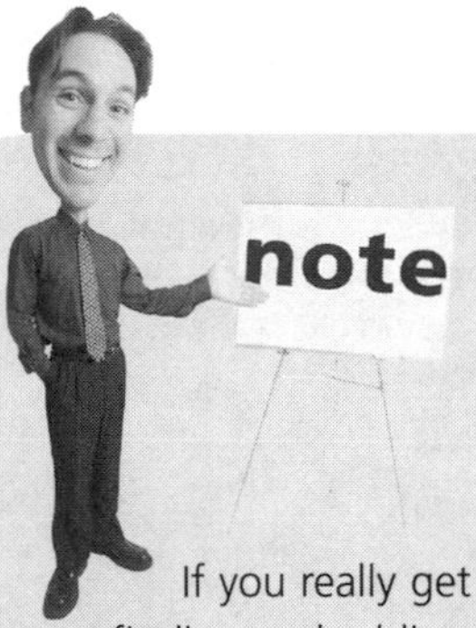

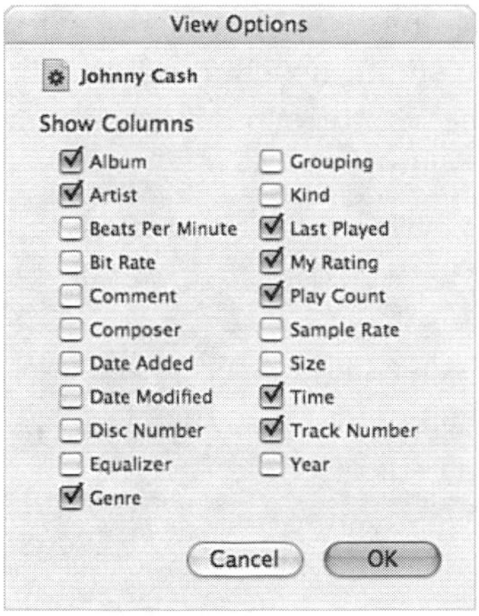

FIGURE 17.14

You can set the columns shown in the Content pane with the View Options dialog box.

View Options

⚙ Johnny Cash

Show Columns

☑ Album   ☐ Grouping
☑ Artist   ☐ Kind
☐ Beats Per Minute   ☑ Last Played
☐ Bit Rate   ☑ My Rating
☐ Comment   ☑ Play Count
☐ Composer   ☐ Sample Rate
☐ Date Added   ☐ Size
☐ Date Modified   ☑ Time
☐ Disc Number   ☑ Track Number
☐ Equalizer   ☐ Year
☑ Genre

(Cancel) (OK)

3. Check the check boxes next to the columns you want to see.

4. Uncheck the check boxes next to the columns you don't want to see.

5. Click **OK**. When you return to the Content pane, only the columns you selected will be shown (see Figure 17.15).

FIGURE 17.15

If you could view all the columns in this Content pane, you would see that they correspond to the check boxes checked in the previous figure.

If you can't see all the columns being displayed, use the horizontal scrollbar to scroll in the Content pane. You can also use the vertical scrollbar to move up and down in the Content pane.

Following are some other ways to customize the Content pane:

- You can change the width of columns by pointing to the line that marks the boundary of the column in the column heading section. When you do, the cursor will become a vertical line with arrows pointing to the left and right. Drag this to the left to make a column narrower or to the right to make it wider. The rest of the columns will move to accommodate the change.

- You can change the order in which columns appear by dragging a column heading to the left or to the right. When you release the mouse button, the column will assume its new position and the other columns will move to accommodate it.

- As you learned when playing a CD, you can sort the Content pane using any of the columns by clicking the column heading by which you want the pane to be sorted. The songs will be sorted according to that criterion, and the column heading will be

note

The only column you can't change (width or location) is the first one (which usually displays the track if you are viewing a CD or playlist and is empty when you are viewing your Library).

highlighted to show it is the current sort column. To change the direction of the sort, click the sort order triangle, which appears only in the Sort column. When you play a source, the songs will play according to the order in which they are sorted in the Content pane, starting from the top of the pane and playing toward the bottom.

THE ABSOLUTE MINIMUM

Hopefully, this chapter turned out to be more exciting than you might have expected based on its title. Although labeling your music might not be fun in itself, it does enable you to do fun things. Setting options for your music enables you to enhance your listening experience, and adding and viewing artwork is fun. Finally, you saw that the Contents pane can be customized to your preferences. As we leave this chapter, here are some nuggets for you to chew on:

- If iTunes can't find information about a CD, you can enter that information yourself by using the Info window you learned about in this chapter.

- If you want to check for information about a CD on command, select **Advanced**, **Get CD Track Names**. (You can also use this command if you turned off the preference that allows iTunes to automatically perform this task.) iTunes will connect to the Internet and attempt to get the CD's information.

- Occasionally, iTunes will find more than one CD that seems to be the one it looked for. When this happens, you will see a dialog box that lists each candidate iTunes found. Select the information you want to apply to the CD by clicking one of the candidates.

- You can submit track names for a CD, label the CD, and select it. Then select **Advanced**, **Submit CD Track Information**. The CD's information will be uploaded into the CDDB and will be provided to other people who use the same CD.

- When adding artwork to songs, you aren't limited to just the related album cover. You can associate any kind of graphics with your songs. For example, you can use pictures of the artists, scenes that relate to the music, pictures you have taken that remind you of the music, and so on.

- If you have looked at the figures in this chapter, you should be able to guess who at least two of my favorite artists are. Can you remember that far back?

- Learn why playlists might just be the best of iTunes' many outstanding features.

- Collect your favorite music in a standard playlist so you hear only the music you want to hear when you want to hear it.

- Change your playlists whenever the spirit moves you.

- Become an iTunes master by creating your own smart playlists to make iTunes choose music for you to listen to based on your criteria.

- Use the Party Shuffle to keep your iTunes experience fresh and interesting.

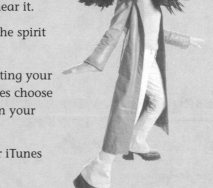

18

CREATING, CONFIGURING, AND USING PLAYLISTS

Of all the cool features iTunes offers (and as you have seen, there lots of cool features), this chapter's topic—playlists—just might be the coolest of them all. Playlists enable you to listen to exactly the music you want to hear, when and how you want to hear it. Do you love a CD but hate a song or two on it? Fine, just set up a playlist without the offensive song. Wish you could hear different songs from a variety of albums? No problem. Ever thought it would be neat if you could pick a style of music and hear your favorites tunes in that style? What about if the tunes you hear are selected for you automatically based on your preferences? With iTunes playlists, you can do all this and more.

Understanding Playlists

Simply put, playlists are custom collections of songs that you create or that iTunes creates for you based on criteria you define. After a playlist has been created, you can listen to it, put it on a CD, move it to your iPod, share it over a network, and more.

There are two kinds of playlists: standard playlists and smart playlists.

The Standard-But-Very-Useful Playlist

A *standard playlist* (which I'll sometimes call just a *playlist* from here on) is a set of songs you define manually. You put the specific songs you want in a playlist and do what you will with them. You can include the same song multiple times, mix and match songs from many CDs, put songs in any order you choose, and basically control every aspect of that music collection (see Figure 18.1).

note

In the Source list, the playlist icon is a blue box with a musical note in its center (see Figure 18.1). A smart playlist has a purple box with a gear inside it (see Figure 18.2). Smart playlists are grouped nearer the top of the Source pane, while standard playlists remain toward the bottom.

FIGURE 18.1

Here is a standard playlist that contains a wide variety of tunes from an assortment of artists.

Playlists are useful for creating CDs or making specific music to which you might want to listen available at the click of the mouse. With a playlist, you can determine exactly which songs are included and the order in which those songs play. Playlists are also easy to create and they never change over time—unless you purposefully change them, of course.

The Extra-Special Smart Playlist

A *smart playlist* is smart because you don't put songs in it manually. Instead, you tell iTunes which kind of songs you want included in it by the attributes of that music, such as genre or artist, and iTunes picks those songs for you (see Figure 18.2). For example, you can create a playlist based on a specific genre, such as Jazz, that you have listened to in the past few days. You can also tell iTunes how many songs to include.

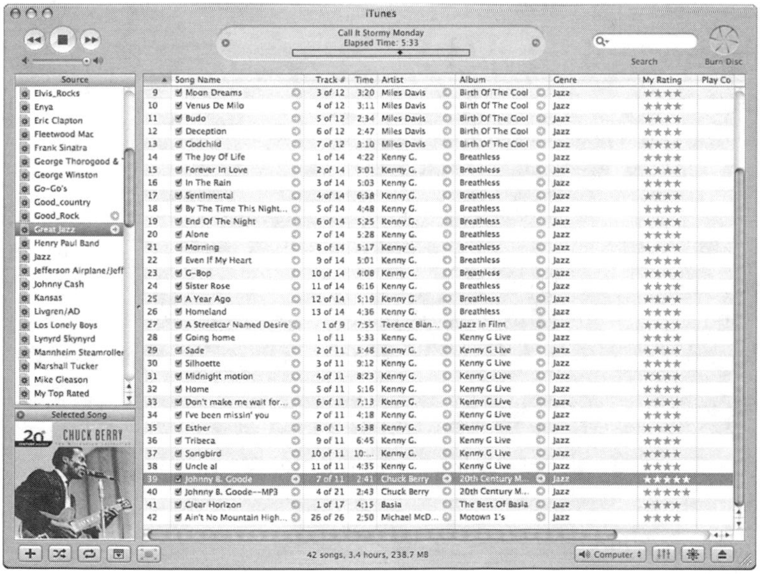

> **caution**
>
> Creating smart playlists depends on your music being properly tagged with information, such as genre, artist, song names, and so on. Sometimes music you add to your Library, such as by MP3 files that are stored on your hard drive, won't have all this information. Before you get going with smart playlists, make sure you have your music properly labeled and categorized. Chapter 17, "Labeling, Categorizing, and Configuring Your Music," explains how you do this.

FIGURE 18.2

On the surface, a smart playlist doesn't look all that different from a playlist, but when you take a closer look, you will see that a smart playlist lives up to its name.

The really cool thing is that smart playlists can be dynamic, meaning the songs they contain are updated over time based on criteria you define. As you add, listen to, or change your music, the contents of a smart playlist can change to match those changes; this happens in real time so the songs included in a smart playlist can change, too. Imagine you have a smart playlist that tells iTunes to include all the music you have in the Jazz genre that is performed by Kenny G, the Pat Metheny Group, Joe Sample, and Larry Carlton. If you make this a "live" smart playlist, iTunes will automatically add any new music from any of the artists to it as you add that music to your Library. The content of a live smart playlist changes over time, depending on the criteria it contains.

note

Whether it's a standard playlist or a smart playlist, the playlist is the starting point for some iTunes activities such as burning a CD. And much of the time, a playlist makes listening to specific music easy and fast.

Building and Listening to Standard Playlists

Although they aren't as smart as their younger siblings, standard playlists are definitely useful because you can choose the exact songs included in them and the order in which those songs will play. In this section, you will learn how to create, manage, and use playlists.

Creating a Standard Playlist

You have two ways to create a playlist. One is to create a playlist that is empty (meaning it doesn't include any songs). The other is to choose songs and then create a playlist that includes those songs.

The place you start depends on what you have in mind. If you want to create a collection of songs but aren't sure which specific songs you want to start with, create an empty playlist. If you know of at least some of the songs you are going to include, choose them and create the playlist. Either way, creating a playlist is simple and you end up in the same place.

Creating an Empty Standard Playlist

You can create an empty playlist from within iTunes by using any of the following techniques:

- Selecting File, New Playlist.
- Pressing Ctrl+N (Windows) or ⌘-N (Mac).
- Clicking the Create Playlist button (see Figure 18.3).

FIGURE 18.3

This playlist has been created and is ready to be renamed.

New playlist

Create Playlist

Whichever method you use will result in an empty playlist whose name will be highlighted to show you that it is ready for you to edit. Type a name for the playlist and press **Enter** (Windows) or **Return** (Mac). The playlist will be renamed and selected. The Content pane will be empty because you haven't added any songs to the playlist yet. You will learn how to do that in the section "Adding Songs to a Playlist" on page **293**.

tip

iTunes keeps playlists in the Source pane in alphabetical order within each group (standard and smart playlists). So, when you rename a playlist, it will jump to the location in the standard playlist section on the Source list to where it belongs.

Creating a Standard Playlist with Songs in It

If you know some songs you want to place in a playlist, you can create the playlist so it includes those songs as soon as you create it. Here are the steps to follow:

1. Browse or search the Library to find the songs you want to be included in the playlist. For example, you can browse for all the songs in a specific genre or search for music by a specific artist.

2. In the Content pane, select the songs you want to place in the playlist.

3. Select **File**, **New Playlist from Selection**. A new playlist will appear on the Source list and will be selected. Its name will be highlighted to indicate that you can edit it, and you will see the songs you selected in the Content pane (see Figure 18.4).

iTunes will attempt to name the playlist by looking for a common denominator in the group of songs you selected. For example, if all the songs are from the same artist, that artist's name will be the playlist's name. Similarly, if the songs are all from the same album, the playlist's name will be the artist's and album's names. Sometimes iTunes picks an appropriate name, and sometimes it doesn't.

tip

You can create a new playlist containing one or more songs by selecting the songs and pressing Ctrl+Shift+N (Windows) or ⌘-Shift-N (Mac).

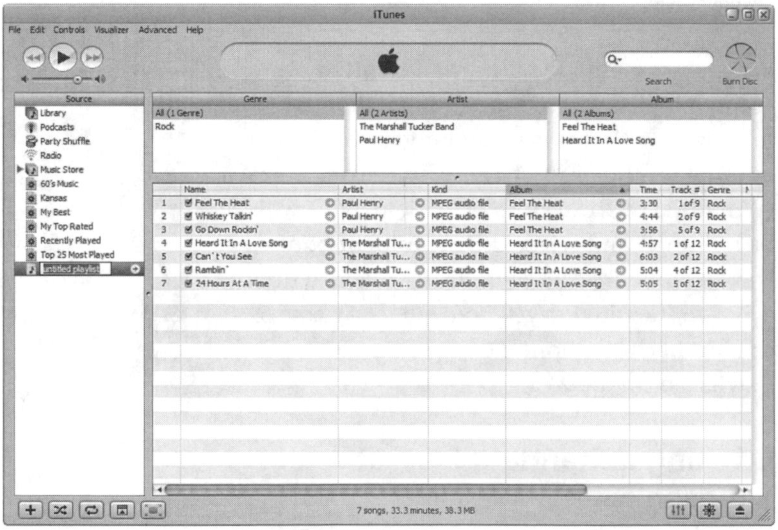

FIGURE 18.4

Because I created a playlist from selected songs, the new playlist contains the songs I selected when I created it.

4. While the playlist name is highlighted, edit the name as needed and then press **Enter** (Windows) or **Return** (Mac). The playlist will be ready for more songs.

Adding Songs to a Playlist

The whole point of creating a playlist is to add songs to it. Whether you created an empty playlist or one that already has some songs in it, the steps to add songs are the same:

tip

You can add the same song to a playlist as many times as you'd like to hear it.

1. Select the **Library** as the source.

2. Browse or search the Library so that songs you want to add to the playlist are shown in the Content pane.

3. Select the songs you want to add to the playlist by clicking them (remember the techniques to select multiple songs at the same time). To select all the songs currently shown in the Content pane, press **Ctrl+A** (Windows) or ⌘-**A** (Mac).

4. Drag the selected songs from the Content pane onto the playlist to which you want to add them. As you drag, you'll see the songs you have selected in a "ghost" image attached to the pointer. When the playlist becomes highlighted and the cursor includes a plus sign (+), release the mouse button (see Figure 18.5). The songs will be added to the playlist.

FIGURE 18.5

You add songs to a playlist by dragging them from the Content pane onto the playlist in the Source pane.

5. Repeat steps 2–4 until you have added all the songs you want to include in the playlist.

6. Select the playlist on the Source list. Its songs will appear in the Content pane (see Figure 18.6). Information about the playlist, such as its playing time, will appear in the Source Information area at the bottom of the iTunes window.

Removing Songs from a Playlist

If you decide you don't want one or more songs included in a playlist, select the songs you want to remove in the playlist's Content pane and press the **Delete** key. A warning prompt will appear. Click **Yes** and the songs will be deleted from the playlist. (If this dialog box annoys you like it does me, check the **Do not ask me again** check box and you won't ever have to see it again.)

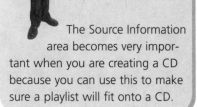

note

The Source Information area becomes very important when you are creating a CD because you can use this to make sure a playlist will fit onto a CD.

FIGURE 18.6

This playlist, called "Songs to Ride By," are tunes that are a good companion while traveling on my motorcycle.

Setting the Order in Which a Playlist's Songs Play

Just like an audio CD, the order in which a playlist's songs play is determined by the order in which they appear in the Content pane (the first song will be the one at the top of the window, the second will be the next one down, and so on). You can drag songs up on the list to make them play earlier or down in the list to make them play later.

Listening to a Standard Playlist

After you have created a playlist, you can listen to it by selecting it on the Source list and using the same controls you use to listen to a CD or music in the Library. You can even search in and browse playlists just as you can the Library or CDs. (That's the real beauty of iTunes; it works the same way no matter what the music source is!)

Deleting a Standard Playlist

If you decide you no longer want a playlist, you can delete it by selecting the playlist on the Source list and pressing the **Delete** key. A prompt will appear; click **Yes** and the playlist will be removed from the Source list. (Be sure to check the **Do not ask me again** check box if you don't want to be prompted in the future.) Even though you've deleted the playlist, the songs in the playlist remain in the Library or in other playlists for your listening pleasure.

note

When you delete a song from a playlist, it *isn't* deleted from the Library. It remains there so you can add it to a different playlist or listen to it from the Library. Of course, if it is included in other playlists, it isn't removed from those either.

Becoming a Musical Genius with Smart Playlists

The basic purpose of a smart playlist is the same as a standard playlist—that is, to contain a collection of songs to which you can listen, put on a CD, and so on. However, the path smart playlists take to this end is completely different from standard playlists. Rather than choosing specific songs as you do in a standard playlist, you tell iTunes the kind of songs you want in your smart playlist and it picks out the songs for you and places them in the playlist. For

tip

You can also change the order in which songs will play by sorting the playlist by its columns. You do this by clicking the column title in the column by which you want the Content pane sorted. You can set the columns that appear for a playlist by selecting Edit, View Options, as you learned to do in the previous chapter.

example, suppose you want to create a playlist that contains all your classical music. Rather than picking out all the songs in your Library that have the Classical genre (as you would do to create a standard playlist), you can use a smart playlist to tell iTunes to select all the classical music for you. The application then gathers all the music with the Classical genre and places that music in a smart playlist.

Understanding Why Smart Playlists Are Called Smart

You create a smart playlist by defining a set of criteria based on any number of tags. After you have created these criteria, iTunes chooses songs that match those tags and places them in the playlist. Another example should help clarify this. Suppose you are a big-time Elvis fan and regularly add Elvis music to your Library. You could create a playlist and manually drag your new Elvis tunes to that playlist. But by using a smart playlist instead, you could define the playlist to include all your Elvis music. Anytime you add more Elvis music to your Library, that music would be added to the playlist automatically so it always contains all the Elvis music in your Library.

You can also base a smart playlist on more than one attribute at the same time. Going back to the Elvis example, you could add the condition that you want only those songs you have rated four stars or higher so the smart playlist contains only your favorite Elvis songs.

As the previous example shows, smart playlists can be dynamic; iTunes calls this *live updating*. When a smart playlist is set to be live, iTunes changes its contents over time to match changes to the music in your Library. If this feature isn't set for a smart playlist, that playlist will contain only those songs that met the criteria at the time the playlist was created.

Finally, you can also link a smart playlist's conditions by the logical expression All or Any. If you use an All logical expression, all the conditions must be true for a song to be included in the smart playlist. If you use the Any option, only one of the conditions has to be met for a song to be included in the smart playlist.

Creating a Smart Playlist

You can create a smart playlist by performing the following steps:

1. Select **File**, **New Smart Playlist** or hold down the **Shift** (Windows) or **Option** (Mac) key and click the **New Playlist** button, which becomes the **New Smart Playlist** button when the Shift or Option key is pressed down. You will see the Smart Playlist dialog box (see Figure 18.7).

> **note**
>
> iTunes includes several smart playlists by default. These include 60's Music (music based on the Year attribute being 1960 to 1969), My Top Rated (all the music you have rated three stars or above), Recently Played (songs you have played within the past two weeks), and Top 25 Most Played (the 25 songs you have played most often). To see the songs that meet these conditions, select a smart playlist and you will see its songs in the Content pane.

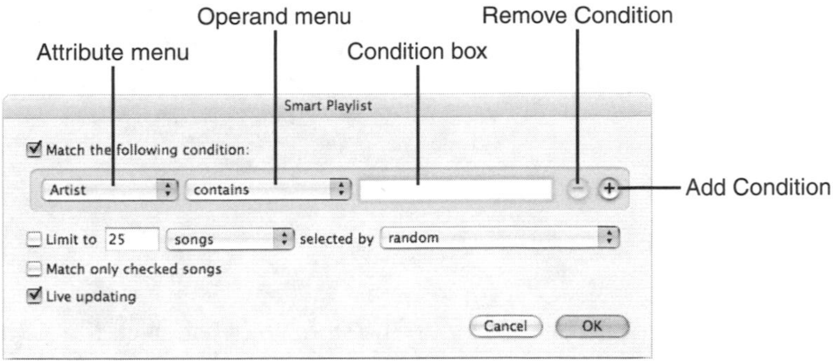

Operand menu

Remove Condition

Attribute menu

Condition box

FIGURE 18.7

The Smart
Playlist dialog
box enables you
to create playlists
based on a single
tag or many of
them.

Smart Playlist

☑ Match the following condition:

Artist ▢ contains ▢ [   ] ⊖ ⊕ ——— Add Condition

☐ Limit to 25 songs ▢ selected by random ▢

☐ Match only checked songs
☑ Live updating

Cancel   OK

2. Select the first tag on which you want
   the smart playlist to be based in the
   Attribute menu. For example, you can
   select Artist, Genre, My Rating, or Year,
   among many others. The Operand
   menu will be updated so that it is applicable to the attribute you selected. For
   example, if you select Artist, the
   Operand menu will include contains,
   does not contain, is, is not, starts with,
   and ends with.

3. Select the operand you want to use on the
   Operand menu. For example, if you want to
   match data exactly, select **is**. If you want
   the condition to be more loose, select
   contains.

4. Type the condition you want to match in
   the **Condition** box. The more you type,
   the more specific the condition will be. As
   an example, if you select Artist in step 1,
   select contains in step 2, and type **Elvis** in
   this step, the condition would look like the
   one shown in Figure 18.8 and would find
   all songs that include Elvis, Elvis Presley,
   Elvis Costello, Elvisiocity, and so on. If you
   typed Elvis Presley in the Condition box
   and left the contains operand, iTunes
   would include only songs whose artist
   includes Elvis Presley, such as Elvis Presley,
   Elvis Presley and His Back-up Band, and
   so on.

tip

You can also create a new
smart playlist by pressing
Ctrl+Alt+N (Windows) or
Option-⌘-N (Mac).

note

As you make selections
on the Attribute menu and
type conditions in the Condition
box, iTunes will attempt to automatically match what you type to
data from the songs in your
Library. If your Library includes Elvis
music and you use Artist as an
attribute, iTunes will enter Elvis
Presley in the Condition box for
you when you start typing "Elvis."

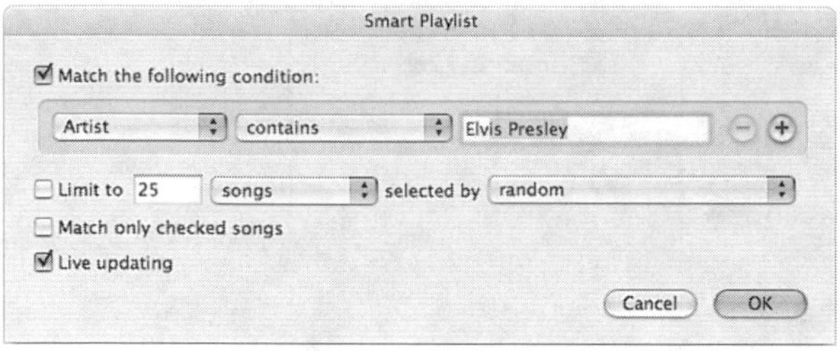

FIGURE 18.8

This smart
playlist is getting
smarter.

5. To add another condition to the smart playlist, click the **Add Condition**
button. A new, empty condition will appear (see Figure 18.9). At the top of
the dialog box, the all or any menu will also appear.

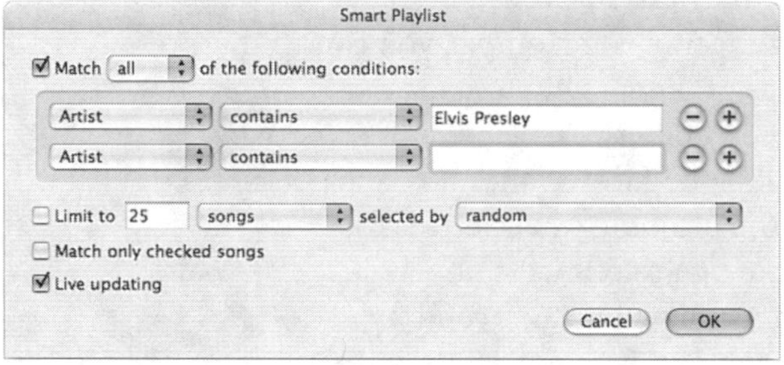

FIGURE 18.9

This smart
playlist now con-
tains two condi-
tions; both are
currently based
on Artist.

6. Select the second tag on which you want the smart playlist to be based in the
second condition's **Attribute** menu. For example, if you want to include
songs from a specific genre, select **Genre** on the menu.

7. Select the operand you want to use in the **Operand** menu, such as contains,
is, and so on.

8. Type the condition you want to match in the **Condition** box. If you selected
Genre in step 6, type the genre from which the music in the playlist should
come. As you type, iTunes will try to match the genre you type with those in
your Library.

9. Repeat steps 5–8 to add more conditions to the playlist until you have all the
conditions you want to include (see Figure 18.10).

FIGURE 18.10

This smart
playlist is
approaching the
genius level; it
now includes
three conditions.

10. Select **all** on the menu at the top of the dialog box if all the conditions must be met for a song to be included in the smart playlist, or select **any** if only one of them must be met. For example, you could create a smart playlist based on multiple Artist conditions and the playlist would feature music by those artists. In this case, you would choose any so that if a song is associated with *any* of the artists for which you created a condition, it would be included in the playlist. As a contrasting example, if you want the playlist to include songs you have rated as three stars or better by a specific artist, you would include both of these conditions and then select all in the menu so that both conditions would have to be met for a song to be included (a song is both by the artist and is rated with three or more stars).

    You can limit the length of a smart playlist based on a maximum number of songs, the time it plays, or the size of the files it includes. You set these limits using the Limit to check box and menus.

11. If you want to limit the playlist, check the **Limit to** check box. If you don't want to set a limit on the playlist, leave the check box unchecked and skip to step 15.

12. Select the attribute by which you want to limit the playlist in the first menu; by default, this menu has songs selected (see Figure 18.11). Your choices include the number of songs (just songs on the menu), the time the playlist will play (in minutes or hours), and the size of the files the playlist contains (in MB or GB).

13. Type the data appropriate for the limit you selected in the **Limit to** box. For example, if you selected minutes in the menu, type the maximum length of the playlist in minutes in the box. If you selected songs, enter the maximum number of songs that can be included in the playlist.

> **tip**
>
> If you want to remove a condition from a smart playlist, click the Remove button for the condition you want to remove.

> **note**
>
> If you include more than one condition based on the same attribute, you usually don't want to use the All option because the conditions will likely be mutually exclusive, and using the All option will result in no songs being included in the playlist because no song will be able to meet all the conditions at the same time.

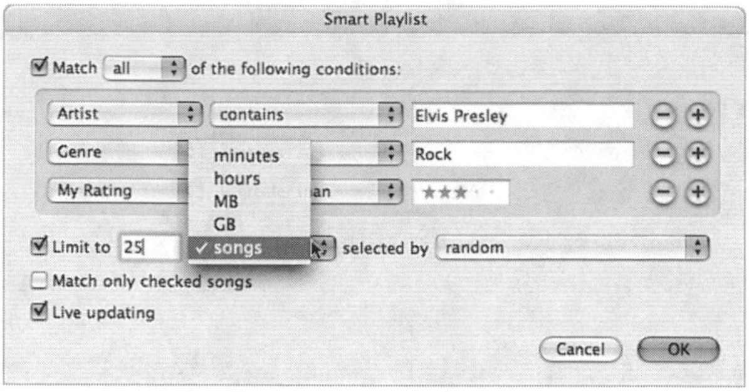

FIGURE 18.11

You can choose
to limit a smart
playlist to a
number of songs,
a length of time,
or by disk space.

14. Select how you want iTunes to choose the songs it includes based on the limit
    you selected by using the **selected by** menu. This menu has many options,
    including to choose songs randomly, based on your rating, how often the
    songs are played, and so on (see Figure 18.12).

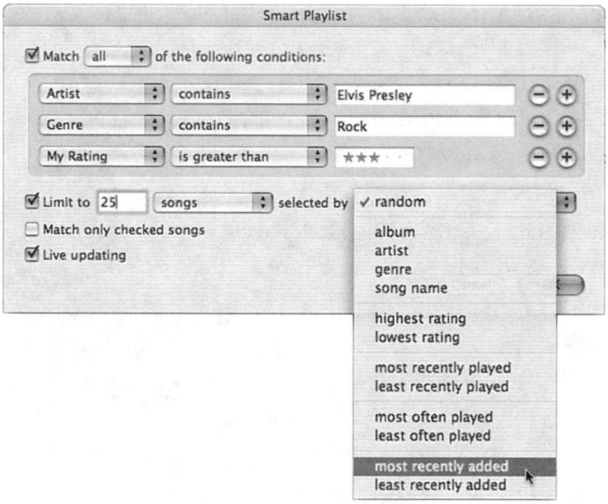

FIGURE 18.12

These options tell
iTunes how you
want it to choose
songs for a smart
playlist when
you limit that
playlist's size.

15. If you want the playlist to include only songs whose check box in the
    Content pane is checked, check the **Match only checked songs** check box.
    If you leave this check box unchecked, iTunes will include all songs that
    meet the playlist's conditions, even if you have unchecked their check box in
    the Content pane.

16. If you want the playlist to be dynamic, meaning that iTunes will update its
    contents over time, check the **Live updating** check box. If you uncheck this
    check box, the playlist will include only those songs that meet the playlist's
    conditions when you create it.

17. Review the playlist to see whether it contains the conditions and settings you
    want (see Figure 18.13).

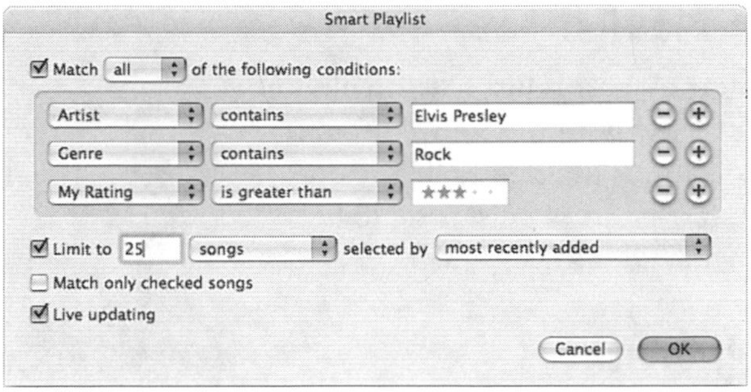

FIGURE 18.13
This playlist will include up to 25 songs of the best (rated at four stars or more) of my Elvis music from the Rock genre; as I add music to my Library, it will also be added to this playlist if it meets these conditions.

18. Click **OK** to create the playlist. You will move to the Source list, the smart playlist will be added and selected, and its name will be ready for you to edit. Also, the songs in your Library that match the criteria in the playlist will be added to it and the current contents of the playlist will be shown in the Content pane.

19. Type the playlist's name and press **Enter** (Windows) or **Return** (Mac). The smart playlist will be complete (see Figure 18.14).

FIGURE 18.14
If you compare the songs in this smart playlist to the criteria shown in the previous figure, you will see they match.

Listening to a Smart Playlist

Listening to a smart playlist is just like listening to other sources: You select it on the Source list and use the playback controls to listen to it. The one difference is that, if a smart playlist is set to be live, its contents can change over time.

Changing a Smart Playlist

To change the contents of a smart playlist, you change the smart playlist's criteria (remember that iTunes actually places songs in a smart playlist). Use the following steps to do this:

1. Select the smart playlist you want to change.

2. Select **File**, **Edit Smart Playlist**. The Smart Playlist dialog box will appear, and the playlist's current criteria will be shown.

3. Use the techniques you learned when you created a playlist to change its criteria (see Figure 18.15). For example, you can remove conditions by clicking their Remove buttons. You can also add more conditions or change the other settings for the playlist.

note

The smart playlist I built as an example in these steps can be interpreted as follows: Include songs by Elvis Presley in the Rock genre that I have rated at four or five stars. Limit the playlist to 25 songs, and if I have more songs that meet the conditions than this time limit allows, select the songs to include based on those I have most recently added to my Library. Finally, keep adding songs that meet these conditions as I add new Elvis music to my Library.

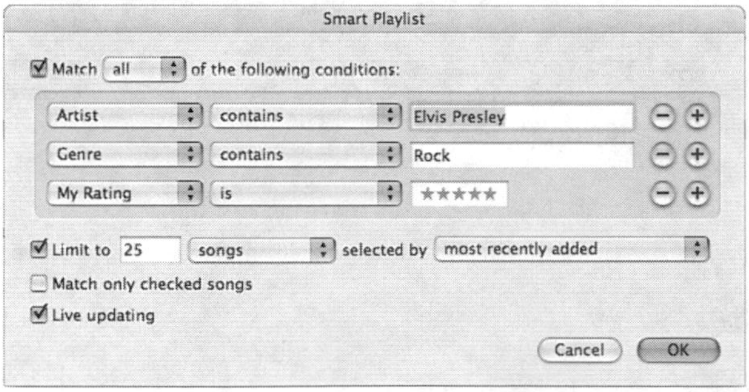

FIGURE 18.15

I changed the conditions on this smart playlist so that only five-star songs are included.

4. Click **OK**. Your changes will be saved and the contents of the playlist will be updated to match the current criteria.

You can also change a smart playlist using the same techniques you use on other sources, such as sorting it, selecting the columns you see when you view it, and so on.

Doing the Party Shuffle

iTunes includes some "built-in" playlists (such as Purchased Music) you might not even recognize as being playlists based on the chapter so far. But, these special playlists are playlists indeed.

One of the most useful of these is the Party Shuffle that you'll see near the top of the Content pane. This is actually a playlist that enables you to play a source you select in shuffle mode. If you like to keep things interesting, the Party Shuffle is a good way to do so because you can hear the songs in any source in a random order without having to change the source itself. After you try this special playlist, you'll probably use it as often as I do, which is to say, quite a lot. To do the party shuffle, follow these steps:

1. Select **Party Shuffle** on the Source pane. You'll see a dialog box explaining what the Party Shuffle is; read it, check the **Do not show this message again** check box, and click **OK**. You'll see songs fill the Content pane and some controls will appear at the bottom (see Figure 18.16).

2. Select the source of music you want to shuffle on the **Source** pop-up menu. You can choose your Library or any playlist (standard or smart).

3. If you want songs you have rated higher to be played more frequently, check the **Play higher rated songs more often**

note

Just like other sources, when you select a smart playlist, its information will be shown in the Source Information section at the bottom of the window. This can be useful if you want to create a CD or just to see how big the playlist is (by number of songs, time, or file size). Remember, though, that because a smart playlist's contents can change over time, its source information can also change over time. So, just because a smart playlist will fit on a CD today doesn't mean it still will tomorrow (or even later today).

tip

You can also edit a smart playlist by selecting it and opening the Info window (which also opens the Smart Playlist dialog box). Plus, you can open the playlist's contextual menu by right-clicking (Windows or Mac) or Ctrl-clicking it (Mac) and selecting Edit Smart Playlist.

check box. This causes iTunes to choose songs with higher star ratings more frequently than those with lower or no star ratings.

4. Use the two **Display** pop-up menus to choose how many songs are shown that have been played recently and that are upcoming. Your choices range from 0 to 100 on both menus. When you make a selection, the songs in the Content pane will reflect your choice.

tip

To delete a smart playlist, select it on the Source list and press **Delete**. Confirm the deletion at the prompt, and the playlist will be removed from the Source list.

FIGURE 18.16

The Party Shuffle source might seem odd to you at first, but once you get to know it, you'll love it.

The current song is always highlighted in the Content pane with a blue bar. Songs that have played are grayed out and are listed above the current song. Songs that will be played are in regular text and appear below the current song.

5. If you want to change the order in which upcoming songs will play, drag them up or down in the Content pane.

6. When you are ready to hear the tunes, use the same playback controls that you use with any other source.

The Party Shuffle source will play forever. After it plays a song, it moves one of the recently played songs off that list, moves the song it just played into the recently played section, highlights and plays the next song, and adds another one to the upcoming songs section. This process will continue until you stop the music.

As the Party Shuffle plays, you can keep moving upcoming songs around to change the order in which they will play. You can also press the right-arrow key to skip to the next song.

In addition, you can manually add songs to the Party Shuffle. View a source to find the song you want to add. Open the song's contextual menu by right-clicking it (see Figure 18.17). Select **Play Next in Party Shuffle** to have the song play next, or select **Add to Party Shuffle** to add the song to the end of the upcoming songs list.

> **note**
>
> The Party Shuffle is one item for which the Source Information data doesn't make a lot of sense. Because the list is always changing, the source information doesn't really mean a lot. It simply shows information based on the songs currently shown in the Content pane, which change after each song is played.

FIGURE 18.17

To add a song to the Party Shuffle, use one of the Party Shuffle commands on its contextual menu.

THE ABSOLUTE MINIMUM

Playlists are a great way to customize the music in your Library for listening purposes, to create a CD, or to manage the music on an iPod. As you learned in this chapter, playlists include a specific collection of songs that you choose, whereas iTunes chooses the songs in a smart playlist based on the conditions you specify.

Playlists are a great way to select specific music to which you want to listen. You can make them as long or as short as you like, and you can mix and match songs to your heart's content.

Use the Party Shuffle playlist to spice up your music experience by keeping it fresh.

Smart playlists can really enhance your listening experience. Following are some ideas you might find interesting for your own smart playlists:

- Be diligent about rating your songs. Then create a smart playlist for one of your favorite genres that also includes a rating condition. Enable this playlist to be updated live. Such a playlist would always contain your favorites songs in this genre, even as you add more songs to your Library.

- Create a smart playlist based only on genre and allow it to be updated live. This playlist would make it easy to listen to that genre, and it would always contain all your music in that genre.

- Create a smart playlist that includes several of your favorite artists (remember to choose Any in the top menu) and limit the number of songs to 20 or so. Have iTunes select the songs in a random order. Playing this playlist might provide an interesting mix of music. If you include a My Rating condition, you can cause only your favorite music to be included in this group. Make a dynamic list, and it will change over time as you add music to your Library.

- Create a smart playlist for your favorite artists and allow them to be updated live. As you add music by the artists to your Library, just play the related playlist to hear all the music by that artist, including the new music you add.

- If you like to collect multiple versions of the same song, create a playlist based on song name. Allow it to be updated live, and this playlist will contain all the versions of this song you have in your Library.

- Get to know the iTunes Equalizer.

- Make your music sound just the way you want it to.

- Use presets to do the same thing, only faster and easier.

- Equalize your music like a pro by adding the Equalizer menu to the iTunes Content pane.

19

EQUALIZING YOUR MUSIC

In addition to the great tools iTunes provides to enable you to choose which music you want to listen to, the application also enables you to control *how* that music sounds. You do this with the Equalizer. Using this feature, you can easily customize how music sounds to suit your system, hearing, and listening preferences.

Touring the iTunes Equalizer

Like a hardware graphic equalizer, the iTunes Equalizer enables you to change the relative volume levels of various frequencies of the sounds of which music is made (see Figure 19.1).

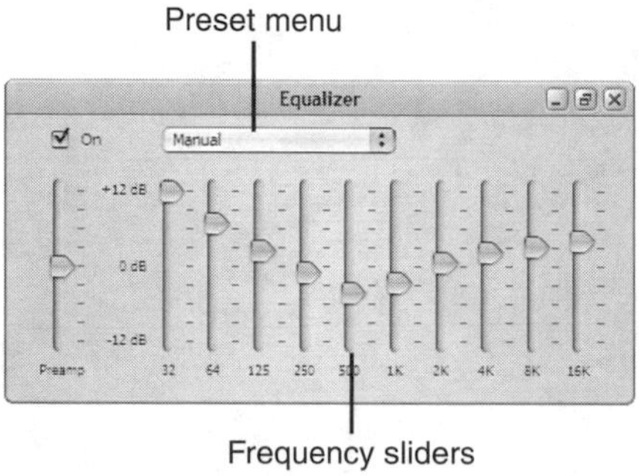

FIGURE 19.1
The Equalizer puts you in charge of how your music sounds.

To open the Equalizer, click the **Equalizer** button on the right side of the bottom of the iTunes window (it contains three blue sliders). On Macintoshes, you can also open the Equalizer by selecting **Window**, **Equalizer** or by pressing ⌘**-2**. The Equalizer window will appear.

At the top of the window, you will see the On check box. When this is checked, the Equalizer is active and will affect how your music sounds. If the check box is not checked, the Equalizer settings don't impact the way your music sounds.

Along the left side of the window is the Preamp slider. The Preamp setting changes the relative volumes of all the frequencies at the same time. For example, if a song is recorded at a low volume level, you can drag the Preamp slider up to make its relative volume louder. Similarly, you can drag the slider down to make a song's relative volume level lower.

When you see the values in the Equalizer window, remember that they are all relative and change only the volume of frequencies relative to one another, not the volume of your system.

The bulk of the window consists of a set of sliders that control the relative volume of a number of sound frequencies that are listed underneath the sliders, from 32Hz to 16KHz (kilohertz). The left end of the range represents lower or bass sound, whereas the middle is the mid-range and the right end is the higher or treble sound. The sliders all have a range from –12 to +12 decibels (dB). This is relative to 0, which means the volume level is not affected.

Above the frequency sliders and to the right of the On check box is the Presets menu. Presets are collections of slider settings, and you can choose to apply them without having to adjust each slider individually. iTunes includes a number of presets, and you can create and save your own presets in the menu.

You can use the Equalizer in a couple of ways: You can set it for all the music you are listening to at a specific time, or you can associate a specific preset with a song so those settings will be used each time that song plays.

As you play with the Equalizer, realize that there are no right or wrong settings. It is entirely up to your listening pleasure. If some adjustment makes the music sound "worse" to you, go onto something else. You might find that some of the default presets don't help the way the music sounds at all. It is all relative to your speakers, the music to which you are listening, and your musical ear.

The abbreviation *dB* stands for *decibels*, which is a measure of the power of sound. Sounds with higher decibels are louder. The decibel measurements are on a logarithmic scale, which means they do not follow a linear progression. In other words, 100 dB is not 10 times louder than 10 dB. To give you an example of this, normal human conversation is about 60 dB, whereas a jet engine at close range is about 150 dB.

Configuring the Equalizer Manually

To configure the Equalizer manually, perform the following steps:

1. Select some music, such as a playlist, and play it.
2. Open the **Equalizer**.
3. Check the **On** check box, if it isn't checked already. This makes the Equalizer active.
4. Select **Manual** on the Presets slider. This puts the Equalizer in the Manual mode. (If you make an adjustment to any of the sliders, the Equalizer will switch to the Manual mode automatically.)
5. If you want to change the relative volume of all the songs you are playing, drag the **Preamp** slider up to make the music louder or down to make the music quieter.
6. Set each of the frequency sliders to change the relative volume of that frequency. Drag a slider up to make its frequency louder or down to make it quieter. For example, to make music more bassy, drag the sliders for the lower end of the frequency scale up. This will increase the volume of lower

sounds and make the bass components of music more prominent. Adjust the other sliders to change the relative volumes of their frequencies until the music sounds "better" to you (see Figure 19.2).

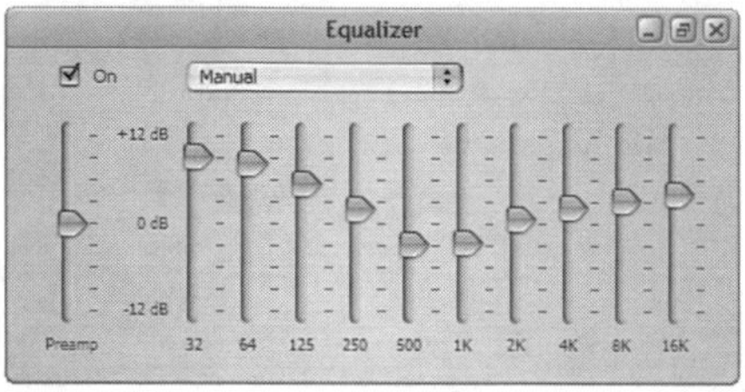

FIGURE 19.2

It's all relative; this classic equalizer pattern enhances both the bass and treble components of music.

7. When you are done making changes, you can click in the iTunes window to make it active or close the Equalizer to get it out of the way (it continues to work even if you can't see it).

Working with Presets

Dragging all the sliders up and down is lots of fun and all, but it isn't something you are likely to want to do a lot. Presets are collections of slider settings that you can apply just by selecting one on the Presets menu. You can use iTunes' default presets or you can create your own.

Selecting a Default Preset

Working with iTunes' default presets is a snap, as you can see from the following steps:

1. Play some music.

2. Open the **Equalizer** and turn it on.

3. Open the **Presets** menu (see Figure 19.3). In the bottom section of the menu, you will see the set of default presets available to you.

4. Select the preset you want to apply. When you return to the Equalizer window, the sliders will be set according to the preset you selected (see Figure 19.4).

5. Continue selecting presets until the music sounds just right.

FIGURE 19.3

Are there enough presets for you?

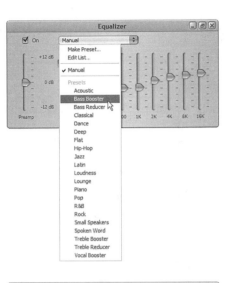

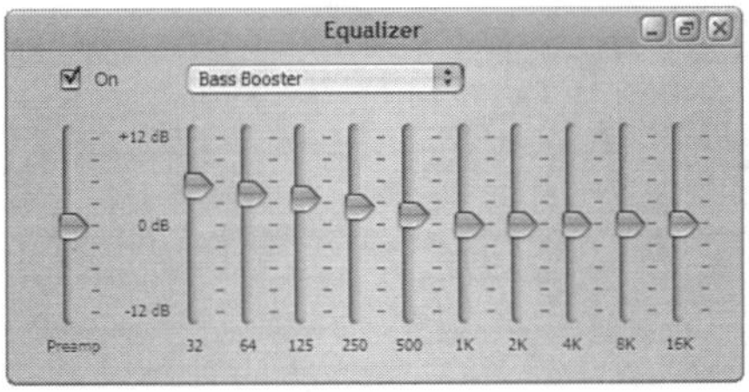

FIGURE 19.4

The Bass Booster preset does just what it sounds like it will.

The specific slider settings you should use depend on many factors, including your sound system; the music to which you are listening; and last, but certainly not least, your personal preferences. For example, if you use speakers that have poor bass performance, you might want to consistently use higher bass settings (assuming you like to hear lots of bass, of course). If you have a system with a powerful subwoofer, you might not need any bass enhancement.

Creating Your Own Presets

If none of the default presets are quite right, you can create your own presets so that you can return to a specific Equalizer configuration easily and quickly. This is useful when a preset of your own making is just what you like and you want to be able to go back to it easily. To create a preset, follow these steps:

1. Open the **Equalizer**, turn it on, and set its sliders to the settings you want to reuse.

tip

A good way to create custom presets is to choose one of the default presets and make changes to it. Then, you can save the preset with your changes as a new preset.

2. Open the **Presets** menu and select **Make Preset**. You'll see the Make Preset dialog box (see Figure 19.5).

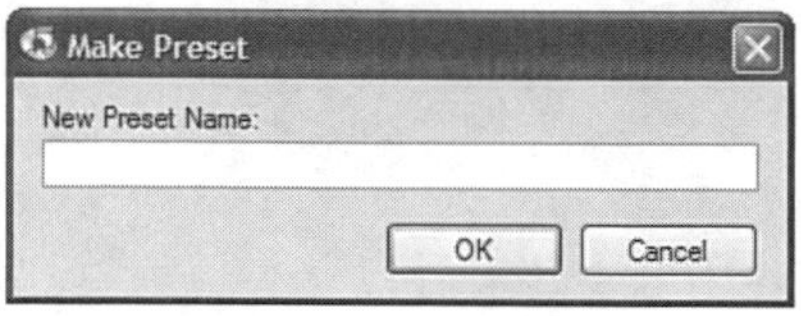

FIGURE 19.5

To save your custom Equalizer settings, you can create your own presets.

3. In the **New Preset Name** box, type a name for your preset.

4. Click **OK**. The preset will be added to the Presets menu, and you can choose it just like one of the defaults (see Figure 19.6).

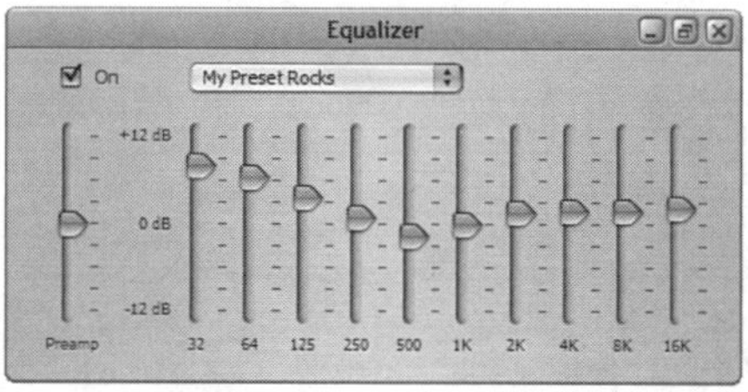

FIGURE 19.6

The preset called "My Preset Rocks" is a creation of yours truly.

Configuring the Preset Menu

As you saw in the previous section, you can add presets to the Presets menu. You can also remove presets from it to create a custom Presets menu. For example, you might want to get rid of presets you will never use so that the menu offers fewer choices. Or, you might want to rename a preset. To do these tasks, use the following steps:

1. Open the **Presets** menu and select **Edit List**. The Edit Presets dialog box will appear (see Figure 19.7).

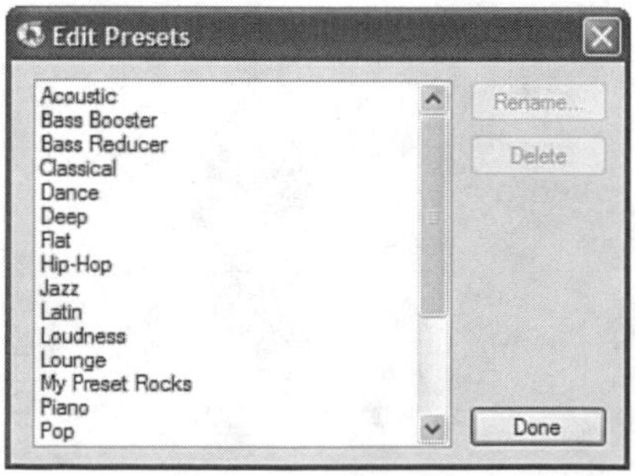

FIGURE 19.7

You can customize the Presets menu so it contains only those presets that are useful to you.

2. To remove a preset from the menu, select it, click **Delete**, and confirm your decision at the prompt by clicking **Yes**. You will see a prompt asking whether you want to remove the preset from the songs that are set to use it as well (you'll learn about this in the next section). Click **Yes** if you want to remove the preset from the songs or **No** if you want to retain the settings even though the preset will be removed from the menu. The preset will be removed from the menu.

3. To rename a preset, select it and click **Rename**. The Rename dialog box will appear. Type a new name for the preset and click **OK**. It will be renamed on the menu.

Setting the Equalizer for Specific Songs

You can apply specific Equalizer presets to individual songs so those songs will always play with the settings you associate with them. You can do this from the Info window or Content pane.

There are several situations in which you might want to set the Equalizer for specific songs. One case might be for songs whose recording level is so low that you have a hard time hearing it—you can use a preset so its volume level is adjusted automatically each time you play it. Or, you might like to use different presets with different types of music. By applying a preset to the songs of a specific type, that preset will be used whenever those songs are played. Suppose you like to listen to both Classical and Rock and have a preset for each. By associating a preset with the Classical music and another with the Rock music, the appropriate preset will be used when you play that music.

Setting the Equalizer in the Info Window

To configure the Equalizer for a specific song, perform the following steps:

1. Select the song to which you want to apply Equalizer settings and open the Info window.

2. Click the **Options** tab.

3. Select the preset you want to apply to the song in the **Equalizer Preset** menu (see Figure 19.8).

4. Click **OK**. The Info window will close and the preset will be associated with the song.

Assuming that the Equalizer is turned on, the preset you associate with a song will be used each time that song plays.

FIGURE 19.8
Remember the
preset "My Preset
Rocks" from ear-
lier in the
chapter? It's
back....

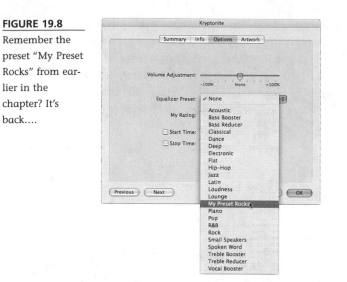

Using the Equalizer from the Content Pane

You can also configure the preset for a song from the Content pane. First, show the Equalizer in the Content pane. Then, you can select a preset for the song.

Showing the Equalizer in the Content Pane

To show the Equalizer in the Content pane, you use the View Options dialog box to show its column. In case you don't remember how, the following steps will lead the way:

1. Select the source for which you want the Equalizer column to be displayed, such as the Library or a playlist.

2. Open the View Options dialog box by selecting **Edit**, **View Options**.

3. Check the **Equalizer** check box and close the dialog box. The Equalizer column will be added to the Content pane for the selected source.

tip

If you can't see the Equalizer column, scroll in the Content pane until you do. Or, drag the Equalizer column to the left in the Content pane so you can see it more easily.

Setting the Equalizer in the Content Pane

After you have added the Equalizer column to the Content pane, you can easily associate a preset with a song. For the song with which you want to associate a preset, click the button that appears on the left side of the Equalizer column. The Presets menu will appear (see Figure 19.9). Select the preset you want to apply to the song. It will be used each time the song is played. To change the preset, select a different one or select None to remove the preset from the song.

FIGURE 19.9

Does this menu look familiar to you?

THE ABSOLUTE MINIMUM

You can use the iTunes Equalizer to fine-tune your music to suit your system, your listening tastes, and the kind of music you listen to. Before we leave this topic, here are a few Equalizer tidbits for you:

- You can reduce the Equalizer window so that you see only the On check box and the Presets menu. This makes it easier to keep the window out of your way, but you can still change its settings by selecting presets to apply. To do this on Windows computers, click the Resize button on the Equalizer window's title bar. On Macs, click the Zoom button in the Equalizer window.

- You can apply the same preset to multiple songs at the same time by selecting the songs to which you want to apply the preset and opening the Info window (which becomes the Multiple Song Information window). Select the preset you want to apply to the selected songs on the Equalizer Preset menu and click OK. The preset will be applied to all the songs you selected.

- Which is more decibels, a jet plane engine up close or a typical rock concert in front of the speakers? In general, the noise levels in these environments are roughly the same. Noises at this level can be damaging to your hearing. So, if you are hanging out next to jet engines or are planning on going to a rock concert, consider wearing hearing protection. After all, you want to protect your hearing so you can take advantage of iTunes, right?

IN THIS CHAPTER

- Know the three disc formats that you can burn.
- Prepare your computer to burn.
- Burn, baby, burn.
- Make that disc look simply marvelous.

20

BURNING YOUR OWN CDs OR DVDs

When you are at your computer, you'll likely use iTunes to listen to your music because you can easily get to the specific music to which you want to listen, such as by using your Library, creating standard playlists and smart playlists, and so on. When you are on the move, you'll probably use your iPod to listen to your tunes. At other times, you might want to put music on a CD to take with you, such as when you are traveling in a car with a standard CD player. Or, you might want to back up your music on a DVD to keep your collection safe. Using iTunes, you can quickly and easily burn CDs or DVDs so they contain any collections of music you want them to.

Understanding the Types of Discs You Can Burn

You can burn several types of disc formats with iTunes, and each of these formats is useful for specific purposes. With iTunes, you can burn the following types of discs:

- **Audio CD**—When you burn a CD in this format, you can play it in any CD player, such as the one in your car, a boombox, or a home theater. And that is the primary benefit of this format: CD players are ubiquitous, so you can play audio CDs just about anywhere.

- **MP3 CD**—You can place your tunes on a CD in the MP3 format and then play those discs using any player that can handle MP3 music. Many newer CD players for cars and home theater systems can play MP3 CDs, so this is a good thing. The benefit of using the MP3 format is just what you might think it is—you can put about three times as much music on a single disc as you can with a disc that uses the Audio CD format.

- **Data CD or DVD**—This format is the same that's used to store music files on your computer's hard drive. In fact, when you choose this format, you simply replicate songs as they are on your computer on a disc. The primary purpose of this format is to back up your music to protect it from loss should something go horribly wrong with your computer. You can also copy songs to a disc to move them from one computer to another.

Getting Your Computer Ready to Burn

To burn CDs or DVDs, your computer must have a drive capable of writing to CD or DVD. Fortunately, most computers include a CD-RW (CD-Rewritable) drive you can use to burn CDs. Many also include a DVD-R, DVD-RW, DVD+R, or DVD+RW drive you can use to create DVDs.

To determine whether your computer is ready to burn, open the **iTunes Preferences** dialog box and open the **Burning** pane (see Figures 20.1 and 20.2). At the top of this pane, you'll see the text CD Burner. If iTunes can find one or more drives capable of burning CDs or DVDs, they will be shown here. If iTunes does recognize a drive, you are good to go and can proceed to the next section.

note

If you have a Mac and it includes a SuperDrive, you can create CDs or DVDs.

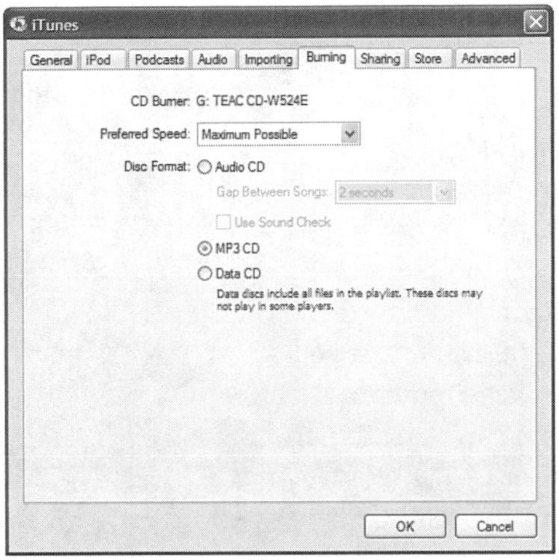

FIGURE 20.1

This Windows computer has a CD burner that is ready to go.

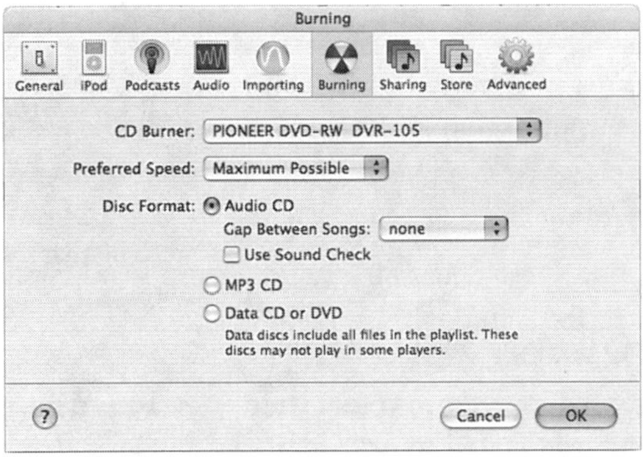

FIGURE 20.2

This Macintosh includes a SuperDrive that can be used to burn CDs or DVDs.

If a drive is not shown on this pane, there are two possibilities. One is that a capable drive is installed but is not functioning correctly, so it's not recognized by iTunes. The other is that your computer doesn't have a capable drive.

If your computer does have a drive capable of writing to a disc but it is not recognized by iTunes, it is likely that your drive is not working. You'll have to use troubleshooting techniques to repair and configure the drive to get it working again. I don't have room in this book to cover this topic because it can be complicated. If you don't know how to do this or you don't know someone who does, you can consult one of the many books

note

In Figure 20.2, you might notice that a menu appears next to the CD Burner text. That's because the machine used for this screenshot includes two drives capable of burning CDs. In this case, you can select from the menu the drive you want iTunes to use to create a disc.

available on this topic to help you get the drive working properly.

Selecting and installing a CD-RW or DVD-RW drive in your computer is beyond the scope of this book. If your computer doesn't have at least a CD-RW drive, it is likely a fairly old machine because these drives have been standard on most computers for a couple of years. Most current machines include a DVD-RW drive, too. If you don't want to purchase a new computer that includes a writable drive, you can purchase an external or internal CD-RW or DVD-RW drive and install it in your computer fairly easily.

Burning Discs

Burning a disc from iTunes is quite straightforward, as you will see from the information in this section.

Preparing Content to Burn

The first phase in the process is to choose the content you want to place onto a disc. You do this by creating a playlist. In Chapter 18, "Creating, Configuring, and Using Playlists," you learned everything you need to know about creating and using playlists, so I don't need to repeat that information here.

One thing you need to keep in mind as you create a playlist for CD or DVD is the size of the playlist. Obviously, you can't put more music on a CD or DVD than there is room to store files on the disc. How large a playlist can be to be put on a disc depends on the format you will be using. If you are burning an Audio CD, you can get about 70 minutes of music on the disc. If you are creating an MP3 disc, you can store about 210 minutes on a disc. If you are creating a data CD, you can store about 750MB of data per disc. On a data DVD disc, you can store at least 5.2GB of files.

note

In many cases, a drive that doesn't work properly can be fixed by updating the driver software for that drive. You might need to download and install the proper driver from your drive's manufacturer; some drivers will be updated automatically when you run Windows Update. If you use a Mac that included a drive when you purchased it, the drivers will be updated when you use the Software Update application.

note

Notice that when you select a playlist, the Action button becomes the Burn Disc button. Does that give you any ideas?

When you are creating an audio CD, use the play time to judge the size of the playlist; keep it to 70 minutes plus or minus a couple minutes. For the other formats, use file size (for example, a CD can typically hold 750MB).

In any case, use the Source Information area to check the playlist to make sure it will fit on the type of disc you are going to create (see Figure 20.3).

FIGURE 20.3

This playlist contains 1.1 hours of music, which will be just right for a CD in the Audio CD format.

Source Information

The name of the playlist will become the name of the CD or DVD, so if you don't want the current playlist name to be used, change it to be what you do want the disc to be called. (To do this, click the playlist name once and pause. It will be highlighted to show you can change it. Type the new name and press **Return** or **Enter**.)

tip

If you click once on the time displayed in the Source Information area, you'll see the exact time to the second instead of the rounded-off time. Click again to return to the rounded-off time.

Preparing for a Burn Session

Next, configure the burn session during which you will create a disc by opening the **Burning** pane of the iTunes Preferences dialog box. Choose the format you want to use for the burning session by clicking the appropriate radio button (see Figure 20.4).

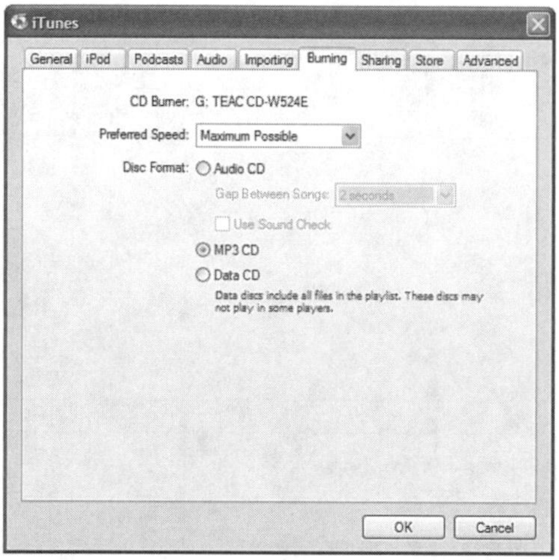

FIGURE 20.4

Because the MP3 CD radio button is selected, the next CD will be burned in that format.

> **note**
>
> If you choose to burn a playlist that contains more music than will fit on the type of disc you are trying to burn, iTunes will warn you about the situation. Then, you can choose to cancel the burn or choose to have iTunes burn the playlist across multiple discs.

If you choose Audio CD, there are two options you can configure. One is the gap between songs, which you choose by making a selection on the Gap Between Songs menu. Your options are none, which causes one song to begin immediately after the previous one ends; 1 second, which places 1 second of silence between tracks; 2 seconds, which places 2 seconds of silence between songs; and so on, up to 5 seconds. The other option is the Use Sound Check box. If you check this box, iTunes applies its Sound Check feature to the music it places on a disc. (If you don't remember from earlier in the book, this feature causes iTunes to attempt to set the relative volume of the songs you play to the same level.)

To select either the MP3 CD or the Data CD or DVD format, simply click the appropriate radio button.

Click **OK** to close the iTunes Preferences dialog box and prepare the burn session.

If you are going to burn a disc in the MP3 CD format, you must make sure all the music in

> **tip**
>
> If you are putting live music on a disc, be sure you select none on the Gap Between Songs menu. Otherwise, the roar of the crowd will be interrupted by the silent gaps, which causes the live feeling to be lost.

the playlist you want to put on disc is in the MP3 format before you can burn the MP3 CD disc. If you are going to create a disc in one of the other formats, you can skip the rest of this section.

To convert songs into the MP3 format, perform the following steps:

1. Open the **Importing** pane of the iTunes Preferences dialog box.

2. Select **MP3 Encoder** on the **Import Using** menu.

3. Click **OK** to close the dialog box.

4. Select the songs you want to convert and right-click (multiple-button mouse) or Ctrl-click (single-button mouse) them to open their contextual menus.

5. Select **Convert Selection to MP3**. Copies of the songs you selected will be made in the MP3 format.

6. Find the MP3 versions of the songs you selected in step 4. Use the Kind information to do this; look for those songs with MPEG audio file as their Kind.

7. Place the MP3 versions of the songs in the playlist you are going to put on an MP3 CD.

Burning a Disc

After you have selected the content and prepared the burning session, actually burning the disc is rather anticlimactic. You burn a disc with the following steps:

1. Make sure the playlist you want to burn is selected.

2. Click the **Burn Disc** button. The drive that is configured on the Burning pane of the iTunes Preferences dialog box will open, you will see a prompt in the Information window, and the Burn button will go radioactive (see Figure 20.5).

3. Insert the appropriate disc into the drive. If you selected the Audio CD or MP3 CD format, use a CD. If you selected the Data format, use a CD or DVD. iTunes will check the disc you inserted. If everything is ready to go, you will see the Click Burn Disc to start prompt in the Information area.

4. Click the **Burn Disc** button again. iTunes will start the burn process and display information about the process in the Information area (see Figure 20.6).

   If the playlist you have selected includes songs you purchased from the iTunes Music Store, you need to authorize your computer for that music before you can burn it to disc. To quickly check this, play the songs you purchased. If you can play them, the computer is authorized. (To learn more about this topic, see Part III, "The iTunes Music Store.")

FIGURE 20.5

iTunes is ready
to burn.

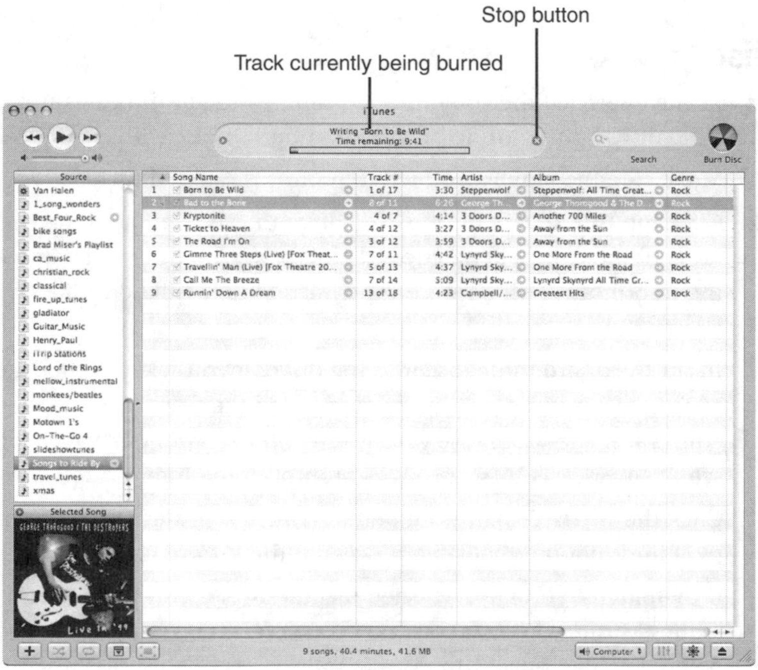

FIGURE 20.6

The playlist
Songs to Ride By
is being put on
an audio CD.

Stop button

Track currently being burned

When the process is complete, iTunes will play a tone to let you know. The
CD you just burned will appear on the Source list and will be selected (see
Figure 20.7).

If the disc can't be burned for some reason, such as there being too much in the selected playlist to fit onto the type of disc being burned, iTunes will let you know what is wrong. You'll have to correct the situation before you can complete the burn. In the case of you selecting too much music for the selected disc format, you'll have the option to burn the playlist on multiple discs.

FIGURE 20.7

The Songs to Ride By playlist has become the Songs to Ride By CD.

5. To eject the disc, click the **Eject** button. You can then use the disc you created in any player or drive that is compatible with its format.

Labeling Your Discs

Now that you can create your own CDs and DVDs, you will probably want to make labels for them to keep them organized and make them look cool. The good news is that iTunes can do some of this for you. The bad news is that it can't do all of it.

tip

To stop the burn before it completes, click the **Stop** button. If you do this, the disc you are trying to burn might be ruined.

Printing Disc Labels

Unfortunately, iTunes can't help you print disc labels—yet. Hopefully, this capability will be added in a future version. For now, if you want to label your discs, you'll need to use a different application. You can use just about any graphics application to create a CD or DVD label; you can also use a word processor to do so. However, to make the process easier and the results better, consider investing in a dedicated disc label creator. If you use a Windows computer, many labeling applications are available, such as AudioLabel CD Labeler. If you use a Mac or a Windows computer, Discus will enable you to create just about any disc label you can imagine (see Figure 20.8).

To print labels, you'll also need a printer and CD labels to print on. For the best results, you should use a color printer, but black-and-white labels can look stylish, too.

> **caution**
>
> Any music you purchase from the iTunes Music Store should be backed up on a CD or DVD. You can download music from the iTunes Music Store only once. If something happens to that music on your computer, you will have to pay for it again to be able to download it again. To protect your investment, create a CD or DVD of all the music your purchase. The easiest way is to put the Purchased Music playlist on disc. If something should happen to your computer, you can restore your purchased music from the backup disc.

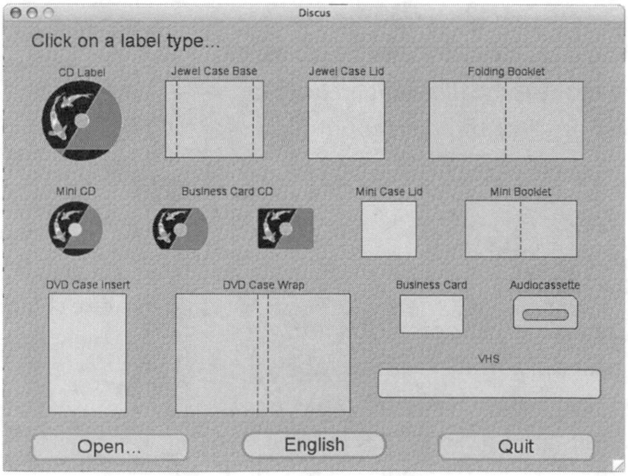

FIGURE 20.8

Discus is a good tool to create disc labels if you use a Macintosh or a Windows computer.

Most CD labeling applications contain templates for specific labels (identified by brand and label number) you purchase. By choosing the right template for the labels you use, the labels you print will be the exactly the same as the labels you design.

Printing Disc Inserts

Although iTunes can't help you with disc labels, it can help you create cool disc inserts so you can label the jewel case in which you store your discs.

For best results, associate artwork with the songs you put on a disc. When you create and print a disc insert, the artwork associated with the songs on the disc will become part of the insert. Refer to Chapter 17, "Labeling, Categorizing, and Configuring Your Music," to learn how to do this.

To create a disc insert, perform the following steps:

1. Select the playlist for which you want to create a disc insert; obviously, this should be the same one you used to burn the disc you are labeling.

2. Select **File**, **Print**. You'll see the Print "*playlistname*" dialog box, where *playlistname* is the name of the playlist you selected in step 1 (see Figure 20.9).

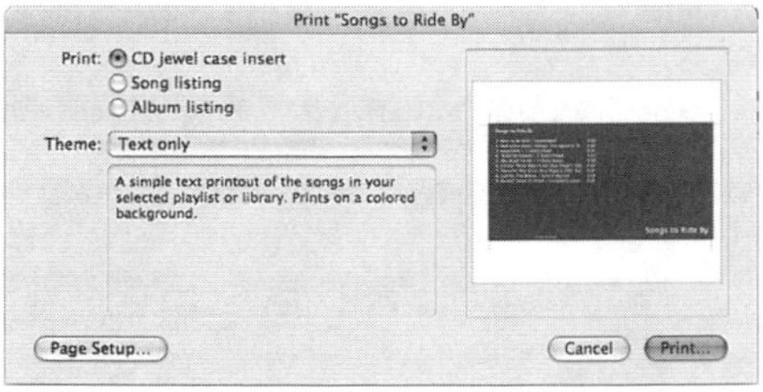

note

To get more information about AudioLabel CD Labeler, go to www.audiolabel.com. To get more information about Discus, visit www.magicmouse.com.

tip

For the ultimate disc labels, consider purchasing a disc burner that can print directly on a disc or etch label information onto the disc's surface. An example of the latter is the LaCie 16X LightScribe external DVD-RW drive.

FIGURE 20.9
Use the Print dialog box to choose the type of jewel case insert you want to print.

3. Click the **CD jewel case insert** radio button.

4. Use the **Theme** pop-up menu to select the type of insert you want to print. Some of the more useful options are explained in the following list:

- **Text only**—Prints a listing of the songs on the disc on the back of the insert over a colored background.

- **Mosaic**—Prints a collage of the artwork associated with songs in the playlist on the front and a list of the songs on the back. This is a color insert.

- **White Mosaic**—This is similar to Mosaic, except it prints on a white background.

- **Single cover**—Places a single graphic on the front; the graphic of the selected song is used. It also includes a list of songs on the back.

- **Large playlist**—It doesn't include any artwork, but it does place the list of songs on the front and back of the insert. As you can tell by its name, it is intended for large playlists that have too many songs to be listed on the back of the other insert types.

- **Black & White versions**—These exist for each of these types in case you don't use a color printer or like the look of black-and-white inserts.

5. Click **Page Setup**. You'll see the Page Setup dialog box.

6. Configure the page setup to match the paper you are using for the insert. If you are using paper designed specifically for this purpose, you might have to experiment a bit to know which selection best matches the insert paper you are printing on. Unfortunately, iTunes doesn't support specific CD insert paper by brand and insert number as a dedicated disc label application does. Maybe in a future version....

7. When you have configure the page setup, click **OK**. You'll move back to the Print dialog box.

8. Click **Print** to print the insert.

9. Cut or tear out the insert and place it in the jewel case. Prepare to be impressed!

Printing Song and Album Listings

In some cases, you might not want to use a disc insert; instead you might want to create just a listing of songs on playlists or even in your entire Library. iTunes can help you do this easily. Here's how:

> **note**
>
> If you choose a mosaic label and the songs included in the playlist have only a single piece of artwork (such as if they are all from the same album), that graphic will fill the front of the insert.

1. Select the source for which you want to print a listing.

2. Select **File**, **Print**. You'll see the Print "*playlistname*" dialog box, where *playlistname* is the name of the source you selected in step 1.

3. Click the **Song listing** radio button to print a listing of songs in the selected source or the **Album listing** radio button to print songs grouped by their albums.

tip

When you use the Album listing option, any artwork associated with an album appears on the list.

4. If you selected the Song listing option, select the theme for the list on the **Theme** drop-down list. The options are the following:

   - **Songs**—Prints the song name, length, artist, and album.

   - **User Ratings**—Adds your rating to the data in the Songs option.

   - **Dates played**—This includes all the information in the Songs option plus the play count and date.

   - **Custom**—Prints the data shown in the current view of the selected source. You can change the data included in the list by changing the View options for the source. (If you don't remember how to do this, refer to Chapter 17.)

5. Click **Print**. The listing will be printed to the printer you have selected (see Figure 20.10).

FIGURE 20.10

Printing song or album lists is useful to keep track of the music you have; in this case, I printed the album listing for a playlist.

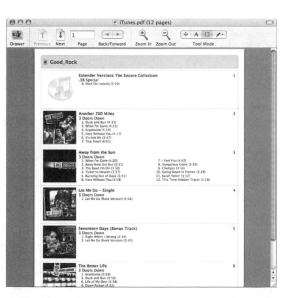

THE ABSOLUTE MINIMUM

Burning a CD or DVD is useful when you want to listen to music apart from iTunes or your iPod or to back up your music collection on disc. It is a relatively simple process, as you have seen in this chapter. As you burn, keep the following points in mind:

- There are three types of discs you can burn with iTunes: Audio CD, MP3 CD, and data CD or DVD discs.

- To prepare your computer to burn discs, you use the Burning tab of the iTunes Preferences dialog box to check that you have a compatible drive.

- To burn a disc, create a playlist containing the content you want to put on disc, configure the settings for the burn session, and then burn the disc.

- If you can't get discs to burn properly, open the Burning pane of the iTunes Preferences dialog box and select a lower burn speed on the Preferred Speed menu. Then try to burn the disc again. Sometimes, using a lower burn speed will correct problems in the burn process.

- The format for a burn session must be compatible with the format of the music you are using. The most likely case that might cause you problems is when you attempt to burn a CD in the MP3 format but the music you are attempting to place on a disc is in the AAC format (such as what you purchase from the iTunes Music Store). In this case, iTunes can't burn the disc because you are trying to place music that is in the AAC format on an MP3 disc. These are different and incompatible formats. If this happens, use the Audio CD or Data CD format instead. Or, if you simply must put AAC music on an MP3 disc, convert the music into the MP3 format before you try to burn the disc.

- Although iTunes can't help you print disc labels, it does a great job with jewel case inserts and listings.

21

SHARING iTUNES MUSIC OVER A NETWORK

With such a great collection of music in your iTunes Library, I'm sure you don't want to keep that music to yourself. So be generous and share that music with others. And, enjoy music that is shared with you.

If two or more computers are connected via a local network—and with the broad use of high-speed Internet connections, networks are becoming common even in homes these days—you can share the music in your iTunes Library with other people on your network. They can listen to that music as if it was stored in their own Libraries. Of course, assuming other folks on your network are also generous, you can listen to music they share with you as well.

If you use the multiuser features of Mac OS X, you can also share your music with other people who use your computer in the same way.

If you want to share your music even with non-computer devices, you can use AirTunes and an AirPort Express to do so.

Understanding How iTunes Music Sharing Works

When iTunes computers can communicate with each other over a network, they can access the Library stored on each computer. This means that you can see music in other iTunes Libraries and other computers can see the music stored in your Library (both cases assume that sharing is enabled on each computer).

note

In case you are wondering, you can't use iTunes to share your music over the Internet. You can only share on a local network, such as the one in your home or business.

When music is shared with you, it appears as a network source on your Source List—if more than one source is available, the Shared Music source will appear. When you share your music with others, your music appears as a network source on their Source lists. In either case, the person using the computer can select the shared source and listen to it using the same tools used to listen to other sources, such as CDs and playlists.

Even better, Windows and Macintosh users can share music with each other on networks that include both kinds of computers.

To share music with others on your network, you configure iTunes to share its music, which is covered in the next section. To access shared music, you configure iTunes to look for music being shared with you; that is the topic of the "Listening to Music Being Shared with You" section, later in this chapter.

Sharing Your iTunes Music with Others

Setting up an iTunes computer to share its music is a two-step process. The first step is to connect your computer to a network or to use the Fast User Switching feature on a Macintosh computer. The second step is to configure iTunes to share your music.

note

Later in this chapter, you'll learn about the amazing AirPort Express wireless hub that you can use to broadcast your music to other devices.

You can also use iTunes to see who is accessing the music you have shared.

Connecting an iTunes Computer to a Network

As I wrote in an earlier note, this is not a book on networking, so I can't provide the information you need to connect computers together on a network. However, to enable sharing over a network, you must be connected to a network, which makes sense because the computers have to have some way to communicate with one another.

The network over which you share iTunes music can be wired, wireless, or both, and it can include Windows and Macintosh computers. If you have such a network and your iTunes computers are connected to it, you are ready to share your music. Otherwise, you will need to build the network before you can share your iTunes tunes.

> **note**
>
> As of iTunes version 4.9, on which this chapter was based, you can't share iTunes music among the user accounts on a Windows XP computer. To listen to another user account's music, you have to import that music into the iTunes Library under each user account. For more information on this, refer to http://docs.info.apple.com/article.html?artnum=93195. Hopefully, this will be corrected soon and Windows users can enjoy the same sharing among user accounts on the same machine that Mac users do.

Sharing Your Music with Other People Who Use Your Mac

If you use a Mac, each user account can share its music with the other user accounts on the same computer (and on the network to which that Mac is connected). Share Libraries on the same Mac act just like Libraries stored on different computers that you access via a network. Using the Fast User Switching feature, you can leave iTunes running under one user account and someone else can log in under another use account and use iTunes to listen to music you share. Likewise, if another user shares her iTunes music and leaves iTunes running when you log in to your user account, you can access her music, too.

For help configuring user accounts on a Mac, see my book *Special Edition Using Mac OS X, v10.4 Tiger.*

Setting Up Your Computer to Share Music

To allow other people to listen to the music in your Library, perform the following steps:

1. Open the iTunes **Preferences** dialog box and then open the **Sharing** pane (see Figure 21.1).

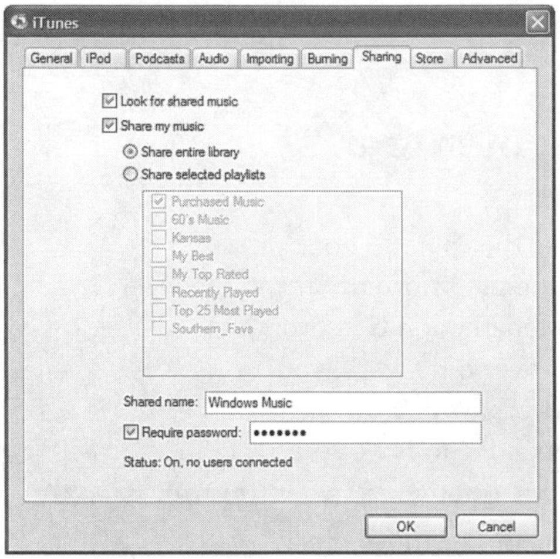

FIGURE 21.1

Using the Sharing pane of the iTunes Preferences dialog box, you can allow other people on your network to listen to your iTunes music.

2. To enable music sharing on your computer, check the **Share my music** check box. When you do so, you will see a prompt reminding you that sharing is for personal use only; click **OK** to clear the prompt.

   When you share music, you have two options for the music you share. You can share your entire Library or you can share only selected playlists.

3. To share your entire Library, click the **Share entire library** radio button.

   To share only specific playlists, click the **Share selected playlists** radio button and then check the check box next to each playlist you want to share. You can scroll through the list of available playlists using the scrollbar located on the right side of the list of available playlists.

4. Enter the name of your shared music collection in the **Shared name** field. By default, this will be the name of your user account on the computer with 's Music added to it. However, you can enter any name you'd like. This name will be how others identify your music on their Source Lists.

5. If you want to require that people enter a password before they can listen to the music you share, check the **Require password** check box and enter the password they will have to use in the box.

6. Click **OK**. The music you selected to share will become available to others on your network.

tip

If you make changes to the sharing configuration in iTunes while other people are accessing your Library, such as changing your sharing name or requiring a password, those users might have to restart their iTunes to be able to access your music again.

7. If you require a password to let others access your music, provide them with the password you created.

Knowing How Many People Are Using Your Music

You can monitor how many people are using the music you are sharing by opening the Sharing pane of the iTunes Preferences dialog box (see Figure 21.2). At the bottom of the pane, you will see the current status of sharing (On or Off) and how many users are currently connected to your music.

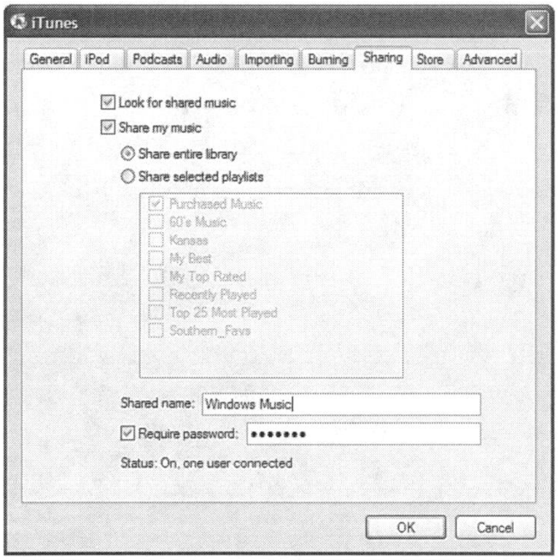

FIGURE 21.2

At the moment, the Status information at the bottom of the pane shows that one user is sharing the iTunes music on this computer.

The Status section shows only those users who are actually accessing your music by selecting it on their Source Lists. If they don't have your music selected, they won't be shown as being connected, even if they can see your music on their Source Lists.

Listening to Music Being Shared with You

Two steps are required to listen to music being shared with you. The first one, which must be done only once, is to tell iTunes to look for any music being shared with you. The second one is to access and listen to that music.

Accessing iTunes Music Being Shared with You

To have iTunes look across the network and identify music that is available to you, open the **Sharing** pane of the iTunes Preferences dialog box (see Figure 21.3). Then, check the **Look for shared music** check box and click **OK**.

When you return to the iTunes window, you will see music that is being shared with you on your Source List.

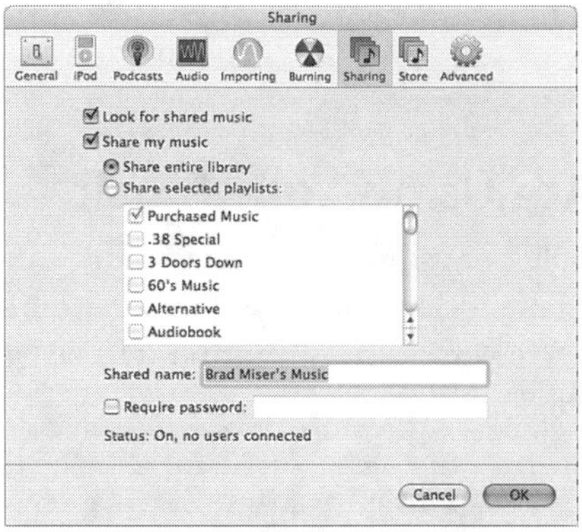

FIGURE 21.3

When the Look for shared music check box is checked, iTunes will look for any music being shared with you.

If only one source of shared music is available, you will see the name of that source with a set of dark blue boxes and a musical note as its icon. Click the expansion triangle next to that source to see the playlists being shared with you. Select the source to see all the music in its Library.

If more than one shared source is available, you'll see the Shared Music source instead (see Figure 21.4).

FIGURE 21.4

Because the source called Shared Music is on its Source List, you know that this computer has access to at least two sources of shared music.

The Shared Music source will have an expansion triangle next to it. Click this triangle to expand the Shared Music source to see each of the music sources being shared with you. Likewise, click the expansion triangle next to each source of shared music to view the playlists being shared with you (see Figure 21.5).

FIGURE 21.5

Under the expanded Shared Music source, you can see that two computers are currently sharing music with this machine; the source called Windows Music has been expanded so you can view its contents.

If a music source requires that you provide a password to listen to it, you will see the padlock icon in the lower-right corner of the source's icon. If you see this icon, you'll need to know the password for this source before you can listen to its music.

Listening to Shared iTunes Music

To listen to shared music, do the following steps:

1. Select the source to which you want to listen by clicking its icon. Your computer will attempt to connect to that music source.

2. If the source is protected by a password, you will be prompted to enter the password for that source. Do so and click **OK**.

   After you have entered the correct password, or if no password is required, the source's music will be shown in the Content pane (see Figure 21.6).

3. If the shared source has one or more playlists, you can view the playlists for that source by clicking the expansion triangle next to the source's name. When it expands, you will see the playlists it contains.

> **note**
>
> If only selected playlists on a source have been shared, when you select the source, you will see all the songs in the shared playlists rather than all the music in that machine's Library (which is what you see if the entire Library has been shared).

FIGURE 21.6

The Windows Music source is selected and its songs appear in the Content pane; the playlists it contains are shown under its icon.

4. Select a playlist under the shared source, and its songs will be shown in the Content pane (see Figure 21.7).

FIGURE 21.7

The shared source Windows Music has a number of playlists available; the Southern_Favs playlist is selected.

5. Play music on the share source just like music in your Library—by selecting it and clicking Play. Other playback tools, such as sorting the Content pane to change the order in which songs play, also work just they do when you are listening to the music in your Library.

Sharing Your Music Anywhere with AirTunes and an AirPort Express Base Station

Sharing music with other computers is very cool, but what if you want to listen to your music someplace that doesn't have a computer? Using an AirPort Express wireless hub and iTunes's AirTunes feature, you can share your music with audio devices such as a home stereo.

> **note**
>
> It probably goes without saying, but I'll say it anyway: If the computer sharing music with you stops running or if iTunes on that computer is closed (such as when the user logs out), the shared music source will disappear and you will no longer be able to use it. If you share music with others, keep iTunes running as much as you can.

You can use an AirPort Express for a lot more than just sharing your iTunes music. It is a full-featured wireless hub—not that you would ever guess so because it's very small. It also enables you to wirelessly share USB printers and so on. The focus of this section is sharing iTunes music with a non-computer device; explore the AirPort Express documentation to learn about its other features.

The general steps to use an AirPort Express to share music with an audio device are the following:

1. Obtain and install an AirPort Express on your network.
2. Connect your AirPort Express to a home stereo, a set of powered speakers, or another audio device.
3. Use the AirPort Express Assistant to set up a new network.
4. Set iTunes to broadcast music to that network.
5. Listen to the music.

Obtaining and Installing an AirPort Express

You can purchase an AirPort Express at any retail location that carries Apple products, such as the online Apple Store (see Figure 21.8). At press time, an AirPort Express costs $129, which is quite a bargain considering its small size and excellent features.

FIGURE 21.8
An AirPort
Express is a full-
featured wireless
hub that is just
slightly larger
than a deck of
cards.

After you have obtained an AirPort Express, use the installation CD that comes with it to install the AirPort Express software on your computer. This also installs AirTunes, the software required to broadcast your music.

Connecting the AirPort Express to an Audio Device

As you can see in Figure 21.8, on the bottom of the AirPort Express are three ports. You use the Ethernet port to connect the device to a cable modem, DSL modem, or wired network so you can use the AirPort Express as a hub. You use the USB port to wirelessly share a USB printer. Finally, you can use the Line Out port to connect the AirPort express to any audio device that has an input port or to powered speakers.

After you have installed the AirPort Express software, connect the Line Out port on the AirPort Express to the Line In port on an audio device. For example, connect a set of power speakers' output cable to this port. Or, use a mini-jack to RCA stereo cable to connect the AirPort Express Output port to audio input ports on a stereo receiver.

> **note**
>
> To share iTunes music with an audio device using AirPort Express, your computer must have access to a wireless network so it can broadcast its music to the AirPort Express.

Then, plug the AirPort Express into a wall outlet. It will become active and you'll see its activity lights turn on.

That is all the installation that is required. How simple is that!

Setting Up a New AirTunes Network

To broadcast your music to an AirPort Express, you first set up a network for that device:

1. Launch the **AirPort Express Assistant**. On a Windows PC, select **Start**, **All Programs**, **AirPort**, **AirPort Express Assistant**. On a Mac, open **Applications**, **Utilities**, **AirPort Express Assistant**. The Assistant will open and you'll see an information window explaining what you can do.

2. Click **Continue**. Depending on how your current wireless network is set up, you might or might not see prompts that ask you to configure your current wireless connection. These prompts should be self-explanatory so work through them until you see the Introduction screen in the Assistant.

3. Click the **Set up a new AirPort Express** radio button and click **Continue**.

4. If you have an existing wireless network, click **Connect to my current wireless network**. If not, click **Create a new wireless network**. The rest of these steps assume you are creating a new network; using an existing network isn't much different. The computer will scan for the AirPort Express and you will see all available AirPort Express units on the Network Setup screen.

5. Click **Continue** to use the AirPort Express that was found. If multiple Express units were found, select the **AirPort Express** you want to use and click **Continue**. The Assistant will begin setting up configuring the AirPort Express for the existing network. When it finds the network, you will be prompted to connect to it and the Network Setup screen.

6. Enter the name of the network you are creating along with a name for the AirPort Express; then click **Continue**.

7. Continue following the instructions in the Assistant until the AirPort Express is fully configured. The exact steps you use depend on your specific network configuration. Fortunately, the Assistant makes it pretty easy in most situations. When the Assistant has completed its work, your AirPort Express will be ready to use.

Configuring iTunes to Broadcast to a Network

After your AirPort Express has been configured, you set iTunes to broadcast to it.

1. Open the **Audio** pane of the iTunes Preferences dialog box (see Figure 21.9).

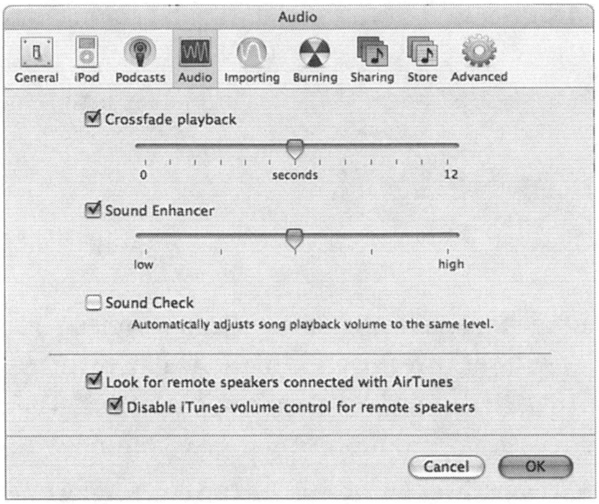

FIGURE 21.9

Use the Audio
pane of the
iTunes
Preferences dia-
log box to con-
figure AirTunes.

2. Check the **Look for remote speakers connected with AirTunes** check
box.

3. Check the **Disable iTunes volume control for remote speakers** check
box if you don't want the position of the Volume slider in iTunes to impact
the volume of the audio device you are broadcasting to. Generally, this is a
good option so that you don't accidentally change the volume at the remote
device when you are using iTunes.

4. Click **OK** to close the Preferences window. You'll return to the iTunes window.

Listening to the Shared Tunes

Now, you can listen to your iTunes music from the remote audio device. Follow
these steps:

1. Choose the remote device on which you want to play music on the **Speaker**
pop-up menu that appears in the lower-right corner of the iTunes window
when the AirTunes software is running
(see Figure 21.10). The name you choose
should be the name of the AirPort
Express connected to the device on
which you want to play the music.

2. Play the music you want to hear, such
as a playlist, a CD, or your Library.
You'll see a message telling you that
iTunes is connecting to the selected
speakers in the Information area. When

tip

You can choose a shared
music source to broadcast
just like any music in your
own Library.

that process is complete, music will begin playing over the device to which the AirPort Express is connected.

FIGURE 21.10

By selecting Express_Station_ Alpha, music I play will be heard on the audio device (in this case, a pair of powered speakers, con- nected to the AirPort Express called Express_Station_ Alpha).

Speaker pop-up menu (appears when connected to AirPort Express)

3. Use the audio device's volume control to adjust the volume. (If you didn't check the Disable iTunes volume control for remote speakers check box, you can also control the volume with the iTunes Volume slider).

Because the music source is iTunes, you control music playback from the computer streaming music to the AirPort Express, such as to start or stop it, change the playlist, and so on. You can control only the volume from the audio device, such as by muting it, increasing it, and so on.

To play iTunes music on the computer again, select **Computer** on the Speaker pop-up menu.

note

Interestingly, if your wireless hub connects wired computers to your network too, you can broadcast music from any computer with iTunes con- nected to the network.

THE ABSOLUTE MINIMUM

The ability to share your music with other computers on your network and being able to listen to the music on other people's computers is pretty cool, don't you think? If you use a Mac, you can just as easily share your music with everyone who has a user account on your computer. And, using an AirPort Express Base Station, you can even share your music by broadcasting to other devices, such as a home stereo receiver.

Following are some points to keep in mind to help your sharing:

- To share music, the computer sharing it must be turned on and cannot be in Standby By (Windows) or Sleep (Mac) mode. If the computer goes to one of these modes or is turned off, the shared music will no longer be available.

- Similarly, iTunes must be running for music to be shared. If you quit iTunes while sharing music, the music you were sharing will no longer be available to others.

- When it comes to sharing, iTunes doesn't care whether a machine is a Windows computer or a Mac. You can share music or listen to shared music from either platform.

- If you use a Mac, configure Fast User Switching to be active so other people can access music in your Library (leave iTunes running whenever your are logged in) when they log in to your computer.

- When you access shared music, you can only listen to it. You can't add it your Library, put it in playlists, change its information, put in on a CD, or other tasks that you can do with the music in your own Library.

- You can share your music with up to five computers at the same time.

- If you access music that was purchased at the iTunes Music Store, you must validate that you have permission to listen to that music by authorizing it. Music that you purchase from the iTunes Music Store can only be used on five computers at a time, and someone sharing music you purchased counts as one of those five. To be able to listen to shared music at all, you must be able to provide the account and username under which it was purchased. You'll learn about this in more detail in Part III, "The iTunes Music Store."

- You can connect an AirPort Base Station to your network to broadcast your iTunes music to other devices, such as a set of powered speakers or to a home stereo system.

IN THIS CHAPTER

- Take care of iTunes, and it will take care of you.

- Be safe, not sorry, by backing up your music.

- Get help with those very rare, but possibly annoying, iTunes problems.

22

MAINTAINING iTUNES AND SOLVING PROBLEMS

As an application, iTunes is so well designed that you aren't likely to have many problems with it. And that is a good thing because who wants problems? However, you can minimize iTunes problems by keeping the application updated to the current release. You should also keep your music collection backed up just in case something bad happens to your computer.

In the rare event that you do have troubles, you can usually solve them without too much effort.

Keeping iTunes Up-to-date

iTunes is one of Apple's flagship applications, especially because it is the only current Apple application that runs on both Macintosh and Windows computers. Because of this, Apple is continuously refining the application to both make it even more trouble free and to enhance its features. You should keep your copy of iTunes current; fortunately, you can set up iTunes so it maintains itself.

Keeping iTunes Up-to-date on Any Computer Automatically

Setting up iTunes so that it keeps itself current automatically is simple. Open the **General** pane of the iTunes Preferences dialog box. Then check the **Check for iTunes updates automatically** check box (see Figure 22.1). Click **OK**.

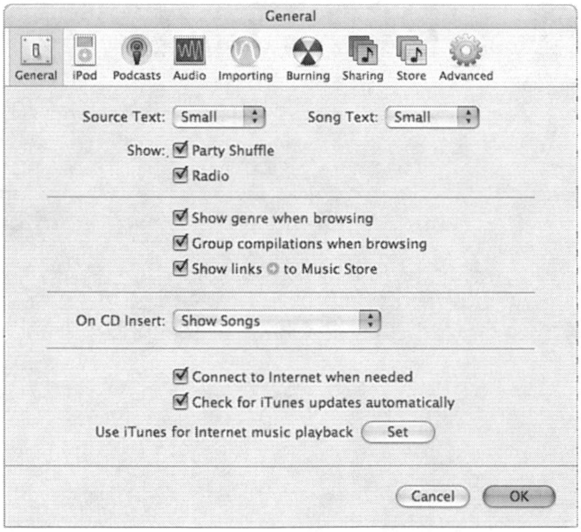

note

For automatic updates to work, you need to allow iTunes to connect to the Internet when it needs to. Check the **Connect to Internet when needed** check box on the General tab of the iTunes Preferences dialog box to grant iTunes permission to do this.

FIGURE 22.1

Using the General pane of the iTunes Preferences dialog box, you can have iTunes keep itself current.

Once per week, iTunes will connect to Apple's servers and check for updates. When it finds an update, you will be prompted to download and install it on your computer.

The benefit of this is that you don't have to remember to check for updates yourself. There isn't really a downside because you have the

caution

For iTunes to perform this check, it must be stopped and started once during the week. In other words, if you never quit iTunes, it won't ever perform this check.

opportunity to decline to install the update if you don't want it installed for some reason.

Keeping iTunes Up-to-date on a Windows PC Manually

You can check for an iTunes update manually any time you think one might be available or if you prefer to do manual updates for some reason. You can check for iTunes updates manually on a Windows computer by selecting **Help**, **Check For iTunes Updates**. iTunes will connect to the Internet and check for a newer version of the application. If a new version is available, you will be prompted to download and install it. If a newer version is not available, you will see a dialog box telling you that you are using the current version.

Keeping iTunes Up-to-date on a Macintosh

Because both Mac OS X and iTunes are Apple products, iTunes is one of the applications tracked by Mac OS X's Software Update feature.

If you have set Software Update to check for updates automatically, it will check for iTunes updates according to the schedule you set. When it finds an update, you will be prompted to download and install it.

To manually check for updates, select **Apple**, **Software Update** (see Figure 22.2). If an iTunes update is available, you will see it in the Software Update window. You can then select it and download it to your Mac. iTunes will then be updated to the latest and greatest version.

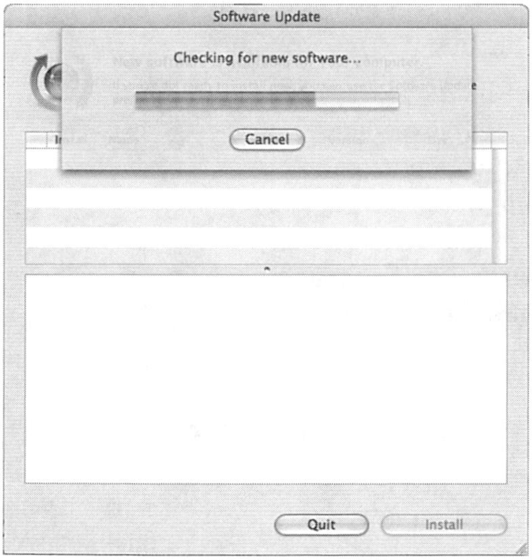

FIGURE 22.2
On a Mac, you can use Software Update to keep your version of iTunes current.

Backing Up Your iTunes Music Library

Hopefully, you have and use a good backup system to protect all your files, including your iTunes Library. If so, you get extra points from me and can skip the rest of this section.

If you don't use a backup system to protect yourself, shame on you. However, you can earn some points back by at least backing up your music collection to CD or DVD. You can do this by creating a playlist containing the music you want to back up. Then, you burn that playlist to a CD or DVD. That will place a copy of your music on disc so you can recover it should you ever need to. For detailed steps to burn discs, refer to Chapter 20, "Burning Your Own CDs or DVDs."

caution

Backing up is especially critical for music you purchase from the iTunes Music Store. If something happens to this music, you can't download it again without paying for it. If you lose music files you have purchased and don't have a backup, they are gone forever.

If the playlist you select contains more songs than will fit on a single CD or DVD, you will be prompted to see whether you want iTunes to place the playlist on multiple discs. If you allow this, iTunes will keep burning discs until all the songs in the playlist have been placed on a disc.

Solving iTunes Problems

iTunes is about as trouble-free as any application gets; this is especially amazing because iTunes offers so many great features. However, even the best application is bound to run into a few hiccups.

Because the odds of me including in this book the specific problem you might experience are small, it is more profitable for you to learn where you can access help with problems you might experience. So, I've included the solution to one problem you are likely to encounter here. Then, you'll learn how to get help for other problems should you experience them.

tip

When you back up your music, make sure you use the data format option, not the Audio CD or MP3 format. If you choose Audio CD format, you won't be able to fit many songs on a single disc. If you choose the MP3 options, music you purchased from the iTunes Music Store won't be able to be burned onto a disc.

Solving the Missing Song File Problem

One problem you might encounter occasionally has nothing to do with iTunes not working properly. This problem occurs when something happens to the file for a song in your Library.

When this happens, iTunes doesn't know what to do because it can't find the song's file. To show its confusion, iTunes displays an exclamation point next to any songs whose files it can't find when you try to play them, or do anything else with them for that matter (see Figure 22.3).

Missing file icon

FIGURE 22.3

The missing file icon means iTunes can't find the file for a song.

To fix this problem, you have to reconnect iTunes to the missing file. Here are the steps to follow:

1. Double-click a song next to which the exclamation point icon is shown. You will see a prompt telling you that the original file can't be found and asking whether you would like to locate it (see Figure 22.4).

caution

iTunes depends on QuickTime to work. If you remove QuickTime from your system, iTunes will stop working. You'll have to reinstall QuickTime or run the iTunes Installer to get it working again.

FIGURE 22.4

When you see this dialog box, iTunes can't find a song's file.

The song "Dry Your Tears, Afrika *" could not be used because the original file could not be found. Would you like to locate it?

Cancel   Yes

2. Click **Yes**. You will see the Open dialog box.

3. Move to the song's file, select it, and click **Open**. You'll return to the iTunes window, and the song will begin to play. This will also restore the link from the iTunes Library to the song's file, and you will be able to play it again like before it was lost.

If the problem was that the file had been moved, you might want to cause iTunes to place it back within the iTunes Music folder to keep your music files nicely organized. To do this, select **Advanced**, **Consolidate Library**. In the resulting prompt, click **Consolidate**. iTunes will place a copy of any missing songs you have reconnected manually back into the proper location (within your iTunes Music folder).

Getting Help with iTunes Problems

When you run into a problem you can't solve yourself, the first place to go for help is Apple's Support website.

If you use iTunes on a Windows computer, go to http://www.apple.com/support/itunes/windows/. This page provides solutions to common problems, and you can search for specific problems you might experience (see Figure 22.5).

FIGURE 22.5

If you use iTunes on a Windows computer, check this website when you have problems.

Mac users are certainly not immune to problems either. For help with those, check out http://www.apple.com/support/itunes/ (see Figure 22.6).

FIGURE 22.6

FIGURE 22.6

Mac users can get help here.

You can also access Apple's general support resources at http://www.apple.com/support.

Many other websites contain useful iTunes troubleshooting help. To find them, go to www.google.com and search for the specific problem you are having. This will often lead you to a forum or other place in which you can find information, including a solution, for many problems.

note

You can also write to me with iTunes questions. My email address is bradmacosx@mac.com.

THE ABSOLUTE MINIMUM

Heck, who wants to spend time solving problems with a music application when the whole point is to spend time listening to and working with music? Not me, that's for sure. Fortunately, iTunes is designed and implemented so well that you aren't likely to experience any problems. If you do, help is available to you on the Web and from other sources.

■ Of course, you can lower the chances that you will ever have problems with iTunes by keeping the application up-to-date. Fortunately, you can set iTunes to do this automatically.

■ Just in case the worst happens, keep your music safe by keeping it backed up separately from your computer, such as on CD or DVD.

■ You aren't likely to need to solve many problems. You might occasionally run into the "missing song file" problem. Fortunately, you learned how to solve that one.

■ If you experience problems with iTunes, you can access the application's help system. You can also get help from the Apple Support web page or by writing to me.

PART III

THE iTUNES MUSIC STORE

TOURING THE ITUNES MUSIC STORE

The iTunes Music Store might just be the best thing to happen to music, well, since iTunes and the iPod. The iTunes Music Store gives you online access to hundreds of thousands of songs and thousands of albums by thousands of artists (that's a lot of thousands!). You can search for or browse for music in many ways. When you find music that interests you, you can preview it to see whether it seems to be up your alley. If it is, you can immediately buy it and download it into your iTunes Library. This all works so well because access to the iTunes Music Store is built in to iTunes so you can make the most of the store using the iTunes tools you already know so well.

Why the iTunes Music Store Rocks

There are many reasons the iTunes Music Store is great. To get you pumped up, here are a few:

- **The one hit wonder**—You know what I mean—that group or artist who put out one great song and that's it. Before the iTunes Music Store, if you wanted to own such a song, you usually had to buy a CD with 11 less-than-good songs to get the one you wanted. Not so with the iTunes Music Store. You can buy individual songs, so you only pay for the music you want.

- **Try before you buy**—You can preview any music in the store to make sure you know as much as possible about a song before you actually buy it.

- **It's legal**—Unlike many other sources of online music, the iTunes Music Store contains only music that is legal for you to buy and download.

- **It's convenient**—Because you access the iTunes Music Store through iTunes, shopping for music is easy and convenient.

- **You can find the music you want**—You can search for specific songs or browse entire genres, artists, and more.

- **Immediate gratification**—Because music is immediately downloaded to your Mac, you don't have to wait for a CD to be delivered.

- **It's cheap**—Individual songs are only $.99. When you buy a CD's worth of songs, the price gets even lower and is usually less than you would pay elsewhere. Plus, there are no shipping costs.

note

Ever hear a song on a commercial or TV show you like? You can often find and buy such a song in just a few minutes.

- **Music allowances**—You can create music accounts that enable someone to purchase music up to a certain amount per period (such as per month). This is a great way to put a cap on the amount someone spends on music in the iTunes Music Store. Because it is so fun and simple to buy music this way, it is easy to get carried away. You might even want to put yourself on a music allowance.

- **Gift certificates**—You can purchase iTunes Music Store gift certificates and send the gift of music via email to someone who uses iTunes. This is a great way to buy music for people even if you aren't sure of the music they have. They can jump into the iTunes Music Store and purchase the music they want.

- **Podcasts**—In the iTunes Music Store, you can subscribe to thousands of podcasts and download them to your iTunes Music Library and an iPod. Most of these are free.

- **Pick and choose**—Because you can buy individual songs, you can pick and choose among songs from a specific artist. Even when you like an artist, sometimes collections from that artist might have only a few songs you like. Rather than getting stuck with several you don't like, you can buy only those you do like.

note

To learn how to subscribe to podcasts, see "Subscribing and Listening to Podcasts" on page **254**.

How the iTunes Music Store Works

Through the rest of the chapters in this part of the book, you will learn how to use the iTunes Music Store in detail. For now, read through the following sections to get an overview of this amazing tool.

Getting an Account

To purchase music from the iTunes Music Store, you need an account (you don't need an account to browse the store or preview music). This account lets you charge music you purchase and prevents you from having to enter your information each time you visit the store. After you create and configure your iTunes Music Store account, you sign in to the store automatically so you don't need to think about it again.

tip

You can use your iTunes Music Store account to log in to the store from any iTunes-equipped computer. You don't need to have an account to subscribe to podcasts.

Accessing the Store

Accessing the store is as easy as clicking the Music Store source in the iTunes Source List (see Figure 23.1). The iTunes Music Store will fill the Content pane, and you can begin browsing or searching for music.

Music Store source

FIGURE 23.1

When you shop at this store, you don't need to worry about parking.

Browsing or Searching for Music

You can use the iTunes Music Store's tools to browse for music by genre, artist, or other attributes. This is a good way to explore the store to look for music you might be interested in but might not be aware of. You can also search for music using the iTunes Search tool, which becomes the Search Music Store tool when the Music Store Source is selected (see Figure 23.2).

FIGURE 23.2

You can use the familiar iTunes Search tool to search for music in the iTunes Music Store.

Previewing Music

When you find a song in which you are interested, you can play a preview of it. The preview typically consists of 30 seconds of the song. This can help you decide whether the song is really one you want.

Buying and Downloading Music

When you find songs you want to add to your iTunes Library, you can buy and download them with a few mouse clicks. The music you buy is automatically placed in a special playlist called Purchased Music (see Figure 23.3).

FIGURE 23.3

As you can see, I have had no trouble finding music to purchase from the iTunes Music Store.

What Happens to Music You Buy?

When you purchase music, it is automatically placed in your iTunes Library. From there, with a few minor exceptions, you can do the same things with iTunes Music Store music as you can with music from CDs you purchase.

What Can You Do with Music You Buy from the iTunes Music Store?

The answer to this question is, just about anything you can do with any other music in your iTunes Library. Of course, "just about" means that there are some limitations on the music you get from the iTunes Music Store. However, you aren't likely to find these very limiting (unless you are trying to do something you shouldn't be doing anyway). So, following are the exceptions that make iTunes Music Store music slightly different from the music you import from a CD:

- **You can listen to music you purchase from the iTunes Music Store on up to five computers at the same time**—For most people, this isn't a limitation because they don't have more than five computers anyway (maybe one at work and a couple at home). Even if you have more than five computers, you can easily authorize and deauthorize computers to enable them to play iTunes Music Store music as needed.

note

The five-computer limit does not apply to iPods. You can place music you purchase from the iTunes Music Store on as many iPods as you want.

- **You can burn to disc the same playlist containing iTunes Music Store up to seven times**—So, you can create up to seven copies of the same CD or DVD. You aren't ever likely to really want to create that many copies of a disc, so this isn't much of a limitation either. Besides, all you have to do is change one song in a playlist and then you can burn the changed playlist onto seven more discs.

- **You are supposed to use the music you purchase for personal use only**—Of course, this is the same limitation for the audio CDs you buy, too.

That's it. You likely will never encounter one of these limits in your regular use of iTunes Music Store music.

Although the iTunes Music Store has an enormous amount of music available in it, it doesn't contain music from every artist. Some music companies have chosen not to place their music in the iTunes Music Store—for now. The inventory in the iTunes Music Store is continually increasing, and because of its dramatic success, my guess is that most of the few holdouts will eventually join the party.

THE ABSOLUTE MINIMUM

The iTunes Music Store is one of the best things to happen to music, ever. Personally, in the first few months the iTunes Music Store was available, I purchased more music than I did in several of the previous years. That's because I have fairly eclectic tastes and don't often want to purchase full CDs because I like only a few songs by some artists. That said, I have purchased a number of full CDs as well. Since the iTunes Music Store opened, I haven't ventured into many other online or brick-and-mortar music retailers. My guess is that once you start using the iTunes Music Store, you, too, might find it to be the only music store you need.

- When you shop in the iTunes Music Store, you can try any song before you buy it!
- To shop in the store, you need to set up an account. This can be done in just a few minutes, and you set up your account using iTunes.
- To visit the iTunes Music Store, simply click the Music Store source.
- You can browse and search the store for specific music you want to hear.
- After you buy music and download it into your Library, you can do all sort of things with it, such as listening to it (duh), adding it to playlists, burning it to CD, and so on.

CONFIGURING iTUNES FOR THE MUSIC STORE

Before you bust through the iTunes Music Store's doors, it is a good idea to configure iTunes for the store so that when you do get there, you can focus on finding and buying cool tunes to add to your collection. And that is the point of this chapter—to help you understand your shopping options and create and configure your iTunes Music Store account.

Understanding Your Shopping Options

When it comes time to buy in the iTunes Music Store, you have two basic options: 1-Click or Shopping Cart. The 1-Click option works best when you have a broadband connection to the Internet. The Shopping Cart method works well for everyone but is primarily intended for people using a slow connection, such as a 56K dial-up account.

1-Click Shopping

This method is aptly named. When it's active, you can click the Buy Album button to purchase an album or the Buy Song button to purchase a song (see Figure 24.1). The item you elected to buy (a collection of songs, such as an album, or a single song) is immediately purchased and downloaded to your iTunes Library. The process requires literally one click (which is where the name came from, I suppose).

FIGURE 24.1

The Buy Album button enables you to purchase and download an album with a single mouse click; the Buy Song button does the same for individual songs.

If you have a broadband Internet connection, such as cable or DSL, this is a useful option because it makes buying music fast and easy. You can click a button, and the purchase and download process take place in the background while you do something else, such as look for more music.

If you have a slow connection, such as a dial-up account, this is probably not a good option for you. Because downloading songs will consume your connection's bandwidth, you won't be able to do anything else while music is being downloaded. So, you will have wait until the download process is complete before continuing to shop. In this case, you should probably use the Shopping Cart method instead.

Shopping Cart Shopping

When you use this method, music you select to purchase is moved into a Shopping Cart, which serves as a holding area for the music you want to purchase. When you find music you want to buy, you click the Add Album or Add Song button. The item whose button you click is moved into your Shopping Cart, which appears on the Source List underneath the Music Store source. When you select the Shopping Cart, you will see the music you have added to it (see Figure 24.2). From there, you can purchase the music by clicking the Buy button for albums or the Buy Song button for songs, at which point the music you purchase is downloaded to your computer and placed in your Library.

FIGURE 24.2

The Shopping Cart holds the music you are interested in.

If you have a slow Internet connection, the Shopping Cart method is useful because you can place music in the cart and then continue shopping for music in the store without being hampered by the music being downloaded to your computer. When you are done shopping, you can pop back to the cart and purchase music and then do something else while that music is downloaded to your computer.

Although the Shopping Cart is designed for slow connections, you can use this method with a fast connection in the same way. The benefit of this is that you can gather a collection of music without actually purchasing it. When you are ready to check out, you can move to the cart and select the music you do actually want to buy. In other words, you can use the Shopping Cart as a holding area for music you find that you might want to buy. When you are ready to purchase music, you move back to your cart and click the Buy buttons for the music you want.

Configuring Your iTunes Music Store Account

To purchase music in the iTunes Music Store, you need to have an account and configure that account on your computer.

Obtaining an iTunes Music Store Account

If you already have an account with AOL, the Apple online store, or .Mac, you already have an account with the iTunes Music Store because it can use any of those accounts.

If you don't have one of these accounts, you can obtain an account in the iTunes Music Store by following these steps:

1. Select the **Music Store** source. The Music Store will fill the Content pane (see Figure 24.3).

2. Click the **Account** button, which is labeled Sign In when you are not signed in to an account. You'll see the Account Login dialog box (see Figure 24.4).

FIGURE 24.3

To sign in to the iTunes Music Store, you click the Account button.

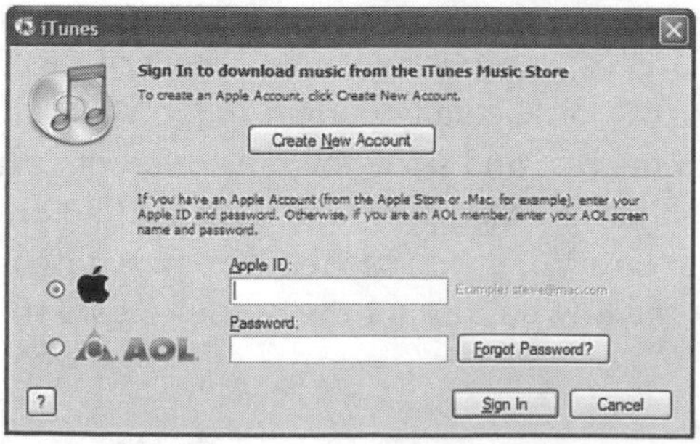

FIGURE 24.4

The Account Login dialog box enables you to log in to an existing account or create a new one.

3. Click the **Create New Account** button. You will return to the Content pane, which will be filled with the first of the three screens you use to create an account.

4. Read the information on the first screen and click the **Agree** button. (The information on the first screen contains the terms of service to which you must agree if you want to use the iTunes Music Store.)

note

Apple uses extensive security measures to protect your credit card information.

5. On the next screen, enter an email address, which will be your account's username (called an Apple ID), and password. Then enter a security question, enter your birth date, and select any information you want to be emailed to you. Then click **Continue**.

6. On the third screen, enter your credit card information and address and then click **Done**.

7. If you are prompted to enter any additional information, do so and click the **Continue** or **Done** button. When the process is complete, you will see a completion screen. You will then be logged in to your new account. Click **Done**. You will return to the iTunes Music Store and you can start shopping (see Figure 24.5).

FIGURE 24.5
When your iTunes Music Store account appears in the Account button, you are logged in to your account and can start shopping for tunes.

Logging In to Your iTunes Music Store Account

To be able to purchase music from the iTunes Music Store, you must log in to your iTunes Music Store account first. To log in to an existing iTunes Music Store account, perform the following steps:

1. Click the **Account** button (this will be labeled Sign In when you aren't signed in to your account). You'll see the Sign In dialog box (see Figure 24.6).

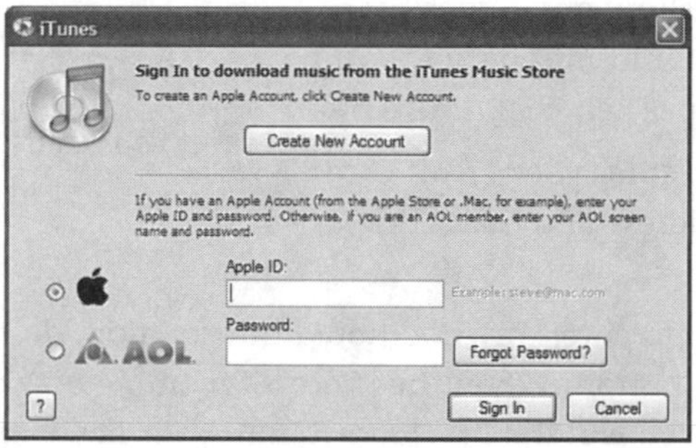

FIGURE 24.6

You can sign in to your iTunes Music Store account by entering your Apple ID or AOL account information in this dialog box.

> **note**
>
> You don't need to log in to an iTunes Music Store account to be able to subscribed to and download podcasts. To learn how to access podcasts in the iTunes Music Store, see "Subscribing and Listening to Podcasts" on page **254**.

2. If you use an Apple ID to sign in to the store, click the **Apple** button (this is selected by default). If you use an AOL account to sign in, click the **AOL** button.

3. Enter your Apple ID in the **Apple ID** field or your AOL screen name in the **AOL Screen Name** field.

4. Enter your password in the **Password** field.

5. Click **Sign In**. You will be logged in to your account. When you return to the iTunes window, you will see your Apple ID or AOL screen name in the Account field. After you are signed in, you can shop for tunes.

Logging Out of Your iTunes Music Store Account

To sign out of your account, click the **Account** button, which shows your Apple ID or AOL account name when you are logged in to your

> **note**
>
> If a different account is currently logged in, you must log out of that account before you can sign in to another one.

account. The Sign In dialog box will appear; click **Sign Out**. You will return to the Music Store and the Account button will again be labeled Sign In.

Changing and Viewing Your iTunes Music Store Account

Times change and sometimes so does your personal information, such as your address or the credit card you want to use in the iTunes Music Store. If such changes occur in your life, you can change your Apple ID account information by using the following steps:

1. Click your iTunes Music Store account name, shown in the Account button, as if you want to sign out. The Sign In dialog box will appear.

2. Enter your password. (Your account name will be filled in already.)

3. Click **View Account**. The Content pane will be replaced by the Apple Account Information screen. On this screen, you will see various buttons that enable you to change your account information and to manage various aspects of your account, such as your music allowances.

4. To change your account information (such as your address), click the **Edit Account Info** button and follow the onscreen instructions to change your information.

5. To change your credit card information, click **Edit Credit Card** and follow the onscreen instructions to change your credit card information.

6. To view your purchase history, click the **Purchase History** button. The screen will be filled with a detailed list of all the transactions for your account (see Figure 24.7). Review the list and click **Done**.

tip

On the View Account screen, you'll also see the number of computers currently authorized to play music you have purchased from the iTunes Music Store. (Unfortunately, it doesn't identify those computers for you.)

7. If you want to change the country your account is associated with (and sometimes the version of the store you use if the country you select has a different version of the store), click the **Change Country** button and follow the onscreen instructions to change the country with which your account is associated.

8. When you are done making changes, click **Done**. You will return to the Music Store.

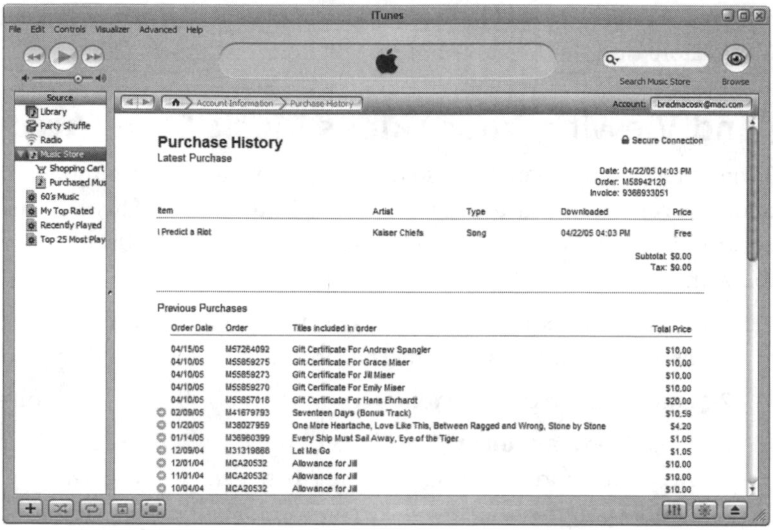

FIGURE 24.7
Yes, I do use the
iTunes Music
Store, as my pur-
chase history
shows.

Setting Up and Managing Music Allowances

You can create a music allowance for an iTunes Music Store account. This enables someone using that account to purchase a certain amount of music per month. This is useful if you have kids who you want to be able to buy music at the store and you want to provide a limited amount of credit for them to use.

If the person to whom you are going to provide an allowance already has an Apple account, you will need her Apple ID and password. Alternatively, you can create an account for that person when you assign an allowance to her.

To create a music allowance, perform the following steps:

1. Access the **Account Information** screen for your account (see the previous section for the steps to do this).

2. Click **Setup Allowance**. You'll see the Set Up an iTunes Allowance screen.

3. Enter your name in the **Your Name** field.

4. Enter the recipient's name in the **Recipient's Name** field.

5. Choose the amount of money the recipient will be able to spend each month in the **Monthly Allowance** menu—this amount will be applied to the

> **tip**
>
> A few other buttons appear on the View Account screen that you aren't likely to use. The Terms and Condition button displays the current terms and conditions for the store. The Privacy Policy enables you to view Apple's privacy policy, and the Reset Warnings button resets all the warning dialog boxes so you see them again the next time they become relevant.

recipient's account on the first day of each
month. You can choose an amount from $10
to $200 per month in $10 increments
between $10 and $100 or in $50 increments
from $100 to $200.

6. If you want the allowance to become available immediately, click the **Send now,
and on the first of next month** radio
button (this is the default option). If you
want the allowance to start on the first of
the next month, click the **Don't send
now, wait until the first of next
month** button instead.

7. If the recipient already has an Apple ID,
check the **Use recipient's existing Apple
Account** radio button and enter the Apple
ID in the two **Apple ID** fields (one is a veri-
fication field). If the recipient does not have
an Apple ID, click the **Create an Apple
Account for Recipient** radio button and
enter an Apple ID for that person in the
two fields.

8. If you want to provide a personal message
about the allowance, write it in the
Personal Message field.

9. Click **Continue**. If you indicated you
wanted to create a new account, you'll
move to the Create an Apple Account
screen. If you chose to use an existing
Apple ID, you'll move to a purchase confirmation screen that summarizes the
allowance you are setting up and can skip
to step 11.

10. Complete the information for the new
iTunes Music Store account you are creating. This includes the recipient's first name,
last name, birthday, and password. When
you have entered this information, click
Create. You'll move to the purchase confirmation screen.

note

If you use an AOL
account to access the store,
you change your account information using the AOL software.

note

Unfortunately, you can't
set up an allowance for the
same account you use to create it.
You must choose a recipient with
an Apple ID different from the one
you are using to create the
allowance. You can get around
this by creating more than one
iTunes Music Store account for
yourself. Log in to one of them
and then create an allowance for
the other. When you log in under
the second account, you'll have
access to the music allowance you
created under the first one.

11. Click **Buy** to start the allowance, **Back** to move back to the previous screen so you can change the information for the allowance, or **Cancel** to stop the transaction.

    You will see a screen that confirms that the allowance has been completed.

12. Click **Done** to complete the process or click **Set Up Another** if you want to set up another iTunes allowance. When you finish setting up allowances, you'll return to the Apple Account Information screen. Click **Done** to return to the iTunes Music Store, or you can continue to work with your account.

tip

You can have multiple iTunes Music Store accounts. If you really do want to set up an allowance for yourself, create a second iTunes Music Store account and then use your first account to create an allowance for your second account. Log in under the second account and you will have access to the allowance you create.

The music allowance's recipient will receive an email containing information about the allowance you set up, including the username and password (if you created one for this person). When recipient signs in, her current balance will be shown next to the username in the Account box. This balance always reflects the amount left for the current month. When the recipient has spent all of this, the account won't be able to purchase more music until the next month.

To change your allowances, return to the Apple Account Information screen. When you have set up at least one allowance, this screen will contain the Manage Allowances button. Click this and you'll move to the Manage Allowances screen. Here, you have the following options:

note

If the recipient doesn't spend an entire month's allowance, it carries over to the next month.

- You can suspend an allowance by clicking the Suspend button. The allowance will remain configured, but any future allowances will be disabled.

- You can restart a suspended allowance by clicking the Activate button. The allowance will receive the allotted amount on the first of the next month.

- You can change the amount of an allowance by selecting a new amount on the pop-up menu (which is active only for current allowances).

- You can remove an allowance entirely by clicking the Remove button. Do this only when you are sure you won't ever use the allowance again.
- You can create a new allowance by clicking the Create New Allowance button.

Purchasing Gift Certificates

If you know music lovers who use iTunes, you can create gift certificates for the iTunes Music Store so the gift recipient can purchase music there. These work similarly to allowances, except that gift certificates are for a set amount and expire when that amount has been spent.

To purchase a gift certificate, click the **Gift Certificate** button on the Apple Account Information screen and follow the onscreen instructions to purchase the certificate. The recipient will receive an email that provides all the information he needs to be able to purchase music up to the full amount of the certificate.

Gift certificates are handy when you want to buy music for someone but don't know what they have already or even what their preferences are.

Managing Your Artist Alerts

If you are interested in specific artists, you can receive an email when new music from that artist is added to the iTunes Music Store.

To create an artist alert, click the **Add Artist Alert** link from the artist's Home screen in the iTunes Music Store (you'll see an example of this later in this part of the book). When music from that artist is added to the store, you'll receive an email letting you know.

To remove an artist alert, click the **Manage Artist Alerts** button on the Apple Account Information screen. You'll see the Manage Artist Alerts screen. Here, you'll see each artist for whom you will receive alert emails. To remove an alert, uncheck the artist's check box and click **Save Changes**. You'll no longer be notified about that artist.

Choosing Your Shopping Preferences

The final step in preparing to shop is to configure your shopping preferences. To do so, follow these steps:

1. Open the iTunes Preferences dialog box.
2. Click the **Store** tab to open the Store pane (see Figure 24.8).
3. To show the iTunes Music Store source, which is the default condition, check the **Show iTunes Music Store** check box. If this box isn't checked, the Music Store won't appear in the Source List.

4. Choose your shopping method by clicking either the **Buy and download
   using 1-Click** radio button or the **Buy
   using a Shopping Cart** radio button.

5. If you want songs that you buy to play
   as soon as you download them, check
   the **Play songs after downloading**
   check box.

6. If you use a slow Internet connection
   and want song previews to download
   completely before they play, check the
   **Load complete preview before
   playing** check box. This will enable the
   preview to play without pauses that
   might be caused by your connection
   speed (or lack thereof).

7. Click **OK**. If you select the Shopping Cart method, the Shopping Cart and
   Purchased Music playlist will appear inside the Music Store source; expand
   the Music Store source to see them. If you use the 1-Click method, you'll see
   the Music Store and Purchased Music playlist separately on the Source List.
   You are now ready to shop!

> **tip**
>
> On the Manage Artist
> Alerts screen, check the
> **Send me Artist Alerts for
> all artists in my Purchase
> History** check box and then
> click **Save Changes** if you
> want to be notified when
> new music from any artist whose
> music you have previously pur-
> chased is added to the iTunes
> Music Store. Click **Clear All** to get
> rid of all your alerts.

THE ABSOLUTE MINIMUM

Shopping at the iTunes Music Store is better than any other music store I have ever seen. Here are some more shopping points to keep in mind:

- When you shop in the iTunes Music Store, you can choose the 1-Click or Shopping Cart method.

- To shop in the store, you need to obtain and configure an account.

- After you have an account, you configure iTunes to shop according to your preference.

- Almost all the music you buy from the iTunes Music Store has artwork associated with it. You can view the artwork by clicking the Show Artwork button.

- The music you buy from the iTunes Music Store is in the Protected AAC audio file format. This is the same AAC format in which you can import music into your Library, but it also includes some protections against copyright violations.

- The best thing about music you buy from the iTunes Music Store might be that you don't have to unwrap a CD. I hate trying to pry them out of their plastic wrapping!

25

SHOPPING IN THE iTUNES MUSIC STORE

Now that you have an account in the iTunes Music Store and have configured iTunes to use it, it is time to start shopping. You can browse or search for music, preview it, and then buy the music you like—all with just a few mouse clicks and keystrokes. To shop in the iTunes Music Store, you use the following general steps:

1. Go to the store (no parking required).
2. Browse or search for music.
3. Preview music.
4. Buy music.

Going into the iTunes Music Store

You learned how to do this step in the previous chapter, but I included it again in this chapter just for completeness's sake. To move into the store, select the Music Store source on the Source List. The iTunes Music Store will fill the Content pane (see Figure 25.1). If your account is shown in the Account button, you are signed in and ready to go. If not, click the **Sign In** button to sign in to your account (refer to Chapter 24, "Configuring iTunes for the Music Store," for help).

As you move around the store, know that just about everything in the iTunes Music Store window is a link, from the album covers to the text you see to the ads showing specific artists. Just about anywhere you click will move you someplace else.

note

I've assumed you already have an iTunes Music Store account, which you need to have before you can purchase music from the iTunes Music Store. If you don't have an account yet, read the previous chapter.

FIGURE 25.1

Shopping at the iTunes Music Store won't make your feet tired.

Browsing for Tunes

Browsing for tunes can be a great way to discover music you might be interested in but don't know about yet. You can click through the store to explore in various ways; when you aren't looking for something specific, browsing can result in lots of great music of which you might not have even been aware.

Browsing the iTunes Music Store Home Page

You have several ways to browse for music from the iTunes Music Store Home page.

You will see several special sections titled New Releases, Exclusives, Pre-Releases, Just Added, and Staff Favorites; these categories of music are relatively self-explanatory (for example, Just Added contains music that is new to the iTunes Music Store). To scroll through the music available in these areas, click the scroll arrows or buttons (see Figure 25.2). When you do so, you will see the next set of albums in that category. If you see an album that interests you, click it. You will see the details of the album on which you clicked (see Figure 25.3). When you get to something that interests you, you can preview and purchase it.

note

Thousands of podcasts are available in the iTunes Music Store. To learn how to access them, see "Subscribing and Listening to Podcasts" on page **254**.

FIGURE 25.2

You can browse the categories on the home page by using the scroll tools.

Scroll buttons

Scroll arrows

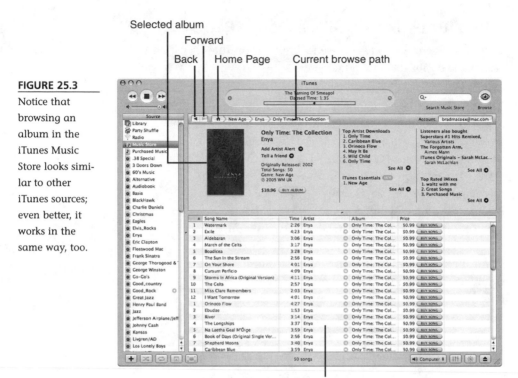

Selected album

Forward

Back | Home Page | Current browse path

FIGURE 25.3

Notice that browsing an album in the iTunes Music Store looks similar to other iTunes sources; even better, it works in the same way, too.

Content pane

You can also browse the iTunes Music Store home page by using the various lists presented on the screen, such as the Today's Top Songs, Today's Top Albums, Featured Artists, Celebrity Playlists, iTunes Originals, and iTunes Essentials. To browse a list, you can click its title or on any of the songs or artists in the list. For example, to see the most downloaded albums on a given day, click the title text of the **Today's Top Album** list. You will see a screen that shows the albums that have been downloaded most on the day you visit the store (see Figure 25.4). You can click an album to view its contents.

In the upper-left area of the home page, you will see a list that enables you to access special areas, including Audio Books, iMix, Music Videos, and so on. Just click a link to move to the related area.

Also on the home page are a number of ads that change over time. These ads feature specific artists, the current sales promotion, and so on. Just click an ad to move to its music.

You can also browse the iTunes Music Store by clicking the iTunes Browse button or the Browse Music link on the iTunes Music Store home page. The Browser pane will appear above the Content pane just as it does when you are browsing your Library. You can browse the store in the same way, too. For example, click a genre to see all the music of that genre in the store. Click the **Browse** button or the **Home page** button to return to the normal store interface.

Browsing by Genre

Browsing by genre is a good way to find music by its style. Start from the home page and choose a genre on the **Genre** menu. The home page will be refreshed, presenting music only in the genre you selected (see Figure 25.5). The tools on the home page will be the same; the content of the music you see will be entirely focused on the genre of music you are browsing.

> **tip**
>
> The iTunes Music Store is a combination of a website and the standard iTunes controls. For example, to move back and forward in the pages you have visited, use the Back and Forward arrows. When you are browsing a specific item, you can jump to any level between it and the home page by clicking anywhere in the current browse path.

FIGURE 25.5

FIGURE 25.5

If you like jazz, as I do, browsing the Jazz genre is a great way to find new music.

Searching for Specific Tunes

Browsing for music is fun, but it can be time-consuming and might not lead you to the music you want. When you want something specific, you can search for music using the iTunes Music Store Search tools. The two kinds of searches are basic search and power search.

When you do a *basic* search, you search by one search term. Basic searches are fast and easy but can sometimes find a lot of songs you aren't interested in. When you perform a *power* search, you can combine several search terms to make searching more precise.

> **note**
>
> When you browse by genre, think of the resulting page as the "home page" for that genre.

Performing a Basic Search

You already learned how to search with iTunes, so you already know how to perform a basic search in the iTunes Music Store because this type of search works in the same way. To perform a basic search, follow these steps:

1. Select **Music Store** as the source. You will see the iTunes Music Store home page.

2. Click the **magnifying glass** icon in the iTunes Search tool (which becomes the Search Music Store tool when the Music Store source is selected) and select the attribute by which you want to search (see Figure 25.6). The options are **All**, **Artists**, **Albums**, **Composers**, **Songs**, **iMixes** (you'll learn about these later in this chapter), and **Power Search** (you'll learn about that one in the next section).

FIGURE 25.6

You can use this menu to choose the attribute by which you want to search for music.

3. In the Search box, type the text or numbers for which you want to search.

4. Press **Return** or **Enter**. The search will be performed and you will be presented with the results window (see Figure 25.7). At the top of the window are the albums relevant to your search. At the upper-right side are the top songs and top artists related to your search. At the bottom of the window, the Content pane lists the specific songs that meet your search criteria.

After you have performed a search, you can click the albums to view their contents, preview songs, purchase albums or songs, and so on.

FIGURE 25.7
In this search, I found all the music in the store with "Basie" as the artist.

Performing a Power Search

Sometimes a basic search just doesn't cut it. Fortunately, you can use a power search if you want to find something very specific. With a power search, you can search by more than one attribute at the same time, such as by artist and composer. To search with power, do the following steps:

1. From the iTunes Music Store home page, click the **Power Search** link located in the upper-left corner of the window. You'll see the Power Search window (see Figure 25.8).

2. For the first attribute for which you want to search, enter text or numbers in its box. For example, to search by artist, enter the artist's name in the **Artist** box.

3. Repeat step 2 for each attribute for which you want to search.

4. If you want to limit the search to a specific genre, select it on the **Genre** menu.

5. When you have configured the search, click **Search**. The window will be refreshed, and you will see the results of your search (see Figure 25.9). Just under the search tools, you will see the top albums, top songs, and top artists that meet your search criteria. At the bottom of the window, you will see the songs that meet your search.

> **note**
>
> Notice that the label under the Search tool reflects the search attribute you selected. For example, if you chose Artists, the tool's label becomes Search Artists.

FIGURE 25.8
Using a power search, you can perform searches based on more than one attribute.

FIGURE 25.9
Here I have searched for music with the artist "Chapman" in the Inspirational genre.

Just like a basic search, after you have performed a power search, you can click the albums to view their contents, preview songs, purchase albums or songs, and so on.

Previewing Tunes

One of the great things about the iTunes Music Store is that you can preview music before you buy. These 30-second previews help you be more sure that the music you are buying is really something you want. For example, you can compare alternative versions of the same songs, listen to songs by artists who are new to you, or listen for any other reason.

To preview a song, you select it in the Content pane of the iTunes Music Store and click the **Play** button or double-click the song (see Figure 25.10). The preview will begin to play, again just like a song on another source, such as a CD or playlist. You can preview as many songs as you'd like, and you can preview the same song as many times as you want.

tip

Any of the black circles with arrows inside them are links to other places (refer to Figure 25.9). For example, when you are viewing a top list, such as top downloads, click the See All arrow to see the entire list.

FIGURE 25.10

When you browse an album or any other content on the iTunes Music Store, you can play a song to preview (or more accurately pre-listen to) it.

Buying Tunes

After you have found music you want to add to your Library, you can purchase it. How you do this depends on which shopping method you selected: 1-Click Shopping or the Shopping Cart method (if you don't know what I am talking about, refer to Chapter 24). With either method, you can build a playlist containing music in which you are interested for later purchase.

Buying Tunes with the 1-Click Method

The 1-Click method is aptly and literally named. It really does require only a single click. To purchase an album, you click the **Buy Album** button next to the album you want to purchase. To purchase a song, you click the **Buy Song** button. In either case, whatever you selected will be immediately purchased and downloaded to your Library (see Figure 25.11). (Because you entered credit card information when you configured your iTunes Music Store account, you don't need to provide any payment information—after you click the Buy button, the store automatically gets the information it needs to complete your purchase.) After the download process is complete, the music will be in your Library and in the Purchased Music playlist and it will be yours to listen to, put on a CD, and so on.

If you like the idea of 1-Click shopping but want to be able to gather music in one place before you purchase it, you can create a "holding" playlist and put music from the store in it. Then, you can preview and purchase that music from the playlist. Create a playlist and name it anything you'd like. Then find music in the store you want to evaluate and drag that music from the store onto the playlist you created. You can select the playlist to preview the songs in it and use the Buy buttons to purchase it. Of course, you can do the same thing with the Shopping Cart method so if you find yourself doing this often, you might want to switch to that method instead.

note

If you have a slow Internet connection and you set the preference to have previews finish downloading before they play, there will be a pause between when you play a preview and when you actually hear it. The length of this pause will depend on how long it takes to download the 30-second preview to your computer.

tip

When you log in to your account, you can indicate whether iTunes should remember your password for shopping purposes. If you allow this, you won't need to enter your password each time you purchase music. If you don't allow this, at some point in the process, you will be prompted to enter the password for the account you are currently signed in under to be able to complete a purchase.

FIGURE 25.11

In the Information area of the iTunes window, you can see that I am currently downloading the album shown because I clicked the Buy Album button.

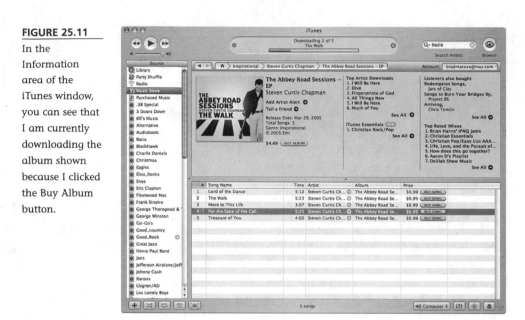

Buying Tunes with the Shopping Cart Method

Whereas the 1-Click method requires a single click to purchase music, the Shopping Cart method requires all of two or three clicks to accomplish the same result—that being to add new music to your Library.

When you find music in which you are interested, click either the **Add Album** button or the **Add Song** button to add an album or song, respectively, to your Shopping Cart source. When you do so, you will see a message in the Information area telling you that the item you selected has been added to your Shopping Cart (see Figure 25.12). Continue adding music to the Shopping Cart as long as you'd like.

note

If you selected the Play songs after downloading option on the Store preference pane, songs will start playing as soon as they have been downloaded to your computer.

FIGURE 25.12

Here I have added an album to my Shopping Cart.

When you are ready to buy music, select the **Shopping Cart** source on the Source List. You will see the music you have added to the cart (see Figure 25.13). You can purchase individual songs, albums, or all the music in the Shopping Cart. (Just like the 1-Click method, you don't need to enter payment information because that is stored as part of your iTunes Music Store account and is provided for you automatically.)

To buy an individual song, click its **Buy Song** button. It will be downloaded to your Library.

To buy an album, click its **Buy** button. All the songs in that album will be added to your Library.

The total cost of all the items in your cart is shown at the bottom of the window. To remove an item from the cart, click its **Remove** button (the *x* on the item's row). The item will be deleted from the cart, and the cost information will be updated. When the cart contains only the music you want to buy, click the **Buy Now** button. The music in the cart will be downloaded to your Library.

After the download process is complete, you can listen to music you purchased, put it in playlists, place it on CD, and so on.

tip

If you don't see the Shopping Cart source, click the expansion triangle next to the Music Store. Music Store will expand and you will see your Shopping Cart along with the Purchased Music playlist.

tip

You can view individual songs on an album by clicking its expansion triangle. This will show you each song on the album. You can't purchase individual songs on the album, though; to do that, you have to add the song to your Shopping Cart by itself.

FIGURE 25.13

You can view the contents of your Shopping Cart and then purchase the music it contains.

FIGURE 25.13

You can view the contents of your Shopping Cart and then purchase the music it contains.

Linking Your Music Library with the iTunes Music Store

The music in your Library can be linked to the iTunes Music Store. The value of this is that you quickly find music in the store that is related to music in your Library by clicking a link (see Figure 25.14). Click the link for an artist to move to that artist's page in the iTunes Music Store, which lets you easily get more music from artists whose music you already have. Clicking the link for a song will take you to that song in the store; this can sometimes help you find similar music or to purchase the album from which the song came. Clicking an album's link will take you to that album if it is available in the store or to an album that is similar if the exact one isn't contained in the store.

By default, the iTunes Music Store links are enabled. If you don't want these links to appear, you can hide them. To do so, open the **General** pane of the iTunes Preferences dialog box and uncheck the **Show links to Music Store** check box.

Music Store links

FIGURE 25.14

These links
enable you to
quickly move to
related music in
the iTunes Music
Store.

iMixing It Up

iMixes are collections of music that are created by iTunes users and published to the
iTunes Music Store. Anyone viewing an iMix can purchase individual songs in the
iMix or buy all of them at once.

Working with iMixes

There are a couple of ways you can access people's iMixes. One is when someone
who knows you sends you a link to it. The other is to browse or search for available
iMixes. To work with iMixes, use the following steps as a guide:

1. Move the iTunes Music Store home page.

2. Click the **iMix** link. You'll move to the iMix home page (see Figure 25.15).
   Existing iMixes are grouped into various categories, including Top Rated,
   Most Recent, and Featured.

3. To view one of the iMixes shown in the categories on the iMix home page,
   click its icon. You'll move to iMix's page and can skip to step 7.

4. To see all the iMixes in a category, click its **See All** link. You'll move to the
   home page for the category and can browse all the iMixes it contains. To
   view an iMix, click its icon. You'll move to the iMix's page and can skip to
   step 7.

FIGURE 25.15

iMixes can be useful when you are looking for new music for your Library.

5. To search for music included in iMixes as an alternative to browsing for it, select the attribute for which you want to search on the pop-up menu at the top of the iMix home page. The options are All, which searches by all attributes and is the default; iMix Name; Artist Name; Album Nam; and Song Name.

6. Enter the text or numbers for which you want to search in the **Search for** box and click the **Search** button, which has the magnifying glass icon. iMixes that contain music that meets your search criterion will appear. Click an iMix's icon to view its contents.

7. When you are viewing an iMix, you can preview the songs it contains just like other music in the store (see Figure 25.16). At the top of the screen, you'll see the iMix's name, its average rating, and a summary of the iMix the publisher created.

tip

When an iMix page contains more iMixes than can be displayed on a single screen, click the More and Back links to move among the screens of those iMixes.

tip

The iMix Search tool appears at the top of all iMix pages so you can refine your browsing. For example, if you view all the Top Rated iMixes, you can search within those to find iMixes containing specific music.

FIGURE 25.16

This iMix was published by yours truly.

8. Use the Buy tools (if you use 1-Click) or Add tools (if you use a Shopping Cart) to purchase any music you like. You can purchase individual songs or all the music in the iMix if all the songs in contains are available for individual purchase in the store. The total cost of the iMix is shown at the top of the window next to the Add All Songs or Buy All Songs button. If either of these buttons is not shown, that means at least one song in the iMix can be purchased only when the entire album is purchased; you'll see the View Album button next to such songs instead of the more common Buy or Add button.

9. To see other iMixes created by the same person, click the **See all iMixes by the user** link or click the **iMixes by this user** button in the path area just above the iMix itself. You'll move to a page showing all iMixes published by the same person.

10. To rate an iMix, click the button for the number of stars you want to give to the iMix and then click **Submit**. The rating buttons will disappear and your rating will be shown. You can rate an iMix only once.

11. To send information about the iMix to other people, click the **Tell a friend** link. You'll see a form on which you enter their email addresses (separated by commas), your name, and a message. When you have completed the form, click **Send** to send it. An email containing a link to the iMix will be sent to each recipient. Click **Done** to move back to the iMix.

Publishing Your Own iMixes

You can publish your own iMixes using music stored in your Library. Then other people can access the iMixes you publish using the steps in the previous section.

When you create an iMix, be aware that only music that is available in the iTunes Music Store will be included in the iMix; music you import from audio CDs that aren't available in the store will be removed from an iMix when you publish it.

To publish an iMix, perform the following steps:

note

Because only music available in the iTunes Music Store can be published via an iMix and all music in the iTunes Music Store has album art associated with it, all the music in iMixes you publish will have art added automatically.

1. Create a playlist containing the music you want to publish in an iMix. (For help creating playlists, refer to Chapter 18, "Creating, Configuring, and Using Playlists").

2. Select the playlist you created and click the arrow button that appears next to it. The first time you publish an iMix, you'll see a warning dialog box explaining what you are doing.

3. Check **Do not show this message again** and then click **Create**. You'll move onto the iTunes Music Store and will see the sign in dialog box.

4. Enter your password and click **Publish**. The iMix will be created, and you'll see an edit screen that enables you to add information to the iMix (see Figure 25.17).

5. Type the name of the iMix in the **Title** box; by default, this will be the name of your playlist.

6. Enter a description of the iMix in the **Description** box.

7. When you are ready to publish the iMix, click the **Publish** button. You'll see your iMix (see Figure 25.18). If all the songs in the iMix are available for individual purchase, you'll see the total cost of your iMix along with the Buy or Add button and the Rating buttons. (Yes, you can rate your own iMix. If you give your own iMix less than five stars, is that a problem?)

8. To send information about your iMix to others, click **Tell a Friend**. You'll see a form on which you enter their email addresses (separated by commas), your name, and a message. When you have completed the form, click **Send** to send it. An email containing a link to the iMix will be sent to each recipient. Click **Done** to move back to the iMix.

FIGURE 25.17

Use this screen to add information to your iMix, such as a description.

FIGURE 25.18

Like fast-paced rock with plenty of guitar? Check out this iMix.

You'll receive an email from Apple informing you that your iMix has been published and providing a list of all the songs it contains along with a link to take you to it.

THE ABSOLUTE MINIMUM

You now have all the skills you need to find, preview, and buy music from the iTunes Music Store. If you are like me, you will be hooked after your first trip. Following are some pointers to help you shop like an iTunes Music Store master:

- When you search and iTunes can't find any music that matches your search, it will prompt you with its best guess about what you meant to search for. For example, if you were searching for music from the group Lynyrd Skynyrd and searched for "lynnrd" (who can ever spell that name right anyway!), iTunes would present a prompt in the search results asking whether you meant to search for "Lynyrd" because it can match that to its database. If you click the search text in the prompt, iTunes will search for that term instead.

- No matter which shopping method you use, the price for everything is listed next to the buttons you use to purchase the song or album or to add it to your Shopping Cart. Songs are $.99 each. The cost of albums varies, but in most cases, the price per song works out slightly less when you buy an album than when you buy the same music by the song.

- Some albums are available only as a partial album; this is indicated by the term "Partial Album" next to the album. This means you can purchase one or more of the songs on the album, but not all the songs on the album or the album itself.

- Some songs are available only as part of an album. This means you can only purchase the song by buying the album of which it is a part. Songs in this category are indicated by the text "Album Only" in the Price column of the Content pane.

- Even if you have a fast connection, you might prefer the Shopping Cart method because you can use the cart as a holding area for the music you might want to buy. This gives you a chance to think about it before you complete the purchase. When you use the 1-Click method, however, as soon as you click the Buy button, the deal is done.

26

WORKING WITH PURCHASED MUSIC

The title of this chapter is somewhat misleading because it implies there is a lot different about working with music you have purchased than with other music in your Library, such as music you've imported from audio CDs. Although there are some unique aspects of music you purchased from the iTunes Music Store, mostly you can use it in the same way as any other music you have added to your own iTunes Library. But, there are just a few things of which you need to be aware, and that is where this chapter comes in.

Understanding What Happens When You Buy Music from the iTunes Music Store

When you download music from the iTunes Music Store, whether you use 1-Click or the Shopping Cart, that music is added to your Library (see Figure 26.1). From there, you can listen to it, add it to playlists, burn it to disc, move it to an iPod, share it, and so on. In other words, it becomes mostly like music you have added to your Library from other sources.

note

The most important difference between music you purchase from the iTunes Music Store and other music in your Library is that a computer must be authorized to play music from the iTunes Music Store. You'll learn about this concept later in this chapter.

FIGURE 26.1

This music came from the iTunes Music Store; it doesn't look any different from other music in the Library and acts only a bit differently.

Using the Purchased Music Playlist

Immediately after your first purchase from the iTunes Music Store, the Purchased Music source will become available on your Source List (see Figure 26.2). This source is actually a special smart playlist that will capture all the music you purchase from the iTunes Music Store. You can always return to your purchased music by using the Purchased Music source.

You can use the Purchased Music playlist like other playlists. To see its contents, select **Purchased Music** on the Source List. The first time you select it, you will see a dialog box explaining the function of the playlist (see Figure 26.3). Read the information and click **OK** to move to the Purchased Music playlist.

note

Also, just like other music in your Library, if you define one or more smart playlists with live updating enabled and then purchase music from the iTunes Music Store that meets the criteria for those playlists, your purchased music will be added to the appropriate playlists automatically.

You can then browse the Purchased Music playlist, search in it, play it, and so on. Of course, you can also configure view options for it, sort it, and do the other playlist tasks with which you are hopefully familiar by now.

FIGURE 26.2

The Purchased Music source is actually a special playlist that always contains all the music you have purchased from the iTunes Music Store.

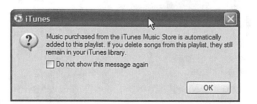

Understanding Authorization

The music you purchase from the iTunes Music
Store is protected in the sense that it has certain
limitations on what you can do with it.
Fortunately, these limitations are not very limiting!

One of these limits is that you can play iTunes
Music Store music on only up to five computers at
the same time. To implement this limit, the computer on which you play iTunes Music Store music
must be *authorized*. When you authorize a computer, iTunes will connect to the Internet and register that computer with the iTunes Music Store to
play the music purchased under the user account
you used to buy it.

To state this another way, you actually authorize
the music for a specific user account on up to five
computers at a time. When you authorize a computer, you authorize all the songs you have purchased under an iTunes Music Store account; you
can't authorize some of the songs you buy on one
machine and a different set on another computer.
When a computer is authorized, it can play all the
music that has been purchased under an iTunes
Music Store account. If it isn't authorized, you
won't be able to play any of the music you purchased.

Fortunately, it is easy to authorize or deauthorize a
computer, as you will see in the next sections.

note

You can also move
music from your Library that
you didn't purchase from the
iTunes Music Store into the
Purchased Music playlist, but I
don't recommend that you do so
because that will dilute its purpose.

note

You can store the music
you purchase on as many
computers as you'd like. Then you
can easily authorize the machines
on which you want to play the
music and deauthorize the ones
you aren't using at the moment.

Authorizing a Computer

The first time you purchase music on a computer, you must authorize that computer before you can play the music you purchase. After that, the computer remains authorized until you deauthorize it.

To authorize a computer to play purchased music, try to play the music you have purchased from the iTunes Music Store. If the current computer has been authorized, the music will begin to play. If it hasn't been authorized, you will see the Authorize Computer dialog box. Enter the username and password that was used to purchase the music and click **Authorize**. iTunes will connect to the Internet and authorize the computer. When that process is complete, the music will play.

If you attempt to authorize more than five computers under the same user account, you will see a warning prompt explaining that you can have only five computers authorized at the same time. You must deauthorize one of the computers to be able to authorize the current one.

Deauthorizing a Computer

To deauthorize a computer, select **Advanced**, **Deauthorize Computer**. You will see the Deauthorize Computer dialog box (see Figure 26.4). Click the **Deauthorize Computer for Music Store Account** radio button and click **OK**. You will see another Deauthorize Computer dialog box. Enter the username (Apple ID or AOL screen name) and password for the account you want to deauthorize on the machine and click **OK**. iTunes will connect to the Internet and deauthorize the computer. When the process is complete, you will see a dialog box telling you so. Click **OK**. The computer will no longer count against the five-computer limit for the user account. (It won't be able to play music purchased under that iTunes Music Store account either.)

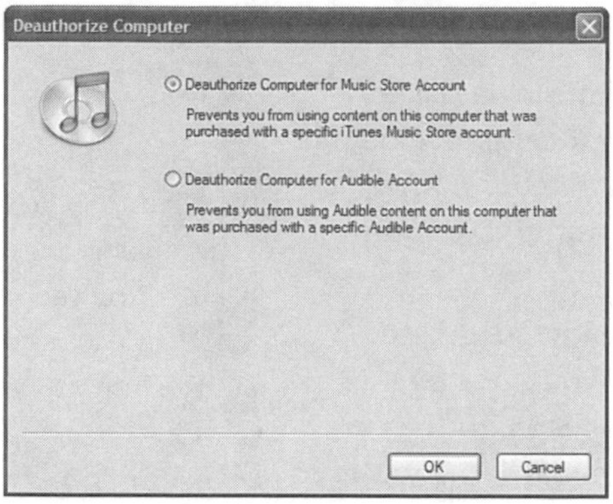

FIGURE 26.4

You use this dialog box to deauthorize a computer.

You can authorize a computer again by attempting to play purchased music and providing the user account and password for which you want to authorize the machine. As you can see, authorizing and deauthorizing computers is simple.

Moving Purchased Music to Other Computers

You can move any music between computers, but usually it is just as easy to import music from audio CDs to each computer on which you want to create a Library. However, if you have more than one computer, you might want to move music you purchased from the iTunes Music Store to the other computers so you can play it from there.

Understanding the Ways You Can Move Your Tunes

First, you need to move the song files from the computer on which they are stored (the machine from which you purchased the music) onto the machine you want to be able to play that music on.

To move files to another computer, you need to know where those files are located. From Part II, "iTunes," you know that iTunes keeps all the files in the Library organized in the iTunes Music folder (assuming you followed my recommendations and

note

You can purchase music on a machine that isn't authorized to play it. If you do this, you will see a warning dialog box that will explain that you won't be able to play the music on the machine you are using to purchase it until you authorize that computer. You can also store music purchased under different iTunes Music Store accounts on the same computer. To authorize the computer to play that music, you must authorize it for the iTunes Music Store account under which the music you want to play was purchased.

set the preferences to allow this). You can move to this folder to find the files you want to move.

You can also find the location of song files by selecting them and selecting **File**, **Show Song File** or pressing **Ctrl+R** (Windows) or ⌘-**R** (Mac). iTunes will open a window showing the location of the files for the songs you have selected (see Figure 26.5).

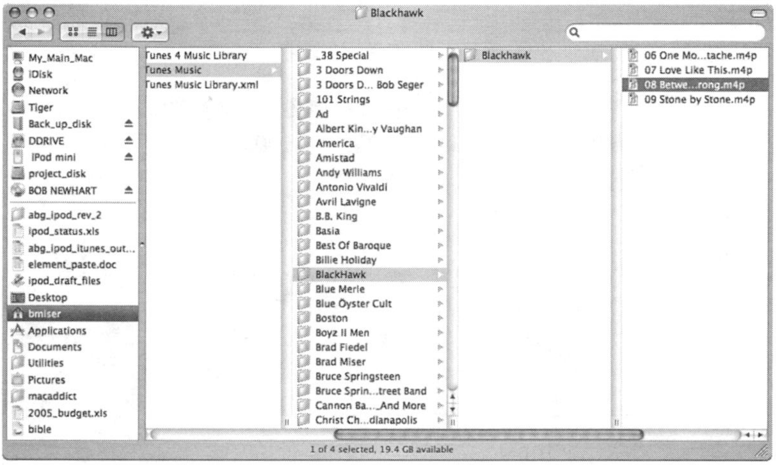

FIGURE 26.5

When you use the Show Song File command, iTunes opens a window to show you where the song's file is located on your computer.

After you have located the song files, you need to make them available to the computer to which you want to move them. There are many ways to do this, including the following:

- **Create a data CD or DVD containing the music you want to move**—You can do this from within iTunes by changing the Burning preferences to use the Data CD or Data DVD format and then burning a disc. This process is easy to do and works regardless of there being a network connection between the computers. The primary limitations are the size of the discs you use and the time it takes to burn the discs.

- **Use a network to share files on the computer from which you bought music with the one to which you want to move the files**—This method is simple and doesn't place a limit on the sizes of the files you move. You also don't

tip

You can share music you have purchased with other computers on your network. However, for other machines to be able to play your purchased music, they must be authorized to do so and therefore count against the five-computer limit. Fortunately, as you have seen, it is simple to authorize and deauthorize computers, so you can keep up to five authorized quite easily.

need to spend time or money to burn discs. The downside is that you have to have the computers connected via a network.

■ **Create an audio CD of purchased music and import that into the other computer's iTunes Library**—This is also an easy process, but you are limited to the amount of music that can fit onto an audio CD.

■ **Move the song files onto a networked drive, such as a server**—For example, if you use a .Mac account, you can use your iDisk to transfer files by copying them to your iDisk. This has the same pros and cons as moving files directly across a network.

■ **Copy the files onto a portable hard drive, such as a FireWire or USB drive**—This is faster than and doesn't have the same space limitations as using a CD or DVD. Of course, the disadvantage is that you have to have such a drive available.

Lastly, you need to add the files you are moving into the Library stored on the computer to which you have moved the music files. This involves using the Add to Library command and then moving to and selecting the files you want to add.

Moving Purchased Music Files over a Network

The following steps provide an example of how to move files that are shared over a network and add them to the Library:

1. Share the files on the original machine with the network.

2. From within iTunes on the computer to which you want to move the songs, select **File**, **Add to Library**. You will see the Add to Library dialog box.

3. Move to and select the files or the folder containing the files you want to add to the Library (see Figure 26.6).

4. Click **Open**. The songs you selected will be copied into your Library (see Figure 26.7). If the music you moved into the Library was purchased on a different computer, you need to authorize the current computer to play that music (see the next section).

> **note**
>
> On Windows PCs, you can select the Add to Folder command, which enables you to select a folder to add. This works in the same way as adding files.

> **tip**
>
> The keyboard shortcut for the Add to Library command is Ctrl+O (Windows) or ⌘-O (Mac).

FIGURE 26.6

Here, I am accessing song files that are stored on a computer on the network.

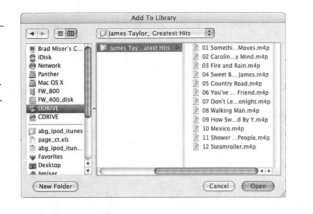

FIGURE 26.7

You can see that the files I selected in the previous figure are now in the Library.

Viewing the Music You Have Purchased

You have a couple ways to see the music you have purchased.

The first way you have already read about. Select the **Purchased Music** source and you will see all the music you have obtained from the iTunes Music Store. (This assumes you haven't removed any songs from this playlist.)

tip

Purchased songs that you move to a different computer won't be added to the Purchased Music playlist automatically. You can drag them onto that playlist from the Library if you want to put them there.

The second way is to view the entire purchase history for a user account. To do so, perform the following steps:

1. While signed in under the user account whose history you want to see, click the **Account** button (you need to select the Music Store source to see this button). You will be prompted to enter the password for that account.

2. Enter the account's password and click **View Account**. The Content pane will be filled with the Apple Account Information window, which provides, amazingly enough, information about the user account.

3. Click the **Purchase History** button. The data will be retrieved, and the Content pane will show the music purchased during each shopping session (see Figure 26.8).

4. To view the detail for a shopping session, click its **Detail** button. The screen will be refreshed, and you will see a detailed list of all the music purchased during that session (see Figure 26.9).

5. When you are done viewing the history of your purchases, click the **Done** button; you'll need to click it twice if you are viewing a detail screen. You'll return to the Apple Account Information screen.

6. Click **Done**. You'll move back to the iTunes Music Store.

note

You can create an audio CD from music you purchase from the iTunes Music Store and then import that music into a Library on another computer. Because the music is converted into the Audio CD format when you do this, it doesn't count against the five-computer limit for music you purchase from the iTunes Music Store. However, if you use this technique to play music you have purchased on more than five computers at the same time, you will violate the spirit and letter of the license agreement you accept when you purchase music from the store. I recommend that you only use this method if this won't result in more than five computers playing this music at the same time. This can be particularly useful if one of the machines on which you will be playing music can't connect to the Internet, which is required for authorization to take place.

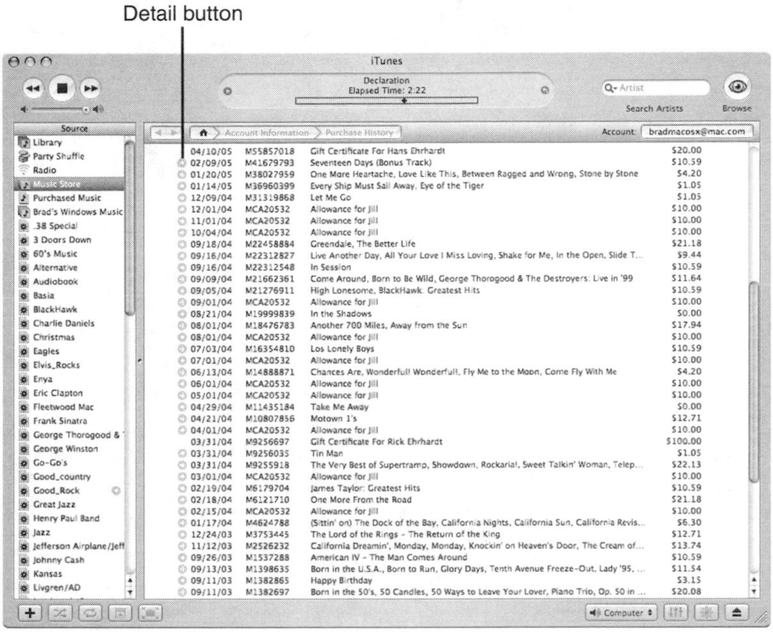

FIGURE 26.8

Your purchase history will be organized by shopping sessions.

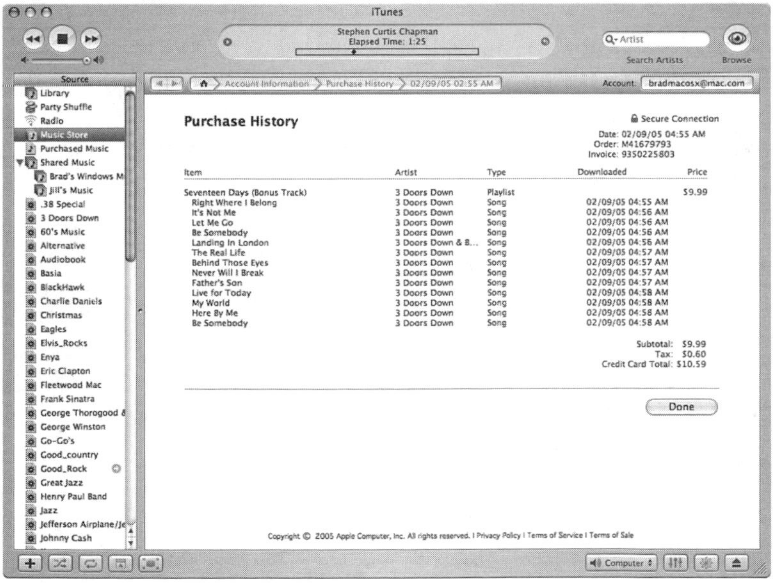

Detail button

Date	Order	Description	Price
04/10/05	M55857018	Gift Certificate For Hans Ehrhardt	$20.00
02/09/05	M41679793	Seventeen Days (Bonus Track)	$10.59
01/20/05	M38027959	One More Heartache, Love Like This, Between Ragged and Wrong, Stone by Stone	$4.20
01/14/05	M36960399	Every Ship Must Sail Away, Eye of the Tiger	$1.05
12/09/04	M31319868	Let Me Go	$1.05
12/01/04	MCA20532	Allowance for Jill	$10.00
11/01/04	MCA20532	Allowance for Jill	$10.00
10/04/04	MCA20532	Allowance for Jill	$10.00
09/18/04	M22458884	Greendale, The Better Life	$21.18
09/16/04	M22312827	Live Another Day, All Your Love I Miss Loving, Shake for Me, In the Open, Slide T...	$9.44
09/16/04	M22312548	In Session	$10.59
09/09/04	M21662361	Come Around, Born to Be Wild, George Thorogood & The Destroyers: Live in '99	$11.64
09/05/04	M21276911	High Lonesome, BlackHawk: Greatest Hits	$10.59
09/01/04	MCA20532	Allowance for Jill	$10.00
08/21/04	M19999839	In the Shadows	$0.00
08/01/04	M18476783	Another 700 Miles, Away from the Sun	$17.94
08/01/04	MCA20532	Allowance for Jill	$10.00
07/03/04	M16354810	Los Lonely Boys	$10.59
07/01/04	MCA20532	Allowance for Jill	$10.00
06/13/04	M14888871	Chances Are, Wonderfull Wonderfull, Fly Me to the Moon, Come Fly With Me	$4.20
06/01/04	MCA20532	Allowance for Jill	$10.00
05/01/04	MCA20532	Allowance for Jill	$10.00
04/29/04	M11435184	Take Me Away	$0.00
04/21/04	M10807856	Motown 1's	$12.71
04/01/04	MCA20532	Allowance for Jill	$10.00
03/31/04	M9256697	Gift Certificate For Rick Ehrhardt	$100.00
03/31/04	M9256035	Tin Man	$1.05
03/31/04	M9255918	The Very Best of Supertramp, Showdown, Rockaria!, Sweet Talkin' Woman, Telep...	$22.13
03/01/04	MCA20532	Allowance for Jill	$10.00
02/19/04	M6179704	James Taylor: Greatest Hits	$10.59
02/18/04	M6121710	One More From the Road	$21.18
02/15/04	MCA20532	Allowance for Jill	$10.00
01/17/04	M4624788	(Sittin' on) The Dock of the Bay, California Nights, California Sun, California Revis...	$6.30
12/24/03	M3753445	The Lord of the Rings - The Return of the King	$12.71
11/12/03	M2526232	California Dreamin', Monday, Monday, Knockin' on Heaven's Door, The Cream of ...	$13.74
09/26/03	M1537288	American IV - The Man Comes Around	$10.59
09/13/03	M1398635	Born in the U.S.A., Born to Run, Glory Days, Tenth Avenue Freeze-Out, Lady '95, ...	$11.54
09/11/03	M1382865	Happy Birthday	$3.15
09/11/03	M1382697	Born in the 50's, 50 Candles, 50 Ways to Leave Your Lover, Piano Trio, Op. 50 in ...	$20.08

FIGURE 26.9

You can also view the detail for any shopping session.

Purchase History

🔒 Secure Connection

Date: 02/09/05 04:55 AM
Order: M41679793
Invoice: 9350225803

Item	Artist	Type	Downloaded	Price
Seventeen Days (Bonus Track)	3 Doors Down	Playlist		$9.99
Right Where I Belong	3 Doors Down	Song	02/09/05 04:55 AM	
It's Not Me	3 Doors Down	Song	02/09/05 04:56 AM	
Let Me Go	3 Doors Down	Song	02/09/05 04:56 AM	
Be Somebody	3 Doors Down	Song	02/09/05 04:56 AM	
Landing In London	3 Doors Down & B...	Song	02/09/05 04:56 AM	
The Real Life	3 Doors Down	Song	02/09/05 04:57 AM	
Behind Those Eyes	3 Doors Down	Song	02/09/05 04:57 AM	
Never Will I Break	3 Doors Down	Song	02/09/05 04:57 AM	
Father's Son	3 Doors Down	Song	02/09/05 04:57 AM	
Live for Today	3 Doors Down	Song	02/09/05 04:58 AM	
My World	3 Doors Down	Song	02/09/05 04:58 AM	
Here By Me	3 Doors Down	Song	02/09/05 04:58 AM	
Be Somebody	3 Doors Down	Song	02/09/05 04:58 AM	

Subtotal: $9.99
Tax: $0.60
Credit Card Total: $10.59

Done

Backing Up Purchased Music

Because you don't have music that you purchase from the iTunes Music Store "backed up" on a disc (like you do for the music you have on audio CD), you should make sure you back up the music you buy. The easiest way to do this is to burn a disc from the Purchased Music playlist. Of course, if you have purchased more than can fit on a single CD or DVD, you will need to use multiple discs to back up the entire collection.

tip

On the Apple Account Information screen, you will see the Computer Authorizations section that shows how many computers are currently authorized to play music from the account you are logged in under.

Consider creating a smart playlist whose criteria is based on the date you added music to your Library and for which live updating is enabled. When you purchase new music, update the criteria so that the added date is just before you made your most recent purchase. Then, all the music you purchased since that date will be added to the playlist. Burn that playlist to disc, and you will have backed up the new music you purchased since the last time you did this.

THE ABSOLUTE MINIMUM

The iTunes Music Store is well designed and makes finding and buying music—from individual songs from your favorite one-hit wonder to complete collections of classic artists—easy. As you work with the tunes you buy, remember the following musical morsels:

- When you purchase music from the iTunes Music Store, it is downloaded into your Library.

- By default, all the music you purchased from the iTunes Music Store is stored in the Purchased Music playlist.

- To play purchased music on a computer, that computer must be authorized. You can have up to five computers authorized at the same time. You can deauthorize a computer by selecting the Deauthorize Computer command.

- To play purchased music on a computer that is different from the one on which you purchased it, you can move the purchased music to another computer. There are several ways to do this.

- There are a couple of ways to see the music you have purchased. One is to use the Purchased Music playlist. You can also use the Purchase History information for your iTunes account to see a list of all the music you have purchased from the iTunes Music Store.

- You should back up the music you purchase from the iTunes Music Store. The easiest way is to do this is to burn a CD or DVD of the Purchased Music playlist.

27

SOLVING ITUNES MUSIC STORE PROBLEMS

You will see that this is a short chapter. The reason is simple: You just aren't likely to encounter that many problems when working with the iTunes Music Store. The store, like iTunes and the iPod, is well designed and works flawlessly most of the time. If you do encounter a problem, this chapter will help you find the solution.

Recovering Music That Wasn't Downloaded Successfully

If the download process for music you purchased wasn't completed for some reason (for example, you lost your Internet connection in the middle of the process), you can restart the download process to recover music you have purchased but weren't able to download successfully.

To do this, select **Advanced**, **Check for Purchased Music** (see Figure 27.1). You will be prompted to enter the user account and password for the account under which the music was purchased. Do so and then click **Check**.

FIGURE 27.1

You use the Check for Purchased Music command to recover music you've purchased but weren't able to download for some reason.

Advanced	
Switch to Mini Player	Ctrl+M
Open Stream...	Ctrl+U
Subscribe to Podcast...	
Convert	
Consolidate Library...	
Get CD Track Names	
Submit CD Track Names	
Join CD Tracks	
Deauthorize Computer...	
Check for Purchased Music...	
Convert ID3 Tags...	

The music you have purchased will be checked against the music that has been successfully downloaded. If music is found that hasn't been downloaded successfully, you will be able to download it again. If you have successfully downloaded all the music you have purchased, you will see a message stating so (see Figure 27.2).

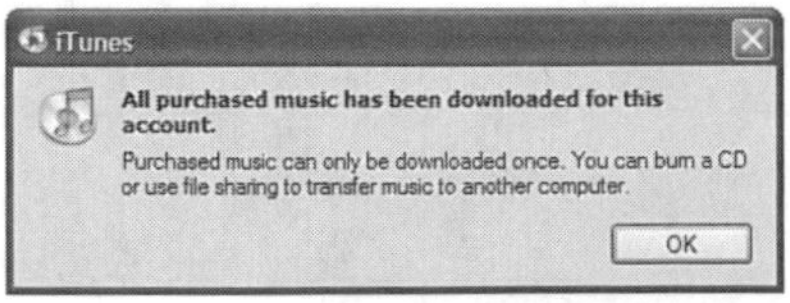

FIGURE 27.2

When you see this message, you have downloaded all the music you have purchased.

> **iTunes**
>
> **All purchased music has been downloaded for this account.**
>
> Purchased music can only be downloaded once. You can burn a CD or use file sharing to transfer music to another computer.
>
> OK

note

No, you can't use this technique to download music you have purchased to more than one computer, nor can you use it to download music more than one time on the same computer. When you successfully download music, that music is marked as having been downloaded. The iTunes Music Store doesn't care to which computer you have downloaded it. When you buy music, you are entitled to download it once and only once. (Back up your purchased music in case something happens to it on your computer.)

Solving the "Not Authorized to Play" Problem

As you learned in the previous chapter, you can play music you have purchased on up to five computers at the same time. If you try to play purchased music and see the `This Computer Is Not Authorized to Play This Music` message, you need to authorize the computer before you can play the purchased music. If you already have five computers authorized, you need to deauthorize at least one before you can authorize another. (If you need help doing these tasks, refer to Chapter 26, "Working with Purchased Music.")

The challenge can sometimes be remembering how many and which computers you have authorized. The "how many" part is easy. Just access the **Apple Account Information** screen for your account. The Computer Authorizations section will tell you how many computers are currently authorized to play music for the account (to learn how to access this screen, refer to "Viewing the Music You Have Purchased" on page **405**).

> **note**
>
> If you use iTunes on only one computer, you never have to think about authorization because it is handled for you automatically. If you use five or fewer computers, it still isn't a problem because after you sign in to your account on each machine, you don't have to bother with it again. Only when you use six or more computers to play music you have purchased from the iTunes Music Store do you need to concern yourself with this topic.

The "which ones" part is a bit more difficult. The easiest way to tell is to try playing purchased music from each computer you might have authorized. If it plays, the computer is authorized.

Correcting Problems with Your iTunes Music Store Account

You can change information for your iTunes Music Store by accessing the Apple Account Information page and using its tools to make changes to your account, such as changing the credit card you use to purchase music. (For help using this page, refer to "Changing and Viewing Your iTunes Music Store Account" on page **369**.)

If something has changed from the iTunes Music Store side of the equation, you will be prompted

> **caution**
>
> If you sell a computer or stop using it, be sure you deauthorize it first. Even if you wipe the machine's hard drive, it still counts as an authorized computer. If you no longer have access to an authorized computer, you will need to contact iTunes Music Store Customer Service to have that machine deauthorized.

to change your account information. The dialog box that appears will also enable you to access your Account Information page to make the required changes.

Getting Help with iTunes Music Store Problems

Hopefully you won't ever have any problems with the iTunes Music Store, and if you do, the information in this chapter should help you solve them. If not, don't despair because help is just a few clicks away.

To access the iTunes Customer Service page, select **Help**, **iTunes and Music Store Service and Support**. Your default web browser will open and you will move to the iTunes Support page for the type of computer you are using (see Figure 27.3). Use the links and information on this page to get help. For example, you can click the **iTunes Music Store Customer Service** site link to move to the Music Store Customer Service page on which you can click the **Get help with computer authorization** link to get help deauthorizing a computer to which you no longer have access.

FIGURE 27.3

This is the iTunes Support page for Windows users.

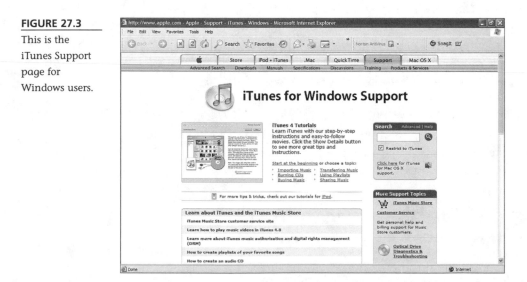

Reporting Music You Can't Find in the Store

Although the iTunes Music Store is great, it isn't perfect. Its major flaw, which is a perfectly understandable one, is that it doesn't contain every song ever produced (as if that were even possible). The good news is that Apple is continually adding music to the store, especially as music producers and record companies see what a great way it is for them to distribute their music.

If you can't find the music you want to buy in the store, you can let Apple know about it. (Who knows, your contact might be the one that causes some specific artist or music to be added to the store!)

To request music, perform the following steps:

1. Open the Music Store Customer Service page by selecting **Help**, **iTunes and Music Store Service and Support** and then clicking the **iTunes Music Store Customer Service** site link.

2. In the FAQ section, click the **Request a song or artist** link. You'll move to the Request Music web page.

3. Complete the onscreen form by entering your name, email address, type of request (such as requesting an artist or album), and the specific request you are making in the **Comments** box.

4. Use the drop-down lists and check boxes to supply the additional information that is requested.

5. Click **Send Feedback**. Your request will be submitted, and you will see a confirmation screen that explains that you won't get a personal response to your request. Hopefully, at some point, the music you requested will be added to the store.

THE ABSOLUTE MINIMUM

The iTunes Music Store is a great tool to search for and add music to your iTunes Library. In fact, you might never purchase a CD again (okay, that's a bit dramatic, but you get the idea). Fortunately, the iTunes Music Store works very well and you aren't likely to have any problems using it, which is a good thing.

Just in case, in this chapter, you learned how to do the following tasks:

- Recover music you didn't download successfully.
- Solve the "Not Authorized to Play" issue.
- Fix problems with your iTunes Music Store account.
- Get help from Apple.
- Request music you can't find in the store.

If you do have problems and none of the information in this chapter helps you, you can always write to me at bradmacosx@mac.com, and I will do my best to help you get back into your best shopping form.

Index

A